TOWARD

A

NEW

CHRISTIANITY:

Readings
in the
Death
of God
Theology

TOWARD A NEW CHRISTIANITY:

Readings in the Death of God Theology

edited by Thomas J.J. Altizer

EMORY UNIVERSITY

HARCOURT, BRACE & WORLD, INC.
New York / Chicago / San Francisco / Atlanta

FOR GREGOR SEBBA
AND
WALTER A. STRAUSS

Contents

TOWARD

A

NEW

CHRISTIANITY:

Readings
in the
Death
of God
Theology

Introduction
to the Readings

Hopefully a new day has dawned for theology, a revolutionary day in which the gradual but decisive transformation of faith that has occurred in the modern world will be recognized, even though doing so may promise the end of most if not all of the established religious forms of the West. At the moment, and for perhaps well into the future, the most radical theological revolution is promised by the death of God theology, a theology grounded by one means or another in the death of the Christian God. This is not to say that this theology, if such it can be called, is the only new or even revolutionary theology at hand. The majority of Christian theologians, whether Catholic or Protestant, acknowledge the end of Western Christendom as we have known it, and with it the end of those cultural and social forms which once assumed a Christian name. Everywhere today theologians are either struggling for new forms of faith and community or are engaged in a desperate battle to preserve the old forms at whatever cost. Until recently it was possible for many theologians to take a neutral stance in this conflict, but increasingly the crisis at hand is driving both the theologian and the believer to a choice between a strange and largely unknown future and a seemingly archaic and irrelevant past.

Left and right or radical and conservative are inescapable poles of conflict in both politics and theology. Let it be granted that the distinction is often unclear, that individuals commonly move back and forth between the poles and may live different aspects of their lives simultaneously in each, and that in our time the root opposition between right and left is entering a new form. Nonetheless the opposition remains real, and it witnesses to a vital struggle. In the West, at least, and increasingly in the world at large, the gulf between right and left is created by the movement of history, and more particularly by the advent of revolutions in consciousness and society which threaten to sweep away all the forms and orders of the past. Although differing in power and intensity, these revolutions occur in every area of human life, and only cease to be revolutionary when they either reveal themselves to be impotent or succeed instead in assimilating and transforming the order and authority which they initially opposed. The questions inevitably asked of any revolutionary movement are: What power does it embody both potentially and actually? To what extent does it demand a break with the past? While there is no instrument at hand to measure the exact power of a revolutionary theological movement, we can reach some conception of its nature by understanding the kind of break which it demands from the past.

✠   ✠   ✠

Probably the least violent break with the past will be demanded of Catholic theologians. Certainly a series of powerful new theological movements are engulfing the Roman Catholic Church, but rather than being destroyed by them the Church has been moved to reinterpret the Catholic tradition so as to insure its place in a new future and to reconstruct both the meaning and the practice of faith and worship so as to open them to the realities of the twentieth century. It is here, and many Protestants would insist only here, that a Church theology is possible which builds upon the Christian tradition in such a manner as to open the way to an evolutionary development which moves into the future by preserving but enlarging the forms of the past. This is not to say that revolutionary as opposed to evolutionary movements have not also occurred in Catholic theology—one has only to remember the work of Teilhard de Chardin—but the specifically Catholic form of theology as we know it has not yet reached the point where it is prepared to make a radical break with the Christian tradition. It is significant that over the past generation so many conservative Protestant theologians have given their best energy to an ecumenical theology promising to reconcile Protestantism and Catholicism; for the future of a Christianity preserving the history of the Church clearly seems to lie with Rome.

But no serious contemporary theological inquiry can afford to ignore the world of Judaism. Indeed, the Christian theologian has been deeply affected both by the awesome suffering of the Jew in the twentieth century and by the peculiar quality of modern Jewish faith. No religious community has embodied a more realistic attitude toward the world than Judaism, and we can see in a religious thinker like Martin Buber a theologian who dared to open the center of faith to the actuality of our time. Buber was the first theologian to confess the eclipse of God in our time just as he was the first to call for a transformation of faith in response to the eclipse of God. Today this radical movement of Jewish thinking is most fully being carried forward by Richard Rubenstein, who was the first Jewish theologian to identify himself with a death of God theology. In the future we may expect a rich dialogue between Christian and Jewish death of God theologians.

There was a time when Protestant theology could claim to be in the intellectual vanguard of the Christian faith. It certainly was more progressive than Catholic theology, and in a limited sense it could still be said to be so right up into our time. Yet the revolution—or, more accurately, counterrevolution against the modern world—which took place in Protestant theology following World War I was directed against any form of faith reflecting or embodying the actuality of human consciousness and society. Initially and most profoundly inspired by Karl Barth, this counterrevolution sought an absolutely autonomous form of faith, grounded solely in the Word of God's revelation and free from the idolatrous presence of any purely human voice. Underlying this most influential of modern Protestant theological movements was the collapse of liberal or cultural Protestantism in Europe and indeed the approaching end of Western Christendom, already manifest in 1914. The great creators of modern Protestant theology, even including a theologian so distinctly on the left as Paul Tillich, were deeply affected if not originally moved by this eclipse of God in modern culture. Hence, while they sought inspiration from premodern theologians such as Luther, Calvin, and Augustine, their quest was also shaped—perhaps in equal measure—by the works of the nineteenth-century prophets who had foreseen the end of Christendom. Indeed, modern Protestant theology has been as much influenced by such atheistic thinkers among those prophets as Marx, Nietzsche, and Freud as by such Christian thinkers as Kierkegaard and Dostoevski.

During the twenties the new movement in Protestant theology had not yet become "neo-orthodox," and, assuming the name *crisis theology* or *dialectical theology,* it attempted a genuine mediation between faith and the world. True, the world of Western history and culture was rapidly losing its Christian character, and no major modern theologian has thought otherwise; but the erosion or disappearance of a specifically Christian culture could be welcomed by a theology positing an antithesis or opposition between culture and faith. If human expressions of faith are inevitably idolatrous, and if their very humanity and historicity must negate revelation itself, then only by maintaining a chasm between faith and culture can either faith or culture most truly be itself. In Barth's early writings, the Word of God and the word of man are antithetical: God's Word always comes as a No to a guilty and creaturely humanity, just as every human word negates and turns away from God's self-revelation. However, a humanity which abandons its own striving toward God and redemption can become open to God's free gift of Himself in Christ. Therefore the absence or eclipse of God in modern culture can free man from an idolatrous and self-destructive seeking after God and at the same time advance the proclamation of the gospel by clearing away a serious obstacle to its reception, a culture falsely and demonically proclaiming itself to be Christian. The task of the theologian becomes one of attacking every idolatrous pretense of an all too human culture, thereby maintaining an antithetical relationship between faith and culture so that neither will claim to be or act as the other, and each can be free to be solely itself. Inevitably, the "crisis" or "dialectical" theologian initially approached the great modern atheistic prophets as theological allies, for he could greet the death of God in modern culture announced by them as a way to the original ground and reality of faith.

A rift began to appear in dialectical theology about 1930 when Barth abandoned the dialectical method and gave himself wholly to the task of writing a church dogmatics or a theology grounded solely in the dogmas of the Church. Grave problems had already beset the Barthian school, however, if only because its positive ground in the Bible had been threatened by modern Biblical scholarship; and it had been perilously posed above the widening chasm between the interior human reality of faith and the claim that faith is absolutely autonomous. Unlike Catholicism, modern Protestantism had not only accepted critical Biblical scholarship, but it had in large measure created it. But Biblical scholarship is likewise the product of modern culture; it shares the radical relativity of the modern historical consciousness, and it assaults the traditional Christian understanding of the Bible as the record of an organic and continuous body of revelation. Moreover Biblical scholarship tends to challenge the relevance of the Bible for modern man, including modern Christian man, by reaching a historical understanding of the Bible as the product of an ancient and diverse body of peoples, whose beliefs and values are far removed from our own. What Barth hailed as the strange new world of the Bible is also strange to the modern Christian, and Barth carried the majority of his fellow theologians with him in his insistence that the historical understanding of the Bible must be subordinate to a "pneumatic," or, more accurately, dogmatic interpretation. Unlike the theologians, few Biblical scholars were willing to follow Barth at this point.

Intimately related to the problem of the alienation of the modern man of faith from the Bible is the dilemma posed by a theological condemnation of all cultural expressions of faith, or, at least, of all positive cultural expressions. If the Word of God cannot be given expression in art, philosophy, science, or society, then what actual or living meaning can it have for the existing man of faith? Nineteenth-century Protestant liberalism was finally driven to reducing faith to an ethical way of life, but neither Barth nor any other European theologian in our century has had anything except scorn for such a humanistic transformation of faith. What then? Must faith be silent, existing in the void of the human heart, and unspeakable in either the objective or subjective language of modern history? Is the proclamation of the Word simply the repetition of the words of the Bible without any regard shown for the meaning of these words for modern man? Protestant evangelists may accept these consequences, but they are impossible for the theologian who is in quest of the meaning of the contemporary reality of faith.

While Barth and his followers were constructing a total form of faith isolated from both modern history and modern culture, other Protestant theologians such as Paul Tillich and Rudolf Bultmann carried forward the earlier dialectical program of mediating between faith and culture. Nevertheless, at certain crucial points, these theologians have been both less radical and less realistic than Barth. Almost from the beginning, Barth has betrayed a compelling sense of the death of God in the modern world: hence his abandonment of a positive or dialectical mediation between faith and modern culture. Those theologians, however, who have maintained a dialectical stance have been committed to belief in a mutual and integral relation between faith and culture, a relation permitting a common language of communication and one demanding an interaction between its opposing poles. Tillich's method of "correlation," for example, allows culture to pose the ultimate questions, although insisting that ultimate answers can only be given by faith. Yet if God is dead in modern culture, how can culture's questions be met by faith's ultimate answer of God (or, for that matter, Tillich's "God above God")? Inevitably, Tillich was forced to deny the death of God in modern culture, and he has been accused from both the right and the left of the theological world for artificially perpetuating a nineteenth-century form of cultural Christianity.

Tillich came to occupy a middle ground between the theological left and right, and perhaps the mere fact that he wrote a systematic theology now precludes the possibility of moving his theology in either direction. With Bultmann the case is far different, not simply because he has not written systematically, but also because there is a living school of Bultmannian theologians whose movements are directed as much by the development of Biblical scholarship as they are by systematic considerations. Furthermore, while Tillich moved to the right as his work progressed, Bultmann has opposed the conservative movement of many of his followers, apparently aligning himself with the Bultmannian left, although not its extreme left. Bultmann's thinking has always been dialectical, if only because it has continually been drawn to two poles: on the one hand we can see the Christian influence of Luther and Kierkegaard, for example, and, on the other, the non-Christian impact of Dilthey and Heidegger. Bultmann is concerned to preserve the full Word of faith, yet he demands that it be expressed in the language of contemporary man. This project is precisely what he understands by the term *demythologizing*. Not only does demythologization rest upon an act of faith, but it is itself an act of faith, a living proclamation of the Word in the "now" of history. Unfortunately, Bultmann's own language obscures the meaning of the now of faith, and the Bultmannian school as a whole has shrouded the meaning of history in ambiguity. In part this ambiguity derives from the distinction in German between *Geschichte* and *Historie*—very roughly, and dangerously, these words might be translated as "internal history" and "external history"—the decisive point being that faith is grounded in *Geschichte* but not in *Historie*. Faith can abandon all of the objective or mythological language of the Bible, and must do so, but the *Geschichte* of faith remains ever the same.

A central ambiguity of the Bultmannian theological program is the nature of the transition for which it calls from the ancient, mythological, and objective language of the Bible and the Christian tradition to the modern and existential language of contemporary faith and witness. Bultmann believes that demythologizing began with the Gospel of John, but the advent of the scientific consciousness and of our modern history demands a more radical transformation of the language of faith than that which was effected by the Fourth Gospel. All theological language deriving from the prescientific and mythical age of humanity must now be negated; or, rather, it must be translated into the contemporary language of the existing man of faith. In no sense does such a program envision the diminution of the Christian faith; on the contrary, it insists that insofar as faith is understood and proclaimed in an objective and mythological language it is pre-Christian or anti-Christian. For the Word of true faith can never be understood or heard by way of the flesh, inasmuch as the Word is invisible and silent to the natural or given faculties of man. Here we see a contemporary theological appropriation of Paul's dichotomy between flesh (*sarx*) and spirit; and for Bultmann it serves to integrate the understanding of faith in Luther and Paul with Kierkegaard's existential dichotomy between "objectivity" and "subjectivity."

Yet the Bultmannian school has not met the problem of the decisive difference between the kind of demythologizing occurring in the Gospel of John and that which must take place in the modern world. Bultmann recognizes that modern man has lost the sense of a transcendent realm standing over man and the world, but he contends that belief in a purely transcendent realm is both mythological and foreign to the faith of the New Testament. He maintains that the Christian faith speaks of a transcendent that is to be sought and found in the midst of this world. The Christian Word is the unconditional in the conditional, the beyond in the here and now, the transcendent in the immanent or in the moment at hand. Does this mean that the loss of the sense of the reality of pure transcendence in the modern world has removed a barrier to faith? Or is the contemporary Christian called to an existential faith transcending the actual or living faith of primitive Christianity? Do the collapse of mythical thinking and the advent of the modern consciousness make possible a forward movement of faith itself? These questions are not answered by Bultmann, and, in fact, are never asked. Bultmann never speaks of going beyond the New Testament, and he refuses to surrender the "saving message" (*kerygma*) of the New Testament proclamation. The inner core of faith remains ever the same, even though it must be translated anew in every changing situation. Consequently, Bultmann, and thus far the great majority of his followers, must be characterized as being unable and unwilling to face the challenge of a world which has lost or abandoned all sense of the reality of transcendence.

In certain respects, as noted above, Barth has remained far more contemporary and even more realistic than Bultmann and Tillich. Tillich has surpassed both Barth and Bultmann in his willingness to meet and to engage in dialogue with modern culture; but the very fact that Barth established an impassable barrier between faith's surrender to the revealed Word of God on the one hand, and the historical actuality of consciousness and experience on the other, preserved his theology from the direct assault of the modern world and allowed it to exist in the presence of the most powerful expressions of unbelief. Tillich's program, on the contrary, stands or falls with the reality of transcendence in the world, even in the form of the "depth" underlying concrete existence; while Bultmann's demythologizing must also collapse, in form if not in substance, should it fail to discover a contemporary existence which is open to transcendence. In fact, all three of these most influential expressions of modern Protestant theology refuse to admit the reality of atheism. True, Tillich concedes the provisional reality of atheism, but he insists that if it remains in a state of "ultimate concern" it must become aware of the reality of transcendence. Bultmann can accept the fact of common and even mass atheism, but to do so he simply assigns it the status of unbelief, and he can by no means admit the possibility that a total existential decision could be atheistic. Barth, who is probably the most ruthlessly consistent theologian in the history of Protestantism, flatly denies that there can be genuine atheism of any kind. The sovereignty of God is such that it can be challenged by no man. When God's grace reveals His Word, it is open to no human refusal. The human reality of atheism is simply irrelevant, nor can the historical reality of atheism be of any consequence, for an atheism which is a turning away from the gift of God's Word is impossible.

If Protestant theology has reached the point where it is closed to the challenge of atheism, then it has ceased to be the intellectual vanguard of Christianity. Must Protestantism now attempt to teach Rome that a genuine dialogue with the world is no longer possible? Must the Protestant theologian join those reactionaries in the Vatican who condemned Teilhard de Chardin's call for a radical transformation of faith, or give support to orthodox Judaism in its resistance to the creation of a contemporary Jewish theology? Is the Christian situation so desperate that the primary task of the contemporary theologian is one of creating a fortress of faith which is unapproachable by the world, or of maintaining that faith is faith and the world is the world, neither undergoing a basic change in relation to the other, and both forever preserving their original forms? These questions are now driving Protestant theology to the wall, a wall where it will have to decide whether or not it continues to have a genuine theological vocation. A generation ago Tillich could ask if the Protestant era had come to an end. Is Protestantism no more than an ideological expression of the bourgeoisie, as the Marxists contend? Must it fade away with our passage into a new historical era? If Protestant theology began not simply as a rebellion against medievalism but as a counterrevolution against the Renaissance inspired by the goal of returning to the primitive Christian faith, must Protestant theology end with a counterrevolution against the modern world?

✠   ✠   ✠

Whether or not Protestant theology has now reached a point where such basic decisions are inescapable, the time has come to take stock of the genuine, positive achievements of modern Protestant theology, and to ask whether this theology admits of transformation into a new form. At least three major motifs of this theology still seem very relevant. All three revolve about the promise of a radical theological transformation, each potentially demands a break with theology's past, and each is a genuine theological response to the new world upon our horizon. These motifs are: (1) the collapse of theology or the doctrine of God into Christology or the doctrine of Christ, (2) the transformation of theological into anthropological language, and (3) a new understanding of how transcendence is dialectically united with immanence. In one way or another these motifs occur throughout modern Protestant theology, although they never achieve a consistent exposition, and they are continually threatened by regressions to pre-modern theological expressions. By examining them we can learn of the present significance of the conservative and radical poles of theology; we can also see that at every point these motifs are thwarted from achieving an intrinsic and consistent resolution by an impasse arising from a coming together of a conservative attachment to the past and a radical demand for a revolutionary movement into the future.

(1) In nineteenth-century Protestant and Anglican theology, Christology began to assume a new form, partly in response to scholastic and modern philosophical conceptions of God which increasingly conceived God in abstract, impassive, and alien and lifeless forms. Parallel to this development in formal philosophy, the modern imagination, as witness the great body of Western literature since the Enlightenment, envisioned either a wholly distant and inactive God or a hostile and oppressive deity who crushes the life and energy of humanity. Post-Reformation expressions of both Catholic and Protestant pietism centered their devotions upon the

passion and love of Jesus rather than upon the compassion and mercy of God—a seemingly all too modern piety that actually has deep theological foundations in Luther and late medieval Christianity. Thus the new Christologies which appeared in the nineteenth century were notably kenotic: they attempted to understand Christ as the embodiment in time and history of the self-sacrifice or self-emptying of the glory and sovereignty of God.

In the twentieth century the collapse of theology into Christology became more explicit still. Even Barth, who throughout most of his career rebelled so violently against nineteenth-century theology, carried forward the kenotic doctrine of the nineteenth-century Christologies, reaching in his *Church Dogmatics* a radical conception of the sovereignty of God derived from the image of God provided by the lowliness and self-sacrifice of Christ. Tillich, too, formulated a kenotic Christology, centered in the total self-negation of Jesus. An implicit ground of this theological motif is the principle that the nature and reality of God are to be understood solely by means of the deity or ultimate power which is revealed in the acts and words of Jesus Christ. The Christian God is the God who is manifest in His Incarnate Word, and theology should accordingly negate every idea and image of God which is foreign to the life and passion of Christ. Yet this theological goal was not pursued because of theology's bondage to the idea of the absolute sovereignty and transcendence of God.

(2) The second motif in modern Protestant theology, the transformation of theological into anthropological language, has been adopted as a program by the Bultmannian movement. This seems strange at first sight because this school has done most of its work in the context of New Testament exegesis and exposition. But it is precisely the theologian who works most intimately with the Bible who is most deeply aware of modern man's estrangement from the world of the Bible and who knows that the Word of the Bible can now become meaningful and real only by means of a transformation of its apparent, literal, or even historical (*Historie*) meaning. Historians might remark that such a transformation has always been the primary means by which Christianity has understood the Bible, but after the rise of the modern historical consciousness a gulf arose between the Church's dogmatic interpretation of the Bible and the measuring of the Bible reached by an objective and critical analysis of its text. Consequently, the contemporary transformation of theological into anthropological language has a historical ground. It is the modern man of faith who is increasingly alienated from the ancient theological language of the Church, and it is faith itself which demands to be given an expression in contemporary language.

No modern school of theology has taken language so seriously as the Bultmannians, but their goal of reaching a contemporary language of faith is now shared by most Catholic and Protestant theologians. From almost every quarter, we hear the demand that the Christian act and speak in history and that a faith which cannot speak in its own present has ceased to be faith. Inasmuch as our history has moved through a radical process of secularization, the claim is made that it is only an anthropological or purely human language which is now meaningful and real. And faith must speak in this language if it is to continue to speak. But how can theology reach a consistently anthropological language apart from effecting a radical break with its own traditional modes of speaking about God?

(3) The third motif in modern Protestant theology, a new understanding of how the transcendence and immanence of God are dialectically united, builds on a long tradition. Beginning with Luther, Protestant theology was in large measure grounded in a dialectical conception of the relation between the immanence and the transcendence of God. It is the sovereign and transcendent Creator who becomes immediately present and real in Christ; in Christ the wrath and judgment of God fully pass into compassion and forgiveness, and insofar as man lives in faith he lives here and now in the actual presence of God. Thus the true man of faith is released from bondage to the "law" and is ultimately bound to no power or authority save the redemptive love and presence of Christ.

This dialectical conception of a union between the transcendence and immanence of God was quickly lost by Protestant scholasticism, but it was reborn interiorly in Protestant mysticism and pietism and then received a new theological expression in the writings of Friedrich Schleiermacher and his nineteenth-century followers. Despite the fact that Barth initiated a counterrevolution to Schleiermacher's theological movement, if only because it threatened to collapse transcendence into immanence, he and his theological contemporaries progressively abandoned the language of pure transcendence and sought a conception uniting by one means or another transcendence and immanence.

The goal sought by modern Protestant theologians should not be confused with the Catholic scholastic conception of a God who is simultaneously transcendent and immanent. That conception was always resisted by Protestant theology, for it threatens the sovereignty of God and diminishes the centrality of the work and person of Christ. In any case, by the twentieth century Protestantism had finally effected a full theological break with its scholastic roots. The problem now set for Protestant theology derived from the necessity of reaching a conception of a God who is at once transcendent and immanent, not in the sense that God is simultaneously both transcendent and immanent, but rather in the sense that transcendence and immanence are fully united or finally indistinguishable in God. This situation has now become critical for the Protestant theologian who is forced to mediate between the radical transcendence of his own theological tradition and the radical immanence of the contemporary sensibility. How can he bring about a union between transcendence and immanence when the very movement of history would seem to have split them asunder and decreed that each can have life only at the cost of negating the other? Thus we see that each of the major theological motifs of the twentieth century has reached a common impasse deriving from the present necessity of establishing a radical break from the previous form of Christian faith and understanding.

✠ ✠ ✠

Perhaps contemporary radical theology can best be understood by its response to the problems it inherited. These problems can even be viewed as having come together in one primary question: How can the Christian faith exist and be real in a world and history in which God is dead? Radical theologians are united in their insistence that faith must exist fully in the actuality of our history, abandon all nostalgia for the lost world of Christendom, and seek that Christ who is real here and now for us. This insistence is reflected in the persistent demand that Christianity must cease to be "religious." Barth began his counterrevolution against liberal Protestantism and modern culture with a prophetic judgment upon all forms of religion. Every human quest for God and redemption, he declared, must culminate either in a false self-righteousness or a nihilistic self-destruction. The gulf between God and man can be crossed by God alone; the human voyager upon the seas of religion must be destroyed by the yawning chasm which his voyage unveils. Faith is absolutely opposed to religion because faith is an acceptance of the gift of grace, whereas religion is the product of a creaturely power alone. Since Barth grounded his theology in the full revelation of the Bible and accepted all the major creeds and confessions of the Church, however, his judgment upon religion seemed to be little more than a repetition of the Protestant principle of justification by faith alone, and it provoked contempt from historians of religions because of its naive conception of religion and its seemingly arbitrary assumption that neither the Bible nor Christianity is religious.

Dietrich Bonhoeffer was the first to give a radical form to Barth's modern expression of the Protestant principle of justification by faith alone. In his late letters and papers, Bonhoeffer openly acknowledged that the Christian era has come to an end, and he called for a "religionless Christianity" as the next stage of faith. God allows Himself to be edged out of the world and onto the Cross, and in a world come of age the man of faith must live without God, even while somehow living with the God before whom we are ever standing.

Only this conjunction of a "religionless Christianity" with a life without God may be judged to be fully radical. The conjunction obviously proceeds from the collapse of the Christian religious tradition and represents a genuine and serious theological response to it: for if Christendom has come to an end, then there can no longer be a living or actual ground for faith in the Christian God. The symbol of the death of God affords a clear dividing line between conservatives and radicals in Protestant theology today. Conservatives, too, often call for the end of religion, but their call envisions a return to Biblical faith, and a ground for faith in the Biblical as opposed to an idolatrous God. True radicals, on the contrary, while often concerned with preserving a Biblical ground of faith, maintain that the end of religious Christianity has brought with it the end of the Christian God, and they call for a faith transcending the religious and theological forms of the Bible.

Contemporary radical theologians inherit the nineteenth-century Catholic and Protestant theological conceptions of the evolutionary development of Christianity, but recognizing that the forward historical movement of Christianity has led to the eclipse or silence of God, they call for a radical break from the God who was once manifest and real in faith, and hence for a renunciation or negation of the sovereign and transcendent God of the Christian tradition. Indeed, radical theologians have discovered that genuinely contemporary forms of faith are already freed from everything which the Bible and Christianity have known as the sole or autonomous *deity* of God. Thus a death of God theology is a theology grounded in the death or dissolution of the Christian God; at the very least it demands an abolition of all God language in the positive expressions of both faith and theology, which means that it will admit nothing of what either the Bible or the Christian tradition has known as the God apart from Jesus Christ.

When so formulated we can see that a death of God theology fully inherits the work of its theological predecessors; it could even be said that the death of God theology attempts to carry that work to its own and therefore radical conclusion. So far from working to abolish or negate theology, the death of God theologian fully accepts the actual historical movement of Christian faith and theology, believing that it is the movement of faith which has now reached a negation and transcendence of the reality of God.

Remarkably enough, most theological opponents of a death of God theology have spoken in the name of the mystery of God, repudiating any attempt to speak of God in contemporary language. Such a refusal to permit a contemporary language of faith proceeds from a conviction that when God is silent, faith and theology must be silent too, and that the fundamental task of theology is accordingly to protect the center of faith from exposure to an alien and hostile world. But this theological tactic is simply a regression to the early position of Barth, or even to a more ancient and now empty fortress of faith, and it offers no hope for a theological movement into the future. If faith itself has now passed through a decisive break with its past, and if the idea and image of the Christian God is the foundation of the faith of the past, then not until theology moves through a negation of the Christian God will it be open to its own future. It is precisely for this reason that it is now necessary for the Christian theologian to speak of the *death* of God; apart from a negation of theology's former ground, no fundamental transformation of theology is possible. A death of God theology offers the hope of a truly new theology. It envisions a total reconstruction of the language and the form of theology which will be at once a fulfillment of the previous movement of theology and a radical movement into the future before us. Acknowledging that the "death" of God can only truly be known in the "life" of faith, it lays claim to a Christ of the future who even now is active in our present.

America looms large in the thinking of the American radical theologian, not as the literal nation about us, but rather as the place where the public and social expressions of secularization are most advanced in Western European civilization. Believing that the movement of secularization is finally a consequence of faith, and of faith in the Christ who lies in our future, the radical theologian is concerned with opening the corporate and communal body of faith to the new and more universal body of Christ which is dawning about and before us. Insofar as the new world lying upon our horizon is negating and transcending the world of the past, theology will be able to enter that new world only by effecting a radical break with its own past and by passing through a dissolution of its inherited form and language. In this sense, the death of the theological tradition is at bottom its rebirth into new life.

✠   ✠   ✠

There are a number of radical theologies at present, although it is not yet possible to assess their respective goals. Aside from Catholic and Jewish developments, we should note the vigorous state of Protestant "secular" theologies which are in quest of a fully secular language and mode of understanding. Thus far, however, these theologies have avoided the problem of God and have given themselves to other and seemingly more pragmatic theological tasks. A new and potentially radical understanding of God is probably most successfully being reached in America by process theology, a growing school of philosophical theology inspired by Whitehead's metaphysical conception of God and the world that is expected most profoundly to challenge a death of God theology.

Significant though the work of new schools of theology may be, it is necessary to insist that many if not most of the most important theological developments are taking place outside the academic precincts of theology, even outside ecclesiastical and public circles of faith; and all radical theologians are influenced as much or more by these developments as they are by forces within the professional theological world. The common charge that radical theologians are simply in quest of the modern at any cost fails to take account of this fact. For these theologians are persuaded that the witness of faith is present wherever there is life and energy, and in a world come of age the primary duty of the theologian is to listen to the world. What should be noted in these radicals is above all their conviction that the life and energy of Christ is present wherever the world is most active and real.

The death of God theologians are a small if enlarging circle within the body of Protestant theology. Some are on college, university, and seminary faculties, but included also are some pastors of almost every sort and a scattering of genuine if "lay" theologians. German radical theology has begun to move in a death of God direction, but thus far the fullest statements of a death of God theology—limited and fragile as they may be— have occurred in America. It should also be noted that the first Jewish death of God theology was conceived by an American theologian, Richard Rubenstein.

This anthology of the death of God theology attempts to draw together a body of materials reflecting both the ground of this new theology and its most important initial expressions. It is divided into three parts: (1) the death of God in the modern world, (2) radical expressions of European theology, and (3) the death of God theology in America. Since no understanding of radical theology is possible apart from a confrontation with the death of God in the modern consciousness and sensibility, the first part of the anthology offers a series of essays examining in depth the meaning of the death of God in the writings of those great prophetic figures who have most fully unveiled it. These essays also embody a conclusive demonstration of the rich theological creativity which is present outside the professional theological world. The rest of the anthology is more arbitrary because it is for the most part limited to Protestant theology and also to those theologians who have most explicitly articulated a death of God theology. Limitations of space in part dictated this decision but a more important reason is that Catholic theology is a world in itself, and its radical expressions cannot so easily be aligned with their Protestant counterparts as can those of Jewish theology. The most grievous omission from this anthology may be the Catholic Teilhard de Chardin, who thus far has been our most radical and most far seeing theologian. However, it is not clear whether his work envisions the death of God, since Teilhard chose to retain a traditional language about God even in the context of foreseeing a convergence of the universe into the "Omega Point" of God.

Just as Catholic theology is already undergoing a metamorphosis in response to its own reformation, Protestant theology must now undergo a radical transformation if it is to justify its continued existence. Ultimately a death of God theology may prove to be a false way out of our present theological crisis, but at the moment it points the way to a theological revolution, and at the very least it is forcing theology to meet questions which it can only continue to ignore by ceasing to exist.

Part One   THE DEATH OF GOD IN THE MODERN WORLD

1
WILLIAM
BLAKE

William Blake was the first seer to envision and proclaim the death of God. His revolutionary proclamation initially appeared in 1793 in his first fully prophetic poem, "America." While "America" is a fragmentary and cryptic poem, its closing lines record a clear and powerful vision of the death of the Christian God, whom Blake names Urizen:

> *Over the hills, the vales, the cities, rage*
> *the red flames fierce;*
> *The Heavens melted from north to south;*
> *and Urizen who sat*
> *Above all heavens in thunders wrap'd,*
> *emerg'd his leprous head*
> *From out his holy shrine, his tears in*
> *deluge piteous*
> *Falling into the deep sublime! flag'd with*
> *grey-brow'd snows*
> *And thunderous visages, his jealous wings*
> *wav'd over the deep;*
> *Weeping in dismal howling woe he dark*
> *descended howling*
> *Around the smitten bands, clothed in*
> *tears and trembling shudd'ring cold.*
> *His stored snows he poured forth, and*
> *his icy magazines*
> *He open'd on the deep, and on the Atlan-*
> *tic sea white shiv'ring.*
> *Leprous his limbs, all over white, and*
> *hoary was his visage.*

Blake's later work moved far beyond his vision in "America," but already in this passage we can see how he succeeded in reversing the mythological imagery and the theological tradition of Christianity so as to unveil a whole new form of faith.

It is safe to say that no modern artist poses more difficulties than Blake; not until a century after his death did a critical understanding of his work come into existence. Perhaps for this reason, and perhaps also because the critical studies of

Blake that do exist almost invariably discuss his work in either modern humanistic or traditional mystical terms, theologians have thus far completely ignored Blake; but no theology of the death of God can afford to ignore its greatest modern prophet. The selection which follows here is the second chapter of Northrop Frye's *Fearful Symmetry*; by almost unanimous consent among Blake scholars, this work has been recognized as the most authoritative study of Blake. Of course, Frye's book is not and cannot be a definitive work. Few Blake scholars accept Frye's thesis that a complete system underlies Blake's work, and the study as a whole is seriously limited in that it considers Blake only as a thinker and poet, thereby disregarding both his plastic creations and his mystical genius. Furthermore, Frye has a tendency to understand Blake's multiple vision of "The Eternal Great Humanity Divine" in purely esthetic terms, and he surely minimizes and distorts the Christian foundations of Blake's vision. Nevertheless, Frye marvelously succeeds in unravelling the incredibly complex religious vision of Blake.

Northrop Frye # The Religious Vision of William Blake

[1]

Samuel Johnson attempted to refute Berkeley by kicking a stone: in doing so he merely transferred his perception of the stone to another sense, but his feeling that the stone existed independently of his foot would possibly have survived even a mention of that fact. Berkeley's argument was that there is a reality about things apart from our perception of them, and, as all reality is mental, this reality must be an idea in the mind of God. Now God and man are different things to Berkeley, and this sudden switch from one to the other leaves a gap in the middle of his thought. Blake, by postulating a world of imagination higher than that of sense, indicates a way of closing the gap which is completed by identifying God with human imagination:

> Man is All Imagination. God is Man & exists in us & we in him.
>
> The Eternal Body of Man is The Imagination, that is, God himself. . . .
>   It manifests itself in his Works of Art (In Eternity All is Vision).[1]

Man in his creative acts and perceptions is God, and God is Man. God is the eternal Self, and the worship of God is self-development. This disentangles the idea . . . of the two worlds of perception. This world is one

[1] Marginal annotations to page 219 of Berkeley's *Siris*, K775; *Laocoön Aphorisms*, K776. [In the notes to this selection, K with a number refers to the page number in *The Complete Writings of William Blake*, ed. by Geoffrey Keynes. ("Oxford Standard Authors.") (London: Oxford University Press, 1966)—T. J. J. A.]

FROM Northrop Frye, *Fearful Symmetry: A Study of William Blake* (Princeton: Princeton University Press, 1947), pp. 30-54. Reprinted by permission of the Princeton University Press. Copyright, 1947, by Princeton University Press.

of perceiver and perceived, of subject and objects; the world of imagination is one of creators and creatures. In his creative activity the artist expresses the creative activity of God; and as all men are contained in Man or God, so all creators are contained in the Creator.

This doctrine of God further explains how a visionary can be said to be normal rather than abnormal, even though his appearance may be rare. The sane man is normal not because he is just like everyone else but because he is superior to the lunatic; the healthy man is normal because he is superior to the cripple. That is, they are most truly themselves. The visionary is supreme normality because most of his contemporaries are privative just as cripples and lunatics are. Whatever he is from their point of view, he is more of a man than they, and it is his successes that make him truly "human," not his failures or weaknesses, as they are apt to say. Hence the visionary expresses something latent in all men; and just as it is only in themselves that the latter find God, so it is only in the visionary that they can see him found. As imagination *is* life, no one is born without any imagination except the stillborn, but those who cut their imagination down as far as they can, deny, as far as they can, their own manhood and their divinity which is that manhood. They will therefore turn their backs on the genius who greatly acts and greatly perceives; but they retain the power to enter into kinship with him:

> The worship of God is: Honouring his gifts in other men, each according to his genius, and loving the greatest men best: those who envy or calumniate great men hate God; for there is no other God.[2]

The identity of God and man is qualified by the presence in man of the tendency to deny God by self-restriction. Thus, though God is the perfection of man, man is not wholly God: otherwise there would be no point in bringing in the idea of God at all. On the other hand, the infinite variety of men is no argument against the unity of God. Such ideas as *mankind* and *humanity* are only generalized; but the fact that an acorn produces only an oak indicates the fact of species or class as clearly as it indicates the fallacy of a generalized tree. Blake's word *form* always includes this unity of species: he says, for instance:

> The Oak is cut down by the Ax, the Lamb falls by the Knife,
> But their Forms Eternal Exist For-ever.[3]

Similarly, God is not only the genius but the genus of man, the "Essence" from which proceed the individuals or "Identities" mentioned in Blake's note on Swedenborg:

[2] *The Marriage of Heaven and Hell,* plates 22-24, K158.
[3] *Milton,* plate 32, K522.

Essence is not Identity, but from Essence proceeds Identity & from one Essence may proceed many Identities.

If the Essence was the same as the Identity, there could be but one Identity, which is false. Heaven would upon this plan be but a Clock.[4]

(Blake is attacking what seems to him a tendency to pantheism in Swedenborg.) Just as the perceived object derives its reality from being not only perceived but related to a unified imagination, so the perceiver must derive his from being related to the universal perception of God. If God is the only Creator, he is the only Perceiver as well. In every creative act or perception, then, the act or perception is universal and the perceived object particular. And we have already met the converse of this principle, that when the perception is egocentric the perceived object is general. There are thus two modes of existence. The ego plays with shadows like the men in Plato's cave; to perceive the particular and imagine the real is to perceive and imagine as part of a Divine Body. A hand or eye is individual because it is an organ of a body: separated from the body it loses all individuality beyond what is dead and useless. That is why the imagination is constructive and communicable and why the "memory" is circular and sterile. The universal perception of the particular is the "divine image" of the *Songs of Innocence*; the egocentric perception of the general is the "human abstract" of the *Songs of Experience*. This is the basis of Blake's theory of good and evil . . . .

There are two corollaries of this. One is that we perceive *as* God: we do not perceive God. "No man hath seen God at any time," because true perception is creation, and God cannot be created. We may see the divine aspect of great men, but when we do the divine in us recognizes itself. The other is, that, as we cannot perceive anything higher than a man, nothing higher than Man can exist. The artist proves this by the fact that he can paint God only as a man, though if he is reproducing senile and epicene ideas of God he will paint an enfeebled old man out of compliment to them. But there is no form of life superior to our own; and the acceptance of Jesus as the fullness of both God and Man entails the rejection of all attributes of divinity which are not human:

Man can have no idea of any thing greater than Man, as a cup cannot contain more than its capaciousness. But God is a man, not because he is so perceiv'd by man, but because he is the creator of man.[5]

Naturally those brought up on abstract ideas will begin by denying both of these postulates, so let us see what success they have with their theology.

[4] Marginal annotations to page 24 of Swedenborg's *Divine Love and Divine Wisdom*, K91.
[5] Marginal annotations to page 11 of *ibid.*, K90.

[2]

We have quoted Blake as saying that the idea of *proportion* means nothing except in relation to a concrete thing which possesses it. The proportions of a real thing are part of its "living form." We can only detach the idea of proportion from reality through what he calls "mathematic form"—generalized symmetry without reference to perceived objects. Now this idea of "mathematic form" has always had a peculiar importance for abstract reasoners, who try to comprehend God's creative power through the abstract idea of creation, or "design."

Hence there is a recurrent desire to believe that some simpler pattern, expressible perhaps in some mathematical formula, underlies the complications of our universe. I say complications, for this line of thought takes the world as complicated rather than complex. Pythagoras began with the patterns of simple arithmetic and the cardinal numbers; the *Timaeus* attempted to work out the geometrical shapes considered most fitting (this word will meet us again) from which to deduce all phenomena; and with the elaboration of the Ptolemaic universe the tendency spread in all directions. Many of its manifestations, particularly those that still survive, are occult, or at least highly speculative. But actually the whole tendency to symmetrical pattern-making in thought is very inadequately described as occultism, which is only a specialized department of it. Pattern-making extends over philosophy from Pythagoras to the Renaissance as a kind of intermediate stage between magic and science.

These latter two are psychologically very similar, we are told; both attempt to manipulate the laws of nature for man's purposes. And if this tendency to explain the world as a complication of simple mathematical formulae is, as we suggest, intermediate between magic and science and psychologically allied to both, we should expect Blake's attitude to it to be much the same as his attitude to science. Briefly, it may be said that the whole Pythagorean tradition in thought, from the *Timaeus* to our own day, has nothing to do with Blake and appears in him only in the form of parody. He simply did not believe in "the mystical Mathematicks of the City of Heaven." "The Gods of Greece & Egypt were Mathematical Diagrams—See Plato's Works," [6] he says. It sounds flippant, but it was the most serious criticism he had to offer.

It is worth insisting on this, because occultists are frequently attracted to Blake, and the above statement may well surprise anyone who has noticed the role that recurring cardinal numbers and even diagrams play in the later prophecies. But real things have mathematical principles inherent in them,

[6] *Laocoön Aphorisms,* K776. The preceding phrase is from Browne, *The Gardens of Cyrus.*

and a work of art, which is a synthesis of real things, has mathematical principles inherent in its unity. Blake distinguishes between the art of "mathematic form," like Greek architecture, which displays a tendency to generalized symmetry, and the art of "living form," like Gothic architecture, which has kept that symmetry properly subordinated.[7] But the Gothic arch and spire would soon collapse without mathematical principles. The Apocalypse in the Bible is an imaginative and visionary work of art, but it is not the less so for making a symbolic use of the number seven. The recurrence of this number is part of its unity as a poem, not an attempt to indicate a sevenfold aspect of things in general. Similarly in Blake all recurrent numbers and diagrams must be explained in terms of their context and their relation to the poems, not as indicating in Blake any affinity with mathematical mysticism.

[3]

The poetic basis of symmetrical thought is now fairly clear to us since the Copernican universe replaced the Ptolemaic one. But the later system has developed new methods of conceiving an impersonal and abstract God which are equally antithetical to Blake, and these, being more contemporary, bear the main brunt of his attack and form the basis for his treatment of Newton. The vast size of the Copernican universe has encouraged many timid souls to feel that the creation of it must be ascribed to an impersonal Power, whose nature can be understood only through our ideas of mechanical force. Hence the true followers of such a God are "men of destiny"—men of force or cunning rather than intelligence or imagination, and those unfortunate enough to possess the latter would do well to avoid him, or rather it. It is true that the more striking manifestations of this religion are later than Blake: when to the ice-cold and ether-breathing deity of the Copernican system there was added the immense stretch of geological time, in which nothing particularly cheerful seems to have occurred, gods like the "immanent Will" of Hardy's *Dynasts* were developed of a ferocity unknown to Blake's age. Blake, however, in his depiction of the chilling terror of his character Urizen, the god of empty space and blind will, shows a remarkably prophetic insight into these dinosaur-haunted theologies.

He himself regards the "immanent Will" account of God as superstitious. Not, of course, because he has any more faith in the benevolent avuncular God who explains away all suffering and injustice at the Last Judgment and proves himself to have had the best intentions all along. Nor does he agree with those who accept it negatively and feel that its

[7] *On Homer's Poetry & on Virgil,* K778.

"right worship is defiance." [8] He disagrees with it on the same ground that he disagrees with Locke's account of abstract ideas. Locke extends involuntary and automatic reflexes to include the passive reception of sense impressions, which to Blake should be the products of an active consciousness. Similarly, the worshiper of "immanent Will" is extending the subconscious activity of the heartbeat from sense experience to the whole universe. And he does it by exactly the same process of trying to find a least common denominator for his general principles. A man, a dog and a tree are all alive; therefore life must be inherently and really some kind of "life force" common to them which can only be identified with the lowest possible limit of life—protoplasm, perhaps. But as the boundary between living things and moving things is difficult to trace, the "immanent Will" is bound to sink below "life force" to take in all other forms of motion in a more inclusive generalization still.

It is much better, as in the previous case, to go to work the other way. A man, a dog and a tree are all alive; but the man is the most alive; and it is in man that we should look for the image, or form, of universal life. There can be no "life force" apart from things possessing it: universal life is the totality of living things, and God has intelligence, judgment, purpose and desire because we are alive and possess these things.

The Darwinian universe merely adds the tyranny of time and will to the tyranny of space and reason with which Blake was already acquainted, and suggests a generalized energy abstracted from form supplementing the generalized form abstracted from energy which we find in Locke's conception of substance. "No Omnipotence can act against order," Blake says.[9] If Blake had lived a century later he would undoubtedly have taken sides at once with Butler and Shaw and claimed that alterations in an organism are produced by the development of the organism's "imagination"; and the doctrine of environmental stimulus in time would have fitted into the same plane in his thought as Locke's doctrine of involuntary sense perception in space.

As a matter of fact Blake does use the persistence of life as an argument that the hold of life on the world is not precarious. Lightning may kill a man, but it cannot beget him: life can come only from life, and must go straight back to the creation at least, which implies the primacy of creative over destructive energy. Worshipers of the "immanent Will" see its most striking effects in the latter, and in the irony and tragedy it suggests, but this must be subordinate to the power of incubation. We have already noticed that Blake's words *form* and *image* mean a species persisting through time: "The Oak dies as well as the Lettuce, but Its Eternal Image

[8] *Moby Dick*, chapter cxix.
[9] Marginal annotations to page 426 of Lavater's *Aphorisms on Man*, K78.

& Individuality never dies, but renews by its seed." [10] Further, when Blake says, "Each thing is its own cause and its own effect," [11] he means that life is not itself caused by anything external to it, and that there is no causality which is not part of an organic process. Accidents happen, but when they do they are not part of a larger superhuman scheme; they are part of the breakdown of human schemes, and their "meaning" depends on what the human mind does with them.

Blake was familiar enough with the earlier manifestations of life-force worship in eighteenth-century primitivism. That postulated a "nature" as the body of life from which man has sprung, and that too attempted to cut parts away from the human imagination by asserting that the latter was diseased and adulterated insofar as it had developed away from nature. Blake had no use for the noble savage or for the cult of the natural man; he disliked Rousseau enough to give an attack on him a prominent place in *Jerusalem*. Civilization is in more than one sense supernatural: it is something which man's superiority over nature has evolved, and the central symbol of the imagination in all Blake's work is the city. "Where man is not, nature is barren," [12] he says. Of all animals, man is the most hopelessly maladjusted to nature: that is why he outdistances the animals, the supreme triumph of the imagination which has developed and conquered rather than survived and "fitted."

[4]

Thus we find ourselves unable to conceive of anything superhuman in the direction of either design or power. The same thing happens when we try to conceive a "perfect" God. Perfection, when it means anything, means the full development of all one's imagination. This is what Jesus meant when he said "Be ye therefore perfect." But many timid abstract thinkers feel that this is irreverent, and that perfection lies in the completeness with which a quality is abstracted from a real thing. God is thus thought to be "pure" goodness. Such a God could never have created Falstaff, to whom he would be vastly inferior. If this idea of "pure" perfection is pressed a little further it dissolves in negatives, as all abstract ideas do. God is infinite, inscrutable, incomprehensible—all negative words, and a negative communion with some undefined ineffability is its highest develop-

[10] Note to pp. 68-69 ["A Vision of the Last Judgment"] *From the Note-book,* K605.
[11] Marginal annotations (conclusion) to Lavater's *Aphorisms on Man,* K88.
[12] *The Marriage of Heaven and Hell,* plate 10, K152.

ment. What Blake thinks of this he has put into one of his most brilliant epigrams:

> God Appears & God is Light
> To those poor Souls who dwell in Night,
> But does a Human Form Display
> To those who Dwell in Realms of day.[13]

It is an old quibble that God cannot move because to move is to alter and to alter would be to lessen his perfection. As long as this means abstract perfection, the argument is unanswerable: a negatively perfect God is not a Creator.

In the first chapter of Genesis we read of a God, or Gods, called Elohim, who can be reconciled with a philosophical First Cause. So completely is he a God of unconscious and automatic order that he created the sun, moon and stars chiefly to provide a calendar for Jewish ritual, and rested on the Sabbath to institute a ceremonial law. In the next chapter we come across a folklore God named Jehovah, a fussy, scolding, bad-tempered but kindly deity who orders his disobedient children out of his garden after making clothes for them, who drowns the world in a fit of anger and re-peoples it in a fit of remorse. Such a God has much to learn, but he comes far closer to what Jesus meant by a Father than the other, and gets a correspondingly higher place in Blake's symbolism.[14]

Even when we try to think of the superhuman in terms of intelligence and imagination we run into difficulties. To be is to be perceived, and we perceive nothing higher than man. The one certain inference from this is that we cannot conceive an essentially superhuman imagination, and when we try to imagine above human nature we always imagine below it. It has been said that grasshoppers are like gods in that they are without blood or feeling. Such gods are therefore as much inferior to man as grasshoppers are, or would be if they could exist. We can imagine men who can do things we cannot; who can fly, who perspire instead of excreting food, who converse by intuition instead of words. But these are differences in attributes, not in substance: the latter we cannot imagine. In Blake there are no characters who represent anything qualitatively superior to man in the way that a man is superior to a fish. There is no "chain of being" in Blake and no trace of any of the creatures invented by those who believe in a chain of being: no gods, no eons, no emanations (in the Gnostic sense: Blake's use of this term is different), no world-soul, no angelic intelligences bound

---

[13] "Auguries of Innocence," lines 129-32, K434.
[14] [See chapter 5 of Frye's complete *Fearful Symmetry*—T. J. J. A.]; and cf. H. Crabb Robinson, *Reminiscences of Blake*, s. 1826 (*Selections*, ed. Morley, 23).

on the spindle of necessity. If they had any intelligence they would get off it, as man got off the spindle of nature.

This is important as throwing some light on Blake's idea of inspiration. It is true that Blake often makes remarks implying an external spiritual agency. He speaks, for instance, of his poems as "dictated," and of himself as their "secretary." [15] But usually the term *angel* or *spirit* in Blake, when not used in an ironic sense, means the imagination functioning as inspiration, and the fact that inspiration often takes on a purpose of its own which appears to be independent of the will is familiar to every creative artist. Blake says, for instance: "Every man's leading propensity ought to be call'd his leading Virtue & his good Angel." [16] It is the same with the "dictation" of his poetry:

> When this Verse was first dictated to me, I consider'd a Monotonous Cadence . . . to be a necessary and indispensible part of Verse. But I soon found . . .

If the inspiration were anything external to Blake he would have had no choice in the matter. "Spirits are organized men," he says, and he would agree with Paul that "the spirits of the prophets are subject to the prophets." [17]

The spirit which is the organized man may also be, however, the imagination which has got itself disentangled from its present world through the process we call death. The imagination cannot exist except as a bodily form, but the body is only what others on the same plane of existence see of the soul or mind. Hence when the imagination changes its world it can change its bodily form as completely as the lepidoptera which have suggested most of the images of immortality. Christianity has always insisted on the resurrection of the body, though the two facts that the risen body is spiritual and that it is a body are hard to keep both in mind at once. All belief in ghosts or shades or in any form of spirit conceived as less than bodily is superstitious: there is no *animula vagula blandula*[18] in Blake.

[5]

There is no divinity in sky, nature or thought superior to our selves. Hence there is in Blake no acceptance of the *données* of existence as such, no

---

[15] Letter to Thomas Butts, July 6, 1803, K825.
[16] Marginal annotations (conclusion) to Lavater's *Aphorisms on Man*, K88; cf. *Jerusalem*, plate 3, K621.
[17] *A Descriptive Catalogue of Pictures* . . . , number IV, K576-77; cf. I Cor. 14:32.
[18] A famous and untranslatable Latin phrase of Hadrian's referring most simply to the individual human soul.—T. J. J. A.

Leibnitzian idea of the perfection of *established* order. Nor is there any idea of finding in nature external hints or suggestions of God; all such intuitions are implanted by the mind on nature. Nature is there for us to transform; it is neither a separate creation of God nor an objective counterpart of ourselves. Blake criticized Wordsworth sharply for ascribing to nature what he should have ascribed to his own mind and for believing in the correspondence of human and natural orders:

> How exquisitely the individual Mind
> (And the progressive powers perhaps no less
> Of the whole species) to the external World
> Is fitted:—and how exquisitely, too—
> Theme this but little heard of among men—
> The external World is fitted to the Mind.

"You shall not bring me down to believe such fitting & fitted," is Blake's comment on this passage.[19]

We arrive at the emotions of acceptance and obedience only at the price of stifling part of our imaginations. In terms of man's desires, we see nothing outside man worthy of respect. Nature is miserably cruel, wasteful, purposeless, chaotic and half dead. It has no intelligence, no kindness, no love and no innocence. Man under natural law is more pitiful than Diogenes' plucked cock. In a state of nature man must surrender intelligence for ferocity and cunning, kindness and pity for a relentless fight to survive, love for the reproductive instinct, innocence for obedience to humiliating laws.

When we look up from the earth to the whizzing balls of ice and fire in the sky we see there merely an extension of nature. It is instinctive with the ignorant to worship the sun as the giver of life, and superstition of this sort is described by Blake as ignorant honesty, beloved of God and man.[20] The advance of knowledge in revealing the deadness and remoteness of the sun should not destroy this instinct for worship, but it should eliminate the sun as a possible object of it. Unthinkable distances and endless resources for killing anyone who might conceivably approach them is all the response the heavens afford to the exploring imagination. They therefore cannot be connected with any feeling of love, reverence, loyalty or anything else we associate with a personal God. And an impersonal God can be worshiped only by the servile, the self-hypnotized, the hypocritical, or at most the resigned.

[19] Marginal annotations, pp. xii-xiii, *The Recluse* . . . by William Wordsworth, K784.
[20] Marginal annotations, pp. 342, Lavater's *Aphorisms on Man*, K74-75.

However, it is all very well to abuse nature, but the divinity in us which Blake postulates is hardly more reassuring. We are capable of depths of cruelty and folly that sink below anything in nature. Yet is not the source of evil the natural weakness of man's body, the form his mind takes in the physical world? Our sight is feeble compared to the lynx; our movements stumbling and foolish compared to a bird; our strength and beauty grotesque compared to the tiger. Once we begin to think in terms of wish and desire, we find ourselves beating prison bars. Our desire to see goes far beyond any telescope. We are ashamed of our bodies, and though the shame itself is shameful, particularly when we realize that they are the forms of our souls, it is there, and it is hard to love a Creator who could, for instance, make our "places of joy & love excrementitious." [21] We are fearfully and wonderfully made, but in terms of what our imaginations suggest we could be, we are a hideous botch. The man who does not use his imagination is the natural man, and the natural man, according to all versions of Christianity except Deism, can do nothing good; yet what does the imagination do except reveal to us our own impotence?

The realization that the world we desire and create with our imaginations is both better and more real than the world we see leads us to regard the latter world as "fallen." It is a cheap print or reproduction of what was once the vision of the unbounded creative power of God, and all great visions in art lead up to visions of the unfallen world, called Paradise in the Bible and the Golden Age in the Classics. "The Nature of my Work is Visionary or Imaginative," said Blake; "it is an Endeavour to Restore what the Ancients call'd the Golden Age." [22] In Christian terms, this means that the end of art is the recovery of Paradise. The Bible tells us that in Paradise man was integrated with God: nature to him was not ocean and wilderness but his own property, symbolized by a garden or park which is what the word *Paradise* means; animals were neither ferocious nor terrified, and life had no pain or death.

In Blake there are certain modifications of the orthodox account of the Fall. One is that as all reality is mental, the fall of man's mind involved a corresponding fall of the physical world. Another is, that as God is Man, Blake follows some of the Gnostics and Boehme in believing that the fall of man involved a fall in part of the divine nature. Not all, for then there would be no imagination left to this one; but part, because it is impossible to derive a bad world from a good God, without a great deal of unconvincing special pleading and an implicit denial of the central fact of Christianity, the identity of God and Man. The conclusion for Blake, and

---

[21] *Jerusalem,* plate 88, K734.
[22] Note to pages 71-72 of ["A Vision of the Last Judgment"] *From the Note-Book,* K605.

the key to much of his symbolism, is that the fall of man and the creation of the physical world were the same event.

All works of civilization, all the improvements and modifications of the state of nature that man has made, prove that man's creative power is literally supernatural. It is precisely because man is superior to nature that he is so miserable in a state of nature. Now in a state of nature, in which we use as little imagination as possible, our minds exist in the form only of our dirty, fragile, confined bodies, and from that point of view man is a speck of life precariously perched on a larger speck in a corner of a huge, mysterious, indifferent, lifeless cosmos. When the subject exists in a cramped distortion the object will necessarily exist in a monstrous distortion. The visionary insists that everything in the physical world which we call real is a matter of perspective and associations:

> How do you know but ev'ry Bird that cuts the airy way,
> Is an immense world of delight, clos'd by your senses five? [23]

There is nothing particularly lovable about a wolf or a fox, but there may be about a dog. Man has caught and trained the dog; he has developed the dog's intelligence and has projected his own imagination on him. He loves the dog more than the wolf because there is more of man in the dog. We get out of nature what we put into it, and the training of a dog is an imaginative victory over nature. So an artist catches and trains the objects of his vision; he can put human imagination into them, make them intelligible and responsive. In a picture every detail is significant and relevant to the whole design. That is an image of the world the visionary wants to live in; a world so fully possessed by the human imagination that its very rocks and clouds are more alive and more responsive than the dogs in this world are. Up to a point we can talk to a dog and make him talk back; we cannot make a tree talk back, but in a higher world we could create the tree as completely as we create sons and daughters in this world. The Classical dryad represents a partial attempt to transform an object of perception into a creature:

> . . . the forms of all things are derived from their Genius, which by the Ancients was call'd an Angel & Spirit & Demon.[24]

The *Metamorphoses* of Ovid record the converse process, of humanized creatures dwindling into objects of perception, which implies that they are images of the fall of man. As our imaginations expand the world takes on

---

[23] *The Marriage of Heaven and Hell,* plate 7, K150.
[24] *All Religions Are One,* K98. For Ovid cf. note to page 79 of ["A Vision of the Last Judgment"] *From the Note-Book,* K607.

a growing humanity, for to see things as created by God and in God is the same as seeing things as created by Man and in Man:

> . . . Each grain of Sand,
> Every Stone of the Land,
> Each rock & each hill,
> Each fountain & rill,
> Each herb & each tree,
> Mountain, hill, earth & sea,
> Cloud, Meteor & Star,
> Are Men seen Afar.[25]

The fallen world is the world of the *Songs of Experience*: the unfallen world is the world of the *Songs of Innocence*. Naturally those who live most easily in the latter are apt to be, from the point of view of those absorbed wholly in the former, somewhat naïve and childlike. In fact most of them are actually children. Children live in a protected world which has something, in epitome, of the intelligibility of the state of innocence, and they have an imaginative recklessness which derives from that. The child who cries to have the moon as a plaything, who slaps a table for hurting him when he bumps his head, who can transform the most unpromising toy into a congenial companion, has something which the adult can never wholly abandon without collapsing into mediocrity.

The paradisal Eden of the Bible is described in terms of a pastoral placidity which may suggest to an unsympathetic reader that Adam fell because he outgrew it: the suggestion is much stronger in *Paradise Lost*. Yet this association of innocence with naïveté is by no means adequate. An unfallen world completely vitalized by the imagination suggests human beings of gigantic strength and power inhabiting it, such as we find hinted at in the various Titanic myths. The vision of such beings would be able to penetrate all the mysteries of the world, searching into mountains or stars with equal ease, as in this description of the bound Titan Orc:

> His eyes, the lights of his large soul, contract or else expand;
> Contracted they behold the secrets of the infinite mountains,
> The veins of gold & silver & the hidden things of Vala,
> Whatever grows from its pure bud or breathes a fragrant soul;
> Expanded they behold the terrors of the Sun & Moon,
> The Elemental Planets & the Orbs of eccentric fire.[26]

Even in those moments when most "we feel that we are greater than we know," this feeling is not so much one of individuality as of integra-

---

[25] Poem in Letter to Thomas Butts, October 2, 1800, K804-05.
[26] *Vala or The Four Zoas,* Night V, lines 121-26, K308.

tion into a higher unit or body of life. This body, of course, is ultimately God, the totality of all imagination. But even men who cannot reach the idea of God believe in the reality of larger human bodies, such as nations, cities or races, and even speak of them as fathers or mothers. It takes a genuine faith to see a nation or race as a larger human being, or form of human existence, and a good deal of such faith is undoubtedly idolatry. Still, there is a partial idea of God in it, and in a Utopia or millennium it would become direct knowledge or vision, such as Milton suggests when he says that "a Commonwealth ought to be but as one huge Christian personage, one mighty growth, and stature of an honest man." [27] Hence these gigantic forms which inhabit the unfallen world are, on nearer view, human aggregates of the kind which inspire loyalty even in this world:

> . . . these various States I have seen in my Imagination; when distant they appear as One Man, but as you approach they appear multitudes of Nations. [28]

This exactly fits what we have just said, that the fall of man involved a fall in part but not all of the divine nature. The particular "Giant form" or "Eternal" to which we belong has fallen, the aggregate of spirits we call mankind or humanity and Blake calls Albion (Adam in Blake has his regular place as the symbol of the physical body or the natural man). When Albion or mankind fell, the unity of man fell too, and although our imagination tells us we belong to some larger organism even if we cannot see it as God, in the meantime we are locked up in separated opaque scattered bodies. If the whole of mankind were once more integrated in a single spiritual body the universe as we see it would burst.

Theology distinguishes between "natural" and "revealed" religion, the former being the vision of God which man develops with his fallen reason and the latter the vision communicated to him by inspired prophets. To Blake "There Is No Natural Religion." The only reason that people believe in it is that they are unwilling to believe in the identity of God and Man. If there is evil in nature, it must be our fault and not God's; therefore God created the world good, the extent to which man's fall altered that goodness being a disputed point. But if we stop trying to rescue the credit of an abstract and pure goodness, we can easily see that all religion is revealed. The Greek word for revelation is *apocalypse,* and the climax of Christian teaching is in the "Revelation" or Apocalypse at the end of the

[27] John Milton, *Of Reformation Touching Church Discipline in England,* Book ii, Introduction.
[28] Note to pages 76-77 of ["A Vision of the Last Judgment"] *From the Note-Book,* K607.

Bible which tells us that there is an end to time as well as a beginning and a middle, a resurrection as well as a birth and a death; and that in this final revelation of the unfallen world all mystery will vanish: John's symbol is the burning of the Great Whore who is called Mystery. Such a revelation involves the destruction of the present world, when the sun will be turned into darkness and the moon into blood and the stars will fall from heaven like ripe figs. It moves on to a new heaven and earth (i.e., an earth renewed or revealed in the form of heaven), in which the chaos of nature becomes our own garden, as in Paradise, a world no longer continuously perceived but continually created:

> In futurity
> I prophetic see
> That the earth from sleep
> (Grave the sentence deep)
> Shall arise and seek
> For her maker meek;
> And the desart wild
> Become a garden mild.[29]

Now when something is revealed to us we see it, and the response to this revelation is not faith in the unseen or hope in divine promises but vision, seeing face to face after we have been seeing through a glass darkly. Vision is the end of religion, and the destruction of the physical universe is the clearing of our own eyesight. Art, because it affords a systematic training in this kind of vision, is the medium through which religion is revealed. The Bible is the vehicle of revealed religion because it is a unified vision of human life and therefore, as Blake says, "the Great Code of Art." [30] And if all art is visionary, it must be apocalyptic and revelatory too: the artist does not wait to die before he lives in the spiritual world into which John was caught up. To quote Wordsworth again in a passage which explains why Blake admired as well as criticized him:

> . . . The unfettered clouds and region of the Heavens,
> Tumult and peace, the darkness and the light—
> Were all like workings of one mind, the features
> Of the same face, blossoms upon one tree;
> Characters of the great Apocalypse,
> The types and symbols of Eternity.[31]

According to Wordsworth the perceived forms of the eternal world are

[29] *Songs of Innocence,* "The Little Girl Lost," K112-13.
[30] *Laocoön Aphorisms,* K777.
[31] William Wordsworth, *The Prelude,* vi, 634-39.

those which are constantly perceived in this one, and it is not in the grandiose or exceptional experience that "the types and symbols of Eternity" are to be found. Blake is merely extending this principle when he says in "Auguries of Innocence":

> To see a World in a Grain of Sand
> And a Heaven in a Wild Flower,
> Hold Infinity in the palm of your hand
> And Eternity in an hour.[32]

Such perception, as the title of the poem makes clear, is an "augury" of the paradisal unfallen state. The last two lines bring us to the next step in the argument.

Those who, like Locke, attempt to separate existence from perception are also separating time from space, as we exist in time and perceive in space. Those who, like the artists, accept the mental nature of reality know that we perceive a thing at a definite moment and that there is thus a quality of time inherent in all perception; and, on the other hand, that existence is in a body, which has a spatial extension. We are back again to Blake's doctrine that "Reason is the bound or outward circumference of Energy," that energy and form, existence and perception, are the same thing. Consequently every act of the imagination, every such union of existence and perception, is a time-space complex, not time plus space, but time *times* space, so to speak, in which time and space as we know them disappear, as hydrogen and oxygen disappear when they become water.

This is what the words *eternal* and *infinite* mean in Blake. Eternity is not endless time, nor infinity endless space: they are the entirely different mental categories through which we perceive the unfallen world. A spiritual world which is visualized as a world of unchanging order, symbolized by the invariable interrelations of mathematics, is not an eternal world but a spatial one, from which time has simply been eliminated. And, to complete the antithesis, a spiritual world visualized as one of unchanging duration is a world of abstract time, from which the "bounding outline" or spatial limits of existence have been eliminated. The Lockian can conceive of eternity and infinity only in either or both of these ways: that is why he uses two words, one suggesting time and the other space, for the same thing. But his two categories have nothing to do with real infinity and eternity; nor, in fact, has he two of them: all he has in each case is the indefinite, which is the opposite of the infinite or eternal, and one of the most sinister words in Blake's symbolism.

Clock time is a mental nightmare like all other abstract ideas. An

---

[32] "Auguries of Innocence," lines 1-4, K431.

impalpable present vanishing between an irrevocable past and an unknown future, it is the source of all our ideas of fate and causality. It suggests an inexorable march of inevitably succeeding events in which everything is a necessary consequence of causes stretching back to an unknown God as a First Cause and stretching on into a future which would be completely predictable if it were not too complicated. Its only possible symbol not only for Blake but even for those who believe in it is the chain, which is also a symbol of slavery. At best time is "the mercy of Eternity";[33] its swiftness makes more tolerable the conditions of our fallen state.

To the imaginative eye there is a more definite shape to time. In most religious allegories, including Blake's, this is indicated by the boundaries ascribed to it, a beginning at the creation or fall and an end at the apocalypse. This is a convenient way of expressing the fact that the fallen world is temporal and the unfallen eternal, but it is not essential, and is even misleading when carried too far. "In the beginning God created the heaven and earth": if we try to visualize what happened *before* that, we get an impression of extraordinary bleakness. This is because we cannot think of eternity except by extending time indefinitely, when we think of it as a continuation of this world:

> Many suppose that before the Creation All was Solitude & Chaos. This is the most pernicious Idea that can enter the Mind. . . . Eternity Exists, and All things in Eternity, Independent of Creation which was an act of Mercy.[34]

Orthodox ideas of the joys of heaven and the torments of hell also deal with the indefinite rather than the eternal.

The religious idea of "salvation" depends on transcending this view of time. The man survives the death of the natural part of him as the total form of his imaginative acts, as the human creation out of nature which he has made. When Blake says, "Eternity is in love with the productions of time," [35] he means in part that every imaginative victory won on this earth, whether by the artist, the prophet, the martyr, or by those who achieve triumphs of self-sacrifice, kindliness and endurance, is a permanent reality, while the triumphs of the unimaginative are lost. Existence and perception being the same thing, man exists eternally by virtue of, and to the extent of, his perception of eternity. Any doctrine of personal immortality which conceives of it either as the survival of the individual or of the disappearance of the individual into some objective form of generalized

---

[33] *Milton*, plate 24, K510.
[34] Note to pages 91-92 of ["A Vision of the Last Judgment"] *From the Note-Book*, K614.
[35] *The Marriage of Heaven and Hell*, plate 7, K151.

being, such as matter or force or the collective memory of posterity, is again thinking of the eternal as the indefinite.

The same principles apply to space. The universe stretches out to indefiniteness in all directions, and to the fallen eye it is without any kind of limit or outline. All that this suggests to the imagination is the latter's own insignificance and helplessness. Yet somehow we manage to shrug it off and go on with our own concerns. By doing so we indicate that as far as our lives go there is something about time and space that is not real, and something about us that is. However man may have tumbled into this world of indefinite space, he does not belong to it at all. Real space for him is the eternal here; where we are is always the center of the universe, and the circumference of our affairs is the circumference of the universe, just as real time is the "eternal Now" [36] of our personal experience. The ordinary man assumes, as a working hypothesis, that all the universe outside his range is not worth bothering one's head about unduly. The visionary sees, as the final revelation of the Word which God speaks to his mind, that the whole "outside" universe is a shadow of an eclipsed Man.

[6]

According to Locke ideas come from space into the mind; according to Blake space is a state of mind. But, as fallen man sees around him only the ruins of a fallen world which his own fall produced, space is a low state of mind. In higher states, where the world we live in is not objective but created, space is no longer an indefinite extent but the form of what we create. This portion of Blake's argument comes, *mutatis mutandis,* from Swedenborg.[37] Let us now return to that crucial passage about the two suns. . . .

> Error is Created. Truth is Eternal. Error, or Creation, will be Burned up, & then, & not till Then, Truth or Eternity will appear. It is Burnt up the Moment Men cease to behold it. I assert for My Self that I do not behold the outward Creation & that to me it is hindrance & not Action; it is as the dirt upon my feet, No part of Me. "What," it will be Question'd, "When the Sun rises, do you not see a round disk of fire somewhat like a Guinea?" O no, no, I see an Innumerable company of the Heavenly host crying, "Holy, Holy, Holy is the Lord God Almighty." I Question not my Corporeal or Vegetative Eye any more

[36] Marginal annotations to page 407 of Lavater's *Aphorisms on Man,* K77.
[37] See especially *Divine Love and Divine Wisdom,* i, 40-82. Cf. M. O. Percival, *William Blake's Circle of Destiny* (New York: Columbia University Press, 1938), p. 83 f.

than I would Question a Window concerning a Sight. I look thro' it &
not with it.

We have said that there are at least three levels of imagination. The
lowest is that of the isolated individual reflecting on his memories of perception and evolving generalizations and abstract ideas. This world is single,
for the distinction of subject and object is lost and we have only a brooding
subject left. Blake calls this world Ulro; it is his hell, and his symbols for
it are symbols of sterility, chiefly rocks and sand. Above it is the ordinary
world we live in, a double world of subject and object, of organism and
environment, which Blake calls Generation. No living thing is completely
adjusted to this world except the plants, hence Blake usually speaks of it
as vegetable. Above it is the imaginative world, and Blake divides this into
an upper and a lower part, so that the three worlds expand into four.

Imagination very often begins with a vision of wonderful and unearthly
beauty. The writings of many visionaries are full of a childlike delight in
a paradisal world which is the same world that other people see, but seen
differently. Traherne's *Centuries of Meditations* is a typical book of this
kind: the feeling that with the purging of vision one is enabled to possess
the entire universe is particularly strong there. Sexual love dwells in the
same paradisal state, and from such a love we may proceed up a ladder of
love to an imaginative awakening, as in the traditional philosophy of love
derived from the *Symposium*.

Love and wonder, then, are stages in an imaginative expansion: they
establish a permanent unity of subject and object, and they lift us from a
world of subject and object to a world of lover and beloved. Yet they
afford us only a lower Paradise after all. Wonder would doubtless have
been defined by Blake differently from Johnson's "effect of novelty upon
ignorance," [38] but perhaps he would only have substituted *innocence* for
the last word. Ultimately, our attitude to what we see is one of mental
conquest springing from active energy. Love and wonder are relaxations
from this state: they do not produce the visions of art but an imaginative
receptivity. The "Renaissance of Wonder" to Blake could be nothing more
than a preliminary imaginative revolt from the fallen world. The imaginative intensity which finds delight and beauty in considering the lilies may
remain suffusing us with a vague and unlocalized joy, and with this we may
well be content. But the impulse to make some kind of creation out of it
is still there, and poetry and painting are the result of the perseverance of
vision into conquest. The highest possible state, therefore, is not the union
of lover and beloved, but of creator and creature, of energy and form.
This latter is the state for which Blake reserves the name Eden. The lower
Paradise he calls Beulah, a term derived from Isaiah which means "mar-

[38] *Lives of the Poets*: "Yalden."

ried" and is used to describe the relation of a land to its people.[39] Eden in Blake's symbolism is a fiery city of the spiritual sun; Beulah is the garden of Genesis in which the gods walk in the cool of the day.

As Ulro is a single and Generation a double world, so Beulah is triple, the world of lover, beloved and mutual creation; the father, the mother and the child. In Eden these three are contained in the unified imagination symbolized in the Bible by the four "Zoas" or living creatures around the throne or chariot of God, described by Ezekiel and John.[40] This world therefore is fourfold, expanding to infinity like the four points of the compass which in this world point to the indefinite. To recapitulate:

> Now I a fourfold vision see,
> And a fourfold vision is given to me;
> 'Tis fourfold in my supreme delight
> And threefold in soft Beulah's night
> And twofold Always. May God us keep
> From Single vision & Newton's sleep! [41]

(The twofold vision here, however, is not that of Generation, but the ability to see an unfallen world as well as a fallen one.)

[7]

We began . . . by showing that for Blake there can be no question of finding God through either the understanding or the will. That is because the distinction between them, which it is necessary to make first in order to get rid of one of them later, is a distinction based on the "Two Horn'd Reasoning, Cloven Fiction" of the Lockian universe. Those for whom subject and object, existence and perception, activity and thought, are all parts of a gigantic antithesis, will naturally conceive of man as split between an egocentric will and a reason which establishes contact with the nonego. Believers in the cloven fiction tend to come to rest finally in either a will-philosophy or a reason-philosophy, trying in each case to minimize the importance of the one they reject, because they are seeking to unify their ideas by reducing the problem from the double world of Generation to the single world of Ulro. One group assumes that will and energy exist by themselves *in vacuo,* and the other makes similar assumptions about necessity and established order.

[39] Isa. 62:4.
[40] Ezek. 1; Rev. 4.
[41] Poem in Letter to Thomas Butts, November 22, 1802, K818.

[For] Blake the subjective navel-gazer and the objective atomist make the identical blunder of chopping the world in two and differ only about which piece of it they are to seize. Those who seek understanding and power form a similar, or rather part of the same, false contrast. One group pursues God into an indefinite omnipotence, the other into an indefinite omniscience, and both lose sight of his humanity and personality. We may put the same point in another way. The will and the reason may be good or bad: if they are to be good, they must meet the standards or conditions of goodness. The will has to meet the standards ordinarily called justice and morality; the reason has to meet the standard of truth. Now these forms of the "good" as we should expect, have in common the impersonal and general quality of law. That two and two make four is equally true for everyone; that a murderer shall be hanged applies to all members of the state which adopts such a law. Here again, the "subject" with which we start seems to get lost in both directions, and to disappear into the uniformity of guinea-sun perceivers.

Hence the "good" is traditionally threefold in division, and includes a middle term of *beauty* which, unlike the other two, seems to have a personal and human reference, and, though it undoubtedly possesses laws, they are laws of a much more flexible kind, which are able to allow for the differences that actually do exist among human beings. Now it is clear that Blake's dislike of antithetical modes of thought will not be appeased by adding a middle term, even one regarded as a *tertium quid*. "Beauty" to Blake is not a third form of the good, but good itself, the union in which the reality of the other two consists; it is pursued not by feeling or emotion or any part of the personality, but by the imagination which is "the Real Man." [42] The product of "beauty" is art; art is civilization; and it is only civilization that can give any value or any meaning to those impersonalizing tendencies of the mind which build up the imaginative forms of science and morality. Thus Blake's identification of religion with art is utterly different from the Romantic identification of the religious and aesthetic experiences. There is no place in his thought for aesthetics, or general theories of abstract beauty.

[8]

If the highest state of man is fourfold in Blake's symbolism, we should expect him to reject the doctrine of a threefold God. Here Blake follows his master Swedenborg, who attacked the orthodox Trinity as tritheistic. In *Paradise Lost,* Blake complains, "the Father is Destiny, the Son a

[42] Marginal annotations to page 241 of Berkeley's *Siris,* K775.

Ratio of the five senses, and the Holy Ghost Vacuum." [43] In theology something is usually done with the conceptions of power and wisdom, but the middle term, as in the ethical diagram, is apt to prove embarrassing and be tacitly dropped. Yet the conception of God as a Holy Spirit, the giver and incubator of life, the indwelling person of God, the eternal Self, is, once again, the unity in which the reality of the other two consists. It was the Holy Spirit that spoke by the prophets, which means that it continues to speak by the artists who have prophetic imaginations. The "inspiration" which artists have is therefore the breath or spirit of God which dwells in the artist and is the artist. Such inspiration is the only proof we have of the existence of a spiritual power greater than ourselves. Art, then, is "the gift of God, the Holy Ghost." [44]

What did the Holy Spirit that spoke by the prophets speak about? It prophesied the Messiah; that is, it saw God as man and understood that "God becomes as we are, that we may be as he is." [45] In Milton this Messiah is a ratio of the five senses because he created the fallen world with its guinea-sun. Such a creative principle is a Nous, a reason or mathematical order, the automatism by which nature maintains enough permanence to keep from dissolving into nonexistence. This Nous is to be visualized as a Father rather than a Son, a hoary "Ancient of Days" such as stretches out his compasses (notice the mathematical symbol) in the frontispiece to *Europe*.[46] Jesus is not a Nous but a Logos, a compelling Word who continually recreates an unconscious floundering universe into something with beauty and intelligence. The Son and the Holy Spirit are therefore the same thing. And this Son or Spirit is also the universal Man who is the unified form of our scattered imaginations, and which we visualize as a Father. The three persons of the Trinity are to be connected by or's rather than and's, and the real God is fourfold, power, love and wisdom contained within the unity of civilized human imagination. This God is a God-Man, the Jesus in whose eternal and infinite risen body we find our own being after we have outgrown the imaginative infancy which the orthodox conception of the Fatherhood of God implies for us. The final revelation of Christianity is, therefore, not that Jesus is God, but that "God is Jesus." [47]

The life of man is polarized between the Creator and the Creation, more abundant life in the larger human mind and body of God and acceptance of the minimum life of nature and reason. Any real religion contains much to encourage the imagination, but it is likely also to try to give

[43] *The Marriage of Heaven and Hell,* plates 5-6, K150.
[44] *A Descriptive Catalogue of Pictures* . . . , number V, K579.
[45] *There Is No Natural Religion* [Second Series], K98.
[46] See Illustration 1, and note, page 433, in the complete *Fearful Symmetry*.
[47] *Laocoön Aphorisms,* K777. Cf. *Faust* I, lines 1224-37.

some divine sanction to the fallen world. Hence when its followers come to the place where they should make the supreme effort to become part of a universal human and divine creator (this place in Blake is the upper limit of Beulah), they find nature and reason blocking the way in a divine disguise. Here they must choose between the Word and the World, and if their choice is wrong they will be like Goethe's Faust, who, unable to grasp the meaning of *"das Wort,"* translates it as *"die That,"* the thing made as opposed to its Maker, and falls into the power of a devil.

A certain amount of natural religion exists in all Christian Churches, but it is only in Blake's own time that the cult of reason and nature has been precipitated from Christianity and made into a dogmatic system with all loopholes for the imagination sealed off. This system is Deism, a term Blake associates, not only with both Voltaire and Rousseau, but with the whole culture of the Age of Reason and the return to nature. For Deism, God is a hypothesis necessary to account for the beginning of the chain of causality; otherwise human life should be confined to nature and reason. That is, its Father is destiny, its Logos the ratio of the five senses, and its Spirit of love and beauty a vacuum—the faults of Milton's thinking unified into a single systematic falsehood. Locke was responsible for Deism, whether he was a Deist himself or not; for his cloven fiction is the source of its separation of the divine and the human. This cleavage in religion produces an antithesis of idolaters: one the egocentric contemplative who broods over his soul, the other the antinomian who pursues a life of selfish expediency. Now while one may find handsome crops of both kinds of tares in all religions, it is only in Deism, which plants no wheat, that they cease to become hypocrites.

We shall never understand why Blake so hated Deism unless we understand not only what it was to him, but what he saw that it would soon become. That is, we must accept in Blake a certain amount of prophecy in the literal sense of anticipating the probable future, and must see in his conception of Deism a mental attitude which is still with us, the monstrous hydra which is the perverted vision of human society as an atomic aggregate of egos instead of as a larger human body. The closer man comes to the state of nature, the more he clings to the "reason" which enables him to deal with nature on its own terms. The natural society, whether we see it in primitive tribes or in exhausted civilizations, is a complicated mechanism of prescribed acts which always have a rational explanation, but make no sense whatever in terms of passion, energy, insight or wisdom. The natural man is not the solitary majestic lion that he would like to be: he is a buzzing and spineless insect, a flying head cut off at the neck, like the cherubs in Reynolds, equipped with a venomous sting and a stupefied sense of duty. So at least he appears in Blake, both as the Deist of Blake's time and as the "Druid" which Blake predicted he would soon become.

An apocalyptic mind, however, is apt to feel that his own time is the darkest hour before the dawn, and to Blake the appearance of this consolidated system of error suggested that it might well be followed by some prophet who, by refuting it, might be the herald of a genuine apocalypse. Swedenborg had said that the Last Judgment took place in the spiritual world in 1757. This did not impress Blake unduly, but neither did he forget altogether that he had been born in that year.[48]

---

[48] Swedenborg, *True Christian Religion,* 115. Cf. *The Marriage of Heaven and Hell,* plate 3, K149.

2

GEORG WILHELM FRIEDRICH HEGEL

Despite the violent reaction against Hegel which took place in the century following his death, he is increasingly being recognized as the philosophical father of the modern world just as Aristotle was of the ancient world. Surely no other thinker has originated so many ideas which later were to become dominant in history and consciousness. Christian theologians, however, although few of them are acquainted with more than his posthumously published lectures, almost universally have been hostile to Hegel, for his thought is profoundly threatening to the inherited dogmatic and ecclesiastical forms of Christianity.

Much recent criticism indicates that the central method of Hegel's thinking is grounded in a deeply radical but nevertheless consistent faith in Christ. Moreover, there is scarcely room to doubt that Hegel's thinking is also grounded in the death of God. A primary problem for the theologian is the relation in Hegel's thinking between the kenotic or self-emptying movement or method of "pure negativity" and the consequent negation of the transcendence and the once-and-for-all-ness of God. Any extensive investigation of this problem would eventually necessitate a direct examination of Hegel's two most important works, the *Phenomenology of Spirit* (1807) and the *Science of Logic* (1812); the discussion of Christianity and religion in the former might well become a seminal text for the future evolution of theology. However, the complexity and depth of Hegel's philosophical language poses as many problems for the reader as does the poetic language of Blake. Therefore the selection which follows here is from J. N. Findlay's lucid and scholarly analysis and recapitulation of Hegel's *Phenomenology of Spirit*.

J. N.
Findlay

Hegel's Study of the Religious Consciousness

RELIGION IN GENERAL

The long section on *Religion* . . . is one of the most important in the *Phenomenology*. Hegel . . . arrived at the main insights of his system in the course of those long broodings on the meaning of the Christian faith which occurred during his stay at Bern and Frankfurt. His whole system may in fact be regarded as an attempt to see the Christian mysteries in everything whatever, every natural process, every form of human activity, and every logical transition. If this is the case, it is important to know what interpretation Hegel put upon these mysteries, and upon the whole religious frame of mind of which Christianity was for him the highest expression.

Hegel begins his treatment of the Religious Consciousness by noting how often in the previous development we have come on phases that deserved the name *religious*. There was something religious in the activities of the Scientific Understanding, when it located explanatory forces and laws *beneath* the surface of objective existence. We were studying a mood of Religion when we dealt with the anguish of the Unhappy Consciousness and its perpetual hopeless yearning for the Unchangeable. In the ethical sphere, likewise, we dealt with a religious phase that was concerned with mysterious family- and blood-ties, with ancestral allegiances and the powers of the "Nether World." In the world of the Enlightenment we dealt with a religious phase which placed its object safely and aseptically beyond all Rational Insight: *il y a un Etre Suprême* became the whole *Credo* of religion. We also studied the unsatisfactory games played with a

REPRINTED with the permission of The Macmillan Company from [pp. 131-43 of] *Hegel: A Re-Examination* by J. N. Findlay. Copyright © 1958 by J. N. Findlay. Also with the permission of George Allen & Unwin Ltd., publisher.

Divine Legislator by the Moral Consciousness, a Legislator whose function vanished entirely once Conscience became sure of itself and of its power and right to make its own moral decisions. But in this Moral Consciousness there was still a distinction, Hegel tells us, between the self-determining moral personality, and the "world" within which his moral choices were exercised, whether this "world" were a world of objects in nature or of other persons making *their* moral decisions. The self-conscious spiritual individual then rose to the height of its development: in the consciousness of loving forgiveness, which broke down the barriers between persons, it at length overcame the "otherness of the other." Henceforth, according to Hegel, it has surmounted even *consciousness:* it can have no *alien* object before it, but only itself. In other words, it has achieved the vision of itself as the "truth," the *raison-d'être* of everything. The consciousness in which it first gains possession of this truth is called by Hegel "Religion," which is thereby given a content identical with the central theses of his own philosophy. This Religious Consciousness only differs from the philosophical in that it retains what Hegel calls "a form of representation" (*Vorstellung*): it remains tied up with an imaginative picture or story, and with whatever misleading suggestions of externality and finitude such a picture or story may suggest. The religious view will, further, have varying degrees of development according to the development of the "world," the natural and social order, of which it represents the explanatory restatement.

In all this Hegel may be held to have given a merely "persuasive definition" of *Religion*. He has (it may be held) defined Religion, not as it would be defined by those who normally talk of it, but in a manner to suit himself, his main motive being to secure for the difficult theses of his philosophy the approval normally accompanying the words *Religion* and *religious. Religion* and *religious* are terms mainly of praise, not of abuse, and were certainly more so in Hegel's day than our own: Hegel, it may be claimed, is simply "cashing in" on this widespread approval and securing its advantages for his own system. He did in fact gain much approval in his lifetime by being thought to be a defender of religious and political orthodoxy, neither of which he could with any depth of truth be held to be. That Hegel's characterization of Religion *is* persuasive, and that it is also largely arbitrary, can scarcely be gainsaid: Hegel might have stressed its "form of representation" rather than its notional content and might have emphasized its supersession, rather than its preservation, in ultimate philosophical truth. But from another point of view Hegel's account of Religion is by no means indefensible. For the states of mind called "religious" *do* show some tendency to develop from a stage where they seem merely to be talking of facts comparable to the presence of rats in a barn or of cockroaches in the kitchen, to a stage where they express little beyond a wholly new way of viewing life and experience, and a way which has many of the distinction-overriding features of Hegel's "Spirit" and "Idea." And we may also plead, in extenuation of Hegel's account, that he did not foist philosophical theses, independently arrived at, on the religion he found about him: these theses were the fruits of brooding on that religion and may even claim to be among that religion's most profound reflective expressions. It was in the course of his wanderings in the neighborhood of Golgotha and Gethsemane, rather than in his sojourn in Athenian gardens and colonnades, that Hegel first met "the Idea."

In the phases of the Religious Consciousness now to be gone through, Hegel tells us that the previous phenomenological relations of Spirit to its "world" will all be resumed. There will be a sensory, a perceptual, a scientifically-understanding, a customary-ethical, a disintegratedly-enlightened, and a moralistic phase of Religion. These stages will also divide themselves into: (A) Natural Religion, in which the religious consciousness assumes the form of Consciousness Proper, of the awareness of an object, a thing, in which the self-conscious and the spiritual are implicit; (B) The Religion of Art, the product of the Hellenic Spirit, which corresponds to Self-consciousness Proper, and finally (C) Absolute or Revealed Religion, the expression of Christian civilization, in which the actual form of religion is said to be adequate to its "notion."

PRE-CHRISTIAN RELIGION

The first form of Natural Religion studied by Hegel is the Religion of Light, of which he holds the ancient Zoroastrian religion to have been the historic expression. In this the "self-conscious essence which is all truth, and which knows all reality as itself" becomes aware of itself in the mode of *Sense-certainty*. It beholds itself, Hegel tells us, in the form of "being," i.e., of something immediate, "out there," not, however, as endowed with one or other of the contingent qualities of sense, but as manifesting a certain "form of formlessness" (*Gestalt der Gestaltlosigkeit*), which will make it into a "being filled with the notion of Spirit," i.e., into a fit sensuous symbol of self-conscious Spirit. This "form of formlessness" the religious consciousness finds ready to hand in the "pure, all containing, all pervading light of the morning," which may disperse itself over natural shapes, but which remains always the same "simple, impalpable, splendid essence." [1]

But just as Sense-certainty finds that it cannot keep its vague object, the immediate "this," before it, but must proceed to turn it into some more definite object of *Perception,* so too the Religious Consciousness cannot

---

[1] *Phen.*, pp. 528-29 (B., pp. 699-700). [The texts cited are, first, Hegel's *Phänomenologie des Geistes* (Hamburg, 1952) and then, marked "B" and in parentheses, J. B. Baillie's translation, *The Phenomenology of Mind,* 2nd ed. (New York: Macmillan, 1955)—T. J. J. A.]

rest content with an object so formless, but must go on to particularize it into a variety of vegetable and animal forms. We leave the pure radiance of the Iranian dayspring, for the pollulating multiplicity of the Indian religious fancy, which, though it may at times show itself in the peaceful innocence of flowers, more often expresses itself in the murderous, guilty forms of warring animal species, each representing some particular national spirit. (Hegel, we may note, held a singularly ill-informed and unsympathetic view of one of the most Hegelian of peoples and religions.)

The warring variety of this type of religious expression is obviously inadequate to the Religious Consciousness: it therefore "rubs itself away" into the regular expressions characteristic of the *Scientific Understanding*. Spirit becomes an Artificer, revealed to itself in various crystalline, pyramidal and needle-like forms, "simple combinations of straight lines with flat surfaces and equality of parts, in which the incommensurability of the round is avoided." These it constructs in an *instinctive* manner like the building habits of bees. We have passed over to the religious expressions of ancient Egypt. In these the creative unrest of consciousness is present mainly in the artificer and not in his work, but it tends gradually to *invade* his monumental products, showing itself in stylized animal forms faintly touched with humanity, or in hieroglyphs carrying remote and irrelevant meanings. The inadequacy of such instinctive art to self-consciousness then becomes manifest in the form of sphinxes, "ambiguous beings, a riddle even to themselves, the conscious fighting with the unconscious, the simple interior with the polymorphous exterior, coupling obscurity of thought with clearness of expression." [2] In the sphinx this stylized, instinctive, constructive religious consciousness may be said to break down: Spirit demands to see itself in a form made self-consciously rather than instinctively, and expressing self-consciousness in a more adequate manner. We pass from the Nature-religions of the early East to the "Art religion" of Greece.

The next longish subsection (B) is as much a treatment of Greek art and literature as of Greek religion. In the *Phenomenology* the two modes of spiritual consciousness are not kept apart, as they are in the treatment of "Absolute Spirit" in the *Encyclopaedia*.[3] Hegel's treatment of Greek religion as a "Religion of Art" is characteristic of German romanticism. So too is the view that while art may be an expression of the ethical life of the free city-community, with which the individual feels himself at one, the *Religion* of art arises only when the individual's naïve trust in his secure communal ways has been shaken or shattered. Only when Spirit has cause to mourn over the loss of its secure ethical background, will it begin to bring forth an "absolute art" which is raised high above reality, and whose forms, according to Hegel, shadow forth "the night in which the Ethical Substance was betrayed, and made into a Sub-

[2] *Ibid.*, p. 534 (B., p. 707).
[3] The reference is to Hegel's *Encyclopædia*—T. J. J. A.

ject." [4] (Again a reminiscence of Gethsemane.) Works of art are said to be the vessels chosen by Spirit to enshrine its sorrow and body forth its pathos. We, living long after the age of Winckelmann, will find in this pathos little beyond a pathetic fallacy.

The artistic religious consciousness has its first typical expression in the *statue* of the God, which combines the externality of nature with an idealized expression of self-consciousness. Here the exact, crystalline forms beloved by the Understanding are discarded: there is a movement towards forms which, though more exact than those of living bodies, still show the essential incommensurability of the rounded forms of life. The human figure is set free from anything natural or brutal, this being left to the Titans or the older generations of Gods. It is Hegel's view that each such marble God stands for the ethical life of a particular people: in worshiping its God, the community is really achieving self-consciousness. Hence the temples of the Gods are for the use of the citizens, their treasure may in time of need be expended by the state, their honor is the honor of "a high-minded people rich in its art."

The joyous immobility of religious statuary will, however, afford an inadequate expression of the suffering and effort in the artistic self-consciousness that produced it. This spiritual suffering and effort demand another medium for their expression, and this Hegel finds in various forms of religious speech, such as the hymn and the oracular utterance: he also finds it in the combination of speech and action which occurs in the religious cult. "The cult," says Hegel, "is constituted by a two-sided movement in which a godlike form, moving in the affective element of self-consciousness, and the same form at rest in the element of thinghood, give up their distinct determinations, so that the unity, which is the notion of their essence, comes into existence. In this the self achieves the consciousness of the descent of the Divine Essence from its transcendent beyondness, while what was previously the unreal and merely objective, achieves thereby the genuine reality of self-consciousness." [5] This two-sided movement occurs elaborately in the religious sacrifice, where the objects sacrificed are said to express both the worshiper's surrender of his own personality, and the descent into actuality and touch with humanity of the God to whom the objects are sacrificed. In other words, the sacrificial ceremony does not merely bring the worshipers to their knees: it also performs the task, at once Voltairean and mystical, of bringing to earth the aloof and self-sufficient Gods. An even more intimate amalgamation of the divine with the human occurs in the various religious mysteries connected with Demeter and Dionysus. These are mysterious and mystical not in the sense of involving hidden secrets, but in the sense that in them "the self knows itself as one with the Essence, and that the latter is accordingly revealed."

[4] *Phen.,* p. 540 (B., p. 714).
[5] *Ibid.,* p. 445 (B., p. 720).

Here the Absolute Being achieves the position of a thing seen, handled, smelled and tasted, it becomes an object of desire and is made one with the self in actual enjoyment.[6] There remains, however, something unself-conscious, something largely natural in this form of religious amalgamation: hence its ready expression in the wild curvets of a swarm of rapt women. "Its self-conscious life is therefore merely the mystery of the Bread and the Wine, of Ceres and Bacchus, not of the genuine upper Gods, whose individuality includes self-consciousness as an essential element in itself. Spirit has not yet offered itself up to this consciousness as self-conscious Spirit, and the mystery of the Bread and Wine is not as yet the mystery of Flesh and Blood." [7] In other words, we are as yet only dealing with a confused anticipation of the Word made Flesh and its continuance in the life of the religious community.

At this point Hegel might have made a wholly natural and easy transition to his Absolute or Revealed Religion, which was for him historically manifest in Christianity. He prefers, however, to linger longer among the forms of the classical "Art-religion," though some of these have only minor relevance to the theme on hand. Very characteristically, he treats the activities connected with the major athletic festivals as purely religious activities. Athletes are for Hegel "animated, living works of art, matching strength with beauty": they represent the "Essence" in general and also the essence of their people, "not in the petrifaction of a God, but in the highest bodily expressiveness."

Neither Olympic athleticism nor Dionysian enthusiasm can, however, be wholly adequate expressions of the union of self-consciousness with the "essence" of things: in the former there is too spiritless a clearness, in the latter too much confusion and wild stammering. It is in a form of speech more coherent than an oracle's, and less emotional and narrow in its direction than that of a hymn, that such an expression must be found. Hegel therefore passes on to the consideration of the spiritual attitudes lying behind the epic, tragic and comic literature of antiquity, which are for him religious phenomena. We shall not here sum up all the deep and perceptive things he says on these themes. Suffice it to say that he regards the epic as expressing in verbal form the same relations between the human and the divine which are actively expressed in the cult. In the epic, however, the individual self-conscious person is inadequately emphasized, being present merely as the anonymous, background singer. This unemphasized individual person then claims a more adequate expression in the tragic form of literature, where he speaks directly, even if behind a stylized mask, and against the less individualized background comment of the Chorus of Elders. At length, in the comic form of literature, the individual claims his complete and absolute due: he silences the gnomic wisdom of the Chorus,

[6] *Ibid.*, p. 551 (B., p. 728).
[7] *Ibid.*, p. 551 (B., p. 728).

liquidates the abstract forms of the Gods, and reveals himself, under all high masks and appearances, as the everyday, commonplace, vulgar man, at one with actor and audience alike. He performs, in short, in ironical fashion, the same liquidation of the transcendently divine that is more solemnly carried out in the sacrificial cult.

From the resolution of all absolutes in the individualistic comic irony, Hegel now leaps dialectically to the individualized Incarnate Word of Christianity. This extreme leap resembles that from phrenology to the reasonable self in society, or from the death-dealing guillotine to the Categorical Imperative of Kant. The comic consciousness is summed up in the light-hearted proposition: "I, the Self, am the Absolute Essence" but this light-hearted utterance at once permits conversion to the serious statement: "The Absolute Essence is I, the self," in which self-consciousness is merely an adjunct, a predicate to something more substantial. The comic consciousness therefore has as its reverse side all the more or less unhappy abstract forms of self-consciousness which were studied earlier in the *Phenomenology,* and which arose when the secure ethical life of the ancient city-state passed away in the dissolved atomicity and abstract right of the Roman imperial period. We are back once more with the abstract self-sufficiency of Stoicism, the uncommitted freedom of Scepticism, and with the Unhappy Consciousness, which Hegel now sees exemplified, not in the self-abasing, ascetic spirit of the middle ages, but in the intellectual and moral *malaise* of the age of Pater's *Marius,* a *malaise* for which the Incarnate Word could provide the only possible medicine. This Unhappy Consciousness is aware only of its total *loss* of all that previously reassured and filled it: its anguish might find expression in the words of the Lutheran hymn "God is dead."

This mortal rupture between the outward and substantial, on the one hand, and the inward and self-conscious, on the other, can be healed (Hegel tells us) only by a twofold movement: by a movement of the Substantial towards the Subjective, and of the Subjective towards the Substantial. In part this need is met by a one-sided spread of undisciplined subjectivity over the whole territory recognized as objective, as in Gnosticism and the Mystery-religions: nature, history and the established faiths become overrun by interpretations and myth, and consciousness wanders crazed in a murky night of its own making. This night passes away only when this one-sided movement of subjectivity towards objectivity is met by a balancing movement from the objective towards the subjective, when self-consciousness finds itself in what is *independently* and *immediately* there. Hegel is here pointing to the essential superiority of the Word made Flesh over the "Aeons" of Valentinus[8] or the Unconquered Sun of Mithraism. We encounter the former in the concrete particularity of sense, whereas the latter has merely the shadowy, projected being of private fantasy.

[8] An ancient Christian Gnostic —T. J. J. A.

"This fact," says Hegel, "that Absolute Spirit has given itself the form of self-consciousness both *in* itself, and also *for* its own consciousness, now appears inasmuch as it is the belief of the world that the Spirit is there as a self-consciousness, i.e., as an actual human being, that it is there for immediate sense-certainty, that the believing consciousness sees and feels and hears the Godhead. In this manner it is no imagination, but an actuality in the believer. Consciousness therefore does not start from the inner life of thought, and the existence of the God; rather does it start from what is immediately present and recognizes the God in it." [9]

It will be noted in the above passage that what Hegel thinks important is not the *Incarnatio Filii Dei*,[10] but the *belief* in such an incarnation: if this incarnation is said to be actual and not imaginary, its actuality is one *in* the believer, rather than in the historical person of Jesus. That person was no doubt the vehicle through which "Absolute Religion," the realization that the divine nature must achieve self-consciousness in man, first became explicit: the realization rather than the vehicle remains the important thing for Hegel. Hegel may therefore fitly be regarded as the father of "modernism," that ever assailed but unsuppressible and authentic expression of Christian belief.

ABSOLUTE OR REVEALED RELIGION (CHRISTIANITY)

Absolute Religion, to which Hegel now turns, is also what he means by "Revealed Religion," i.e., a religion in which the Divine Being is known for what it is, a being whose nature it is to be self-conscious, to reveal itself to itself. Hegel remarks: "There is something secret to consciousness in its object, as long as this appears strange and alien to itself, and is not known *as* itself. This secretness ceases when the Essence becomes objective to Spirit *as* Spirit. . . . Itself is only manifest to itself in its own certainty of self, its object is the self: self, however, is nothing foreign, but inseparable unity with itself, the immediate universal." [11] It is this *immediate universality* which is the true content of a belief in the Incarnation. Hegel uncompromisingly holds that it is only in speculative knowledge that God can be truly reached: he holds indeed that God's being *consists* solely in speculative knowledge. The content of this knowledge is, however, held to be one with that of Revealed Religion. Philosophy is therefore alike the saviour and the salvation of men, though this need not be in every way patent to those whom it saves.

[9] *Phen.*, p. 576 (B., pp. 757-58).
[10] Incarnation of the Son of God —T. J. J. A.
[11] *Phen.*, pp. 577-78 (B., p. 759).

The religious presentation of speculative truth is, as we saw, an imaginative, pictorial presentation: it has not yet risen to the pure universality of conceptual thought. The union of universality with immediacy remains for it their union in the individual self-consciousness of Jesus, which excludes the believer's own self-consciousness. The movement towards a fuller universalization even of such universality-in-particularity, begins when the Incarnation shifts into the *past,* when its present reality becomes a matter of memory or tradition. This shift, for Hegel, does not veil vision, but rather adds to its acuteness. For only if the Absolute loses the sensuous immediacy of the flesh, can it achieve spiritual resurrection in the experience of the community. Reference to the past is, however, only a semi-pictorial form of universality: though the content of what is thus referred has become universal—what is past is always a *such* rather than a *this*—it is still pictured *as if* present to sense. The Religious Consciousness, according to Hegel, never wholly rises above the externality of imaginative presentation. When it seeks for the roots of its spiritual life, it tends mistakenly to go back to the historical circumstances of its origin, to the "soulless recollection of an ideally constructed individual figure and its existence in the past." [12] To seek for the historical Jesus is for Hegel to lose touch with the risen and ascended Christ.

Hegel now gives a lengthy phenomenological restatement of the doctrines of the Trinity, Creation, Fall, etc., which throws considerable light on his own system. Spirit, says Hegel, conceived abstractly as a "Substance" in the element of pure thought, is the "simple, self-identical, eternal Essence"—the Essence which Hegel afterwards called "the Idea," and which religion knows as "the Father." But, says Hegel, this simple, eternal Essence would be spiritual merely in name, were it conceived *merely* as such an abstract Essence. It must present itself, become objective to something, and in so far as the religious imagination transforms this conceptual entailment into an historical process, the eternal Essence may be said to give birth to something other than itself (God the Son begotten before all worlds). But this procession to otherness is at the same time a return to self, since the conscious Son, and the Father of whom He is conscious, are one and the same spiritual reality. We have therefore the materials for a Trinity consisting of the Essence, of the self-conscious being that knows it, and of the knowledge of the former in the latter. If the self-conscious element represents the Divine word "which being spoken externalizes and empties the speaker, but which is just as immediately apprehended," it seems that the Spirit is represented by the active identification of the two aspects. "So that," says Hegel, "the differences that are made are as immediately dissolved as they are made, and are as immediately made as

[12] *Ibid.,* p. 583 (B., pp. 764-65).

they are dissolved, and the True and Real is just this movement turned circlewise on itself." [13] The whole Trinity therefore lives enshrined in the Cartesian *Cogito*. The imagination of the religious community cannot, however, rise to this pitch of abstraction: for it the moments of self-conscious Spirit fall apart in quasi-independence and in consequent quasi-sequence and interaction.

The same logical entailment which connects the elements of self-consciousness, and which is misleadingly represented as a temporal process, now leads to the existence of a World. The distinction between the pure Essence of Divinity and the self-conscious Word that is conscious of it, is too abstract and categorial to be a *real* distinction: it is, says Hegel (perhaps remembering Augustine's account of the Trinity) a distinction of *love,* in which there is no sufficient opposition of nature. For such a merely categorial distinction to have substance, and to be something that can be genuinely seen through and overcome, it must be exemplified in the immediacy and separateness of sensuous being. The eternal abstract Spirit must therefore create a World, the word *creation* being merely an imaginative symbol for the entailment holding between the being of an abstract notion and the being of cases in which it may be instantiated. The Spirit which is the sense of the World must itself show an initial aspect of separateness and immediacy: it must at first appear as a natural individual in this world, and must regard the world as a system of things foreign to itself. As so individualized, Spirit may be styled "innocent," but it cannot as yet be called "good." Being Spirit, it must, however, progress from the immediacy of sense-experience to the inwardness of pure thought, and must in the process lose its innocence: it must become conscious of what is good, i.e., of its thinking being, on the one hand, and of what is bad, i.e., its sensuous being, on the other. This epistemological progress from sense-experience to perception and thought is turned by the religious imagination into the story of the temptation and expulsion from paradise. The same imagination translates this progress into the region of pure thought, into the myth of the fall of Lucifer and his angels.

The world in which the merely natural, self-retreating (*insichgehend*) and therefore bad self-consciousness has a place, must find a place also for the good self-consciousness, i.e., for Spirit returning to self out of sensuousness. This return the religious imagination depicts in the form of a free act of "self-humbling" on the part of the Absolute Essence, whereby sensuous man is redeemed. Religion is right, Hegel thinks, in attributing such redemption to the universal abstract Godhead rather than to the individual spirit that is conscious of it, precisely because it is *necessary* for the abstract Godhead to instantiate itself, in order to have any real being at all. It is the *abstractness* of God which forces Him to come down from

[13] *Ibid.,* pp. 584-85 (B., pp. 766-67).

heaven, and to suffer death by exemplification. The descent of the abstract universal into sensuous embodiment is also, of course, the elevation of what is sensuous into what is abstract and notional: the death of God leads to His Resurrection and Ascension. What is remarkable in the passage before us is the wholly logical or epistemological interpretation put upon the Christian mysteries.

From this brief, embarrassed encounter with the Word made Flesh, Hegel passes on to a stage where Spirit is conscious of itself in universal form, as the Spirit inspiring a religious community. The Divine Man who has died is the communal self-consciousness implicit: the community must make His self-consciousness explicitly its own. The death and resurrection of the Redeemer must lose their simple, natural significance as events in the life-history of a particular individual: they must become phases in the life of a Spirit which lives and dies daily in the religious community.[14] The death involved is a death to particularity, which presumably here covers both the particularity of sense and the particularity of interest and impulse, and a resurrection to universality. It is also the death of all imaginative religious presentations, and a resurrection to a more inward, notional form of religious experience. The death of the Mediator must be appropriated by the religious community: His independent, objective self-consciousness must be set aside, and transformed into a universal self-consciousness. With this dissolution of the Mediator in the communal consciousness, will also go the death of the divine Essence, as something abstract and apart: we must learn to sing, not despairingly but exultingly, that God Himself has died. "This hard saying," says Hegel, "is the expression of the innermost simple knowledge of self, the return of consciousness into the deep night of I = I, that can no more distinguish or know anything outside of itself." [15] The ultimate fate of all imaginative religious presentations is therefore to hand over their majesty and authority to self-conscious Spirit, that the latter may be all in all. The religious community does not, of course, realize how revolutionary, how Voltairean a role it is playing. It *feels* its union with the Divine in the form of love, without embracing this in a clear concept.

Though Hegel has veiled his treatment of Religion in much orthodox-sounding language, its outcome is quite clear. Theism in all its forms is an imaginative distortion of final truth. The God outside of us who saves us by His grace, is a misleading pictorial expression for saving forces *intrinsic* to self-conscious Spirit, wherever this may be present. And the religious approach must be transcended (even if after a fashion preserved) in the final illumination. At the same time it would be wrong to regard Hegel as some sort of humanist: he has not dethroned God in order to put Man, whether as an individual or group of individuals, in His place. The

[14] *Ibid.,* p. 597 (B., p. 780).
[15] *Ibid.,* p. 598 (B., p. 782).

self-conscious Spirit which plays the part of God in his system is not the complex, existent person, but the impersonal, reasonable element in him, which, by a necessary process, more and more "takes over" the individual, and becomes manifest and conscious in him. Hegel's religion, like that of Aristotle, consists in "straining every nerve to live in accordance with the best thing in us."

3

SØREN AABAYE KIERKEGAARD

Kierkegaard has so frequently been taken as the representative of the conservative reaction to Hegel, and therefore as the antipode of Marx, that the revolutionary nature of his own thinking is often neglected. Kierkegaard carried through the attack upon the modern consciousness begun by Blaise Pascal (compare his "La Mystère de Jésus" in the *Pensées*), reaching the inevitable conclusion that the "objectivity" of the modern consciousness and sensibility is the antithesis of faith. By means of a radical negation of this objectivity, Kierkegaard found the way to the "subjectivity" of faith. Here, everything depends upon the interior and contemporaneous reality of faith and thus upon the passion of the existing man of faith. But because the objectivity of consciousness is so distinctively and even uniquely dominant in the modern world, a contemporary expression of subjectivity must be deeply affected by the actual objective world which it confronts. Kierkegaard was led to believe that modern Protestantism had surrendered to this objectivity to the point that it had totally betrayed and negated the original Christian faith. His answer to this dilemma was an existential language of "subjectivity," a mode of expression dependent upon the present and fully human reality of faith. If only because of this dependence, theologians have again and again withdrawn from a full or consistent employment of Kierkegaard's language, and Barth was also impelled to reject Kierkegaard when he took up the task of evolving a dogmatic theology grounded solely in the Church's confession of faith.

Another pervasive motif in Kierkegaard's reflections and meditations is the

all too modern one of the total transcendence and alien distance of God.
Kierkegaard, who so frequently identified
himself with Job, fully opened himself
to the interior eclipse of transcendence
in the modern sensibility, and did so as a
consequence of his choice to seek the
reality of faith in that actual subjectivity
which can become present and real in
the immediacy of the moment. The
following essay on Kierkegaard by John
Updike astutely captures in a contemporary form the Kierkegaardian motif of
the radical transcendence of God, a
theme which plays a significant role in
Updike's novels.

John
Updike # The Fork

It is not certain that the United States needs still more translations of
Kierkegaard. The Kierkegaard bibliography in this country is already
amply confusing; led by the dauntless Walter Lowrie, a campaign of translation coincident with the Second World War endowed the English-speak-
ing world with almost all of the torrential *œuvre* that the Danish thinker
had created a century before. Eight books, including the immense *Concluding Unscientific Postscript,* were published here in 1941 alone. The
current index of books in print lists twenty-two Kierkegaard titles, not
counting duplications and anthologies. Distributed among a number of
commercial, university, and religious presses (notably Harper, Princeton,
and Augsburg) and bedevilled by overlappings and omissions (*Stages on
Life's Way* seems to be out of print, whereas some of the *Discourses* crop
up repeatedly), the list is nevertheless the fullest outside of Germany and
Denmark itself. We lack in English only Kierkegaard's doctoral disserta-
tion on irony . . . , some topical and humorous trifles, and the very vo-
luminous total of the journals and stray papers.

The Last Years: Journals, 1853-1855, edited and translated by Professor Ronald Gregor Smith,[1] draws upon the papers from 1853 onward and
the journals from their resumption, on March 1, 1854, after a four-month
gap. This material, which represents Kierkegaard in his most haranguing
and repetitious phase, is not unknown to previous translation. The final fifty-

[1] (New York: Harper & Row, 1965).

FROM John Updike, "The Fork," *The New Yorker* (February 26, 1966), pp. 115-36.
Reprinted by permission; © 1966 The New Yorker Magazine, Inc. The extracts from
Kierkegaard's journals quoted in this review are from *The Last Years,* by Søren
Kierkegaard, edited and translated by Ronald Gregor Smith, copyrighted 1965 by
Ronald Gregor Smith, used by permission of Harper & Row, Publishers, Inc.; also
with the permission of Collins Publishers.

five pages of Alexander Dru's selection derive from the same portion of the journals. Professor Smith, though he compiles three hundred and forty pages, omits half of what Dru includes. Absent in Smith are some of the most pungent entries in Dru:

> Oh, Luther, Luther; your responsibility is great indeed, for the closer I look the more clearly do I see that you overthrew the Pope—and set the public on the throne.

> Hypocrisy is quite as inseparable from being a man as sliminess is from being a fish.

> What could be more ridiculous than to use a jack to pick up a pin— or to make use of the eternal punishment of hell in order to make men into that half-demoralized, half-honest bagatelle which is roughly what it means to be a man.

Professor Smith prefers the extensive to the epigrammatic, and he might claim that his selection emphasizes Kierkegaard's religious thought—the ideas that were projected outward in his pamphleteering attack upon the established Christianity of Denmark. But the pamphlets (ten in all, called *The Instant*) and the open letters that Kierkegaard issued have been already rendered into English by Lowrie, under the title *Attack upon "Christendom."* This book relates to *The Last Years* much as the outside of a sock relates to the inside; the pattern is not identical, but the threads are the same. After minimizing the considerable duplication, the editor of *The Last Years* justifies its publication by saying, "The last years of Kierkegaard's life saw a remarkable concentration of the motifs which controlled his whole authorship. This comes vividly to life in the present selection from the journals and papers of that time, and casts light on all that went before it." True, if "concentration" is taken to mean a narrowing. The prolix philosophizing of the "aesthetic works" and the fervent exhortation of the "religious works" have been succeeded by a third stage—an apostolic or pathological vehemence. *The Last Years* shows Kierkegaard's mind narrowed to a very hard point. More precisely, it shows his mind and life, those antagonistic twins, both narrowed to a very hard point, the point of attack, which becomes the point of vanishing.

Søren Aabye Kierkegaard (the name means "churchyard," and is pronounced "Kĕrkĕgör") was born in Copenhagen in 1813—"the year," he was to say, "when so many worthless notes were put in circulation." His father, Michael, was a man of great force and complexity. A shepherd lad from the desolate West Jutland heath, he had become a prosperous cloth merchant and grocer in the city, only to retire at the age of forty, perhaps to devote himself to religious brooding. Within a year of his first wife's death, Michael married a household servant, Ane Lund, who bore him a child four months after their wedding. This marriage was to produce seven children, of whom Søren Aabye (as distinguished from his older brother, Søren Michael) was the last. His father was fifty-six, his mother forty-five; the advanced age of his parents accounts in part for Kierkegaard's physical frailty, and his position as the family Benjamin for his pertness and conceit. His nickname within the family was Fork—bestowed when, rebuked for shovelling food greedily at the table, he announced, "I *am* a fork, and I will stick you." Descriptions of his childhood abound in his journals:

> I was already an old man when I was born. . . . Delicate, slender and weak, deprived of almost every condition for holding my own with other boys, or even for passing as a complete human being in comparison with others; melancholy, sick in soul, in many ways profoundly unfortunate, one thing I had: an eminently shrewd wit given me presumably in order that I might not be defenseless.

But many weak boys with sharp tongues are born into the world, and Kierkegaard's heightened sense of himself reaches for more:

> I am in the deepest sense an unfortunate individual who has from the earliest age been nailed fast to one suffering or another, to the very verge of insanity, which may have its deeper ground in a disproportion between my soul and my body.

And in *The Last Years,* in the last entry, within a few weeks of his death, this sense of initial misfortune attains a frightening pitch:

> Through a crime I came into existence, I came into existence against God's will. The fault, which in one sense is not mine, even if it makes me a criminal in God's eyes, is to give life. The punishment fits the fault: it is to be deprived of all joy of life, to be brought to the supreme degree of disgust with life.

His adult life consisted of a series of quixotic, or expiatory, gestures. His father wanted him to study for the ministry, so he spent his youth in frivolity, drunkenness, and dandyism. His father died, so he settled down to pass the theological examination. He fell in love with and successfully courted Regine Olsen; then he broke off the engagement and buried himself in a frenetic literary activity dedicated to her. He became, under his own name and under the open secret of his pseudonyms, the most remarkable writer in Denmark, the only author above attack by the scurrilous magazine the *Corsair*; so he incited the *Corsair*, though its editor, Meïr Goldschmidt, revered him, to attack, which it did with such success that Kierkegaard's personal life was made a torment and the name Søren became a byword for the ridiculous. Lastly, he who had long been on the verge of becoming a country parson mounted a savage attack upon organized Christianity, exhorting true Christians to abstain from the sin of church worship; he refused the Eucharist, since it could not be administered by a layman, on his deathbed.

Kierkegaard's American reputation was long deferred and is still esoteric, but in Denmark Kierkegaard was a celebrity. Indeed, he seems to have been the Benjamin of Copenhagen, the marketplace capital of a small and homogeneous country. His break with Regine was surrounded by so much gossip that it amounted to a public event. His pseudonyms, with their interlocking prefaces and compliments, must have been private jokes to a considerable group. His books, surprisingly, sold well enough to make money. During the *Corsair* persecution, his twisted back and uneven trouser legs were caricatured every week for a year, and the students at the university produced a comedy whose ridiculous hero was called Søren Kirk. Children taunted him on the streets. In his journals, he lamented, "To let oneself be trampled by geese is a slow way of dying," and complained that "when . . . I have sought recreation by driving ten or twelve miles, and my body has gradually become somewhat weak . . . when I alight from the carriage . . . there is sure to be someone at hand who is jolly enough to call me names." Astonishingly, the very name Søren, up to then the most common male baptismal name, became opprobrious, and Danish parents, according to Lowrie, took to admonishing their children, "Don't be a Søren." Though helpless under such assault, Kierkegaard was not without power. A staunch monarchist, he was on conversational terms with King Christian VIII, and Lowrie asserts that in the relationship it was Kierkegaard who "held himself a little aloof." (In his journals, Kierkegaard dryly noted, "On the whole, Christian VIII has enriched me with many psychological observations. Perhaps psychologists ought to pay particular attention to kings, and especially to absolute monarchs; for the freer a man is, the better he can be known.") Kierkegaard's satirical pen was a feared weapon. He undoubtedly ruined the life of a former friend, P. S. Møller, with a personal attack published in the newspaper *Fatherland*. So his assault upon the ecclesiastical establishment was delivered from the strength of notoriety, and, far from being the private fulminations of an obscure aesthete and mystic, was a demagogic assault, a well-publicized uproar reverberating throughout Scandinavia. (*The Instant* was immediately translated into Swedish and, not needing translation in Norway, aroused the interest of young Ibsen, to become the basis of *Brand*.) Kierkegaard's expectation of arrest and imprisonment was not fulfilled, but at his funeral a crowd of students gathered to protest the church's appropriation of the body, and a riot was barely averted. W. H. Auden, in introducing his own Kierkegaard anthology, regards *The Attack upon "Christendom"* as not a book but an act: "What for the author was the most important book of his life is for us, as readers, the least, for to us the important point is not what it contains but the fact that Kierkegaard wrote it."

Certainly, the journals of *The Last Years* are difficult to enjoy. How different are, say, the *Last Diaries* of Tolstoy, wherein the old man, honored all over the world, a sacred figure to his countrymen, struggles with the naïveté of a child to become good! Kierkegaard never had Tolstoy's candid willingness to learn and grow. He was endowed from birth with a somewhat elderly mind. Though he read voraciously and could be gregarious and charming, only five people seem to have really interested him: Jesus, Socrates, Hegel, Regine Olsen, and his father. Though his ability to vary and extend his voice is marvellous, a single field of ideas appears to have been in his possession since the beginning. It remained only for him to explore it and to arrive at the ultimate conclusion. One does not find in *The Last Years* those categories—"the absurd," "the leap," "dread" —that modern Existentialism has made fashionable; they were expounded in the earlier "aesthetic works." What one does find, theologically, is a wholehearted insistence upon the inhumanity of God. Through the bitter clamor of these journals—the outrageous but telling satires on bourgeois Christianity, the complaints about priests and professors and Bishop Mynster, the searching diagnoses of Luther and Schopenhauer, the not always tender deprecations of women, the copious self-dramatization, the tedious extollation of "the individual," the slashing dismissals of "knavish religiosity," "scoundrelly posterity," and the "increasing mass of drivel which is called science"—there sounds a note that attains a crescendo in the last pages: Christianity is torture, and God a torturer:

> In Christianity God is spirit—and therefore so immensely severe, from love: for he longs for spirit from man. . . . God is never so severe with those he loves in the Old Testament as he is with the apostles, for example, whose life was sheer suffering and then a martyr's death. . . . In the Old Testament, when the prophet is in need, God always finds a way out—but as for the apostle . . . there is no talk of unexpected help which shall bring him his strictest necessities; no, God just leaves him in the lurch, leaves him to die of hunger and thirst—it can be as severe as that.

> If I were a pagan and had to speak Greek, I should say that God has arranged everything for his own entertainment; he amuses himself like a man who puts a piece of bacon in a mousetrap and watches all the tricks of the mice to get the bacon out without being trapped— so God amuses himself at the leaps and springs and contortions of these millions of men to get hold of the truth without suffering.

> . . . What torture! If a man is really to be the instrument of God, for the infinite will that God is, then God must first take all his will from him. What a fearful operation! And it is natural that no one

knows how to examine so painfully as one who is omniscient and omnipotent. Certainly with other forms of torture there are doctors present to estimate how long the tortured man can hold out without losing his life. Yet mistakes can happen, and the tortured man can die before their eyes. This never happens with one who is omniscient.

> To be a Christian is the most terrible of all torments, it is—and it must be—to have one's hell here on earth. . . . One shudders to read what an animal must suffer which is used for vivisection; yet this is only a fugitive image of the suffering involved in being a Christian —in being kept alive in the state of death.

The vision is so terrible that Kierkegaard almost relents: "What I write is from a Christian standpoint so true, so true, and from a Christian standpoint this is how I must write. And yet I can say that what I write here tortures me to produce . . . it is repugnant to me." Again: "Ah, it is with sorrow that I write this. In melancholy sympathy, though myself unhappy, I loved men and the mass of men. Their bestial conduct toward me compelled me, in order to endure it, to have more and more to do with God."

And what is the essence of God's nature, that makes "having to do" with Him so painful? Majesty:

> Suffering, that there must be suffering, is connected with the majesty of God. His majesty is so infinite that it can be characterized or expressed only by a paradox: it is the paradox of the majesty which is bound to make the beloved unhappy . . . Suffering depends on the fact that God and man are qualitatively different, and that the clash of time and eternity in time is bound to cause suffering.

A little later, the formula is given a personal turn:

> O infinite majesty, even if you were not love, even if you were cold in your infinite majesty I could not cease to love you, I need something majestic to love. . . . There was and there is a need of majesty in my soul, of a majesty I can never tire of worshiping.

Yet elsewhere this majesty acquires human attributes, even weaknesses. God knows sorrow. "Alas, the more I think about it the more I come to imagine God as sitting in sorrow, for he most of all knows what sorrow is." God loves, out of need. "It is God's passion to love and to be loved, almost infinite love!—as though he himself were bound in this passion, in the power of this passion, so that he cannot cease to love, almost as though it were a weakness. . . ." And: "I know that in love you suffer with me, more than I, infinite Love—even if you cannot change."

The paragraph preceding this last quotation is revealing:

If my contemporaries could understand how I suffer, how Providence, if I may dare to say so, maltreats me, I am certain that they would be so profoundly moved that in human sympathy they would make an attempt (as sometimes happens with a child which is being maltreated by its parents) to wrest me free from Providence.

The hypothetical cruel parents return in another metaphor:

As the child of a tight-rope walker is from his earliest years made supple in his back and in every muscle so that, after daily practice, he is sheer suppleness and can carry out every movement, absolutely every movement, in the most excruciating positions, yet always easily and smiling: so with prayer to the absolute majesty.

And in a third image, world history is likened to "the uproar and hubbub which children make in their playroom, instead of sitting still and reading their books (as their parents would like)." With these similes, we touch a central nerve of Kierkegaard's thought—the identification of God with his father, whom he both loved and hated, who treated him cruelly and who loved him.

Much is known of Kierkegaard's relation with his father, but more is unknown. Kierkegaard wrote in his journals: "Perhaps I could recount the tragedy of my childhood, the fearful secret explanation of religion, suggesting an apprehensive presentiment which my imagination elaborated, my offence at religion—I could recount it in a novel entitled *The Enigmatical Family*." And another entry reads:

It is terrible whenever for a single instant I come to think of the dark background of my life, from the very earliest time. The anxious dread with which my father filled my soul, his own frightful melancholy, the many things which I cannot record—I got such a dread of Christianity, and yet I felt myself so strongly drawn to it.

A childhood classmate later wrote, "To the rest of us who led a genuinely boyish life S. K. was a stranger and an object of compassion, especially on account of his dress. . . . This [his costume, which resembled the costume of charity schools] procured him the nickname of Choirboy, which alternated with Søren Sock, in allusion to his father's previous business as hosier. S. K. was regarded by us all as one whose home was wrapped in a mysterious half-darkness of severity and oddity." And in his autobiographical *The Point of View for My Work as an Author,* Kierkegaard wrote, "As a child I was strictly and austerely brought up in Christianity; humanly speaking, crazily brought up. A child crazily travestied as a melancholy old man. Terrible!"

Yet the boy's relation to his father was also intimate and admiring. One of Kierkegaard's pseudonyms, Johannes Climacus, reminisces:

> His father was a very severe man, apparently dry and prosaic, but under this rough coat he concealed a glowing imagination which even old age could not quench. When Johannes occasionally asked of him permission to go out, he generally refused to give it, though once in a while he proposed instead that Johannes should take his hand and walk back and forth in the room. . . . While they went back and forth in the room the father described all that they saw, they greeted passersby, carriages rattled past them and drowned the father's voice; the cake-woman's goodies were more enticing than ever. He described so accurately, so vividly, so explicitly even to the least details, everything that was known to Johannes and so fully and perspicuously what was unknown to him, that after half an hour of such a walk with his father he was as much overwhelmed and fatigued as if he had been a whole day out of doors. . . . To Johannes it seemed as if the world were coming into existence during the conversation, *as if the father were our Lord and he were his favorite,* who was allowed to interpose his foolish conceits as merrily as he would; for he was never repulsed, the father was never put out, he agreed to everything.

I have abbreviated this often quoted passage and italicized a revealing clause. By the same light, Kierkegaard did not expect to live past the age of thirty-three (the age of Christ) and did expect his father, though fifty-seven years older, to outlive him (to be immortal). In fact, his father lived to the patriarchal age of eighty-two and Kierkegaard died when he was only forty-two, so the premonition was in spirit correct. There is no doubt that his father fearfully dominated the household. Incredibly, in all of Kierkegaard's writings there is not one mention of his mother. And an age that has been able to peruse Kafka's diaries need not be reminded that, severity aside, the *competence,* the very wonderfulness of a father can be felt as a crushing tyranny. "It is a fearful thing," Kierkegaard wrote, "to fall into the hands of the living God."

To all this add a precocious compassion. In his journals Kierkegaard writes of the perils of religious education:

> The most dangerous case is not when the father is a free thinker, and not even when he is a hypocrite. No, the danger is when he is a pious and God-fearing man, when the child is inwardly and deeply convinced of it, and yet in spite of all this observes that a profound unrest is deeply hidden in his soul, so that not even piety and the fear of God can bestow peace. The danger lies just here, that the child in this relationship is almost compelled to draw a conclusion about God, that after all God is not infinite love.

It does not seem to me contradictory to posit a father who appears as both God and a victim of God. Such a paradox, after all, is fundamental to Christian theology, and Kierkegaard's imagination often returns to the forsaken Christ's outcry on the Cross. Duplicity was the very engine of Kierkegaard's thought, a habit he elevated to a metaphysical principle— the principle of "indirect communication," which he found both in Socrates' intellectual midwifery and in God's decision to embody Himself in a scorned and mocked sufferer. In all Kierkegaard's production, nothing is more powerful, more beautiful and typical, than the sweeping Prelude to *Fear and Trembling,* wherein the story of Abraham and Isaac is pursued through a sequence of differing versions. All portray, in similar language, Abraham and Isaac rising in the morning, leaving Sarah, and travelling to Mount Moriah, where God has told Abraham he must sacrifice his son. In the first version, Abraham, whose face has shown sorrow and "fatherliness," turns away a moment, "and when Isaac again saw Abraham's face it was changed, his glance was wild, his form was horror. He seized Isaac by the throat, threw him to the ground, and said, 'Stupid boy, dost thou then suppose that I am thy father? I am an idolator. Dost thou suppose that this is God's bidding? No, it is my desire.' Then Isaac trembled and cried out in his terror, 'O God in heaven, have compassion upon me. God of Abraham, have compassion upon me. If I have no father upon earth, be Thou my father!' But Abraham in a low voice said to himself, 'O Lord in heaven, I thank Thee. After all it is better for him to believe that I am a monster, rather than that he should lose faith in Thee.' " Here, in this shocking twist of a myth, that nerve is bared. Here, in this play of ironies and deceits carried out under the highest pressure of anguish, we feel close to Kierkegaard's mysterious and searing experience of his father.

A specific revelation about his father troubled Kierkegaard's young manhood and was transmuted, or absorbed, into a gnawing guilt or uneasiness that he refers to in his journals as "the thorn in my flesh," which in turn seems to be synonymous with his singularity, his fate, as "the individual," to suffer a martyrdom not incomparable with Christ's. Some crucial confidence was imparted on his twenty-second birthday: "Then it was that the great earthquake occurred, the frightful upheaval which suddenly forced upon me a new infallible rule for interpreting the phenomena one and all. Then I surmised that my father's great age was not a divine blessing, but rather a curse. . . . Guilt must rest upon the whole family, a divine punishment must be impending over it." The exact nature of the "earthquake" is forever buried in the portentous secrecy Kierkegaard assigned it. Possibly the old man's confession had to do with sex. On the mere statistical records, Michael Kierkegaard seduced his housekeeper in the year of mourning his first wife, married the woman when she was five months pregnant, and fathered upon her a total of seven children, the last, Søren Aabye, being born when the parents, if not as ancient as Abraham and Sarah, were of an age when, in Lowrie's delicate phrase, "no such blessing was expected." Kierkegaard frequently speaks of his own existence as a "mistake," and in the journals of *The Last Years* this sense of himself has spread to include all humanity: "This whole human existence, dating from the Fall, and which we men are so puffed up about as a devilish *tour de force* . . . is merely the consequence of a false step." Of a hypothetical son he writes:

> Concerning himself he learns that he was conceived in sin, born in transgression—that his existence is therefore a crime, that therefore his father in giving him life, has done something which is as far as possible from being well-pleasing to God.

His vivid, even sensual awareness of Original Sin, of life itself as a crime, may be traceable to an embarrassment he felt about being himself living proof of an elderly couple's concupiscence. He ranged from the heights of conceit to abysmal depths of shame; near the end of his life, he suffered a stroke while visiting friends and, falling helpless to the floor, rejected the attempts to lift him up by saying, "Oh, leave it [his body] until the maid clears it away in the morning." In the last journals, he thanks God "that no living being owes existence to me," urges celibacy upon all Christians, faces cheerfully the consequence that the race would die out, and asserts that "human egoism is concentrated in the sexual relation, the propagation of the species, the giving of life."

Or the "earthquake" may have been learning that his father, as an eleven-year-old boy, had cursed God. An entry in the journals of 1846 reads:

> How terrible about the man who once as a little boy, while herding the flocks on the heaths of Jutland, suffering greatly, in hunger and in want, stood upon a hill and cursed God—and the man was unable to forget it even when he was eighty-two years old.

The first editor of Kierkegaard's papers, Barfod, showed this passage to Bishop Peter Kierkegaard, the one surviving sibling, who confirmed that this was indeed his father, and that, since shortly thereafter the shepherd boy was adopted by an uncle and set on the road to prosperity, he regarded this prosperity as an inverted curse, as God's vengeance for, to quote Peter, "the sin against the Holy Ghost which never can be forgiven." It seems likely that this, and not a sexual confession, is the matter of the "earthquake." And it seems to me, furthermore, that in some sense Kierkegaard's attack upon Christendom is a repetition of his father's curse —an attack, ostensibly directed against the Danish Protestant Church, upon God Himself, on behalf of the father who had suffered, and yet also against this same father, who had made his son suffer and bound him to Christian belief.

In 1849, Kierkegaard wrote in his journals, under the heading *Something about myself which must always be remembered:* "If, with my imagination, and with my passions, etc., I had been in any ordinary human sense a man, then I should certainly have forgotten Christianity entirely. But I am bound in agonizing misery, like a bird whose wings have been clipped, yet retaining the power of my mind undiminished, and its undoubtedly exceptional powers." And the pamphlets comprising *The Attack* have been, in every language except English, the first things by Kierkegaard to be translated, as anticlerical, anti-Christian literature. The "Christendom" Kierkegaard denounced was popularly taken to be synonymous with Christianity, and perhaps it was. It is hard to account otherwise for the strange qualities of the attack as found in *The Instant* and in these journals. Are specific abuses, as in Luther's attack upon the Papal church, named? No: "Luther nailed up ninety-five theses on the church door; that was a fight about doctrine. Nowadays one might publish one single thesis in the papers: 'Christianity does not exist'; and offer to dispute with all parsons and dons." This is from a journal of 1851; by 1854, Kierkegaard had developed a piercing critique of Luther, stated wittily as:

> Luther suffered extremely from an anxious conscience, he needed treatment. Very well: but is that a reason for completely transforming Christianity into a matter of calming anxious consciences?

Kierkegaard does not want consciences to be calmed; he wants them to be exacerbated by the truth about Christianity. "My task is to put a halt to a living diffusion of Christianity, and to help it to shake off a mass of nominal Christians." And what is the truth about Christianity?

> The ideal means hatred of man. What man naturally loves is finitude. To face him with the ideal is the most dreadful torture . . . it kills in him, in the most painful way, everything in which he really finds his life, in the most painful way it shows him his own wretchedness, it keeps him in sleepless unrest, whereas finitude lulls him into enjoyment. That is why Christianity is called, and is, hatred of man.

Now, is such advocacy not a hidden prosecution? It may be argued that harsh words were a needed corrective to an existing complacency and that the New Testament itself is sternly world-denying. But I notice that, just as liberal apologists are troubled to explain away the "hard" sayings of Jesus, Kierkegaard is embarrassed by the Gospels' softer moments—the genial miracle at the wedding of Cana, the sufferance of little children, the promise to the thief on the cross. Kierkegaard says, "Men live their life in the strength of the assurance that of such as children is the kingdom of

God, and in death they look for consolation to the image of the thief. That is the whole of their Christianity, and, characteristically enough, it is a mixture of childishness and crime." Surely here he is attacking something essential to Biblical teaching—the forgivingness that balances majesty. He seems impatient with divine mercy, much as a true revolutionary despises the philanthropies whereby misery is abated and revolution delayed. The "Christendom" he attacks has strangely little substance, apart from the person of Bishop Mynster, his father's pastor, who is criticized only for his urbanity and eloquence and his refusal to confess that "what he represented was not really Christianity but a milder form of it." Indeed, the whole attack is an invitation to the Church to commit suicide: "Yes, truly, suicide, and yet an action well-pleasing to God." Any specific reform— a revival of monasteries, an abolition of "livings"—he explicitly disavows. The one concrete result he expects from his attack is his own imprisonment and death. Though the Church's functionaries barely troubled to respond even in writing, he did die. He suffered his fatal stroke while returning from the bank with the last scrap of his fortune. He had nowhere further to go, and his death, whose causes eluded diagnosis, seems willed.

In the hospital, he told his only intimate friend, the pastor Emil Boesen, "The doctors do not understand my illness; it is psychic, and they want to treat it in the ordinary medical way." His conversations with Boesen, a kind of continuation of the journals (printed as such by Dru), have a relaxed sweetness; his terrible "task" is done, and he is happy that so much in his life has "come out right" and melancholy that he cannot share his happiness with everyone. He refuses to put flowers sent him into water: "it is the fate of flowers to blossom, smell, and die." Of *The Instant,* whose tenth number lay unpublished on his desk, he said, "You must remember that I have seen everything from the inmost center of Christianity, it is all very poor and clumsy. . . . I only said it to be rid of evil, and so to reach an Alleluia! Alleluia! Alleluia!" This "Alleluia," it may be, could be reached only through a scandal in which, alone like a shepherd boy on the Jutland heath, Kierkegaard execrated God. At any rate, with Kierkegaard, as with Proust, we feel writing as a demon—the one way to set a bent life straight.

Kierkegaard would hardly be pleased to know that more than any other thinker of the nineteenth century—not excluding Newman and Dostoevski —he has made Christianity intellectually possible for the twentieth. Not that the "millions of men falling away from Christianity" that he foresaw and desired has not occurred. But, by giving metaphysical dignity to "the subjective," by showing faith to be not an intellectual development but a movement of the will, by holding out for existential duality against the tide of all the monisms, materialist or spiritualized or political, that would absorb the individual consciousness, Kierkegaard has given Christianity new life, a handhold, the "Archimedean point." From Jaspers and Barth, Unamuno and Marcel, Heidegger and Sartre, his thought has filtered down through the seminaries to the laity. He has become, as he angrily predicted, the property of those men "more abominable and gruesome than the cannibals," professors and clergymen, and he is used, in the form of a few phrases or a bolder style, to prop up the feeble, always tottering faith of contemporary "Christians." He has become an instrument in the conspiracy to "make a fool of God." Those who read him eat the aesthetic coating and leave the religious pill, and "neo-Orthodox" Protestantism, his direct beneficiary, has accepted the antinomianism and ignored the savage austerity, the scornful authoritarianism. Yet Kierkegaard himself, this two-tined Fork with his trouser legs of unequal length, this man in love with duplicity and irony and all double-edged things, lived luxuriously to the last and is nowhere quite free of sophism and vanity. (His sermons, for example, so symphonic and ardent, somehow belong with the memorable sermons of fiction, like those of Father Mapple in *Moby Dick* and of Père Paneloux in *The Plague*.) In the journal of 1849 he reminded himself, "It must never be forgotten that Christ also succored temporal and worldly needs. One can also, untruly, make Christ so spiritual that he becomes sheer cruelty." If this is what Kierkegaard seemed to do in the end, he also remembered that infinite majesty infinitely relents. Late in *The Last Years* we find this surprising entry: "For with such clarity as I have, I must say I am not a Christian. For the situation as I see it is that in spite of the abyss of nonsense in which we are caught, we shall all alike be saved."

4

FEODOR MIKHAILOVICH DOSTOEVSKI

No writer has more deeply affected the modern quest for faith than Dostoevski, and yet his work continues to elude the nets of all those who have sought to capture it by a systematic or purely rational formulation. Dostoevski invariably provokes a passionate response, and it is not possible to find a neutral treatment of his work. One critic has called Dostoevski the last Christian, and it would seem as though he was the last major artist or thinker who could respond in depth to the redemptive promise of the Christian God. While theologians have thus far given the bulk of their attention to *The Brothers Karamazov,* it is *The Possessed* which contains Dostoevski's most radical vision, and for many years now one of its characters, Kirillov, has been enshrined as a sacred hero to seekers of a radical form of faith. The following selections from the novel record the dialogues which are perhaps most revealing of Kirillov's quest.

*Feodor
Mikhailovich
Dostoevski*

Kirillov's Quest

[1]

"Are you fond of children?"

"I am," answered Kirillov, though rather indifferently.

"Then you're fond of life?"

"Yes, I'm fond of life! What of it?"

"Though you've made up your mind to shoot yourself."

"What of it? Why connect it? Life's one thing and that's another. Life exists, but death doesn't at all."

"You've begun to believe in a future eternal life?"

"No, not in a future eternal life, but in eternal life here. There are moments, you reach moments, and time suddenly stands still, and it will become eternal."

"You hope to reach such a moment?"

"Yes."

"That'll scarcely be possible in our time," Nikolay Vsyevolodovitch responded slowly and, as it were, dreamily; the two spoke without the slightest irony. "In the Apocalypse the angel swears that there will be no more time."

"I know. That's very true; distinct and exact. When all mankind attains happiness then there will be no more time, for there'll be no need of it, a very true thought."

"Where will they put it?"

"Nowhere. Time's not an object but an idea. It will be extinguished in the mind."

FROM *The Possessed,* translated by Constance Garnett (New York: Modern Library, 1936), pp. 239-41, 626-30.

"The old commonplaces of philosophy, the same from the beginning of time," Stavrogin muttered with a kind of disdainful compassion.

"Always the same, always the same, from the beginning of time and never any other," Kirillov said with sparkling eyes, as though there were almost a triumph in that idea.

"You seem to be very happy, Kirillov."

"Yes, very happy," he answered, as though making the most ordinary reply.

"But you were distressed so lately, angry with Liputin."

"H'm . . . I'm not scolding now. I didn't know then that I was happy. Have you seen a leaf, a leaf from a tree?"

"Yes."

"I saw a yellow one lately, a little green. It was decayed at the edges. It was blown by the wind. When I was ten years old I used to shut my eyes in the winter on purpose and fancy a green leaf, bright, with veins on it, and the sun shining. I used to open my eyes and not believe them, because it was very nice, and I used to shut them again."

"What's that? An allegory?"

"N-no . . . why? I'm not speaking of an allegory, but of a leaf, only a leaf. The leaf is good. Everything's good."

"Everything?"

"Everything. Man is unhappy because he doesn't know he's happy. It's only that. That's all, that's all! If anyone finds out he'll become happy at once, that minute. That mother-in-law will die; but the baby will remain. It's all good. I discovered it all of a sudden."

"And if anyone dies of hunger, and if anyone insults and outrages the little girl, is that good?"

"Yes! And if anyone blows his brains out for the baby, that's good too. And if anyone doesn't, that's good too. It's all good, all. It's good for all those who know that it's all good. If they knew that it was good for them, it would be good for them, but as long as they don't know it's good for them, it will be bad for them. That's the whole idea, the whole of it."

"When did you find out you were so happy?"

"Last week, on Tuesday, no, Wednesday, for it was Wednesday by that time, in the night."

"By what reasoning?"

"I don't remember; I was walking about the room; never mind. I stopped my clock. It was thirty-seven minutes past two."

"As an emblem of the fact that there will be no more time?"

Kirillov was silent.

"They're bad because they don't know they're good. When they find out, they won't outrage a little girl. They'll find out that they're good and they'll all become good, every one of them."

"Here you've found it out, so have you become good then?"

"I am good."

"That I agree with, though," Stavrogin muttered, frowning.

"He who teaches that all are good will end the world."

"He who taught it was crucified."

"He will come, and his name will be the man-god."

"The god-man?"

"The man-god. That's the difference."

"Surely it wasn't you lighted the lamp under the ikon?"

"Yes, it was I lighted it."

"Did you do it believing?"

"The old woman likes to have the lamp and she hadn't time to do it to-day," muttered Kirillov.

"You don't say prayers yourself?"

"I pray to everything. You see the spider crawling on the wall, I look at it and thank it for crawling."

His eyes glowed again. He kept looking straight at Stavrogin with firm and unflinching expression. Stavrogin frowned and watched him disdainfully, but there was no mockery in his eyes.

"I'll bet that when I come next time you'll be believing in God too," he said, getting up and taking his hat.

"Why?" said Kirillov, getting up too.

"If you were to find out that you believe in God, then you'd believe in Him; but since you don't know that you believe in Him, then you don't believe in Him," laughed Nikolay Vsyevolodovitch.

[2]

"No, you were right in what you said; let it be comfort. God is necessary and so must exist."

"Well, that's all right, then."

"But I know He doesn't and can't."

"That's more likely."

"Surely you must understand that a man with two such ideas can't go on living?"

"Must shoot himself, you mean?"

"Surely you must understand that one might shoot oneself for that alone? You don't understand that there may be a man, one man out of your thousands of millions, one man who won't bear it and does not want to."

"All I understand is that you seem to be hesitating. . . . That's very bad."

"Stavrogin, too, is consumed by an idea," Kirillov said gloomily, pacing up and down the room. He had not noticed the previous remark.

"What?" Pyotr Stepanovitch pricked up his ears. "What idea? Did he tell you something himself?"

"No, I guessed it myself: if Stavrogin has faith, he does not believe that he has faith. If he hasn't faith, he does not believe that he hasn't."

"Well, Stavrogin has got something else wiser than that in his head," Pyotr Stepanovitch muttered peevishly, uneasily watching the turn the conversation had taken and the pallor of Kirillov.

"Damn it all, he won't shoot himself!" he was thinking. "I always suspected it; it's a maggot in the brain and nothing more; what a rotten lot of people!"

"You are the last to be with me; I shouldn't like to part on bad terms with you," Kirillov vouchsafed suddenly.

Pyotr Stepanovitch did not answer at once. "Damn it all, what is it now?" he thought again.

"I assure you, Kirillov, I have nothing against you personally as a man, and always . . ."

"You are a scoundrel and a false intellect. But I am just the same as you are, and I will shoot myself while you will remain living."

"You mean to say, I am so abject that I want to go on living."

He could not make up his mind whether it was judicious to keep up such a conversation at such a moment or not, and resolved "to be guided by circumstances." But the tone of superiority and of contempt for him, which Kirillov had never disguised, had always irritated him, and now for some reason it irritated him more than ever—possibly because Kirillov, who was to die within an hour or so (Pyotr Stepanovitch still reckoned upon this), seemed to him, as it were, already only half a man, some creature whom he could not allow to be haughty.

"You seem to be boasting to me of your shooting yourself."

"I've always been surprised at every one's going on living," said Kirillov, not hearing his remark.

"H'm! Admitting that's an idea, but . . ."

"You ape, you assent to get the better of me. Hold your tongue; you won't understand anything. If there is no God, then I am God."

"There, I could never understand that point of yours: why are you God?"

"If God exists, all is His will and from His will I cannot escape. If not, it's all my will and I am bound to show self-will."

"Self-will? But why are you bound?"

"Because all will has become mine. Can it be that no one in the whole planet, after making an end of God and believing in his own will, will dare to express his self-will on the most vital point? It's like a beggar inheriting a fortune and being afraid of it and not daring to approach the bag of gold, thinking himself too weak to own it. I want to manifest my self-will. I may be the only one, but I'll do it."

"Do it by all means."

"I am bound to shoot myself because the highest point of my self-will is to kill myself with my own hands."

"But you won't be the only one to kill yourself; there are lots of suicides."

"With good cause. But to do it without any cause at all, simply for self-will, I am the only one."

"He won't shoot himself," flashed across Pyotr Stepanovitch's mind again.

"Do you know," he observed irritably, "if I were in your place I should kill some one else to show my self-will, not myself. You might be of use. I'll tell you whom, if you are not afraid. Then you needn't shoot yourself to-day, perhaps. We may come to terms."

"To kill some one would be the lowest point of self-will, and you show your whole soul in that. I am not you: I want the highest point and I'll kill myself."

"He's come to it of himself," Pyotr Stepanovitch muttered malignantly.

"I am bound to show my unbelief," said Kirillov, walking about the room. "I have no higher idea than disbelief in God. I have all the history of mankind on my side. Man has done nothing but invent God so as to go on living, and not kill himself; that's the whole of universal history up till now. I am the first one in the whole history of mankind who would not invent God. Let them know it once for all."

"He won't shoot himself," Pyotr Stepanovitch thought anxiously.

"Let whom know it?" he said, egging him on. "It's only you and me here; you mean Liputin?"

"Let every one know; all will know. There is nothing secret that will not be made known. *He* said so."

And he pointed with feverish enthusiasm to the image of the Saviour, before which a lamp was burning. Pyotr Stepanovitch lost his temper completely.

"So you still believe in Him, and you've lighted the lamp; 'to be on the safe side,' I suppose?"

The other did not speak.

"Do you know, to my thinking, you believe perhaps more thoroughly than any priest."

"Believe in whom? In *Him?* Listen." Kirillov stood still, gazing before him with fixed and ecstatic look. "Listen to a great idea: there was a day on earth, and in the midst of the earth there stood three crosses. One on the Cross had such faith that he said to another, 'To-day thou shalt be with me in Paradise.' The day ended; both died and passed away and found neither Paradise nor resurrection. His words did not come true. Listen: that Man was the loftiest of all on earth, He was that which gave meaning to life. The whole planet, with everything on it, is mere madness without that Man. There has never been any like Him before or since, never, up to a miracle. For that is the miracle, that there never was or never will be another like Him. And if that is so, if the laws of nature did not spare even Him, have not spared even their miracle and made even Him live in a lie and die for a lie, then all the planet is a lie and rests on a lie and on mockery. So then, the very laws of the planet are a lie and the vaudeville of devils. What is there to live for? Answer, if you are a man."

"That's a different matter. It seems to me you've mixed up two different causes, and that's a very unsafe thing to do. But excuse me, if you are God? If the lie were ended and if you realized that all the falsity comes from the belief in that former God?"

"So at last you understand!" cried Kirillov rapturously. "So it can be understood if even a fellow like you understands. Do you understand now that the salvation for all consists in proving this idea to every one? Who will prove it? I! I can't understand how an atheist could know that there is no God and not kill himself on the spot. To recognize that there is no God and not to recognize at the same instant that one is God oneself is an absurdity, else one would certainly kill oneself. If you recognize it you are sovereign, and then you won't kill yourself but will live in the greatest glory. But one, the first, must kill himself, for else who will begin and prove it? So I must certainly kill myself, to begin and prove it. Now I am only a god against my will, and I am unhappy because I am *bound* to assert my will. All are unhappy because all are afraid to express their will. Man has hitherto been so unhappy and so poor because he has been afraid to assert his will in the highest point and has shown his self-will only in little things, like a schoolboy. I am awfully unhappy, for I'm awfully afraid. Terror is the curse of man. . . . But I will assert my will, I am bound to believe that I don't believe. I will begin and will make an end of it and open the door, and will save. That's the only thing that will save mankind and will re-create the next generation physically; for with his present physical nature man can't get on without his former God, I believe. For three years I've been seeking for the attribute of my godhead and I've found it; the attribute of my godhead is self-will! That's all I can do to prove in the highest point my independence and my new terrible freedom. For it is very terrible. I am killing myself to prove my independence and my new terrible freedom."

5

FRIEDRICH WILHELM NIETZSCHE

Friedrich Nietzsche is the foremost modern spokesman of the death of God. His first full proclamation of the death of God occurs in a section entitled "The Madman" in *The Gay Science,* which was first published in 1882. This passage has finally become a seminal text for Christian theology after having deeply influenced a wide variety of artists and thinkers; it is included here along with a second passage, "The Background of Our Cheerfulness," added to the second edition of *The Gay Science* in 1887. All of Nietzsche's mature work is grounded in his vision of the death of the Christian God or the collapse of all transcendence as it has been known in the Western philosophic and religious tradition. Between 1883 and 1885 Nietzsche wrote *Thus Spoke Zarathustra,* his most comprehensive work, a work which was intended to be a dialectical reversal and transformation of the Christian gospel. Nietzsche's Zarathustra is an Anti-Christ, but he is also a liberator who has come to free man from the life-negating power of guilt and revenge. We include two sections of the fourth part of *Thus Spoke Zarathustra,* both of which are primarily concerned with the meaning of the death of God.

Until recently, theologians have thought of Nietzsche as the foremost modern enemy of faith and have employed his work only to point to the antithesis of faith. So likewise philosophers such as Martin Heidegger and Karl Jaspers have regarded Nietzsche as the primary source of modern nihilism, and Heidegger believes that Nietzsche's proclamation of the death of God recorded the end of the metaphysical tradition of the West. Nietzsche thought of himself, however, as an enemy of nihilism, a nihilism which he conceived as an ultimate No-saying to life and the world. As opposed to all No-saying, Nietzsche proclaimed a "Dionysian" Yes-saying, a passionate affirmation of and total immersion in the brute reality of the world; such Yes-saying becomes fully possible only when the world and human existence are known as being meaningless and absurd. Most critics have misunderstood Nietzsche's Yes-saying as a return to classical paganism or a regression to madness. But Erich Heller, who has re-created Nietzsche's thinking perhaps most fully in our own time, understands Nietzsche as a philosopher and prophet who created a uniquely contemporary mode of thinking and experience, the chief foundation of which is the actualization in the modern consciousness of the death of God.

Passages on the

Friedrich Wilhelm
Nietzsche

Death of God

THE MADMAN

Have you not heard of that madman who lit a lantern in the bright morning hours, ran to the market place, and cried incessantly, "I seek God! I seek God!" As many of those who do not believe in God were standing around just then, he provoked much laughter. Why, did he get lost? said one. Did he lose his way like a child? said another. Or is he hiding? Is he afraid of us? Has he gone on a voyage? or emigrated? Thus they yelled and laughed. The madman jumped into their midst and pierced them with his glances.

"Whither is God" he cried. "I shall tell you. *We have killed him*—you and I. All of us are his murderers. But how have we done this? How were we able to drink up the sea? Who gave us the sponge to wipe away the entire horizon? What did we do when we unchained this earth from its sun? Whither is it moving now? Whither are we moving now? Away from all suns? Are we not plunging continually? Backward, sideward, forward, in all directions? Is there any up or down left? Are we not straying as through an infinite nothing? Do we not feel the breath of empty space? Has it not become colder? Is not night and more night coming on all the while? Must not lanterns be lit in the morning? Do we not hear anything yet of the noise of the gravediggers who are burying God? Do we not smell anything yet of God's decomposition? Gods too decompose. God is dead. God remains dead. And we have killed him. How shall we, the murderers of all murderers, comfort ourselves? What was holiest and most powerful of all that the world has yet owned has bled to death under our knives. Who will wipe this blood off us? What water is there for us to

FROM *The Portable Nietzsche,* trans. and ed. by Walter Kaufmann. Copyright 1954 by The Viking Press, Inc. Reprinted by permission of The Viking Press, Inc.

83

clean ourselves? What festivals of atonement, what sacred games shall we have to invent? Is not the greatness of this deed too great for us? Must not we ourselves become gods simply to seem worthy of it? There has never been a greater deed; and whoever will be born after us—for the sake of this deed he will be part of a higher history than all history hitherto."

Here the madman fell silent and looked again at his listeners; and they too were silent and stared at him in astonishment. At last he threw his lantern on the ground, and it broke and went out. "I come too early," he said then; "my time has not come yet. This tremendous event is still on its way, still wandering—it has not yet reached the ears of man. Lightning and thunder require time, the light of the stars requires time, deeds require time even after they are done, before they can be seen and heard. This deed is still more distant from them than the most distant stars—*and yet they have done it themselves.*"

It has been related further that on that same day the madman entered divers churches and there sang his *requiem aeternam deo.* Led out and called to account, he is said to have replied each time, "What are these churches now if they are not the tombs and sepulchers of God?"

THE BACKGROUND OF OUR CHEERFULNESS

The greatest recent event—that "God is dead," that the belief in the Christian God has ceased to be believable—is even now beginning to cast its first shadows over Europe. For the few, at least, whose eyes, whose *suspicion* in their eyes, is strong and sensitive enough for this spectacle, some sun seems to have set just now. . . . In the main, however, this may be said: the event itself is much too great, too distant, too far from the comprehension of the many even for the tidings of it to be thought of as having *arrived* yet, not to speak of the notion that many people might know what has really happened here, and what must collapse now that this belief has been undermined—all that was built upon it, leaned on it, grew into it; for example, our whole European morality. . . .

Even we born guessers of riddles who are, as it were, waiting on the mountains, put there between today and tomorrow and stretched in the contradiction between today and tomorrow, we firstlings and premature births of the coming century, to whom the shadows that must soon envelop Europe really *should* have appeared by now—why is it that even we look forward to it without any real compassion for this darkening, and above all without any worry and fear for *ourselves?* Is it perhaps that we are still too deeply impressed by the first consequences of this event—and these first consequences, the consequences for *us,* are perhaps the reverse of what one might expect: not at all sad and dark, but rather like a new, scarcely describable kind of light, happiness, relief, exhilaration, encouragement, dawn? Indeed, we philosophers and "free spirits" feel as if a new dawn were shining on us when we receive the tidings that "the old god is dead"; our heart overflows with gratitude, amazement, anticipation, expectation. At last the horizon appears free again to us, even granted that it is not bright; at last our ships may venture out again, venture out to face any danger; all the daring of the lover of knowledge is permitted again; the sea, *our* sea, lies open again; perhaps there has never yet been such an "open sea."

Retired

Not long, however, after Zarathustra had got away from the magician, he again saw somebody sitting by the side of his path: a tall man in black, with a gaunt pale face; and *this* man displeased him exceedingly. "Alas!" he said to his heart, "there sits muffled-up melancholy, looking like the tribe of priests: what do *they* want in my realm? How now? I have scarcely escaped that magician; must another black artist cross my way so soon— some wizard with laying-on of hands, some dark miracle worker by the grace of God, some anointed world-slanderer whom the devil should fetch? But the devil is never where he should be: he always comes too late, this damned dwarf and clubfoot!"

Thus cursed Zarathustra, impatient in his heart, and he wondered how he might sneak past the black man, looking the other way. But behold, it happened otherwise. For at the same moment the seated man had already spotted him; and not unlike one on whom unexpected good fortune has been thrust, he jumped up and walked toward Zarathustra.

"Whoever you may be, you wanderer," he said, "help one who has lost his way, a seeker, an old man who might easily come to grief here. This region is remote and strange to me, and I have heard wild animals howling; and he who might have offered me protection no longer exists himself. I sought the last pious man, a saint and hermit who, alone in his forest, had not yet heard what all the world knows today."

"What does all the world know today?" asked Zarathustra. "Perhaps this, that the old god in whom all the world once believed no longer lives?"

"As you say," replied the old man sadly. "And I served that old god until his last hour. But now I am retired, without a master, and yet not free, nor ever cheerful except in my memories. That is why I climbed these mountains, that I might again have a festival at last, as is fitting for an old pope and church father—for behold, I am the last pope—a festival of pious memories and divine services. But now he himself is dead, the most pious man, that saint in the forest who constantly praised his god with singing and humming. I did not find him when I found his cave; but there were two wolves inside, howling over his death, for all animals loved him. So I ran away. Had I then come to these woods and mountains in vain? Then my heart decided that I should seek another man, the most pious of all those who do not believe in God—that I should seek Zarathustra!"

Thus spoke the old man, and he looked with sharp eyes at the man standing before him; but Zarathustra seized the hand of the old pope and long contemplated it with admiration. "Behold, venerable one!" he said then; "what a beautiful long hand! That is the hand of one who has always dispensed blessings. But now it holds him whom you seek, me, Zarathustra. It is I, the godless Zarathustra, who speaks: who is more godless than I, that I may enjoy his instruction?"

Thus spoke Zarathustra, and with his glances he pierced the thoughts and the thoughts behind the thoughts of the old pope. At last the pope began, "He who loved and possessed him most has also lost him most now; behold, now I myself am probably the more godless of the two of us. But who could rejoice in that?"

"You served him to the last?" Zarathustra asked thoughtfully after a long silence. "You know when he died? Is it true what they say, that pity strangled him, that he saw how *man* hung on the cross and that he could not bear it, that love of man became his hell, and in the end his death?"

The old pope, however, did not answer but looked aside, shy, with a pained and gloomy expression. "Let him go!" Zarathustra said after prolonged reflection, still looking the old man straight in the eye. "Let him go! He is gone. And although it does you credit that you say only good things about him who is now dead, you know as well as I *who* he was, and that his ways were queer."

"Speaking in the confidence of three eyes," the old pope said cheerfully (for he was blind in one eye), "in what pertains to God, I am— and have the right to be—more enlightened than Zarathustra himself. My love served him many years, my will followed his will in everything. A good servant, however, knows everything, including even things that his master conceals from himself. He was a concealed god, addicted to secrecy. Verily, even a son he got himself in a sneaky way. At the door of his faith stands adultery.

"Whoever praises him as a god of love does not have a high enough opinion of love itself. Did this god not want to be a judge too? But the lover loves beyond reward and retribution.

"When he was young, this god out of the Orient, he was harsh and vengeful and he built himself a hell to amuse his favorites. Eventually, however, he became old and soft and mellow and pitying, more like a grandfather than a father, but most like a shaky old grandmother. Then he sat in his nook by the hearth, wilted, grieving over his weak legs, weary of the world, weary of willing, and one day he choked on his all-too-great pity."

"You old pope," Zarathustra interrupted at this point, "did you see that with your own eyes? Surely it might have happened that way—that way, and also in some other way. When gods die, they always die several kinds of death. But—well then! This way or that, this way and that—he is gone! He offended the taste of my ears and eyes; I do not want to say anything worse about him now that he is dead.

"I love all that looks bright and speaks honestly. But he—you know it, you old priest, there was something of your manner about him, of the priest's manner: he was equivocal. He was also indistinct. How angry he got with us, this wrath-snorter, because we understood him badly! But why did he not speak more cleanly? And if it was the fault of our ears, why did he give us ears that heard him badly? If there was mud in our ears—well, who put it there? He bungled too much, this potter who had never finished his apprenticeship. But that he wreaked revenge on his pots and creations for having bungled them himself, that was a sin against *good taste*. There is good taste in piety too; and it was this that said in the end, 'Away with *such* a god! Rather no god, rather make destiny on one's own, rather be a fool, rather be a god oneself!'"

"What is this I hear?" said the old pope at this point, pricking up his ears. "O Zarathustra, with such disbelief you are more pious than you believe. Some god in you must have converted you to your godlessness. Is it not your piety itself that no longer lets you believe in a god? And your overgreat honesty will yet lead you beyond good and evil too. Behold, what remains to you? You have eyes and hands and mouth, predestined for blessing from all eternity. One does not bless with the hand alone. Near you, although you want to be the most godless, I scent a secret, sacred, pleasant scent of long blessings: it gives me gladness and grief. Let me be your guest, O Zarathustra, for one single night! Nowhere on earth shall I now feel better than with you."

"Amen! So be it!" said Zarathustra in great astonishment. "Up there goes the way, there lies Zarathustra's cave. I should indeed like to accompany you there myself, you venerable one, for I love all who are pious. But now a cry of distress urgently calls me away from you. In my realm no one shall come to grief; my cave is a good haven. And I wish that I could put everyone who is sad back on firm land and firm legs.

"But who could take *your* melancholy off your shoulders? For that I am too weak. Verily, we might wait long before someone awakens your god again. For this old god lives no more: he is thoroughly dead."

Thus spoke Zarathustra.

The Ugliest Man

And again Zarathustra's feet ran over mountains and through woods, and his eyes kept seeking, but he whom they wanted to see was nowhere to be seen: the great distressed one who had cried out. All along the way, however, Zarathustra jubilated in his heart and was grateful. "What good things," he said, "has this day given me to make up for its bad beginning! What strange people have I found to talk with! Now I shall long chew their words like good grains; my teeth shall grind them and crush them small till they flow like milk into my soul."

But when the path turned around a rock again the scenery changed all at once, and Zarathustra entered a realm of death. Black and red cliffs rose rigidly: no grass, no tree, no bird's voice. For it was a valley that all animals avoided, even the beasts of prey; only a species of ugly fat green snakes came here to die when they grew old. Therefore the shepherds called this valley Snakes' Death.

Zarathustra, however, sank into a black reminiscence, for he felt as if he had stood in this valley once before. And much that was grave weighed on his mind; he walked slowly, and still more slowly, and finally stood still. But when he opened his eyes he saw something sitting by the way, shaped like a human being, yet scarcely like a human being—something inexpressible. And all at once a profound sense of shame overcame Zarathustra for having laid eyes on such a thing: blushing right up to his white hair, he averted his eyes and raised his feet to leave this dreadful place. But at that moment the dead waste land was filled with a noise, for something welled up from the ground, gurgling and rattling, as water gurgles and rattles by night in clogged waterpipes; and at last it became a human voice and human speech—thus:

"Zarathustra! Zarathustra! Guess my riddle! Speak, speak! What is *the revenge against the witness?* I lure you back, here is slippery ice. Take care, take care that your pride does not break its legs here! You think yourself wise, proud Zarathustra. Then guess the riddle, you cracker of hard nuts—the riddle that I am. Speak then: who am I?"

But when Zarathustra had heard these words—what do you suppose happened to his soul? *Pity seized him;* and he sank down all at once, like an oak tree that has long resisted many woodcutters—heavily, suddenly, terrifying even those who had wanted to fell it. But immediately he rose from the ground again, and his face became hard.

"I recognize you well," he said in a voice of bronze; "*you are the murderer of God!* Let me go. You could not *bear* him who saw *you*—who always saw you through and through, you ugliest man! You took revenge on this witness!"

Thus spoke Zarathustra, and he wanted to leave; but the inexpressible one seized a corner of his garment and began again to gurgle and seek for words. "Stay!" he said finally. "Stay! Do not pass by! I have guessed what ax struck you to the ground: hail to you, O Zarathustra, that you stand again! You have guessed, I know it well, how he who killed him feels—the murderer of God. Stay! Sit down here with me! It is not for nothing. Whom did I want to reach, if not you? Stay! Sit down! But do not look at me! In that way honor my ugliness! They persecute me; now *you* are my last refuge. *Not* with their hatred, *not* with their catchpoles: I would mock such persecution and be proud and glad of it!

"Has not all success hitherto been with the well-persecuted? And whoever persecutes well, learns readily how to *follow;* for he is used to going after somebody else. But it is their *pity*—it is their pity that I flee, fleeing to you. O Zarathustra, protect me, you my last refuge, the only one who has solved my riddle: you guessed how he who killed him feels. Stay! And if you would go, you impatient one, do not go the way I came. *That* way is bad. Are you angry with me that I have even now stammered too long —and even advise you? But know, it is I, the ugliest man, who also has the largest and heaviest feet. Where *I* have gone, the way is bad. I tread all ways till they are dead and ruined.

"But that you passed me by, silent; that you blushed, I saw it well: that is how I recognized you as Zarathustra. Everyone else would have thrown his alms to me, his pity, with his eyes and words. But for that I am not beggar enough, as you guessed; for that I am too rich, rich in what is great, in what is terrible, in what is ugliest, in what is most inexpressible. Your shame, Zarathustra, honored me! With difficulty I escaped the throng of the pitying, to find the only one today who teaches, 'Pity is obtrusive' —you, O Zarathustra. Whether it be a god's pity or man's—pity offends the sense of shame. And to be unwilling to help can be nobler than that virtue which jumps to help.

"But today that is called virtue itself among all the little people—pity. They have no respect for great misfortune, for great ugliness, for great failure. Over this multitude I look away as a dog looks away over the backs of teeming flocks of sheep. They are little gray people, full of good wool and good will. As a heron looks away contemptuously over shallow ponds, its head leaning back, thus I look away over the teeming mass of gray little waves and wills and souls. Too long have we conceded to them that they are right, these little people; so that in the end we have also conceded them might. Now they teach: 'Good is only what little people call good.'

"And today 'truth' is what the preacher said, who himself came from among them, that queer saint and advocate of the little people who bore witness about himself: 'I am the truth.' This immodest fellow has long given the little people swelled heads—he who taught no small error when he taught, 'I am the truth.' Has an immodest fellow ever been answered more politely? You, however, O Zarathustra, passed him by and said, 'No! No! Three times no!' You warned against his error, you, as the first, warned against pity—not all, not none, but you and your kind.

"You are ashamed of the shame of the great sufferer; and verily, when you say, 'From pity, a great cloud approaches; beware, O men!'; when you teach, 'All creators are hard, all great love is over and above its pity'

—O Zarathustra, how well you seem to me to understand storm signs. But you—warn yourself also against *your* pity. For many are on their way to you, many who are suffering, doubting, despairing, drowning, freezing. And I also warn you against myself. You guessed my best, my worst riddle: myself and what I did. I know the ax that fells you.

"But he *had* to die: he saw with eyes that saw everything; he saw man's depths and ultimate grounds, all his concealed disgrace and ugliness. His pity knew no shame: he crawled into my dirtiest nooks. This most curious, overobtrusive, overpitying one had to die. He always saw me: on such a witness I wanted to have revenge or not live myself. The god who saw everything, *even man*—this god had to die! Man cannot bear it that such a witness should live."

Thus spoke the ugliest man. But Zarathustra rose and was about to leave, for he felt frozen down to his very entrails. "You inexpressible one," he said, "you have warned me against *your* way. In thanks I shall praise mine to you. Behold, up there lies Zarathustra's cave. My cave is large and deep and has many nooks; even the most hidden can find a hiding-place there. And close by there are a hundred dens and lodges for crawling, fluttering, and jumping beasts. You self-exiled exile, would you not live among men and men's pity? Well then! Do as I do. Thus you also learn from me; only the doer learns. And speak first of all to my animals. The proudest animal and the wisest animal—they should be the right counselors for the two of us."

Thus spoke Zarathustra, and he went his way, still more reflectively and slowly than before; for he asked himself much, and he did not know how to answer himself readily. "How poor man is after all," he thought in his heart; "how ugly, how wheezing, how full of hidden shame! I have been told that man loves himself: ah, how great must this self-love be! How much contempt stands against it! This fellow too loved himself, even as he despised himself: a great lover he seems to me, and a great despiser. None have I found yet who despised himself more deeply: that too is a kind of height. Alas, was *he* perhaps the higher man whose cry I heard? I love the great despisers. Man, however, is something that must be overcome."

The Modern German Mind: The Legacy of Nietzsche

Erich Heller

In 1873, two years after Bismarck's Prussia had defeated France, a young German who happened to live in Switzerland, teaching classical philology in the University of Basel, wrote a treatise concerned with "the German mind." It was an inspired diatribe against, above all, the German notion of *Kultur* and against the philistine readiness to believe that military victory proved cultural superiority. This was, he said, a disastrous superstition, symptomatic in itself of the absence of any true culture. According to him, the opposite was true: the civilization of the vanquished French was bound more and more to dominate the victorious German people that had wasted its spirit upon the chimera of political power.

This national heretic's name, rather obscure at the time, was Friedrich Nietzsche. What, almost a century ago, he wrote about the perverse relationship between military success and intellectual dominance proved true: not then, perhaps, but now; and it was precisely through him, through his intellectual vision of a world to come, that Germany appears to have invaded vast territories of the world's mind at the very moment when the German body politic was utterly prostrate. Among all the thinkers of the nineteenth century he is, with the possible exceptions of Dostoevski and Kierkegaard, the only one who would not be too amazed by the amazing scene upon which we now move in sad, pathetic, heroic, stoic, or ludicrous bewilderment. Much, too much, would strike him as *déjà vu:* yes, he had foreseen it; and he would understand: for the Modern Mind speaks Ger-

FROM Erich Heller, "The Modern German Mind: The Legacy of Nietzsche," *French and German Letters Today: Four Lectures,* presented under the auspices of the Gertrude Clarke Whittall Poetry and Literature Fund (Washington, D.C.: Library of Congress, 1960).

man, not always good German, but fluent German nonetheless. It was, alas, forced to learn the idiom of Karl Marx, and was delighted to be introduced to itself in the language of Sigmund Freud; taught by Ranke and, later, Max Weber, it acquired its historical and sociological self-consciousness, moved out of its tidy Newtonian universe on the instruction of Einstein, and followed a design of Oswald Spengler's in sending from the depth of its spiritual depression most ingeniously engineered objects higher than the moon. Whether it discovers, with Heidegger, the true habitation of its *Existenz* on the frontiers of Nothing, or meditates, with Sartre and Camus, *le Néant* or the Absurd; whether—to pass to its less serious moods—it is nihilistically young and profitably angry in London or rebelliously debauched and buddhistic in San Francisco—*man spricht deutsch.* It is all part of a story told and foretold by Nietzsche.

As far as modern German literature and thought are concerned—and this is, of course, what we mean by the somewhat giddy abstraction "the modern German mind"—it is hardly an exaggeration to say that they would not be what they are if Nietzsche had never lived. Name almost any poet, man of letters, philosopher, who wrote in German during the twentieth century and attained to stature and influence; name Rilke, George, Kafka, Thomas Mann, Ernst Jünger, Musil, Benn, Heidegger, or Jaspers—and you name at the same time Friedrich Nietzsche. He is to them all— whether or not they know and acknowledge it (and most of them do)— what St. Thomas Aquinas was to Dante: the categorical interpreter of a world which they contemplate poetically or philosophically without ever radically upsetting its Nietzschean structure. Therefore, and in order to escape the embarrassment of vague generalities, I have elected to equate the modern German mind of my title with the mind of Friedrich Nietzsche.

Nietzsche died sixty years ago, after twelve years of a total eclipse of his intellect, insane—and on the threshold of this century. Thinking and writing to the very edge of insanity, and with some of his last pages even going over it, he read and interpreted the temperatures of his own mind; but by doing so, he has drawn the fever-chart of an epoch. Indeed, much of his work reads like the self-diagnosis of a desperate physician who, suffering the disease on our behalf, comes to prescribe as a cure that we should form a new idea of health, and live by it.

He was convinced that it would take at least fifty years before a few men would understand what he had accomplished; and he feared that even then his teaching would be misinterpreted and misapplied. "I am terrified," he wrote, "by the thought of the sort of people who may one day invoke my authority." But is this not, he added, the anguish of every great teacher? He knows that he may prove a disaster as much as a blessing. The conviction that he was a great teacher never left him after he had passed through that period of sustained inspiration in which he wrote the first part of *Zarathustra*. After this, all his utterances convey the disquieting self-confidence and the terror of a man who has reached the culmination of that paradox which he embodies, a paradox which we shall try to name and which ever since has cast its dangerous spell over some of the finest and some of the coarsest minds.

Are we then, at the remove of two generations, in a better position to probe Nietzsche's mind and to avoid, as he hoped some might, the misunderstanding that he was merely concerned with the religious, philosophical, or political controversies fashionable in his day? And if this be a misinterpretation, can we put anything more valid in its place? What is the knowledge which he claims to have, raising him in his own opinion far above the contemporary level of thought? What is the discovery which serves him as a lever to unhinge the whole fabric of traditional values?

It is the knowledge that God is dead.

The death of God he calls the greatest event in modern history and the cause of extreme danger. Note well the paradox contained in these words. He never said that there was no God, but that the Eternal had been vanquished by Time and the Immortal suffered death at the hands of mortals: God is dead. It is like a cry mingled of despair and triumph, reducing, by comparison, the whole story of atheism and agnosticism before and after him to the level of respectable mediocrity and making it sound like a collection of announcements of bankers who regret they are unable to invest in an unsafe proposition. Nietzsche, for the nineteenth century, brings to its *perverse* conclusion a line of religious thought and experience linked with the names of St. Paul, St. Augustine, Pascal, Kierkegaard, and Dostoevski, minds for whom God was not simply the creator of an order of nature within which man has his clearly defined place; but to whom He came rather in order to challenge their natural being, making demands which appeared absurd in the light of natural reason. These men are of the family of Jacob: having wrestled with God for His blessing, they ever after limp through life with the framework of Nature incurably out of joint. Nietzsche is just such a wrestler; except that in him the shadow of Jacob merges with the shadow of Prometheus. Like Jacob, Nietzsche too believed that he prevailed against God in that struggle, and won a new name for himself, the name of Zarathustra. But the words *he* spoke on his mountain to the angel of the Lord were: "I will not let thee go, except thou curse me." Or, in words which Nietzsche did in fact speak: "I have on purpose devoted my life to exploring the whole contrast to a truly religious nature. I know the Devil and all his visions of God."

"God is dead"—this is the very core of Nietzsche's spiritual existence, and what follows is despair, *and* hope in a new greatness of man, visions of catastrophe *and* glory, the icy brilliance of analytical reason, fathoming with affected irreverence those depths hitherto hidden by awe and fear, and, side-by-side with it, the ecstatic invocations of a ritual healer. Without knowing Hölderlin's dramatic poem *Empedocles,* the young Nietzsche, who loved what he knew of Hölderlin's poetry, at the age of twenty planned to write a drama with Empedocles as its hero. His notes show that he saw the Greek philosopher as the tragic personification of his age, as a man in whom the latent conflicts of his epoch attained to consciousness, as one who suffered and died as the victim of an unresolvable tension: born with the soul of *homo religiosus,* a seer, a prophet, and poet, he yet had the mind of a radical sceptic; and defending his soul against his mind and, in turn, his mind against his soul, he made his soul lose its spontaneity, and finally his mind its rationality. Had Nietzsche ever written the drama *Empedocles,* it might have become, in uncanny anticipation, his *own* tragedy.

It is a passage from Nietzsche's *Gaya Scientia* [*The Gay Science*] which conveys best the substance and quality of the mind, indeed the whole spiritual situation, from which the pronouncement of the death of God sprang. The passage is prophetically entitled "The Madman." Here is a brief extract from it:

> Have you not heard of that madman who, in the broad light of the forenoon, lit a lantern and ran into the market-place, crying incessantly: "I am looking for God!" . . . As it happened, many were standing there who did not believe in God, and so he aroused great laughter . . . The madman leapt right among them . . . "Where is God?" he cried. "Well, I will tell you. *We have murdered him*—you and I . . . But how did we do this deed? . . . Who gave us the sponge with which to wipe out the whole horizon? How did we set about unchaining our earth from her sun? Whither is it moving now? Whither are we moving? . . . Are we not falling incessantly? . . . Is night not approaching, and more and more night? Must we not light lanterns in the forenoon? Behold the noise of the grave-diggers, busy to bury God . . . And we have killed him! What possible comfort is there for us? . . . Is not the greatness of this deed too great for us? To appear worthy of it, must not we ourselves become gods?"—At this point the madman fell silent and looked once more at those around him: "Oh," he said, "I am too early. My time has not yet come. The news of this tremendous event is still on its way . . . Lightning and thunder take time, the light of the stars takes time to get to us, deeds take time to be seen and heard . . . and *this* deed is still farther from them than the farthest stars—*and yet it was they themselves who did it!*"

and elsewhere, in a more prosaic mood, Nietzsche says: "People have no notion yet that from now onwards they exist on the mere pittance of inherited and decaying values"—soon to be overtaken by an enormous bankruptcy.

The story of the Madman, written two years before *Zarathustra* and containing *in nuce* the whole message of the Superman, shows the distance that divides Nietzsche from the conventional attitudes of atheism. He is the madman, breaking with his sinister news into the market-place complacency of the pharisees of unbelief. They have done away with God, and yet the report of their own deed has not yet reached them. They know not what they have done, but He who could forgive them is no more. Much of Nietzsche's work ever after is the prophecy of their fate: "The waters of religion," Nietzsche writes at the time of *Zarathustra,* "recede and leave behind morasses and shallow pools. . . . Where we live, soon nobody will be able to exist." For men become enemies, and each his own enemy. From now onwards they will *hate,* Nietzsche believes, however many *comforts* they will lavish upon themselves, and hate *themselves* with a new hatred, unconsciously at work in the depths of their souls. True, there will be ever better reformers of society, ever better socialists, and ever better hospitals, and an ever increasing intolerance of pain and poverty and suffering and death, and an ever more fanatical craving for the greatest happiness of the greatest numbers. Yet the deepest impulse informing their striving will not be love and will not be compassion. Its true source will be the panic-struck determination not to have to ask the question "What is the meaning of our lives?" the question which will remind them of the death of God, the uncomfortable question inscribed on the features of those who are uncomfortable, and asked above all by pain and poverty and suffering and death. Rather than have that question asked, they will do everything to smooth it away from the face of humanity. For they cannot endure it. And yet they will despise themselves for not enduring it, and for their guilt-ridden inability to answer it: and their self-hatred will betray them behind the back of their apparent charity and humanitarian concern. For *there* they will assiduously construct the tools for the annihilation of human kind. "There will be wars," Nietzsche writes, "such as have never been waged on earth." And he says: "I foresee something terrible. Chaos everywhere. Nothing left which is of any value; nothing which commands: Thou shalt!" This would have been the inspiration of the final work which Nietzsche often said he would write and never wrote: *The Will to Power,* or, as he sometimes wanted to call it, *The Transvaluation of All Values.* It might have given his full diagnosis of what he termed nihilism, the state of human beings and societies faced with a total eclipse of all values.

It is in defining and examining the (for him *historical*) phenomenon of nihilism that Nietzsche's attack on Christianity sets in (and it has remained the only truly subtle point which, within the whole range of his more and more unrestrained argumentativeness, this Anti-Christ makes against Christianity). For it is at this point that Nietzsche asks (and asks the same question in countless variations throughout his works): What are the *specific* qualities which the Christian tradition has instilled and cultivated in the minds of men? They are, he thinks, twofold: on the one hand, a more refined sense of truth than any other civilization has known, an almost uncontrollable desire for absolute spiritual and intellectual certainties; and, on the other hand, the ever present suspicion that life on this earth is not in itself a supreme value, but in need of a higher, a transcendental justification. This, Nietzsche believes, is a destructive, and even self-destructive alliance, which is bound finally to corrode the very Christian beliefs on which it rests. For the mind, exercised and guided in its search for knowledge by the most sophisticated and comprehensive theology the world has ever known—a theology which through St. Thomas Aquinas has assimilated into its grand system the genius of Aristotle—was at the same time fashioned and directed by the indelible Christian distrust of the ways of the world. Thus it had to follow, with the utmost logical precision and determination, a course of systematically "devaluing" the knowably real. This mind, Nietzsche predicts, will eventually, in a frenzy of intellectual honesty, unmask as humbug and "meaningless" that which it began by regarding as the finer things in life. The boundless faith in truth, the joint legacy of Christ and Greek, will in the end dislodge every possible belief in the truth of any faith. Souls, long disciplined in a school of unworldliness and humility, will insist upon knowing the worst about themselves, indeed will only be able to grasp what is humiliating. Psychology will denigrate the creations of beauty, laying bare the tangle of unworthy desires of which they are "mere" sublimations. History will undermine the accumulated reputation of the human race by exhuming from beneath the splendid monuments the dead body of the past, revealing everywhere the spuriousness of motives, the human, all-too-human. And science itself will rejoice in exposing this long-suspected world as a mechanical contraption of calculable pulls and pushes, as a self-sufficient agglomeration of senseless energy, until finally, in a surfeit of knowledge, the scientific mind will perform the somersault of self-annihilation.

"The nihilistic consequences of our natural sciences"—this is one of Nietzsche's fragmentary jottings—"from its pursuits there follows ultimately a self-decomposition, a turning against itself," which, he was convinced, would first show as the impossibility, within science itself, of comprehending the very object of its enquiry within *one* logically coherent system, and would lead to extreme scientific pessimism, to an inclination to embrace a kind of analytical, abstract mysticism in which man would shift himself and his world where, Nietzsche thinks, they were driving "ever since Copernicus: from the center towards an unknown X."

It is the tremendous paradox of Nietzsche that he himself follows, and indeed consciously wishes to hasten, this course of "devaluation"—particularly as a psychologist: and at the onset of megalomania he called himself "the first psychologist of Europe," a self-compliment which Sigmund Freud all but endorsed when, surprisingly late in his life, he came to know Nietzsche's writings. He had good reason to do so. Consider, for instance, the following passage from Nietzsche's *Beyond Good and Evil*:

The world of historical values is dominated by forgery. These great poets, like Byron, Musset, Poe, Leopardi, Kleist, Gogol (I dare not mention greater names, but I mean them)—all endowed with souls wishing to conceal a break; often avenging themselves with their works upon some inner desecration, often seeking oblivion in their lofty flights from their all-too-faithful memories, often lost in mud and almost in love with it until they become like will-o'-the-wisps of the morasses and simulate the stars . . . oh what a torture are all these great artists and altogether these higher beings, what a torture to him who has guessed their true nature.

This does indeed anticipate many a more recent speculation on traumata and compensations, on lusts and sublimations, on wounds and bows. Yet the extraordinary Nietzsche—incomprehensible in his contradictions except as the common strategist of two opposing armies who plans for the victory of a mysterious third—a few pages later takes back the guessing, not without insulting himself in the process: "From which follows that it is the sign of a finer humanity to respect 'the mask' and not, in the wrong places, indulge in psychology and psychological curiosity." And furthermore: "He who does not *wish* to see what is great in a man has the sharpest eye for that which is low and superficial in him, and so gives away—himself."

If Nietzsche is not the first psychologist of Europe, he is certainly a great psychologist—and perhaps really the first who comprehended what his more methodical successors, "strictly scientific" in their approach, did not see: *the psychology and the ethics of knowledge itself;* and both the psychology and the ethics of knowledge are of particular relevance when the knowledge in question purports to be knowledge of the human psyche. It was, strangely enough, Nietzsche's a-moral metaphysics, his doubtful but immensely fruitful intuition of the *Will to Power* being the ultimate reality of the world, that made him into the first *moralist of knowledge* in his century and long after. While all his scientific and scholarly contemporaries throve on the comfortable assumptions that, firstly, there was such a thing as "objective," and therefore morally neutral, knowledge, and that, secondly, everything that *can* be known "objectively" is therefore also *worth knowing,* he realized that knowledge, or at least the mode of knowledge predominant at his time and ours, is the subtlest guise of the Will to Power; and that *as a manifestation of the will it is liable to be judged morally.* For him, there can be no knowledge without a compelling urge to acquire it; and he knew that the knowledge thus acquired invariably reflects the nature of the impulse by which the mind was prompted. It is this impulse which *creatively* partakes in the making of the knowledge, and its share in it is truly immeasurable when the knowledge is about the very source of the impulse: the soul. This is why all interpretations of the soul must to a high degree be self-interpretations: the sick interpret the sick, and the dreamers interpret dreams—or, as the Viennese satirist Karl Kraus—with that calculated injustice which is the prerogative of satire—once said of a certain psychological theory: "Psychoanalysis is the disease of which it pretends to be the cure."

Psychology is bad psychology if it disregards its own psychology. Nietzsche knew this. He was, as we have seen from his passage about "those great men," a most suspicious psychologist, but he was at the same time suspicious of the impulse of suspicion which was the father of his thought. Homer, to be sure, did not suspect his heroes, but Stendhal did. Does this mean that Homer knew less about the heroic than Stendhal? Does it make sense to say that Flaubert's Emma Bovary is the product of an imagination more profoundly initiated into the psychology of women than that which created Dante's Beatrice? Is Benjamin Constant, who created the dubious lover Adolphe, on more intimate terms with the nature of a young man's erotic passion than is Shakespeare, the begetter of Romeo? Certainly, Homer's Achilles and Stendhal's Julien Sorel are different heroes, Dante's Beatrice and Flaubert's Emma Bovary are different women, Shakespeare's Romeo and Constant's Adolphe are different lovers, but it would be naive to believe that they simply differ "in actual fact." Actual facts hardly exist in either art or psychology: both interpret and both claim universality for the meticulously particular. Those creatures made by creative imaginations can indeed not be compared, but they are incommensurable above all by virtue of incommensurable *wills* to know the human person, to know the hero, the woman, the lover. It is not better and more knowing minds that have created the suspect hero, the unlovable woman, the disingenuous lover, but minds possessed by different affections for a different knowledge, affections other than the wonder and pride that know Achilles, the love which knows Beatrice, the passion and compassion which know Romeo. When Hamlet comes to know the frailty of woman, he knows Ophelia not better than when he was "unknowingly" in love with her; he knows her differently and he knows her worse.

All *new* knowledge about the soul is knowledge about a *different* soul. For can it ever happen that the freely discovering mind says to the soul: "This is what you are!"? Must not the soul speak first? And worse: having revealed its secret, the soul is no longer what it was when it lived in secrecy. There are secrets which are *created* in the process of their revelation. And still worse: having been told its secrets, it may cease to be a soul. The step from modern psychology to soullessness is as imperceptible as that from modern physics to the dissolution of matter.

Tell an oyster that its pearl is the result of a pathological irritation. It will neither stop producing healthy pearls nor fall in love with pathology. The human soul, on being similarly enlightened, may do both, and must in fact have subtly done so before the mind could tell. Once it is told, the price of pearls drops in the exchanges of the spirit while the demand for pathological irritations soars. They are sold now as chances for winning a pearl, a poet, an artist—still desirable things even with their value reduced. It is this disturbing state of affairs which made Nietzsche deplore "the torture" of psychologically guessing "the true nature of those higher beings" and, at the same time, recommend "respect for the mask" as a condition of "finer humanity." It is a great pity that those parts of Nietzsche's *Transvaluation of All Values* which, if we are to trust his notes, would have been concerned with the literature of the nineteenth century, never came to be written. For no literary critic of the age has had a more penetrating insight into the "nihilistic" character of that "absolute aestheticism" that, from Baudelaire onwards, is the dominant inspiration of European poetry, an aestheticism the *negative* side of which Nietzsche read in the utterly pessimistic image of reality provided by the realistic and psychological novel of that epoch, and above all in the extraordinary fusion of absolute pessimism, radical psychology, and extreme aestheticism achieved by Flaubert.

For Nietzsche, however, *all* the activities of human consciousness share the predicament of psychology. There can be, for him, no "pure" knowledge, only satisfactions, however sophisticated, of the ever varying intellectual needs of the *will* to know. He therefore demands that man should accept *moral responsibility* for the kind of questions he asks, and that he should realize what *values* are implied in the answers he seeks. "The desire for truth," he says, "is itself in need of critique. Let this be the definition of my philosophical task. By way of experiment, I shall question for once the value of truth." And does he not! And he protests that, in an age which is as uncertain of its values as is his and ours, the search for truth will issue in either trivialities or—catastrophe. We may well wonder how he would react to the pious hopes of our day that the intelligence and moral conscience of politicians will save the world from the disastrous products of our scientific explorations and engineering skills. It is perhaps not too difficult to guess; for he knew that there was a fatal link between the moral resolution of scientists to follow the scientific search *wherever,* by its own momentum, it will take us, and the moral debility of societies not altogether disinclined to "apply" the results, however catastrophic. Believing that there was a hidden identity between *all* the expressions of the Will to Power, he saw the element of moral nihilism in the ethics of our science: its determination not to have "higher values" interfere with its highest value—Truth (as it conceives it). Thus he said of the kind of knowledge which the age pursues with furious passion that it was "the most handsome instrument of perdition."

"God is dead"—and man, in his heart of hearts, is incapable of forgiving himself for having done away with Him: he is bent upon punishing himself for this, his "greatest deed." For the time being, however, he will take refuge in many an evasive action. With the instinct of a born hunter

Nietzsche pursues him into all his hiding-places, cornering him in each of them. Morality without religion? Indeed not: "All purely moral demands without their religious basis," he says, "must needs end in nihilism." What is there left? Intoxication. "Intoxication with music, with cruelty, with hero-worship, or with hatred. . . . Some sort of mysticism. . . . Art for Art's sake, Truth for Truth's sake, as a narcotic against self-disgust; some kind of routine, *any* silly little fanaticism. . . ." But none of these drugs can have any lasting effect. The time, Nietzsche predicts, is fast approaching when secular crusaders, tools of man's collective suicide, will devastate the world with their rival claims to compensate for the lost Kingdom of Heaven by setting up on earth the ideological rules of Love and Justice which, by the very force of the spiritual derangement involved, will issue into the rules of cruelty and slavery; and he prophesies that the war for global domination will be fought on behalf of ideological doctrines.

In one of his notes written at the time of *Zarathustra* Nietzsche says: "He who no longer finds what is great in God, will find it nowhere. He must either deny or create it." These words take us to the heart of that paradox that enwraps Nietzsche's whole existence. He is, by the very texture of his soul and mind, one of the most radically religious natures that the nineteenth century brought forth, but endowed with an intellect which guards, with the aggressive jealousy of a watch-dog, all the approaches to the temple. For such a man, what, after the *denial* of God, is there left to *create?* Souls, not only strong enough to endure Hell, but to transmute its agonies into superhuman delight—in fact: the Superman. Nothing short of the transvaluation of all values can save us. Man has to be made immune from the effects of his second Fall and final separation from God: he must learn to see in his second expulsion the promise of a new paradise. For "the Devil may become envious of him who suffers so deeply, and throw him out—into Heaven."

Is there, then, any cure? Yes, says Nietzsche: a new kind of psychic health. And what is Nietzsche's conception of it? How is it to be brought about? By perfect self-knowledge *and* perfect self-transcendence. But to explain this, we should have to adopt an idiom disturbingly compounded of the language of Freudian psychology and tragic heroism. For the self-knowledge which Nietzsche means all but requires a course in depth-analysis; but the self-transcendence he means lies not in the practice of virtue as a sublimation of natural meanness; it can only be found in a kind of unconditional and almost supranatural sublimity. If there were a Christian virtue, be it goodness, innocence, chastity, saintliness, or self-sacrifice, that could not, however much he tried, be interpreted as a compensatory maneuver of the mind to "transvalue" weakness and frustration, Nietzsche might affirm it (as he is constantly tempted to praise Pascal). The trouble is that there cannot be such a virtue. For virtues are reflected upon by minds; and even the purest virtue will be suspect to a mind filled with suspicion. To think thoughts so immaculate that they must command the trust of even the most untrusting imagination, and to act from motives so pure that they are out of reach of even the most cunning psychology, this is the unattainable ideal, it would seem, of this first psychologist of Europe. "Caesar—with the heart of Christ!" he once exclaimed in the secrecy of his diary. Was this perhaps a definition of the Superman, this darling child of his imagination? It may well be; but this lofty idea meant, alas, that he had to think the meanest thought: he saw in the real Christ an illegitimate son of the Will to Power, a frustrated rabbi who set out to save himself and the underdog humanity from the intolerable strain of impotently resenting the Caesars: *not* to be Caesar was now proclaimed a spiritual distinction— a newly invented form of power, the power of the powerless.

Nietzsche had to fail, and fail tragically, in his determination to create a new man from the clay of negation. Almost with the same breath with which he gave the life of his imagination to the Superman, he blew the flame out again. For Zarathustra who preaches the Superman also teaches the doctrine of the Eternal Recurrence of All Things; and according to this doctrine nothing can ever come into being that had not existed at some time before. Thus the expectation of the Superman, this majestic new departure of life, indeed the possibility of any novel development, seems frustrated from the outset, and the world, caught forever in a cycle of gloomily repeated constellations of energy, stands condemned to a most dismal eternity.

Yet the metaphysical nonsense of these contradicatory doctrines is not entirely lacking in poetic and didactic method. The Eternal Recurrence of All Things is Nietzsche's mythic formula of a meaningless world, the universe of nihilism, and the Superman stands for its transcendence, for the miraculous resurrection of meaning from its total negation. All Nietzsche's miracles are paradoxes designed to jerk man out of his false beliefs—in time before they bring about his spiritual destruction in an ecstasy of disillusionment and frustration. The Eternal Recurrence is the high school to teach strength through despair. The Superman graduates from it *summa cum laude et gloria*. He is the prototype of health, the man who has learned to live without belief and without truth, and, superhumanly delighting in life "as such," actually *wills* the Eternal Recurrence: "Live in such a way that you desire nothing more than to live this very same life again and again!" The Superman, having attained to this manner of existence which is exemplary and alluring into all eternity, despises his former self for craving moral sanctions, for satisfying his will to power in neurotic sublimation, for deceiving himself about the "meaning" of life. What will he be then, this man who at last knows what life *really* is? Recalling Nietzsche's own accounts of all-too-human nature, and his analysis of the threadbare fabric of traditional values and truths, may he not be the very monster of nihilism, a barbarian, not necessarily blond, but perhaps a conqueror of the world, shrieking bad German from under his dark moustache? Yes, Nietzsche feared his approach in history: the vulgar caricature of the Superman. And because he also feared that the liberally decadent and agnostically disbelieving heirs to Christian morality would be too feeble to meet the challenge, having enfeebled the idea of civilized existence and rendered powerless the good, he sent forth from his imagination the Superman to defeat the defeat of man.

Did Nietzsche himself *believe* in the truth of his doctrines of the Superman and the Eternal Recurrence? In one of his posthumously published notes he says of the Eternal Recurrence: "We have produced the hardest possible thought—the Eternal Recurrence of All Things—now let us create the creature who will accept it lightheartedly and joyfully!" Clearly, there must have been times when he thought of the Eternal Recurrence not as a "Truth" but as a kind of spiritual Darwinian test to select for survival the spiritually fittest. There is a note of his which suggests precisely this: "I perform the great experiment: who can bear the idea of the Eternal Recurrence?" This is a measure of Nietzsche's own unhappiness: the nightmare of nightmares was to him the idea that he might have to live his identical life again and again and again; and an ever deeper insight into the anatomy of despair we gain from this note: "Let us consider this idea in its most terrifying form: existence, as it is, without meaning or goal, but inescapably recurrent, without a finale into nothingness. . . ." Indeed, Nietzsche's Superman is the creature strong enough to live forever a cursed existence and even to transmute it into the Dionysian rapture of tragic acceptance. Schopenhauer called man the *animal metaphysicum*. It is certainly true of Nietzsche, the renegade *homo religiosus*. Therefore, if God was dead, then for Nietzsche man was an eternally cheated misfit, the diseased animal, as he called him, plagued by a metaphysical hunger to feed which all the Heavens may be ransacked without result. Such a creature was doomed: he had to die out, giving way to the Superman who would miraculously feed on barren fields and finally conquer the metaphysical hunger itself without any detriment to the glory of life.

Did Nietzsche himself *believe* in the Superman? In the manner in which a poet believes in the truth of his creations. Did Nietzsche believe in the truth of poetic creations? Once upon a time when, as a young man, he wrote *The Birth of Tragedy,* Nietzsche did believe in the power of art to transfigure life by creating lasting images of true beauty out of the meaningless chaos. It had seemed credible enough as long as his gaze was enraptured by the distant prospect of classical Greece and the enthusiastic vicinity of Richard Wagner's Tribschen. Soon, however, his deeply romantic belief in art turned to scepticism and scorn; and his unphilosophical anger was provoked by those "metaphysical counterfeiters," as he called them, who enthroned the trinity of beauty, goodness, and truth. "One should beat them," he said. Poetic beauty *and* truth? No, says Zarathustra, "poets lie too much"—and adds dejectedly: "But Zarathustra too is a poet. . . . *We* lie too much." And he did: while Zarathustra preached the Eternal Recurrence, his author confided to his diary: "I do not wish to live *again*. How have I borne life? By creating. What has made me endure? The vision of the Superman who affirms life. I have tried to affirm life *myself*— but ah!"

Was he, having lost God, capable of truly believing in anything? "He who no longer finds what is great in God will find it nowhere—he must either deny it or create it." Only the "either-or" does not apply. All his life Nietzsche tried to do both. He had the passion for truth and no belief in it. He had the love of life and despaired of it. This is the stuff from which demons are made—perhaps the most powerful secret demon eating the heart out of the modern mind. To have written and enacted the extremest story of this mind—a German mind—is Nietzsche's true claim to greatness. "The Don Juan of the Mind" he once called, in a "fable" he wrote, a figure whose identity is hardly in doubt:

> The Don Juan of the Mind: no philosopher or poet has yet discovered him. What he lacks is the love of the things he knows, what he possesses is *esprit,* the itch and delight in the chase and intrigue of knowledge— knowledge as far and high as the most distant stars. Until in the end there is nothing left for him to chase except the knowledge which hurts most, just as a drunkard in the end drinks absinthe and methylated spirits. And in the very end he craves for Hell—it is the only knowledge which can still seduce him. Perhaps it too will disappoint, as everything that he knows. And if so, he will have to stand transfixed through all eternity, nailed to disillusion, having himself become the Guest of Stone, longing for a last supper of knowledge which he will never receive. For in the whole world of things there is nothing left to feed his hunger.

It is a German Don Juan, this Don Juan of the Mind; and it is amazing that Nietzsche should not have recognized his features: the features of Goethe's Faust at the point at which he has succeeded at last in defeating the plan of salvation.

And yet Nietzsche's work, wrapped in paradox after paradox, taking us to the limits of what is still comprehensible and often beyond, carries elements which issue from a center of sanity. No doubt, this core is in perpetual danger of being crushed, and was in fact destroyed in the end. But it is there, and is made of the stuff of which goodness is made. Nietzsche once said that he had spent all his days in philosophically *taking sides against himself.* Why? Because he was terrified by the prospect that all the better things in life, all honesty of mind, integrity of character, generosity of heart, fineness of aesthetic perception, would be corrupted and finally cast away by the new barbarians, unless the mildest and gentlest hardened themselves for the war which was about to be waged against them: "Caesar with the heart of Christ!"

Time and again we come to a point in Nietzsche's writings when the shrill tones of the rebel are hushed by the still voice of the autumn of a world waiting in calm serenity for the storms to break. Then this tormented mind relaxes in what he once called the *Rosengeruch des Unwiederbringlichen*—an untranslatably beautiful lyricism of which the closest equivalent in English is perhaps Yeats'

> Man is in love and loves what vanishes.
> What more is there to say?

In such moments the music of Bach brings tears to his eyes and he brushes aside the noise and turmoil of Wagner; or he is, having deserted Zarathustra's cave in the mountains, enchanted by the gentle grace of a Mediterranean coastline. Contemplating the quiet lucidity of Claude Lorrain, or seeking the company of Goethe in conversation with Eckermann, or comforted by the composure of Stifter's *Nachsommer,* a Nietzsche emerges, very different from that who used to inhabit the fancies of Teutonic schoolboys and, alas, schoolmasters, a Nietzsche who is a traditionalist at heart, a desperate lover who castigates what he loves because he knows it will abandon him and the world. It is the Nietzsche who can with one sentence cross out all the dissonances of his apocalyptic voices: "I once saw a storm raging over the sea, and a clear blue sky above it; it was then that I came to dislike all sunless, cloudy passions which know no light, except the lightning."

In these regions of his mind dwells the terror that he may have helped to bring about the very opposite to what he desired. Then he is much afraid of the consequences of his teaching. Perhaps the best will be driven to despair by it, the very worst accept it? And once he put into the mouth of some imaginary titanic genius what is his most terrible prophetic utterance: "Oh grant madness, you heavenly powers! Madness that at last I may believe in myself . . . I am consumed by doubts, for I have killed the Law . . . if I am not more than the Law, then I am the most abject of all."

Small wonder that few can think in Germany without thinking of Nietzsche. He is the master-mind of modern Germany—a country with open frontiers.

6

SIMONE WEIL

France has given the twentieth century two of its most illuminating and original mystical visionaries in Simone Weil and Pierre Teilhard de Chardin. Each has given a deeply religious expression to the underlying currents of our century. Just as Simone Weil has baptized the horror of our world with her vision of the impotence of God, so Teilhard de Chardin has named Christ as the center of the primal energy leading forward the movements of consciousness and life. If Teilhard embodies the triumphant Yes-saying of the Christian faith, a Yes-saying which must ever be held in balance by the No-saying of the prophetic tradition, then that No-saying has surely been given a contemporary voice in Simone Weil.

In the selection that follows Susan Anima Taubes claims that Simone Weil has given a new kind of atheism its most uncompromising formulation, a mystical atheism embodying Nietzsche's announcement that God is dead.

Susan A. Taubes

The Absent God

[1]

When Nietzsche announced that God is dead, he planted the seed for a new kind of atheism which has become a major theme of European thinkers in our century and which found its most uncompromising formulation in the posthumously published notes of the French philosopher-mystic-saint, Simone Weil. Atheism, which used to be a charge leveled against skeptics, unbelievers, or simply the indifferent, has come to mean a *religious* experience of the death of God. The godlessness of the world in all its strata and categories becomes, paradoxically and by a dialectic of negation, the signature of God and yields a mystical atheism, a theology of divine absence and nonbeing, of divine impotence, divine nonintervention, and divine indifference.

Religious atheism is distinct from secular atheism from the start, in that it invests the natural world, from which divine presence and providence have been totally excluded, with theological significance. He who, seeking God, does not find him in the world, he who suffers the utter silence and nothingness of God, still lives in a religious universe: a universe whose essential meaning is God, though that meaning be torn in contradiction and the most agonizing paradoxes. He lives in a universe that is absurd, but whose absurdity is significant, and its significance is God. God, however negatively conceived, explains the world, explains the nothingness of God in the world. The thesis of religious atheism has been most boldly formulated by Simone Weil: the existence of God may be denied without denying God's reality.

REPRINTED FROM "The Absent God," *The Journal of Religion* (January, 1955), by Susan A. Taubes, by permission of the University of Chicago Press. Copyright 1955 by the University of Chicago.

God's absence is not a temporary ill brought about by the sinfulness of a generation, as when the prophet Isaiah laments that God has turned away from his people and hid his face from man, believing that there was a time when God was present and that there will be a time when he will show his face again. Simone Weil has universalized the historical experience of the death of God into a theological principle. The unworldliness of God, his silence, and nothingness are his most essential features. God can be present to us only in the form of his absence.

The situation that Nietzsche represented by the image of the death of God grew out of several revolutions in consciousness, each of which voiced its particular challenge to Christianity. These movements range from the critical investigation of sacred Christian history to the final shattering of faith in divine providence in the moral catastrophe of the twentieth century. They encompass the scientific technological transformation of a hierarchically created universe into a blind mechanical process; the empirical investigation of the religions of the world leading to the relativization of Christian dogma and institutions; the progressive undermining of faith, first, by Marxian theory, that exposed religion as political ideology, and then by psychological and psychoanalytical theory, that reduced "religious experience" to behavioristic and subjective categories. The scientific conception of the universe and the critical inquiry into the nature of man and society have relegated religious "symbols" to the level of useful or useless, dangerous or therapeutic, fictions.

The march of optimistic humanism was, however, almost from the start accompanied by apprehensions, which, under the impact of the political and economic events of the last decades, ripened into an acute anxiety and despair, manifest in the general hunger for religion in our day.

Simone Weil was neither an apologist for the traditional faith, trying to defend it against materialistic attacks, nor a fugitive from the emptiness and confusion of the secular world to the fortress of an orthodox religious frame of reference. Jewish by birth, she refused baptism, choosing to identify herself with the "immense and unfortunate mass of unbelievers." She tried to meet the modern challenge to the authenticity of religious life not by taking issue with the claims of empirical science but by accepting them. The mortification of God in the world becomes the theological starting point for the life of the spirit in God. She discovered the reality of God in the phenomena that seemed to testify most forcibly against it: in the meaningless suffering of the concentration camps, in the futility of manual labor, in the coercive necessity of matter, in the mechanistic behaviorism of the human psyche. And she succeeded in coining a religious vocabulary from the profoundest experience of the absence of God.

The theology that emerges from the notes of Simone Weil is conditioned by the contemporary experience of atheism. But while she has illuminated the depths of contemporary affliction and inhumanity with unfailing purity of insight, she has divorced them from their historical causes and formalized the impotence of the age into a theological category. Thus the uprootedness, the nakedness, and the hopelessness of man today reveal him in his ultimate *essence.*

Affliction does not create human misery, it merely reveals it. It is precisely in the enslavement and degradation of man in our times that she discovers the Christian image of man. Describing her experience at the Renault factory, where she worked for a year in order to share the lot of the workers, Simone Weil writes: "There I received forever the mark of a slave, like the branding of the red-hot iron which the Romans put on the foreheads of their most despised slaves. Since then I have always regarded myself as a slave."

It was through the experience of industrial labor, where the atomization of the individual and the dehumanization of man to a mere thing reaches one of its peaks, that Simone Weil for the first time envisaged Christianity as an answer to human suffering. "There the conviction was suddenly borne in upon me that Christianity is preeminently the religion of slaves, that slaves cannot help belonging to it, and I among others." In the ordeal of twentieth-century fascism and atheism, the Christian symbols regain their significance. Stripped of his humanity, man once more envisages himself in the image of a slave. Simone Weil speaks from the very heart of the Christian experience when she discovers, in the last nudity and wretchedness of man, his genuine spirituality.

She saw the greatness of Christianity in that it does not seek for a supernatural remedy for suffering but for a supernatural *use* of suffering. Her Christianity, however, goes only as far as the Cross, the image of the crucified and humiliated God. And in her *Letter to a Priest,* where she discusses the obstacles to her conversion to the Catholic faith, she repudiates, point by point, the major dogmas of the church regarding resurrection, providence, immortality, miracles, and eschatology.

[2]

Simone Weil's meditations center in the problem of evil and the effect of affliction on the soul. Affliction, in distinction from simple suffering, represents a total uprooting of life in all its parts—social, psychological, as well as physical. Affliction "takes possession of the soul and marks it through and through with its own particular mark, the mark of slavery." It stamps man with the scorn, the disgust, and self-hatred, the sense of guilt and defilement, which crime ought to produce but actually does not. There is a pitiless realism in Simone Weil's analysis of the effect of affliction on the human soul, which seems to defy any attempt to glorify it. We like to believe that affliction ennobles man, but actually the contrary is true, for the afflicted person does not contemplate his affliction; "he has his soul filled with no matter what paltry comfort he may have set his heart on." Affliction degrades whomever it touches and can evoke only the revulsion of those who behold it.

The model of the slave, not the model of the hero or the model of the martyr, determines Simone Weil's insight into affliction. Affliction proceeds from chance and blind mechanism; "affliction is anonymous before all things, it deprives its victims of their personality and makes them into things." The slave emerges as the model of affliction in a technological society whose blind mechanism makes both heroism and martyrdom meaningless as human possibilities and which finds its image in the impotent victim, in the industrial worker, or in the prisoner in a concentration camp, who suffers not as a man in the hands of men but as a thing battered around by impersonal forces. It is a world in which man as such, man as an autonomous person and source of action, has no being; personality and organism crumble in a calculus of forces; and it remains merely to distinguish between two orders of necessity: gravity and grace.

Gravity, whereby Simone Weil understands the strictest Cartesian determinism, governs all natural phenomena, and man's soul as well as his body is caught in the mechanism of the world. Man's social behavior, his imagination, his emotions, desires, and beliefs—in short, all the *natural* movements of the soul—obey quantitative laws as rigid as those that rule physical phenomena. By a law of compensation, suffering is necessarily converted into either violence or hatred. Any blow we suffer, whether in the form of a pain or an insult, is automatically communicated to some person or object outside us in a sense as material as the transfer of force in the action and reaction of atoms.

Affliction cuts one of our innumerable threads of attachment to the world. A vacuum is created in the soul, of which it tries to rid itself either by transferring it to another creature by inflicting a wrong or by "filling" it through the action of a compensatory imagination. The psyche is essentially governed by a *horror vacui.* It cannot tolerate any emptiness, and its basic activity consists in filling up the void that is continually communicated to it by other psyches likewise determined to get rid of the void created in them. Under the law of gravity both forgiveness and compassion are impossible. The realm of human relations presents a field of force where there is a perpetual transmission of evil from man to man. Unless we suppose the action of a force radically different from that of gravity, it would be utterly beyond man's power to arrest evil.

It is through the contemplation of "human mechanics" that Simone Weil is led to conceive of the necessity of grace. The possibility of a power which can withstand the force of gravity and *endure* the void created in the soul through affliction implies the intervention of a force of a different order, the supernatural action of grace.

Grace alone can give the soul the strength to suffer the void, to "go on loving in the emptiness." We do not love God because he exists; our love is the proof and the very substance of his reality. "God is absent from the world except through the existence of those in this world in whom his love lives." Thus to affirm and at the same time to deny God's existence is a "case of contradictories which are true. God exists. God does not. Where is the problem? I am quite sure that there is a God in the sense that I am quite sure my love is not illusory. I am quite sure that there is not a God in the sense that I am quite sure nothing real can be anything like what I am able to conceive when I pronounce this word."

Simone Weil's notion of "atheism as a purification" goes even further. Since God can be present in the world only in the form of absence, "we have to believe in a God who is like the true God in everything except that he does not exist." It is precisely to the extent that we have dissociated from our love of God the least sense of consolation (including the consolation that God exists) that our love is real. The subjective and pragmatic motives that modern psychology and sociology have discovered in all forms of religiosity do not necessarily lead to an attitude of cynicism but, on the contrary, serve to purify our notion of the supernatural.

Simone Weil criticizes the basic Christian doctrines of the immortality of the soul, resurrection, divine providence, and eschatological hope as forms of consolation that are obstacles to faith. While belief in God as a consolation actually insulates the soul from contact with the true God, atheism that endures the emptiness of God's absence is a purification. Doubt is not incompatible with faith, for faith is not identical with *belief;* it is "loving in the emptiness"; it is "fidelity to the void."

Simone Weil's mysticism of atheistic purification bears some resemblance to the "dark night of the soul" of St. John of the Cross, to whom she frequently refers in her notes. But while the Spanish mystic is describing an ecstatic experience of the soul's death prior to its rebirth in God, for Simone Weil the dark night of God's absence is itself the soul's contact with God. When she speaks of an "ineffable consolation" that fills the soul after it has renounced everything, renounced even the desire for grace, she does not mean that supernatural love is something distinct from the acceptance of the void. To endure the void, to suffer evil, is our contact with God. The path of Simone Weil's thought "from human misery to God" has the sense of a "correlation" and not a compensation. Affliction contains the seed of divine love. "By redemptive suffering, God is present in extreme evil. For the absence of God is the mode of divine presence which corresponds to evil—absence which is felt."

[3]

The psychological analysis of affliction brought into light the existence of two irreducibly contrary forces—grace and gravity. On the level of the theological interpretation of evil, however, grace and gravity are shown to be two aspects of the same divine reality. The soul that goes on loving in the emptiness and consents to affliction knows that "this world, in so far as it is completely empty of God, is God himself" and that "necessity, in so far as it is absolutely other than the good, is the good itself." But how can God, who is the source of the good, wear the mask of evil? Why has God hidden himself behind the "screen" of creation, so that we can love him only in the form of the "inconsolable bitterness" of his absence? This is perhaps the most desperate formulation of the question that has haunted theology ever since the Creator of the world was envisaged as one supreme and infinitely good God.

If God is the supreme Creator, then he is responsible for all evil, including the crimes committed by men; if God is not responsible for the evil in the world, then we must suppose that there exists a being whose power is equal to God's. The efforts of orthodox theology have been directed toward maintaining the omnipotence of God without making God responsible for evil. Simone Weil argues that God can be supreme and innocent at the same time because he is impotent. The Son of God was crucified; his Father allowed him to be crucified; these are the two aspects, Simone Weil writes, of God's impotence.

God suffers and consents to evil. But whence does the evil spring originally? Evil arises out of the fact that there is something other than God, namely, the world and all its creatures. Simone Weil does not shrink from saying that, as the creator of the world, God is the author of evil and likewise the author of sin. But creation does not mean the exercise of divine power; it is the abdication of God, the sacrifice of God. Through creation, God renounced being everything.

Creation and sin are the same thing viewed from different perspectives. "The great crime of God against us is that he created us; that we exist. Our great crime against God is our existence. When we forgive God our existence, our existence is forgiven by God." Why God abdicated his power in favor of cosmic necessity, by creating an autonomous universe, remains an incomprehensible mystery for Simone Weil. We must consent to the world, consent to necessity and to the suffering of the innocent, because God has consented. Finally, it is by consenting to God's will that we can expiate the crime of our existence and become nothing.

Man's consent to be nothing is essentially the same as the acceptance of the void and involves the action of grace. Conversely, God's consent not to be everything, God's impotence, manifests itself as the mechanism of gravity. De-creation is a process of uprooting one's self, of accepting and loving the affliction that tears the soul from its social and vital attachments. Indeed, suffering implies the superiority of man over God, and "the incarnation was necessary so that this superiority should not be scandalous."

The paradox of consenting to evil and suffering it to the limit as a way of attaining the good leads to the verge of nihilism. For if affliction is the proof of God's supreme love, why should we not deliberately uproot, degrade, and destroy both ourselves and others? If we were created in order that we should de-create ourselves, why should we not choose suicide, or why should we try to avert or to assuage the suffering of others? If the death of the self is desirable, if existence as such is evil, why should murder and destruction be condemned?

To consent to affliction, Simone Weil claims, is to consent to the will of God. Affliction, therefore, must be inflicted by God and "through his own instruments." The afflictions which we trace to "human mechanism"— social injustice, political oppression, and economic exploitation—are as much an instrument of God, a supernatural device for revealing to man the wretchedness of natural attachments, as are flood, earthquake, and disease. "Human crime, which is the cause of most affliction, is a part of blind necessity." And since extreme affliction always involves social degradation, it is, finally, the "social animal" that gives affliction its specific and absolute stamp.

Whenever we pray "Thy will be done," we should think of "all possible misfortunes added together," because only at the point where suffering becomes intolerable will the cords that attach us to the world break. But at the same time she counsels us not to seek affliction deliberately. "We must not seek the void, for it would be tempting God if we counted on supernatural bread to fill it."

To inflict violence on one's self or on others is therefore contrary to grace. Does it follow that we ought to do good, to prevent evil, or to help those who are afflicted? For Simone Weil the question as such is baseless, for man cannot *do* good. All action is subject to the law of gravity, and "only suffering, useless in appearance and perfectly patient" can arrest evil. The condemnation of crime and suicide springs only from the fact that they are *actions;* the nature of the good, however, is passive, for it reflects the impotence of God. We cannot imitate God through creativity—this necessarily leads to evil—but only through obedience. Simone Weil speaks of acts of charity as supernatural; moreover, at a certain stage of spiritual perfection it is as impossible for a man not to help a creature in need as it is for a stone to defy gravity. Nevertheless, charity remains inexplicable on the plane either of grace or of gravity, and the mystery of charity is analogous to the mystery of creation itself: "Why has God created us?

But why do we feed those who are hungry?" We can no more comprehend the value of charity than the goodness of creation.

The soul's movement toward God in Simone Weil's mysticism is conceived in terms of an intellectual skepsis rather than ecstatic experience. She makes no claim to voices or visions and is suspicious of states of spiritual intoxication. Voices and visions, she writes, result from an illegitimate admixture of imagination in supernatural love; and the lives of the saints would have been still more wonderful without them.

To imagine that one is in paradise is a "horrible possibility," for every paradise is artificial and the mystical experience of eternal blessedness is simply a glorified projection of earthly happiness. The true union with God is not beatific but crucifying, for we become one with God in void and slavery, one with the crucified God.

[4]

The Gnostic[1] traits of Simone Weil's mysticism are striking at first sight. And her notebooks contain ample evidence of her familiarity with Gnostic, Manichaean, and Catharist sources. Her intellectualism in matters of faith, the obsession with purity, the notion of transcendental immanence, and the pathos of the non-existent God place her in the line of Gnostic heretics.

Simone Weil adopts the basic motifs of the *gnosis,*[2] the absent God, the divine void, the world order as an all-embracing predatory mechanism wherein man is imprisoned, the *pneuma* or divine part of the soul that is opposed to both the body and the psyche, and the dialectical unity of the supernatural self and the supernatural God, but eliminates the eschatological drama and the mythological frame. She reinterprets the gnosis by robbing or "purifying" it of its aura of positive transcendence, of its visions of the splendor of the utterly strange and utterly new God, its sense of genuine liberation from the bonds of necessity.

The God of the Gnostics, however strange, absent, and unknown, is yet a God of dazzling splendor, of light and joy, a God of life. The Gnostics, like the early Christians, refer to the divine spark in man as the *life*. Life liberated from the chains of the flesh and death, freedom, a kind of folly and fever, a sense of quickening and ecstasy, and, above all, hope in redemption and resurrection in God characterize the quality of spirit. Where the gnosis is inconsistent, confusing the experience of the nothingness of God with visions of apocalypse and the triumph of the good, Simone Weil is logical to the bitter end. Supernatural love is not a quickening of the soul; it is a kind of death. Once we understand that truth is

---

[1] A reference to ancient Christian Gnosticism, a heretical movement offering a mystical liberation from the evil power of the world —T. J. J. A.

[2] The sacred or redemptive knowledge of the Gnostic mystical vision —T. J. J. A.

on the side of death, we have no right to project even the most sublime image of life on the plane of the supernatural or the hereafter. Freedom and the sense of spiritual exaltation are the illusions of life; they are inextricably bound up with the world we must renounce. Therefore, it is futile to seek through the supernatural "a slackening of the chains of necessity. The supernatural is more precise, more rigorous than the crude mechanism of matter. . . . It is a chain over a chain, a chain of steel over a chain of brass."

The power and the glory and the Kingdom are images of this world. Simone Weil accuses the early Christians and the Gnostics of making God "more," and thereby less, than supernatural. The gospel of Resurrection is still tainted with the attachment to life. The proof of God is not Resurrection but the Cross. "Hitler could die and return to life again fifty times," Simone Weil writes; "I should still not look upon him as the Son of God. And if the gospel omitted all mention of Christ's resurrection, faith would be easier for me. The Cross by itself is enough."

The figure of the crucified Jesus, abandoned by God and dying without hope of resurrection, does not, however, yield the image of man's tragic complaint against a deaf sky—an image not without some human grandeur, for it implies that man in his conscious moral anguish is superior to an amoral universe. The contemporary situation does not lend itself to a tragic interpretation; its image is not the hero fighting against great odds and defeated in the end but the masses of helpless victims subjected to meaningless waste and torture, defeated from the beginning. Its image is not the sinner who wilfully transgresses God's law, but the oppressors and the oppressed alike as mere victims of a mechanism of drives and compensations. Its image is not even that of the martyr, for martyrdom, like heroism, can be chosen; but "one cannot choose the Cross. . . . The Cross is infinitely more than martyrdom. It is the most purely bitter suffering, penal suffering."

[5]

It was surely a profound experience of the pits of unredeemed human suffering in the contemporary world, combined with a pitiless realism regarding the effects of affliction on men's souls, that led Simone Weil to realize that any attempt to resurrect the dead God is doomed to remain romantic rhetoric. Her insight into the fact that God dies in the souls of men subjected to the extremes of torture and humiliation drove her to devise a religion of a dead God: a God who is not so much unmanifest because he is the primordial and inexhaustible source of all that can become manifest, a God who is not so much transcendental because he is beyond the limitations of time, space, and necessity, but a God who does not exist, who emptied himself into the world, transformed his substance in the blind mechanism of the world, a God who dies in the inconsolable pits of human affliction. This God is, finally, more alien to the living person and to the visionary life of the spirit than the blind mechanism of nature, for while nature may constrain and imperil life, this God asks man to renounce his attachment to life altogether.

By way of a negative theodicy, Simone Weil interprets the complete absence of justice, mercy, and the good in the world as the sign of divine justice and goodness. Thereby she defends divine justice, but not without destroying the possibility of man's justice. The negative theodicy attains its most powerful formulation in the image of the crucified God. For it is God himself who suffers in the flesh and soul of every afflicted creature. "God is at once a sacrificial victim and an all-powerful ruler." The theological solution, which represents the murderer and his victim united in the selfsame person of God, merely obscures the fact that, in reality, the murderers are two, standing over against each other, divided by a gulf that separates the living from the dead and that magnifies a human dilemma to cosmic dimensions.

There is no answer to the suffering of the helpless, to the tortures of the concentration camps, to the slow death of manual labor. "To explain suffering," Simone Weil writes, "is to console it; therefore, it must not be explained." And yet, by finding theological uses for suffering, she has, in whatsoever unjust and absurd a manner, striven to justify and to rationalize it. To say that the cries of the afflicted praise God, that supernatural grace fills the voids of the crippled and the humiliated, is finally as grave an insult to the hells of human suffering as to say that the suffering of the innocent is rewarded in heaven or serves God's final purpose. There is no meddling with human suffering, and Simone Weil knew this. The suffering she had in mind was the ultimate hell that reduces men to a mass of shrieking flesh and then to inert matter, that robs them of their capacity to feel and act as men. Simone Weil understood that for this suffering there is no answer. Her deepest insights are those which reveal that extreme affliction plunges the soul beyond the pale of redemption and which show that, in fact, suffering, and not sin, brings damnation. But even while she realized that the soul dies in the hideous pits of affliction, she refused to accept it—the thirst for redemption was sufficient proof for its reality—and thus she tried through a series of spiritual experiments to find a way to strengthen, train, and prepare a part of the soul for the worst affliction.

What is at stake for Simone Weil in the question of the reality of God is the survival of man's soul, his capacity for love, compassion, gratitude, forgiveness, and his joy in reality, even under slavery, degradation, impotence, exile, and pain, even under the most terrible tortures. Life itself and all attachments to this world seemed worth sacrificing if only a spark of love could be made to enter the petrified soul of the afflicted in the concentration camps. She started by asking, How can this cross be borne? She ended by exalting the Cross into the sole union with God and the end of all spiritual striving.

But the hells of the afflicted are unredeemable. This is what Ivan Karamazov meant when he said that it is beyond God's power to make good a single tear from a single child. Simone Weil writes: "We have to say, like Ivan Karamazov, that nothing can make up for a single tear from a single child, and yet to accept all tears and the nameless horrors which are beyond tears. . . . We have to accept the fact that they exist simply because they do exist." But acceptance is as irrelevant as revolt before the irreparable, before that which *simply is*. Revolt at least transcends man's impotence in the face of the particular unredeemable fact, by stating that such a fact should not be possible and by demanding that it should not be permitted to exist. What is meant is not the permission of God but of men.

The Cross, as Simone Weil knew, is more than martyrdom. The sufferings of the destitute, the persecuted, and the oppressed are not a ritual but a reality. Was it her continual failure, despite many efforts, to take this reality upon herself that drove her to construe suffering as a spiritual exercise? For she left the Renault factory after a year's "experience" to return to her academic circle and did not lose herself in the anonymity of the masses. After an accident in the Spanish civil war she accepted the rescuing hand of well-to-do parents, while others died and rotted away in camps. Hitler came, and she followed her parents, if unwillingly, to Portugal, North Africa, the United States, and England. One cannot help suspecting that, by a strange twist of honesty, she felt impelled to confront affliction in spurious ways, on the level of "spiritual experience," because she did not succeed in meeting it in reality.

It is a romantic illusion that one can go to the people and share their lot as long as one retains the possibility of returning to one's former life of security whenever one chooses. The people have no other resources. If one would share the condition of the poor, one must go among them as one enters a cloister, leaving one's securities and resources behind. Otherwise, one remains a spectator. For the gravity of their lot consists just in its hopeless finality.

The attempt to introduce contemplation in physical suffering results in a kind of aestheticism. Affliction, Simone Weil claims, reveals man's essential wretchedness and thus his spirituality. But is this not to confuse man's capacity for moral anguish with the facts of physical pain and social degradation? It would seem that there is a distinction between man's metaphysical reflection on his human condition and the kind of violent physical torment and social dislocation Simone Weil means by affliction. The distinction is rather crucial, for while man's consciousness of his own frailty may indeed reveal his greatness, the tortures of the concentration camps and the ruthless uprooting of human beings reveal, if anything, the abyss of human bestiality.

Simone Weil shows with unfailing insight how man's social dependence, his need for "moral food," reveals his vulnerability; and she uses man's vulnerability as the pivotal point on which man's spirituality turns, by way of detachment from the social as well as the vegetative realm. But the spirituality of human suffering is rooted, if at all, in the spirituality of human existence, the specifically human relations whose destruction can mutilate and even kill man's spirit. The religions that teach the "supernatural value" of suffering exploit man's image of an ideal human community and his longing to realize it, while they bid him to renounce attaining it and to acquiesce in his condition.

It is the specific mark of human suffering that it points beyond the sheer immediacy of pain to an ideal norm which applies to man as such within a historical reality. The chain of the oppressed of all ages burdens man not merely by its physical weight but as a *wrong*. It has been the crime of religion against humanity to teach men that slavery under whatever form is not a wrong but a fate. It reaches its most scandalous expression in the view that the suffering of the innocent is a special sign of the love of God. Thereby religion not only sanctions the present sufferings of the injured but paralyzes the nerves of a historical human community based on a mutual responsibility between the generations.

The purity of Simone Weil's experience of the Cross and her genuine desire for identification with the injured and the oppressed render her religion of suffering all the more tragic. For her mystical atheism offers a religion to the afflicted only at the price of blindfolding one's self to the fact of those who profit from their affliction and consequently serving their ends.

[6]

Simone Weil assimilated both the psychological and the sociological critique of religion. Her analysis of the psychological motivations and social horizon of the early Christian does not fall short of the descriptions of either Marx or Nietzsche and is as devastating. At the same time she answered Nietzsche's contemptuous and Marx's indignant characterization of Christianity as a religion for slaves, by embracing the identity of slavery and religion without apology or reservations. She was fully aware of the role of compensation in traditional religion and tried to develop a theology which could in no way be reduced to a compensatory-escapist mechanism, since it rested on a total renunciation of desire and extinction of hope, on the one hand, and a total surrender to brute actuality, on the other. She envisaged a God whose reality was beyond doubt because he revealed himself only at the point where the mechanism of compensation was arrested and attention was fixed on the point of suffering.

What Simone Weil failed to realize was that the social implications of her negative theology were not essentially different from those of positive theology, so that the sociological critique of religious mystification applied to the God of impotence as well as to the God of power. It would seem, then, that in the end she did not meet the challenge of enlightened humanism to Christianity, for her attempt to purify Christian theological symbols from the element of power remains trapped in the social dialectic of domination. The alternative to domination is not impotence but the elimination of domination. Impotence is only one side of the power relation and presupposes the relation of man's domination over man.

Simone Weil's negative theodicy of divine impotence presupposes a powerful God who voluntarily abdicates his power. Behind the void of divine absence looms the figure of an all-powerful God who, by an act of withdrawal, sets the grim mechanism of necessity in motion and lets evil take its course. Thus, in the end, the human implications of serving the "dead God" and of being in the hands of the living God are equally ambiguous. Simone Weil attacks the living God, represented by the God of Israel, as a form of social idolatry. The religion of power may have been guilty of idolizing the aspirations of a particular community; but is not Simone Weil in her way also guilty of projecting the impotence and the hopelessness of a particular human society into the divine being?

Regarded from the point of view of man, theodicy is an offense against human justice; from the point of view of God, it is blasphemy against the divine being. The book of Job presents the most poignant formulation of the problem of theodicy and at the same time its most powerful refutation. Job believed to the end that the suffering of a just man is unjust and did not speculate on the supernatural uses of suffering. He questioned the justice of God, and the Almighty answered him out of the whirlwind that the Creator of heaven and earth cannot be called to account by his creatures. Otherwise, we must hold with Lucretius that the gods are so remote from the affairs of men that, for all intents and purposes, men must carry on their pursuit as if the gods did not exist.

Part Two **RADICAL EXPRESSIONS OF EUROPEAN THEOLOGY**

7
KARL
BARTH

Karl Barth has certainly been the most influential Christian theologian of the twentieth century. It will be ironic if future historians identify him as the supreme religious genius of our century, for surely no other modern theologian so fully embodies a human passion for the infinite, despite the fact that he condemns such passion as the greatest barrier to faith. Barth's commentary on Paul's Epistle to the Romans succeeded in creating a revolution in Protestant theology. Written while he was serving as a pastor in Switzerland between 1911 and 1921, Barth's commentary on Romans was first published in 1918, but he completely rewrote the volume for its second edition in 1921, and it is this edition which is now established as a theological classic. In it we find a conception of grace as a void within human experience that appears only with the collapse of everything on this side of the abyss between man and God. Grace reveals that there is no God in history or religion but only in the Christ whose absolute self-negation effects the "end" of humanity. Thus Barth, who so powerfully revived the classical theology of the Protestant Reformation, in addition created the possibility of a radical theology proceeding from the total absence of God in human experience. Barth is also a radical theologian insofar as he leads the way to a collapse of theology into Christology. Today's radical theologians commonly feel a firm bond with the Barth of the commentary on Romans while they largely repudiate the mature and ecclesiastical Barth of the *Church Dogmatics*. The following selections are Barth's verse-by-verse commentaries on two passages in Paul's Epistle to the Romans.

Karl
Barth

Two Passages from
The Epistle to the Romans

THE MEANING OF RELIGION

[Rom. 7:7–11]

VERSE 7A   *What shall we say then? That the law itself is sin? God forbid.*

We have now reached the point where we are bound to discuss the effective meaning and significance of that last and noblest human possibility which encounters us at the threshold and meeting-place of two worlds, but which, nevertheless, remains itself on this side the abyss dividing sinners from those who are under grace. Here, at this turning-point, grace and law—religion—the first invisibility and the last visible thing, confront each other. Grace is the freedom of God by which men are seized. Within the sphere of psycho-physical experience this seizure is, however, nothing but vacuum and void and blankness. The seizure, therefore, lies on the other side of the abyss. Though religion and law appear to concern that relationship between men and God with which grace is also concerned, yet in fact they do not do so. Law and religion embrace a definite and observable disposition of men in this world. They hold a concrete position in the world, and are, consequently, things among other things. They stand, therefore, on this side the abyss, for they are not the presupposition of all things. There is no stepping across the frontier by gradual advance or by laborious ascent, or by any human development whatsoever.

FROM *The Epistle to the Romans,* translated by Edwyn C. Hoskyns (New York: Oxford University Press, 1933), pp. 96-99, 240-53. Reprinted with the permission of the Oxford University Press.

125

The step forward involves on this side collapse and the beginning from the far side of that which is wholly Other. If, therefore, the experience of grace be thought of as the prolongation of already existing religious experience, grace ceases to be grace, and becomes a thing on this side. But grace is that which lies on the other side, and no bridge leads to it. Grace confronts law with a sharp, clearly defined "No! Anything rather than such confusion!" The first divine possibility is contrasted with the last human possibility along the whole frontier of religion. There is no bridge between service *in newness of spirit* and *service in oldness of the letter*.[1] What then, we ask, is the meaning of the paradox of this close proximity and this vast separation, this near parallelism and this unbridgeable gulf, this interlocking relationship and this harsh opposition? What attitude are we to adopt to that relationship to God from which no man can escape *as long as he liveth*[2]? How are we to think of religion, if it be also the most radical dividing of men from God?

The law—sin? It seems obvious that we are almost compelled to the judgement that the law is sin. Whenever we have been brought to understand the double position which the law occupies as the loftiest peak of human possibility, we have been on the brink of subscribing to this judgement.[3] And why should we not surrender to the pressure and say roundly that religion is the supremacy of human arrogance stretching itself even to God? Why should we not say that rebellion against God, robbery of what is His, forms the mysterious background of our whole existence? Would not this bold statement represent the truth? And why, then, should we not embark on a war against religion? Would not such an engagement constitute a human possibility far outstripping the possibility of religion? Why should we not enroll ourselves as disciples of Marcion, and proclaim a new God, quite distinct from the old God of the law? Why should we not follow Lhotzky, and play off the "Kingdom of God" against "Religion"? or Johannes Müller, and, transporting men from the country of indirect observation, deposit them in the lost, but nevertheless still discoverable, land of direct apprehension? or Ragaz, and, waving the flag of revolution against Theology and the Church, advance from their barrenness into the new world of complete laicism in religion? Why should we not return to the main theme of the first edition of this commentary, and joining hands with Beck and with the naturalism of the leaders of the old school of Württemberg, set over against an empty idealism the picture of humanity as a growing divine organism? Or finally, why not proclaim ourselves one with the company of "healthy" mystics of all ages, and set forth the secret of a true supernatural religion running at all points parallel to natural religion? Why not? The answer is simply—God forbid! The apparent radi-

[1] 7:6. [Unless otherwise specified verse and chapter numbers refer to Paul's Epistle to· the Romans —T. J. J. A.]
[2] 7:1. [3] 4:15; 5:20; 6:14, 15; 7:5.

calism of all these simplifications is pseudo-radicalism: *Nondum con-siderasti, quanti ponderis sit peccatum* [Do not consider the weight of sin—Anselm]. The corrupt tree of sin must not be identified with the possibility of religion, for sin is not one possibility in the midst of others. We do not escape from sin by removing ourselves from religion and taking up with some other and superior thing—if indeed that were possible. Religion is the supreme possibility of all human possibilities; and consequently grace, the good tree, can never be a possibility above, or within, or by the side of, the possibility of religion. Grace is man's divine possibility, and, as such, lies beyond all human possibility. When, therefore, on the basis of a true perception that law is the supreme dominion of sin over men, men first deduce that sin and law are identical, and then proceed in crude or in delicate fashion to demand the abrogation of law, in order that they may live in this world without law—that is, presumably, without sin!; when men revolt, as Marcion did, and with equally good cause, against the Old Testament; when they forget, however, that a like resentment must be applied to the totality of that new thing which they erect upon the ruins of the old—this whole procedure makes it plain that they have not yet under-stood the criticism under which the law veritably stands. The veritable *krisis* under which religion stands consists first in the impossibility of escape from it *as long as* a man *liveth;* and then in the stupidity of any attempt to be rid of it, since it is precisely in religion that men perceive themselves to be bounded as men of the world by that which is divine. Religion compels us to the perception that God is not to be found in reli-gion. Religion makes us to know that we are competent to advance no single step. Religion, as the final human possibility, commands us to halt. Religion brings us to the place where we must wait, in order that God may confront us—on the other side of the frontier of religion. The trans-formation of the "No" of religion into the divine "Yes" occurs in the dis-solution of this last observable human thing. It follows, therefore, that there can be no question of our escaping from this final thing, ridding ourselves of it, or putting something else in its place. It follows also that we cannot just identify law and sin, or suppose that we can advance out of the realm of sin into the realm of grace simply by some complete or partial abroga-tion of law.

VERSE 7B   *Howbeit, I had not known sin, except through the law: for I had not known coveting, except the law had said, Thou shalt not covet.*

"I had not known sin, except through the law." What then is religion, if it be not the loftiest summit in the land of sin, if it be not identical with sin? The law is quite obviously the point at which sin becomes an observa-ble fact of experience. Law brings all human possibility into the clear light of an all-embracing *krisis*. Men are sinners, only because of their election and vocation, only because of the act of remembering their lost direct dependence upon God, only because of the contrast between their pristine and their present relation to Him. Otherwise they are not sinners. Apart from the possibility of religion, men, as creatures in the midst of other creatures, are sinners only in the secret of God; that is, they sin unobservably and nonhistorically. God knows good and evil. But not so can men be convinced of sin. Sin does not yet weigh them down as guilt and as destiny. They are incompetent to perceive the sword of judgement hanging above their heads; nor can any man persuade or compel them to this fatal perception. Nor is it otherwise with regard to the new creation, which is the obverse side of the condition of men. Men are righteous, only in the secret of God: that is, they are righteous unobservably and nonhistorically. They cannot convince themselves of righteousness. Between these two unobservable realities are set observable law and observable religion. In the midst of other things, whether we recognize it or not, is placed the impress of revelation, the knowledge of good and evil, the perception—more or less clear—that we belong to God, the reminiscence of our Primal Origin, by which we are elected either to blessedness or to damnation. Reference is made, it is true, in verses 13 and 14 to an exception to this general knowledge; but it is, presumably, only a theoretical exception. We are now concerned with the meaning of this peculiar and final apprehension; and the question as to whether there are exceptions is hardly relevant. We are able to see that, compared with other things of which we are aware, religion is a distinct and quite peculiar thing. A numinous perception of any kind has an alarming and disturbing effect upon all other perceptions; a divinity of any kind tends to bring men into a condition which is more or less ambiguous; a cleavage of some form or other is made between their existence and a contrasted and threatening nonexistence; a gulf appears between the concrete world and the real world; there emerges a scepticism as to whether we are competent to elongate possibility into impossibility or to stretch our actual existence into nonexistence. Something of this *krisis* underlies all religion; and the more insistent the tension becomes, the more clearly we are in the presence of the phenomenon of religion, whether or no we ourselves are conscious of it. From the point of view of comparative religion, the evolution of religion reaches its highest and purest peak in the Law of Israel, that is, in the assault made upon men by the Prophets. But what is the real significance of this prophetic *krisis*? It is unintelligible unless we first recognize that precisely in the phenomena of religion there occurs visibly a rising of slaves against the authority of God. Men *hold the truth imprisoned in unrighteousness*. They have lost themselves. Giving pleasurable attention to the words—*Ye shall be as God*—they become to themselves what God ought to be to them. Transforming time into eternity, and therefore eternity into time, they stretch themselves beyond the boundary of death, rob the Unknown God of what is His, push themselves into His domain, and depress Him to their own level. Forgetting the awful gulf by which they are separated from Him, they enter upon a relation with Him which would be possible only if He were not God. They make Him a thing in this world, and set Him in the midst of other things. All this occurs quite manifestly and observably within the possibility of religion. Now the prophetic *krisis* means the bringing of the final observable human possibility of religion within the scope of that *krisis* under which all human endeavor is set. The prophets see what men in fact are: they see them, confronted by the ambiguity of the world, bringing forth the possibility of religion; they see them arrogantly and illegitimately daring the impossible and raising themselves to equality with God. But, if this last achievement of men be the action of a criminal, what are we to say of all their other minor achievements? Clearly, all are under judgement. In the light of the prophetic condemnation of this final achievement we perceive the condemnation also of all previous and lesser achievements. The whole series of human competences becomes to us a series of impossibilities. When the highest competence is seen to be illusion, the lower share inevitably in a general illusoriness. If God encounters and confronts men in religion, He encounters and confronts them everywhere. Remembering their direct relation with Him, its loss becomes an event, and there breaks out a sickness unto death. It is religion, then, which sets a question mark against every system of human culture; and religion is a genuine experience. But what do men experience in religion? In religion men know themselves to be conditioned invisibly by—sin. In religion the Fall of mankind out of its primal union with God becomes the presupposition of all human vitality. *Through the law,* the double and eternal predestination of men to blessedness or to damnation becomes a psychophysical occurrence; and—*sin abounds.*[4]

"I had not known coveting, except the law had said, Thou shalt not covet." The sinfulness of my vitality and the necessary dissolution of my desires are not self-evident truths. This qualification of my whole activity is, apart from religion, merely an opinion. Moreover, all my senses object to being disqualified; they protest vigorously against a suspicion and condemnation which is directed against them and against the natural order as such. Surely, if we exclude from our thoughts the primal and final significance of the possibility of religion, this resistance and protest is wholly justified. Why indeed should mere natural vitality be evil? *I had not known coveting—Apart from the law sin is dead* [5]—unless, that is, with fatal imprudence, I had dared, as a religious man, to leave the region of mere worldliness and press forward into the questionable light of my divine

[4] 5:20.   [5] 5:8.

possibility. Religion in some guise or other overwhelms me like an armed man; for, though the ambiguity of my existence in this world may perhaps be hidden from me, yet nevertheless my desires and my vitality press forward into the sphere of religion, and I am defenseless against this pressure. To put the matter another way: I am confronted, as a man of this world, by the clear or hidden problem of the existence of God. It is, then, inevitable that I should do what I ought not to do: that quite inadequately and unworthily, I should formulate the relation between the infinity of God and my finite existence, between my finite existence and the infinity of God —in terms of religion. When I have surrendered to this seeming necessity, law has entered into my life, and my desires and vitality are then subjected, if not to an absolute, at least to a quite devastating negation; if not to a direct, at least to a brilliant indirect lighting; if not to a final, at least to a penetrating and a vigorous ambiguity. Between the experience of religion and all other human experiences there is a relatively quite radical cleavage: in the religion of the prophets, for example, this cleavage is peculiarly terrible. The "peculiarity" of the Jew is occasioned by his occupation of a position so perilously near the edge of a precipice that its sheer drop may be taken as bearing witness to the sharp edge of that wholly other precipice, by which all human achievements, all concrete occurrences, are bounded; the precipice which separates men from God.[6] Though I may with naïve creatureliness *covet,* so long as I know naught but this coveting creatureliness, yet even this is forbidden me whenever, in venturing to know more than my creatureliness, I have pressed so hard on the frontier of divine possibilities that even my created existence is rendered questionable. When this has once occurred, the desires even of my simple createdness are broken desires. They are no longer innocent, and I am no longer justified in their enjoyment. When religion, supreme among all desires, opens its mouth, it proclaims to all coveting—*Thou shalt not!* When eternity confronts human finite existence, it renders that finite existence sinful. When human finite existence is confronted by the eternity of God, it becomes sin. This applies, however, only when the action of men who have fallen out of their relationship with God is not the action of God Himself. We are not concerned here with the precise form or scope or extent of this *krisis* of human vitality, for such matters belong properly to the study of history. We are concerned only to bring out the peculiar significance of the phenomenon of religion and its relation to other phenomena. We have asked the question: What is the meaning of religion? We have now discovered its meaning to be that our whole concrete and observable existence is sinful. Through religion we perceive that men have rebelled against God, and that their rebellion is a rebellion of slaves. We are now driven to the consideration of that freedom which lies beyond the concrete visibility of sin—the freedom of God which is our freedom.

[6] 3:1-2.

VERSES 8-11   *But sin, taking occasion by the commandment, wrought in me all manner of coveting: for apart from the law sin is dead. And I was alive apart from the law once: but when the commandment came, sin burst into life, and I died; and the commandment, which was unto life, this I found to be unto death: for sin, taking occasion by the commandment, deceived me, and through it slew me.*

"But sin, taking occasion by the commandment, wrought in me all manner of coveting." In speaking of the process by which Word became Myth it is impossible to avoid mythological language! In its primal form, in the secret of God, sin is the possibility that the union between men and God may be broken. Sin is the possibility of predestination to blessedness *or* to damnation. This does not mean, of course, that sin originated in God; but it does mean that He is its final truth. In God men possess—as slaves do—the possibility of rebellion. They can separate themselves from Him who is eternally one. They can lay hold of the shadow which follows the divine glory—but only as its negation—and make it their eternity. Men have the opportunity of making themselves God. The knowledge of this opportunity, and the consequent capacity to make use of it, is sin. When the sluice-gates are opened, the water, by the force of its own inertia, pours through to a lower level. So sin, because its nature is to move downwards and not upwards, because it belongs properly to what is relative, separated, independent, and indirect, bursts into the world of time, breaks into concrete visibility, and stands there in stark contrast with what is unobservable, nonconcrete, and eternal. Sin is sin—in so far as the world is manifested as an independent thing over against creation; in so far as the course of the world runs counter to its existence; in so far as men are opposed to God. And yet, it is not immediately obvious that the sluice-gates of the lock which marks the distinction between God and man have been opened. Originally, there was no separation. Men dwelt in the Garden of Eden, in which there were no absolute and relative, no "Higher" and "Lower," no "There" and "Here": such distinctions marked the Fall. The world was originally one with the Creator, and men were one with God. The natural order then, as such, was holy, because holiness is its characteristic mark. Originally, there was no *coveting:* men were permitted, and indeed commanded, to enjoy all the fruits of the garden. There was, however, one exception. In the midst of the garden stood *the tree of the knowledge of good and evil.* The behavior of men must not be governed by knowledge of the contrast between the primal state and its contradiction. That is God's secret. Men ought not to be independently what they are in dependence upon God; they ought not, as creatures, to be some second thing by the side of the Creator. Men ought not to know that they are merely—men. God knows this, but in His mercy He has concealed it from them. So long as ignorance prevailed, the Lord walked freely in the garden in the cool of the day, as though in the equality of friendship. Look how Michelangelo has depicted the "Creation of Eve": in the fullness of her charm and beauty she rises slowly, posing herself in the fatal attitude of—worship. Notice the Creator's warning arm and careworn, saddened eyes, as He replies to Eve's gesture of adoration. She is manifestly behaving as she ought not. Eve—and we must honor her as the first "religious personality" —was the first to set herself over against God, the first to worship Him; but, inasmuch as *she* worshipped *Him,* she was separated from Him in a manner at once terrible and presumptuous. Then the "well-known serpent" appears upon the scene. He utters words—the archetype of all sermons— about God; he—the first shepherd of the souls of men—first offers advice concerning the commandments of God. Adam's titanic capacity for wisdom already existed before Eve!—now it is turned into tragic reality. Tragic— because, when men, knowing good and evil, become *like God,* when their direct relation with Him gives birth to independent action, then all direct relationship is broken off. When men stretch out their hands and touch the link which binds them to God, when they touch the tree *in the midst of the garden,* which ought not to be touched, they are by this presumptuous contact separated from Him. They have handled death—that barbed wire loaded with electricity. Stretching out to reach what they are not, men en- counter what they are, and they are thereby fenced in and shut out. With open eyes they see that they are separated from God and—naked. Covet- ing, lusting after, passionately desiring corruptible things, they become themselves corruptible. Why is the question concerning God as the Creator and us as His creation a question which, in spite of its insistent, compell- ing, desperate urgency, cannot even be formulated—by us? Yet we know no man who has not done as Adam did. We ourselves have touched the tree; we have formulated the question; and in formulating it we have set ourselves in opposition to God. In opposition to God!—this which God withheld from us for our salvation now governs our lives. Immediately we know good *and* evil, the commandment of God transforms Paradise into —Paradise Lost. Our present existence is discredited and rendered ques- tionable, already, perhaps, accused and condemned as actually evil, by the demand which names a thing *good* which—ought to be so and is not. The covetous desire, which causes men to stretch out their hands towards that one tree, renders also more or less forbidden those many desires to enjoy the fruits of all the other trees. For this one lust sets everything which men think and will and do in direct opposition to the relentless and holy and eternal will of God. This is the triumph of sin. Impetuously sin has sought and found its level in the many-sided vitality of men, and their vitality is now named *lust.* Opposition to God emerges in the critical distinction be- tween seen and unseen, relative and absolute, independence and primal union. And this opposition comes into being through the divine command- ment; through the intrusion of the possibility of religion; through the beguilement of the serpent's sermon on the theme of a direct relation between men and God; through the far too great attention paid to it by men, and especially by women, since they are more acutely disturbed than men are by the riddle of direct relationship. So it is that religion becomes the occasion of sin. Religion is the working capital of sin; its fulcrum; the means by which men are removed from direct union with God and thrust into disunion, that is, into the recognition of their—creatureliness.

"For apart from the law sin is dead. And I was alive apart from the law once." The words *I was alive* can no more refer to the historical past than can the words *we shall live*[7] to some historical future; the reference is to that life which is primal and nonhistorical, just as the previous reference was to that life which is also final and nonhistorical. There is no question here of contrasting a particular epoch in the life of a single individual, or of a group, or indeed of all mankind, with some other epoch, past or future. The passages refer to that timeless age to which all men belong. Only in a parable, and, even so, only with the greatest care, can we speak of the "innocence" of children and of the guilt of those who have passed beyond the "age of innocence"! Only with great circumspection ought we to speak of "Child-races" or "Child-civilizations," etc., or of their "growing up." The life defined as past or future must not be depressed into history, because the contrast is concerned with the opposition between eternal life and our present concrete existence. *I was alive* and sin was dead, because I lived *apart from the law: apart from the law* sin is dead, and men are alive. Only when the creature stands over against the Creator may it be defined as sinful. The creation is not questionable, unless it be thought of as mere Nature, independent of God. The recognition of the opposition of the world to God, and of its consequent sinfulness, becomes acute only with the emergence of the titanic possibility of religion. The creature, in its primal, original, unseen history, lives and moves without touching the line of death which marks the separation between God and man; without touching the tree of destiny which stands in the midst of the garden. In this primal life, the union and distinction between the Creator and the creature is not fraught with the tragic significance which comes into being with the emergence of religion. In the fresco of the "Creation of Adam" Michelangelo depicts God and Adam looking one another straight in the face, their hands stretched out towards one another in a delicious freedom of intercourse. The air is charged with the deep, triumphant, moving peace of the eternal "Moment" of creation. And yet, the scene is heavy with tragedy; for it portrays the direct relation as not yet lost; it portrays the relation in which religion plays no part. And so it draws attention to the distinction between our present existence and, not only the "old" Creation, but also the "new" Creation for which men are now waiting. In this direct relation-

[7] 6:2. A good example of Barth's fundamental distinction between chronological history (*Historie*) and ultimate or eschatological history (*Geschichte*).—T. J. J. A.

ship mankind lives; not this or that individual man, but mankind as created by God, in His own image, and as He will again create them. Out of this relationship, which never has been, and never will be, an event in history, we issue, and towards it we move. Nor can sin destroy this primal union, for it is the act and work of God alone. Marcion described it admirably as the "Wholly Other" which is our unforgettable home; the reality, the proximity, the glory, which we encounter in the last words of the Gospel—Forgiveness, Resurrection, Redemption, Love, God. These are words in which disturbance and promise are joined together; for they direct us towards the realm where there is no law and no religion.[8] Those concrete and historical events which seem to us[9] relatively pure and innocent are harmless and fraught with hope and meaning only when we behold reflected in them that life from which we come and to which we move.

"But when the commandment came, sin burst into life, and I died." Scattered to the winds is the eternal "Now" of the Creation. *The commandment came.* It had to come, when men became as God, bearing the burden of the divine secret, knowing good *and* evil, election *and* damnation, "Yes" *and* "No." The time when there was no commandment is beyond our understanding. All we know is that the union between God and man has been changed from divine presupposition to human supposition, and that, consequently, every human position has suffered dislocation. On the very brink of human possibility there has, moreover, appeared a final human capacity—the capacity of knowing God to be unknowable and wholly Other; of knowing man to be a creature contrasted with the Creator, and, above all, of offering to the Unknown God gestures of adoration. This possibility of religion sets every other human capacity also under the bright and fatal light of impossibility. Such is human capacity; and we are bound to believe and to make known—for only a weak-chested piety fails to perceive it—that men are compelled to advance along a road which ends in "Double Predestination." What then—we are bound to ask the question —are men? *Sin burst into life.* Irrecoverable is the "Moment" of creation; irretrievable the purity and peace of that existence in which God and men were one and not two. The unity of life has been sundered, and God stands over against men as their counterpart—in power; whereas men stand over against God as His counterpart—in weakness. Men are limited by God, and God is limited by men: both are compromised and rendered questionable. *And I died.* Death is the mark of that passing of eternity into time, which is, of course, not an occurrence in time, but a past happening in primal history. Now everything is concrete and indirect. The whole range of the life we now live is contrasted with our life in God, and consequently stamped with the indelible mark of death. The narrow gate through which our perception widens out from what is finite to what is infinite closes and opens only with critical negation. The recognition that

[8] 4:15.   [9] As 5:13.

we must die is forced upon us, and such recognition is the point where we either attain wisdom or remain "fools"—in the most reprehensible sense of the word. In the inexorable "No" of death, the "Yes" of God and of life is presented to us: that is to say, it is presented to us in the contrast between what we are able to observe and what is beyond our observation; it is presented to us in recognizable time, which is past and future, but never present; in the concrete form of Nature, which is mere "world"— *cosmos*—but never Creation; in visible history, which is only process, but never completed occurrence. The only world we can know is the world of time, of things, and of men. The final experience to which we have access in this world is summed up in the words *and I died,* and this is the presupposition of all experience. Now, the religious man is bound to encounter this experience, this presupposition of all experience, precisely because he is a religious man: *Then said I, Woe is me! for I am undone: . . . for mine eyes have seen the King, the Lord of hosts.*[10] There is no escape from this vision or from this undoing.

"And the commandment, which was unto life, this I found to be unto death: for sin, taking occasion by the commandment, deceived me, and through it slew me." The supreme possibility to which we can attain within the range of our concrete existence under the dominion of sin consists in our capacity to grasp the line of death, to know both good and evil, and in the consequent emergence of the distinction between God as God and men as men. Now, that this supreme and urgent necessity of our existence should be identical with that capacity by which our direct union with God was destroyed, constitutes the final paradox of the Fall.

When we ask what it is that directs us towards that lost, but recoverable life in God, standing as we do within the world of time and things and men, there is but one possible answer: we are directed by the *commandment,* by our capacity for religion, by a vast critical negation—in fact, by the recognition that *we must die.* Is there any other road where the unseen becomes visible, any other road along which those men have passed who have *seen clearly* and to whom the thought of God has been revealed,[11] except the narrow way of the "wisdom of death"? Since we cannot take up our position beyond the line of death, and since we must take our stand somewhere, have we any alternative but to stand on the line "across which Adam fell" (Luther)? Daring the best and the highest, our place is on the extremest edge of human possibility, where the "Jesus of History" stands, where Abraham, Job, and all the prophets and apostles stand; the place where men are most evidently men, where they are most completely removed from direct union with God, and where human existence is most heavily burdened with its own questionableness. There is for us no honorable alternative but to be religious men, repenting in dust and ashes, wrestling in fear and trembling, that we may be blessed; and, since we must take up a

[10] Isa. 6:5.　　　　　　[11] 1:20.

position, adopting the attitude of adoration. To all this we are urged by the commandment which directs us unto life. Knowing, then, that we have no alternative, knowing also what that alternative involves, ought we to shrink from advancing to take up our position on the very outermost edge of the precipice, on the very brink of the possibility of religion? We may, however, judge the relentlessness of Calvin, the dialectical audacity of Kierkegaard, Overbeck's sense of awe, Dostoevsky's hunger for eternity, Blumhardt's optimism, too risky and too dangerous for us. We may therefore content ourselves with some lesser, more feeble possibility of religion. We may fall back on some form of rationalism or pietism. Yet these more feeble types of religion are also pregnant with implications pointing towards that outermost edge, and some day they may bring this harsh and dangerous reality to birth. If Adam, easily content with lesser possibilities, should ever forget his proper condition and omit to move to his final possibility, Eve soon reminds him of the possibility of religion, for she is more acutely aware of the loss of direct union with God. And yet—for here is the tragic paradox of religion—should we seriously undertake to turn as pilgrims towards that far-off land which is our home, should we undertake the final concrete human action, we do but display the catastrophe of human impotence in the things of God. What is our action, our taking up of a position, but the supreme betrayal of the true presupposition? What is our undertaking of a visible relationship, our scaling of the summit of human possibility, but our completest separation from the true invisible relationship? Seen from God's standpoint, religion is precisely that which we had better leave undone: *And the commandment—this I found to be unto death.* The necessity of the possibility of religion, the necessity of stretching out towards the tree in our midst, the desire to know good and evil, life and death, God and man—this necessity is no more than a maneuver, undertaken by men within the concrete reality of this world. By it they are defined as evil and passing to corruption; by it they are defined as—men; by it they are thrown into the contrast between relative and absolute, and there imprisoned. At best they are confronted in religion by the "No" in which the "Yes" of God is hidden. Death is the meaning of religion; for when we are pressed to the boundary of religion, death pronounces the inner calm of simple and harmless relativity to be at an end. Religion is not at all to be "in tune with the infinite" or to be at "peace with oneself." It has no place for refined sensibility or mature humanity. Let simple-minded Occidentals (!) retain such opinions as long as they are able. But religion is an abyss: it is terror. There demons appear (Ivan Karamazov and Luther!). There the old enemy of man is strangely near. There sin deceives. There the power of the commandment is deadly—*The serpent beguiled me.*[12] Sin is the place where our destiny becomes a present, concrete possibility, the place where our knowledge of good and evil becomes

[12] Gen. 3:13.

an urgent, direct knowledge. The deception of sin is the illusion that such direct knowledge is life, whereas in fact it is death. Deceit runs its full course, because men do not perceive that the necessity of independent human action is what should not be in the presence of God. It is successful, because human determination to retain the possibility of independence before God reveals men to be—merely men. The commandment is therefore the lever or *occasion* of sin: clothing time with the garment of eternity, it presents piety as a human achievement, evokes worship which knows not how to be silent before God, and names such worship "religion"; concealing from the worshiper, not merely how questionable the world is, but how utterly questionable religion is, it compels him to lift up hands in prayer, then lets them drop back wearily, and in this weariness spurs him unto prayer again. And this is, after all, the situation in which men find themselves under the commandment.

We have now been able to provide a second answer to our question concerning the meaning of religion. Religion is that human necessity in which the power exercised over men by sin is clearly demonstrated. Once again we are compelled to consider what the freedom of God means when it confronts men imprisoned in the closed circle of humanity.

THE RIGHTEOUSNESS OF GOD

[Rom. 3:21–22a]

VERSES 21-22A   *But now apart from the law the righteousness of God hath been manifested, being witnessed by the law and the prophets; even the righteousness of God through his faithfulness in Jesus Christ unto all them that believe.*

☒   ☒   ☒

The righteousness of God is manifested—"through his faithfulness in Jesus Christ." The faithfulness of God is the divine patience according to which He provides, at sundry times and at many divers points in human history, occasions and possibilities and witnesses of the knowledge of His righteousness. Jesus of Nazareth is the point at which it can be seen that all the other points form one line of supreme significance. He is the point at which is perceived the crimson thread which runs through all history. Christ—the righteousness of God Himself—is the theme of this perception. The faithfulness of God and Jesus the Christ confirm one another. The faithfulness of God is established when we meet the Christ in Jesus. Consequently, in spite of all our inadequacy, we are able to recognize the veritable possibility of the action of God in all His divers witnesses in history; consequently also, we are able to discover in the traces of the righteousness of God in the world more than mere chance occurrences, and are in a position to see that our own position in time is pregnant with eternal promise, if—nay, because!—we meet truth of another order at one point in time, at one place in that time which is illuminated throughout by reality and by the answer of God. The Day of Jesus Christ is the Day of all days; the brilliant and visible light of this one point is the hidden invisible light of all points; to perceive the righteousness of God once and for all here is the *hope of righteousness*[13] everywhere and at all times. By the knowledge of Jesus Christ all human waiting is guaranteed, authorized, and established; for He makes it known that it is not men who wait, but God—in His faithfulness. Our discovery of the Christ in Jesus of Nazareth is authorized by the fact that every manifestation of the faithfulness of God points and bears witness to what we have actually encountered in Jesus. The hidden authority of the Law and the Prophets is the Christ who meets us in Jesus. Redemption and resurrection, the invisibility of God and a new order, constitute the meaning of every religion; and it is precisely this that compels us to stand still in the presence of Jesus. All human activity is a cry for forgiveness; and it is precisely this that is proclaimed by Jesus and that appears concretely in Him. The objection that this hidden power of forgiveness and, in fact, the whole subject-matter of religion, is found elsewhere, is wholly wide of the mark, since it is precisely we who have been enabled to make this claim. In Jesus we have discovered and recognized the truth that God is found everywhere and that, both before and after Jesus, men have been discovered by Him. In Him we have found the standard by which all discovery of God and all being discovered by Him is made known as such; in Him we recognize that this finding and being found is the truth of the order of eternity. Many live their lives in the light of redemption and forgiveness and resurrection; but that we have eyes to see their manner of life we owe to the One. In His light we see light. That it is the Christ whom we have encountered in Jesus is guaranteed by our finding in Him the sharply defined, final interpretation of the Word of the faithfulness of God to which the Law and the Prophets bore witness. His entering within the deepest darkness of human ambiguity and abiding within it is *the* faithfulness. The life of Jesus is perfected obedience to the will of the faithful God. Jesus stands among sinners as a sinner; He sets Himself wholly under the judgement under which the world is set; He takes His place where God can be present only in questioning about Him; He takes the form of a slave; He moves to the cross and to death; His greatest achievement is a negative achievement. He is not a genius, endowed with manifest or even with occult powers; He is not a hero or leader of men; He is neither poet nor thinker:—*My God, my God, why hast thou forsaken me?* Nevertheless, precisely in this negation, He is the fulfillment of every possibility of human progress, as the Prophets and the Law conceive of

[13] Gal. 5:5.

progress and evolution, because He sacrifices to the incomparably Greater and to the invisibly Other every claim to genius and every human heroic or aesthetic or psychic possibility, because there is no conceivable human possibility of which He did not rid Himself. Herein He is recognized as the Christ; for this reason God hath exalted Him; and consequently He is the light of the Last Things by which all men and all things are illuminated. In Him we behold the faithfulness of God in the depths of Hell. The Messiah is the end of mankind, and here also God is found faithful. On the day when mankind is dissolved the new era of the righteousness of God will be inaugurated.

"Unto all them that believe." Here is the necessary qualification. The vision of the New Day remains an indirect vision; in Jesus revelation is a paradox, however objective and universal it may be. That the promises of the faithfulness of God have been fulfilled in Jesus the Christ is not, and never will be, a self-evident truth, since in Him it appears in its final hiddenness and its most profound secrecy. The truth, in fact, can never be self-evident, because it is a matter neither of historical nor of psychological experience, and because it is neither a cosmic happening within the natural order, nor even the most supreme event of our imaginings. Therefore it is not accessible to our perception: it can neither be dug out of what is unconsciously within us, nor apprehended by devout contemplation, nor made known by the manipulation of occult psychic powers. These exercises, indeed, render it the more inaccessible. It can be neither taught nor handed down by tradition, nor is it a subject of research. Were it capable of such treatment, it would not be universally significant, it would not be the righteousness of God for the whole world, salvation for all men. Faith is conversion: it is the radically new disposition of the man who stands naked before God and has been wholly impoverished that he may procure the one pearl of great price; it is the attitude of the man who for the sake of Jesus has lost his own soul. Faith is the faithfulness of God, ever secreted in and beyond all human ideas and affirmations about Him, and beyond every positive religious achievement. There is no such thing as mature and assured possession of faith: regarded psychologically, it is always a leap into the darkness of the unknown, a flight into empty air. Faith is not revealed to us by *flesh and blood:* [14] no one can communicate it to himself or to any one else. What I heard yesterday I must hear again today; and if I am to hear it afresh tomorrow, it must be revealed by the Father of Jesus, who is in heaven, and by Him only. The revelation which is in Jesus, because it is the revelation of the righteousness of God, must be the most complete veiling of His incomprehensibility. In Jesus, God becomes veritably a secret: He is made known as the Unknown, speaking in eternal silence; He protects himself from every intimate companionship and from all the impertinence of religion. He becomes a scandal to the Jews and

[14] Matt. 16:17.

to the Greeks foolishness. In Jesus the communication of God begins with a rebuff, with the exposure of a vast chasm, with the clear revelation of a great stumbling block. "Remove from the Christian Religion, as Christendom has done, its ability to shock, and Christianity, by becoming a direct communication, is altogether destroyed. It then becomes a tiny superficial thing, capable neither of inflicting deep wounds nor of healing them; by discovering an unreal and merely human compassion, it forgets the qualitative distinction between man and God" (Kierkegaard). Faith in Jesus, like its theme, the righteousness of God, is the radical "Nevertheless." Faith in Jesus is to feel and comprehend the unheard of "loveless" love of God, to do the ever scandalous and outrageous will of God, to call upon God in His incomprehensibility and hiddenness. To believe in Jesus is the most hazardous of all hazards. This "Nevertheless," this unheard of action, this hazard, is the road to which we direct men. We demand faith, no more and no less; and we make this demand, not in our own name, but in the name of Jesus, in whom we have encountered it irresistibly. We do not demand belief in our faith; for we are aware that, in so far as faith originates in us, it is unbelievable. We do not demand from others our faith; if others are to believe, they must do so, as we do, entirely at their own risk and because of the promise. We demand faith in Jesus; and we make this demand here and now upon all, whatever may be the condition of life in which they find themselves. There are, however, no preliminaries necessary to faith, no required standard of education or intelligence, no peculiar temper of mind or heart, no special economic status. There are no human avenues of approach, no "way of salvation"; to faith there is no ladder which must be first scaled. Faith is its own initiation, its own presupposition. Upon whatever rung of the ladder of human life men may happen to be standing —whether they be Jews or Greeks, old or young, educated or uneducated, complex or simple—in tribulation or in repose they are capable of faith. The demand of faith passes diagonally across every type of religious or moral temperament, across every experience of life, through every department of intellectual activity, and through every social class. For all faith is both simple and difficult; for all alike it is a scandal, a hazard, a "Nevertheless"; to all it presents the same embarrassment and the same promise; for all it is a leap into the void. And it is possible for all, only because for all it is equally impossible.

8

MARTIN

BUBER

Martin Buber has been surpassed by none in his chosen work of making faith meaningful and real to twentieth-century man. Buber's success in recovering the Hasidic way of Judaism in contemporary language, his powerful poetic and philosophic reflections upon faith, his joint translation with Franz Rosenzweig of the Old Testament into German, and his more recent, quite marvelous critical-reflective studies of the Bible, without parallel in Old Testament scholarship, all place Buber at the forefront of modern religious thinking. Famous as these activities have made him, however, the radical thrust of his thinking is seldom appreciated in the Christian world. This radicalness is suggested by the fact that his primal distinction between the "I-Thou" and "I-It" relationships was originated by Ludwig Feuerbach. Buber's classic work *I and Thou* (1922) anticipated Paul Tillich's theological program.[1] From the beginning, Buber recognized the eclipse of both God and the transcendent realm in the modern world, and he gave himself to a quest for a human community grounded in faith, precisely in the context of such a world. In his later years, he could attack modern atheism as a demonic form of Gnosticism (*The Eclipse of God,* 1952). Yet he also could look upon the eclipse of God in the modern world as the occasion for a new manifestation of the reality of God. Of the two selections here, one is taken from his earlier and one from his later work; they illustrate not only the continuity of his thinking but also the way in which it evolved to confront new and differing issues.

[1] Students of Tillich will recognize the relevance to his program of the following statement by Buber: "But when he, too, who abhors the name, and believes himself to be godless, gives his whole being to addressing the *Thou* of his life, as a *Thou* that cannot be limited by another, he addresses God." *I and Thou,* p. 76.

Martin Buber — I, Thou, and It.

The eternal *Thou* can by its nature not become *It*; for by its nature it cannot be established in measure and bounds, not even in the measure of the immeasurable, or the bounds of boundless being; for by its nature it cannot be understood as a sum of qualities, not even as an infinite sum of qualities raised to a transcendental level; for it can be found neither in nor out of the world; for it cannot be experienced, or thought; for we miss Him, Him who is, if we say "I believe that He is"—*He* is also a metaphor, but *Thou* is not.

And yet in accordance with our nature we are continually making the eternal *Thou* into *It,* into some thing—making God into a thing. Not indeed out of arbitrary self-will; God's history as a thing, the passage of God as Thing through religion and through the products on its brink, through its bright ways and its gloom, its enhancement and its destruction of life, the passage away from the living God and back again to Him, the changes from the present to establishment of form, of objects, and of ideas, dissolution and renewal—all are one way, are *the* way.

What is the origin of the expressed knowledge and ordered action of the religions? How do the Presence and the power of the revelation (for all religions necessarily appeal to some kind of revelation, whether through the medium of the spoken word, or of nature, or of the soul: there are only religions of revelation)—how do the Presence and the power received by men in revelation change into a "content"?

The explanation has two layers. We understand the outer psychical layer when we consider man in himself, separated from history, and the inner factual layer, the primal phenomenon of religion, when we replace him in history. The two layers belong together.

Man desires to possess God; he desires a continuity in space and time of possession of God. He is not content with the inexpressible confirmation of meaning, but wants to see this confirmation stretched out as something that can be continually taken up and handled, a continuum unbroken in space and time that insures his life at every point and every moment.

Man's thirst for continuity is unsatisfied by the life-rhythm of pure relation, the interchange of actual being and of a potential being in which only our power to enter into relation, and hence the presentness (but not the primal Presence) decreases. He longs for extension in time, for duration. Thus God becomes an object of faith. At first faith, set in time, completes the acts of relation; but gradually it replaces them. Resting in belief in an *It* takes the place of the continually renewed movement of the being towards concentration and going out to the relation. The "Nevertheless I believe" of the fighter who knows remoteness from as well as nearness to God is more and more completely transformed into the certainty of him who enjoys profits, that nothing can happen to him, since he believes that there is One who will not let anything happen to him.

Further, man's thirst for continuity is unsatisfied by the life-structure of pure relation, the "solitude" of the *I* before the *Thou,* the law that man, though binding up the world in relation in the meeting, can nevertheless only as a person approach and meet God. He longs for extension in space, for the representation in which the community of the faithful is united with its God. Thus God becomes the object of a cult. The cult, too, completes at first the acts of relation, in adjusting in a spatial context of great formative power the living prayer, the immediate saying of the *Thou,* and in linking it with the life of the senses. It, too, gradually replaces the acts of relation, when the personal prayer is no longer supported, but displaced, by the communal prayer, and when the act of the being, since it admits no rule, is replaced by ordered devotional exercises.

Actually, however, pure relation can only be raised to constancy in space and time by being embodied in the whole stuff of life. It cannot be preserved, but only proved true, only done, only done up into life. Man can do justice to the relation with God in which he has come to share only if he realizes God anew in the world according to his strength and to the measure of each day. In this lies the only authentic assurance of continuity. The authentic assurance of duration consists in the fact that pure relation can be fulfilled in the growth and rise of beings into *Thou,* that the holy primary word makes itself heard in them all. Thus the time of human life is shaped into a fulness of reality, and even though human life neither can nor ought to overcome the connection with *It,* it is so penetrated with relation that relation wins in it a shining streaming constancy: the moments of supreme meeting are then not flashes in darkness but like the rising moon in a clear starlit night. Thus, too, the authentic assurance of constancy in space consists in the fact that men's relations with their true *Thou,* the radial lines that proceed from all the points of the *I* to the Center, form a circle. It is not the periphery, the community, that comes first, but the radii, the common quality of relation with the Center. This alone guarantees the authentic existence of the community.

Only when these two arise—the binding up of time in a relational life of salvation and the binding up of space in the community that is made one by its Center—and only so long as they exist, does there arise and exist, round about the invisible altar, a human cosmos with bounds and form, grasped with the spirit out of the universal stuff of the aeon, a world that is house and home, a dwelling for man in the universe.

Meeting with God does not come to man in order that he may concern himself with God, but in order that he may confirm that there is meaning in the world. All revelation is summons and sending. But again and again man brings about, instead of realization, a reflection to Him who reveals: he wishes to concern himself with God instead of with the world. Only, in such a reflection, he is no longer confronted by a *Thou,* he can do nothing but establish an It-God in the realm of things, believe that he knows of God as of an *It,* and so speak about Him. Just as the "self"-seeking man, instead of directly living something or other, a perception or an affection, reflects about his perspective or reflective *I,* and thereby misses the truth of the event, so the man who seeks God (though for the rest he gets on very well with the self-seeker in the one soul), instead of allowing the gift to work itself out, reflects about the Giver—and misses both.

God remains present to you when you have been sent forth; he who goes on a mission has always God before him: the truer the fulfillment the stronger and more constant His nearness. To be sure, he cannot directly concern himself with God, but he can converse with Him. Reflection, on the other hand, makes God into an object. Its apparent turning towards the primal source belongs in truth to the universal movement away from it; just as the apparent turning away of the man who is fulfilling his mission belongs in truth to the universal movement towards the primal source.

For the two primary metacosmical movements of the world—expansion into its own being and turning to connection—find their supreme human form, the real spiritual form of their struggle and adjustment, their mingling and separation, in the history of the human relation to God. In turning the Word is born on earth, in expansion the Word enters the chrysalis form of religion, in fresh turning it is born again with new wings.

Arbitrary self-will does not reign here, even though the movement towards the *It* goes at times so far that it threatens to suppress and to smother the movement out again to the *Thou.*

The mighty revelations to which the religions appeal are like in being with the quiet revelations that are to be found everywhere and at all times.

The mighty revelations which stand at the beginning of great communities and at the turning point of an age are nothing but the eternal revelation. But the revelation does not pour itself into the world through him who receives it as through a funnel; it comes to him and seizes his whole elemental being in all its particular nature, and fuses with it. The man, too, who is the "mouth" of the revelation, is indeed this, not a speaking-tube or any kind of instrument, but an organ, which sounds according to its own laws; and to sound means to *modify*.

The various ages of history, however, show a qualitative difference. There is a time of maturing, when the true element of the human spirit, suppressed and buried, comes to hidden readiness so urgent and so tense that it awaits only a touch from Him who touches in order to burst forth. The revelation that then makes its appearance seizes in the totality of its constitution the whole elemental stuff that is thus prepared, melts it down, and produces in it a form that is a new form of God in the world.

Thus in the course of history, in the transforming of elemental human stuff, ever new provinces of the world and the spirit are raised to form, summoned to divine form. Ever new spheres become regions of a theophany. It is not man's own power that works here, nor is it God's pure effective passage, but it is a mixture of the divine and the human. He who is sent out in the strength of revelation takes with him, in his eyes, an image of God; however far this exceeds the senses, yet he takes it with him in the eye of the spirit, in that visual power of his spirit which is not metaphorical but wholly real. The spirit responds also through a look, a look that is *formative*. Although we earthly beings never look at God without the world, but only look at the world in God, yet as we look we shape eternally the form of God.

Form is also a mixture of *Thou* and *It*. In belief and in a cult form can harden into an object; but, in virtue of the essential quality of relation that lives on in it, it continually becomes present again. God is near His forms so long as man does not remove them from Him. In true prayer belief and cult are united and purified to enter into the living relation. The fact that true prayer lives in the religions witnesses to their true life: they live so long as it lives in them. Degeneration of the religions means degeneration of prayer in them. Their power to enter into relation is buried under increasing objectification, it becomes increasingly difficult for them to say *Thou* with the whole undivided being, and finally, in order to be able to say it, man must come out of the false security into the venture of the infinite—out of the community, that is now overarched only by the temple dome and not also by the firmament, into the final solitude. It is a profound misunderstanding of this impulse to ascribe it to "subjectivism"; life face to face with God is life in the one reality, the only true "objective," and the man who goes out to this life desires to save himself, in the objective that truly *is,* from that which is apparent and illusory, before it has disturbed the truth of the real objective for him. Subjectivism empties God of soul, objectivism makes Him into an object—the latter is a false fixing down, the former a false setting free; both are diversions from the way of reality, both are attempts to replace reality.

God is near His forms if man does not remove them from Him. But when the expanding movement of religion suppresses the movement of turning and removes the form from God, the countenance of the form is obliterated, its lips are dead, its hands hang down, God knows it no more, and the universal dwelling-place that is built about its altar, the spiritually apprehended cosmos, tumbles in. And the fact that man, in the disturbance of his truth, no longer sees what is then taking place, is a part of what has then taken place.

Disintegration of the Word has taken place.

The Word has its essence in revelation, its effect in the life of the form, its currency during the domination of the form that has died.

This is the course and the counter-course of the eternal and eternally present Word in history.

The times in which the living Word appears as those in which the solidarity of connection between *I* and the world is renewed; the times in which the effective Word reigns are those in which the agreement between *I* and the world are maintained; the times in which the Word becomes current are those in which alienation between *I* and the world, loss of reality, growth of fate, is completed—till there comes the great shudder, the holding of the breath in the dark, and the preparing silence.

But this course is not circular. It is the way. In each new aeon fate becomes more oppressive, turning more shattering. And the theophany becomes ever *nearer,* increasingly near to the sphere that lies *between beings,* to the Kingdom that is hidden in our midst, there between us. History is a mysterious approach. Every spiral of its way leads us into both profounder perversion and more fundamental turning. But the event that from the side of the world is called turning is called from God's side redemption.

Martin
Buber

Paulinism in the Modern World

The periods of Christian history can be classified according to the degree in which they are dominated by Paulinism, by which we mean of course not just a system of thought, but a mode of seeing and being which dwells in the life itself. In this sense our era is a Pauline one to a particular degree. In the human life of our day, compared with earlier epochs, Christianity is receding, but the Pauline view and attitude is gaining the mastery in many circles outside that of Christianity. There is a Paulinism of the unredeemed, one, that is, from which the abode of grace is eliminated: like Paul man experiences the world as one given into the hands of inevitable forces, and only the manifest will to redemption from above, only Christ is missing. The Christian Paulinism of our time is a result of the same fundamental view, although it softens down or removes that aspect of the demonocracy of the world: it sees nevertheless existence divided into an unrestricted rule of wrath and a sphere of reconciliation, from which point indeed the claims for the establishment of a Christian order of life is raised clearly and energetically enough, but *de facto* the redeemed Christian soul stands over against an unredeemed world of men in lofty impotence. Neither this picture of the abyss spanned only by the halo of the saviour nor that of the same abyss covered now by nothing but impenetrable darkness is to be understood as brought about by changes in sub-

REPRINTED by permission of The Macmillan Company from [pp. 162-69 of] *Two Types of Faith* by Martin Buber, translated by Norman P. Goldhawk. First published in the United States by The Macmillan Company in 1951. Also with the permission of Routledge & Kegan Paul, Ltd., Publishers.

jectivity: in order to paint them the retina of those now living must have been affected by an actual fact, by the situation now existing.

I will illustrate my position from two books, which are very different from each other; I choose them because the view of which I am speaking comes to light clearly in them. For this reason I have chosen one from the literature of modern Christian theology, because I do not know of any other in which the Pauline view of God is expressed so directly; it is *The Mediator* by Emil Brunner. The other, one of the few authentic similes which our age has produced, is the work of a non-Christian poet, a Jew, Franz Kafka's novel *The Castle*.

I am only concerned in Brunner's book with what he has to say about God, and not about Christ; that is, with the dark foil and not the image of glory which stands out against it. We read: "God cannot allow His honour to be impugned"; "the law itself demands from God the reaction"; "God would cease to be God if He allowed His honour to be impugned." This is said of the Father of Christ; therefore it does not refer to one of the gods and rulers, but to Him of Whom the "Old Testament" witnesses. But neither in this itself nor in any Jewish interpretation is God spoken of in this way; and such a word is unimaginable from the lips of Jesus as I believe I know him. For here in fact "with God all things are possible"; there is nothing which he "could not." Of course the rulers of this world cannot allow their honor to be impugned; what would remain to them if they did! But God—to be sure prophets and psalmists show how He "glorifies His name" to the world, and Scripture is full of His "zeal," but He Himself does not assume any of these attitudes otherwise than remaining superior to them; in the language of the interpretation: He proceeds from one *middah* to the other, and none is adequate to Him. If the whole world should tear the garment of His honor into rags nothing would be done to Him. Which law could presume to demand anything from Him? —surely the highest conceivable law is that which is given by Him to the world, not to Himself:[1] He does not bind Himself and therefore nothing binds Him. And that He would cease to be God—"God" is a stammering of the world, the world of men, He himself is immeasurably more than "God" only, and if the world should cease to stammer or cease to exist, He would remain. In the immediacy we experience His anger and His tenderness in one; no assertion can detach one from the other and make Him into a God of wrath Who requires a mediator.

---

[1] Brunner explains: "The law of His being God, on which all the lawfulness of the world is based, the fundamental order of the world, the consistent and reliable character of all that happens, the validity of all standards . . . ." Precisely this seems to me to be an inadmissible derivation of the nature of the world from the nature of God, or rather the reverse. Order and standards are derived from the act of God, which sets the world in being and gives it the law, and not from a law which would determine His being. See E. Brunner, *The Mediator* (Philadelphia: The Westminster Press, 1934), p. 444.

In the Book of Wisdom, scarcely later than a hundred years before Christ, God is addressed in this fashion: "But Thou hast compassion upon all, since Thou canst do all things"—He is able to have compassion even upon us, as we are!—"and Thou dost overlook the sins of men up to their turning"—He overlooks them, not that we should perish, but turn to Him; He does not wait until we have turned (this is significantly the opposite of the Synoptic characterization of the Baptist's preaching: not repentance for the remission of sins, but the remission of sins for repentance)—". . . for Thou lovest all creatures and abhorrest nothing that Thou hast made"—here the creation is obviously taken more seriously than the Fall—". . . Thou sparest all things because they are Thine, O Lord, Who willest good to the living. For Thine incorruptible Spirit is in all." It is as if the author wished to oppose a doctrine current in Alexandria about the Jewish God of wrath.

Kafka's contribution to the metaphysics of the "door" is known: the parable of the man who squanders his life before a certain open gateway which leads to the world of meaning, and who vainly begs admission until just before his death it is communicated to him that it had been intended for him, but is now being shut. So "the door" is still open; indeed, every person has his own door and it is open to him; but he does not know this and apparently is not in a condition to know it. Kafka's two main works are elaborations of the theme of the parable, the one, *The Trial,* in the dimension of time, the other, *The Castle,* in that of space; accordingly the first is concerned with the hopelessness of man in his dealings with his soul, the second with the same in his dealings with the world. The parable itself is not Pauline but its elaborations are, only as we have said with salvation removed. The one is concerned with the judgment under which the soul stands and under which it places itself willingly; but the guilt, on account of which it has to be judged, is unformulated, the proceedings are labyrinthian and the courts of judicature themselves questionable—without all this seeming to prejudice the legality of the administration of justice. The other book, which especially concerns us here, describes a district delivered over to the authority of a slovenly bureaucracy without the possibility of appeal, and it describes this district as being our world. What is at the top of the government, or rather above it, remains hidden in a darkness, of the nature of which one never once gets a presentiment; the administrative hierarchy, who exercise power, received it from above, but apparently without any commission or instruction. A broad meaninglessness governs without restraint, every notice, every transaction is shot through with meaninglessness, and yet the legality of the government is unquestioned. Man is called into this world, he is appointed in it, but wherever he turns to fulfill his calling he comes up against the thick vapors of a mist of absurdity. This world is handed over to a maze of intermediate beings—it is a Pauline world, except that God is removed into the impenetrable darkness and that there is no place for a mediator. We are reminded of the Haggadic account (Aggadat Bereshit IX)[2] of the sinful David, who prays God that He Himself may judge him and not give him into the hands of the seraphim and cherubim, for "they are all cruel." Cruel also are the intermediate beings of Kafka, but in addition they are disorderly and stupid. They are extremely powerful bunglers, which drive the human creature through the nonsense of life—and they do it with the full authority of their master. Certain features remind us of the licentious demons into which the archons of Paul's conception of the world have been changed in some Gnostic schools.

The strength of Pauline tendencies in present-day Christian theology is to be explained by the characteristic stamp of the time, just as that of earlier periods can explain that at one time the purely spiritual, the Johannine tendency was emphasized, and at another the so-called Petrine one, in which the somewhat undefined conception "Peter" represents the unforgettable recollection of the conversations of Jesus with the disciples in Galilee. Those periods are Pauline in which the contradictions of human life, especially of man's social life, so mount up that they increasingly assume in man's consciousness of existence the character of a fate. Then the light of God appears to be darkened, and the redeemed Christian soul becomes aware, as the unredeemed soul of the Jew has continually done, of the still unredeemed concreteness of the world of men in all its horror. Then to be sure, as we know indeed from Paul too, the genuine Christian struggles for a juster order of his community, but he understands the impenetrable root of the contradiction in the view of the threatening clouds of wrath, and clings with Pauline tenacity to the abundant grace of the mediator. He indeed opposes the ever-approaching Marcionite danger, the severing not only of the Old and New Testaments, but that of creation and salvation, of Creator and Saviour, for he sees how near men are, as Kierkegaard says of the Gnosis, "to identifying creation with the Fall," and he knows that a victory for Marcion can lead to the destruction of Christianity; but—this seems to me to be more strongly recognized again in Christendom today—Marcion is not to be overcome by Paul.

Even Kierkegaard, a century ago, gave expression to the fact that there is a non-Pauline outlook, that is, one superior to the stamp of the age, when he wrote in his Journal a prayer, in which he says: "Father in heaven, it is indeed only the moment of silence in the inwardness of speaking with one another." That to be sure is said from the point of view of personal existence ("When a man languishes in the desert, not hearing Thy voice there"), but in this respect we are not to distinguish between the situation

---

[2] The Mishnah ("second law") is the oldest and most authoritative part of the Talmud, the principal literary production of post-Biblical Judaism. The bulk of the Mishnah is either Halakhah ("usage")—i.e., details of Rabbinic law, mostly based on Scripture—or Haggadah ("narrative"), interpretation of Scripture seeking edification—T. J. J. A.

of the person and that of man or mankind. Kierkegaard's prayer, in spite of his great belief in Christ, is not from Paul or from John, but from Jesus.

A superficial Christian, considering Kafka's problem, can easily get rid of him by treating him simply as the unredeemed Jew who does not reach after salvation. But only he who proceeds thus has now got rid of him; Kafka has remained untouched by this treatment. For the Jew, in so far as he is not detached from the origin, even the most exposed Jew like Kafka, is safe. All things happen to him, but they cannot affect him. He is not to be sure able any longer to conceal himself "in the covert of Thy wings," [3] for God is hiding Himself from the time in which he lives, and so from him, its most exposed son; but in the fact of God's being only hidden, which he knows, he is safe. "Better the living dove on the roof than the half-dead, convulsively resisting sparrow in the hand." He describes, from innermost awareness, the actual course of the world; he describes most exactly the rule of the foul deviltry which fills the foreground; and on the edge of the description he scratches the sentence: "Test yourself on humanity. It makes the doubter doubt, the man of belief believe." His unexpressed, ever-present theme is the remoteness of the judge, the remoteness of the lord of the castle, the hiddenness, the eclipse, the darkness; and therefore he observes: "He who believes can experience no miracle. During the day one does not see any stars." This is the nature of the Jew's security in the dark, one which is essentially different from that of the Christian. It allows no rest, for as long as you live, you must live with the sparrow and not with the dove, who avoids your hand; but, being without illusion, it is consistent with the foreground course of the world, and so nothing can harm you. For from beyond, from the darkness of heaven the dark ray comes actively into the heart, without any appearance of immediacy. "We were created to live in Paradise; Paradise was appointed to serve us. Our destiny has been changed; that this also happened with the appointment of Paradise is not said." So gently and shyly anti-Paulinism speaks from the heart of this Pauline painter of the foreground-hell: Paradise is still there and it benefits us. It is there, and that means it is also here where the dark ray meets the tormented heart. Are the unredeemed in need of salvation? They suffer from the unredeemed state of the world. "Every misery around us we too must suffer"—there it is again, the word from the shoot of Israel. The unredeemed soul refuses to give up the evidence of the unredeemed world from which it suffers, to exchange it for the soul's own salvation. It is able to refuse, for it is safe.

This is the appearance of Paulinism without Christ which at this time when God is most hidden has penetrated into Judaism, a Paulinism therefore opposed to Paul. The course of the world is depicted in more gloomy

[3] Ps. 61:4.

colors than ever before, and yet Emunah[4] is proclaimed anew, with a still deepened "in spite of all this," quite soft and shy, but unambiguous. Here, in the midst of the Pauline domain, it has taken the place of Pistis.[5] In all its reserve, the late-born, wandering around in the darkened world, confesses in face of the suffering peoples of the world with those messengers of Deutero-Isaiah:[6] "Truly Thou art a God Who hides Himself, O God of Israel, Saviour!" So must Emunah change in a time of God's eclipse in order to persevere steadfast to God, without disowning reality. That He hides Himself does not diminish the immediacy; in the immediacy He remains the Saviour and the contradiction of existence becomes for us a theophany.

[4] Emunah: the Hebrew word for faith which Buber employs to speak of the specifically Jewish mode of faith grounded in God's eternal and yet historical covenant with Israel—T. J. J. A.

[5] Pistis: the Greek New Testament word for faith which Buber employs to speak of an individual act or decision of faith as found in Christianity—T. J. J. A.

[6] Isa. 45:15.

9

PAUL
TILLICH

If Karl Barth has exercised the greatest influence upon twentieth-century Protestant theology, it is probably Paul Tillich who has most effectively mediated the theological meaning of the Christian faith to the modern world. Opposing theological dogmatism and modern secularism, Tillich sought a mediating theology which would correlate the questions arising on the boundaries of human existence with the answer in Jesus as the Christ. Faith for Tillich is the state of ultimate concern; it is grounded in the depths of being itself, and it appears throughout the whole gamut of human experience. There are critics who identify Tillich as the first theologian to create a theology founded in an acceptance and affirmation of the death of God. While this judgment seems highly questionable in view of the three volumes of Tillich's *Systematic Theology* (1951-63), it certainly has a measure of validity when applied to the radical essays he wrote in an earlier period. The best of these essays are collected in *The Protestant Era*, and his introduction to the volume, reprinted in the following pages, is one of his most lucid and revealing writings. Unfortunately, he never went beyond the sketch of a justification by doubt which he presents in this introduction. One suspects that Tillich felt ever more deeply threatened by the contemporary crisis of faith, even though he could say in his last years that the real Tillich is the radical Tillich.

Justification by Doubt and the Protestant Principle

Paul Tillich

[1]

This book would not have been published without the initiative and the work of James Luther Adams in Chicago. He has translated the German articles which are presented here for the first time to American readers. He has suggested the organization of the book and the selection of its parts. He has encouraged me again and again to go ahead with the publication. Before anything else I want to express my profound gratitude to him; and I want to include in my thanks some mutual friends who advised us. The hardest task was the translation of some extremely difficult German texts. In many cases the impossibility of an adequate translation made it imperative for me to reproduce whole passages and even articles without keeping to the original text. In all these cases I have used the paraphrasing translations of Dr. Adams, and in no case have I changed the train of thought of the original writing. This Introduction is intended to justify the selection and organization of the material by a retrospective and somewhat personal record of the development which is reflected in the different articles and which has led to the point of view from which the book is conceived.

This point of view, of course, is suggested in the title of the book, *The Protestant Era*. But, since this title itself needs interpretation and since the relation of several of the published articles to the title is not immediately evident, it seems advisable that the collection have an explanatory introduc-

---

REPRINTED FROM *The Protestant Era* by Paul Tillich, translated and with a concluding essay by James Luther Adams, by permission of The University of Chicago Press. Copyright 1948 by The University of Chicago.

tion. There is another, even more important reason for such an introduction.

The collection [*The Protestant Era*] includes material taken from about
twenty years of theological and philosophical work. During these two
decades some of the most monumental historical events have taken place
—the victory of national socialism in Germany and the second World War.
An immediate effect of the first event on my life was my emigration from
Germany and my settlement in New York City. The change of country
and continent, the catastrophe of a world in which I had worked and
thought for forty-seven years, the loss of the fairly mastered tool of my
own language, the new experiences in a civilization previously unknown
to me, resulted in changes, first, of the expression and then, to a certain
degree, of the content of my thinking. These changes were supported by
the dramatic events in Germany under the rule of naziism, especially the
German church struggle, further by two extended trips through the countries of western Europe and my active participation in the Oxford conference of the world churches, and, finally, by the political and spiritual events
preceding and accompanying the second World War. The imminence and
the outbreak of this war and the tremendous problems of postwar reconstruction have forced upon me a larger participation in practical politics
than I ever had intended to give. And, since the key to the interpretation
of history is historical activity, my understanding of the world-historical
situation has become broader and, I hope, more realistic. Besides these
dramatic events, American theology and philosophy have influenced my
thinking in several respects. The spirit of the English language has demanded the clarification of many ambiguities of my thought which were
covered by the mystical vagueness of the classic philosophical German;
the interdependence of theory and practice in Anglo-Saxon culture, religious as well as secular, has freed me from the fascination of that kind
of abstract idealism which enjoys the system for the system's sake; the
cooperation with colleagues and students of Union Theological Seminary,
Columbia University, and other universities and colleges has provided the
experience of a type of Protestant religion and culture very different from
that of Continental Europe; the world perspective, almost unavoidable on
a bridge between the continents like New York and at a center of world
Protestantism like Union Theological Seminary, has had strong effects on
my thinking about the situation of the church universal in our time.

All these influences—and, besides them, the natural growth of a man's
experience and thought in two decades—are mirrored in the different
articles of this book. They betray changes of style, of temper, of emphasis,
of methods, of formulations, which cannot escape any reader.

But more obvious than the changes from the earlier to the more recent
articles in this collection is the continuity of the main line of thought and
the permanence of the basic principles. It sometimes strikes me (and this is

probably a very common experience), when I read some of my earliest writings, how much of what I believed to be a recent achievement is already explicitly or at least implicitly contained in them. This is, first of all, true of the problem that controls the selection of the articles— the problem of Protestantism, its meaning and its historical existence. Since my first years as a student of Protestant theology, I have tried to look at Protestantism from the outside as well as from the inside. "From the outside" meant in those earlier years: from the point of view of a passionately loved and studied philosophy; it meant in later years from the point of view of the powerfully developing comparative history of religion; and it meant, finally, from the point of view of the experienced and interpreted general history of our period. This outside view of Protestantism has deeply influenced my inside view of it. If you look at Protestantism merely as a special denominational form of Christianity to which you are bound by tradition and faith, you receive a picture different from the one you perceive when looking at it as a factor within the world-historical process, influenced by and influencing all other factors. But the converse is also true. The inside view of Protestantism, based on an existential experience of its meaning and power, strongly modifies the outside view. None of the articles contained in this volume considers the situation of Protestantism in a merely factual, "statistical" way, but each of them betrays the author's concern and active involvement. This is not said in order to depreciate detachment and scientific objectivity in the matters dealt with. There is a place for such an attitude even toward religion. But it touches only the surface. There are objects for which the so-called "objective" approach is the least objective of all, because it is based on a misunderstanding of the nature of its object. This is especially true of religion. Unconcerned detachment in matters of religion (if it is more than a methodological self-restriction) implies an a priori rejection of the religious demand to be ultimately concerned. It denies the object which it is supposed to approach "objectively."

The inside and the outside views of Protestantism in their mutual dependence have created an interpretation of its meaning which is set forth, directly or indirectly, in all sections of this book. Protestantism is understood as a special historical embodiment of a universally significant principle. This principle, in which one side of the divine-human relationship is expressed, is effective in all periods of history; it is indicated in the great religions of mankind; it has been powerfully pronounced by the Jewish prophets; it is manifest in the picture of Jesus as the Christ; it has been rediscovered time and again in the life of the church and was established as the sole foundation of the churches of the Reformation; and it will challenge these churches whenever they leave their foundation.

There is no question here as to whether we are now approaching the end of the Protestant principle. This principle is not a special religious or cultural idea; it is not subject to the changes of history; it is not dependent on the increase or decrease of religious experience or spiritual power. It is the ultimate criterion of all religious and all spiritual experiences; it lies at their base, whether they are aware of it or not. The way in which this principle is realized and expressed and applied and connected with other sides of the divine-human relationship is different in different times and places, groups, and individuals. Protestantism as a principle is eternal and a permanent criterion of everything temporal. Protestantism as the characteristic of a historical period is temporal and subjected to the eternal Protestant principle. It is judged by its own principle, and this judgment might be a negative one. The Protestant era might come to an end. But *if* it came to an end, the Protestant principle would not be refuted. On the contrary, the end of the Protestant era would be another manifestation of the truth and power of the Protestant principle. Will the Protestant era come to an end? Is *that* the judgment of the Protestant principle, as it was the judgment of the prophets that the nation of the prophets would be destroyed? This is a question which, of course, is not to be answered by historical predictions but by an interpretation of Protestantism, its dangers and its promises, its failures and its creative possibilities.

All articles of this collection are meant to contribute to the answer. Only a few of them deal directly with Protestantism, but all deal with the Protestant problem; for it is a presupposition of this book that no realm of life can be understood and formed without a relation to the Protestant principle, as it is a presupposition also that Protestantism cannot be understood and formed except in relation to all realms of life. This correlation, which is more fully developed in several places in the book, was decisive for the selection and organization of the articles, as it was decisive for the considerable number of different questions with which I have dealt in my thinking and writing and which appear in this collection as parts of the general problem of the Protestant era.

This Introduction does not intend to sum up the contents of the articles that follow. Its purpose is to show how the questions they ask and try to answer have arisen in connection with the rise of the Protestant problem in my thought. This cannot be done, however, without some autobiographical references, for the line of thought running through this book is based on a unity of experience and interpretation.

[2]

The power of the Protestant principle first became apparent to me in the classes of my theological teacher, Martin Kaehler, a man who in his personality and theology combined traditions of Renaissance humanism and German classicism with a profound understanding of the Reformation and with strong elements of the religious awakening of the middle of the nineteenth century. The historians of theology count him among the "theologians of mediation"—often in a depreciating sense. But *the task of theology is mediation,* mediation between the eternal criterion of truth as it is manifest in the picture of Jesus as the Christ and the changing experiences of individuals and groups, their varying questions and their categories of perceiving reality. If the mediating task of theology is rejected, theology itself is rejected; for the term *theo-logy* implies, as such, a mediation, namely, between the mystery, which is *theos,* and the understanding, which is *logos.* If some biblicists, pietists, evangelicals, and lay Christians are opposed to the mediating function of theology, they deceive themselves, since, in reality, they live by the crumbs falling from the table of the theological tradition which has been created by great mediators. One of the methods of mediation in theology is called "dialectical." Dialectics is the way of seeking for truth by talking with others from different points of view, through "Yes" and "No," until a "Yes" has been reached which is hardened in the fire of many "No's" and which unites the elements of truth promoted in the discussion. It is most unfortunate that in recent years the name "dialectical theology" has been applied to a theology that is strongly opposed to any kind of dialectics and mediation and that constantly repeats the "Yes" to its own and the "No" to any other position. This has made it difficult to use the term *dialectical* to denote theological movements of a really dialectical, that is a mediating, character; and it has resulted in the cheap and clumsy way of dividing all theologians into naturalists and supernaturalists, or into liberals and orthodox. As a theologian who sometimes has been dealt with in this easy way of shelving somebody (for instance, by being called a "neosupernaturalist") I want to state unambiguously my conviction that these divisions are completely obsolete in the actual work which is done today by every theologian who takes the mediating or dialectical task of theology seriously. Therefore, I would not be ashamed to be called a "theologian of mediation," which, for me, would simply mean: a "theo-logian." There is, of course, danger in all mediation performed by the church, not only in its theological function but also in all its practical functions. The church is often unaware of this danger and falls into a self-surrendering adaptation to its environment. In such situations a prophetic challenge like that given by the "neo-Reformation" theology (as it should be called instead of "dialectical theology") is urgently needed. But, in spite of such a danger, the church as a living reality must permanently mediate its eternal foundation with the demands of the historical situation. The church is by its very nature dialectical and must venture again and again a "theo-logy" of mediation.

The example of Martin Kaehler, in reference to whom this excursus on the mediating character of my theology has been made, shows clearly that mediation need not mean surrender. Kaehler's central idea was "justification through faith," the idea that separated Protestantism from Catholicism and that became the so-called "material" principle of the

Protestant churches (the biblical norm being the "formal" principle). He was able not only to unite this idea with his own classical education but also to interpret it with great religious power for generations of humanistically educated students. Under his influence a group of advanced students and younger professors developed the new understanding of the Protestant principle in different ways. The step I myself made in these years was the insight that the principle of justification through faith refers not only to the religious-ethical but also to the religious-intellectual life. Not only he who is in sin but also he who is in doubt is justified through faith. The situation of doubt, even of doubt about God, need not separate us from God. There is faith in every serious doubt, namely, the faith in the truth as such, even if the only truth we can express is our lack of truth. But if this is experienced in its depth and as an ultimate concern, the divine is present; and he who doubts in such an attitude is "justified" in his thinking. So the paradox got hold of me that he who seriously denies God, affirms him. Without it I could not have remained a theologian. There is, I soon realized, no place *beside* the divine, there is no possible atheism, there is no wall between the religious and the nonreligious. The holy embraces both itself and the secular. Being religious is being unconditionally concerned, whether this concern expresses itself in secular or (in the narrower sense) religious forms. The personal and theological consequences of these ideas for me were immense. Personally, they gave me at the time of their discovery, and always since then, a strong feeling of relief. You cannot reach God by the work of right thinking or by a sacrifice of the intellect or by a submission to strange authorities, such as the doctrines of the church and the Bible. You cannot, and you are not even asked to try it. Neither works of piety nor works of morality nor works of the intellect establish unity with God. They follow from this unity, but they do not make it. They even prevent it if you try to reach it through them. But just as you are justified as a *sinner* (though unjust, you are just), so in the status of *doubt* you are in the status of truth. And if all this comes together and you are desperate about the meaning of life, the seriousness of your despair is the expression of the meaning in which you still are living. This unconditional seriousness is the expression of the presence of the divine in the experience of utter separation from it. It is this radical and universal interpretation of the doctrine of justification through faith which has made me a conscious Protestant. Strictly theological arguments for this idea are given in an early German article which I mention mainly because of its title: "Rechtfertigung und Zweifel" ("Justification and Doubt"). In that article . . . the conquest of the experience of meaninglessness by the awareness of the paradoxical presence of "meaning in meaninglessness" is described. References to this idea are given wherever the Protestant principle is mentioned, especially in the chapters on "Realism and Faith," "The Protestant Message and the Man of Today," and "The Transmoral Conscience."

The radical and universal interpretation of the idea of justification through faith had important theological consequences beyond the personal. If it is valid, no realm of life can exist without relation to something unconditional, to an ultimate concern. Religion, like God, is omnipresent; its presence, like that of God, can be forgotten, neglected, denied. But it is always effective, giving inexhaustible depth to life and inexhaustible meaning to every cultural creation. A first, somewhat enthusiastic, expression of this idea was given in a lecture printed in the *Kant-Studien* under the title, "Über die Idee einer Theologie der Kultur" ("On the Idea of a Theology of Culture"). A short time later, in a more systematic fashion, the same idea was explained in a paper that appeared in the same magazine under the paradoxical title, "Die Überwindung des Religionsbegriffs in der Religionsphilosophie" ("Overcoming the Notion of Religion within the Philosophy of Religion"). Both articles . . . try to introduce the larger concept of religion, challenging the undialectical use of the narrower definition.

It was natural that on the basis of these presuppositions the history of religion and of Christianity required a new interpretation. The early and high Middle Ages received a valuation that they never had received in classical Protestantism. I call them "theonomous" periods, in contrast to the heteronomy of the later Middle Ages and the self-complacent autonomy of modern humanism. "Theonomy" has been defined as a culture in which the ultimate meaning of existence shines through all finite forms of thought and action; the culture is transparent, and its creations are vessels of a spiritual content. "Heteronomy" (with which theonomy is often confused) is, in contrast to it, the attempt of a religion to dominate autonomous cultural creativity from the outside, while self-complacent autonomy cuts the ties of a civilization with its ultimate ground and aim, whereby, in the measure in which it succeeds, a civilization becomes exhausted and spiritually empty. The Protestant principle as derived from the doctrine of justification through faith rejects heteronomy (represented by the doctrine of papal infallibility) as well as a self-complacent autonomy (represented by secular humanism). It demands a self-transcending autonomy, or theonomy. These ideas have been developed in my "Religionsphilosophie" ("Philosophy of Religion") which appeared as a section of the *Lehrbuch der Philosophie* ("Textbook of Philosophy," edited by Max Dessoir). Expressions of the same point of view are given in the essays "Philosophy and Fate," "Philosophy and Theology," and "Kairos," in the present volume.

[3]

Most important for my thought and life was the application of these ideas to the interpretation of history. History became the central problem of my theology and philosophy because of the historical reality as I found it when I returned from the first World War: a chaotic Germany and Europe;

the end of the period of the victorious *bourgeoisie* and of the nineteenth-century way of life; the split between the Lutheran churches and the proletariat; the gap between the transcendent message of traditional Christianity and the immanent hopes of the revolutionary movements. The situation demanded interpretation as well as action. Both were attempted by the German religious-socialist movement, which was founded immediately after the war by a group of people including myself. The first task we faced was an analysis of the world situation on the basis of contemporary events, viewed in the light of the great criticism of bourgeois culture during the nineteenth and early twentieth centuries, and with the help of the categories derived from the Protestant principle in its application to religion and culture. In this analysis the central proposition of my philosophy of religion proved its significance: Religion is the substance of culture, culture is the expression of religion. A large section of my published writings and unpublished lectures has been dedicated to such a "theonomous" interpretation of culture. The small, widely received book *Die Religiöse Lage der Gegenwart* (translated in 1932 under the title, *The Religious Situation*) tried to give an all-embracing analysis of the recent decades of our period. A similar, though shorter, analysis has recently appeared as the first section of a symposium, *The Christian Answer*. Among the articles collected in the present volume, practically all those brought together in the fifth part, "The Present Crisis," as well as "The Protestant Principle and the Proletarian Situation" and "The Idea and the Ideal of Personality," contribute to a theonomous interpretation of our period. An analysis of our situation could not have been attempted by me without my participation in the religious-socialist movement. In speaking about it, I first want to remove some misunderstandings concerning its nature and purpose. This is especially necessary in a country like the United States, where everything critical of nineteenth-century capitalism is denounced as "red" and, consciously or through ignorance, confused with communism of the Soviet type. The most unfortunate consequence of this attitude is the barrier that it erects against any real understanding of what is going on in our world, especially in Europe and Asia, and of the transformations that are taking place in all realms of life, in religion as well as in economy, in science as well as in the arts, in ethics as well as in education, in the whole of human existence. Religious socialism was always interested in human life as a whole and never in its economic basis exclusively. In this it was sharply distinguished from economic materialism, as well as from all forms of "economism." It did not consider the economic fact as an independent one on which all social reality is dependent. It recognized the dependence of economy itself on all other social, intellectual, and spiritual factors, and it created a picture of the total, interdependent structure of our present existence. We understood socialism as a problem not of wages but of a new theonomy in which the the question of wages, of social security, is treated in unity with the question of truth, of spiritual security. On the other hand, we realized more than most Christian theologians ever did that there are social structures that unavoidably frustrate any spiritual appeal to the people subjected to them. My entrance into the religious-socialist movement meant for me the definitive break with philosophical idealism and theological transcendentalism. It opened my eyes to the religious significance of political Calvinism and social sectarianism, over against the predominantly sacramental character of my own Lutheran tradition. Religious socialism is not a political party but a spiritual power trying to be effective in as many parties as possible. It had and has sympathizers and foes on the Left as well as on the Right. Yet it stands unambiguously against every form of reaction, whether it be a semifeudal reaction as in Germany; a bourgeois status quo policy as in this country; or the clerical reaction that threatens to develop in large sections of postwar Europe. Religious socialism is not "Marxism," neither political Marxism in the sense of communism nor "scientific" Marxism in the sense of economic doctrines. We have, however, learned more from Marx's dialectical analysis of bourgeois society than from any other analysis of our period. We have found in it an understanding of human nature and history which is much nearer to the classical Christian doctrine of man with its empirical pessimism and its eschatological hope than is the picture of man in idealistic theology.

The most important theoretical work done by religious socialism was the creation of a religious interpretation of history, the first one, so far as I can see, of an especially Protestant character. There were Christian interpretations of history in the early and medieval church, an ecclesiastical or conservative type represented by Augustine and a sectarian or revolutionary type represented by Joachim of Floris. There were and are secular interpretations of history, conservative-pessimistic ones or evolutionary-optimistic ones or revolutionary-utopian ones (see the chapter on "Historical and Nonhistorical Interpretations of History"). Lutheranism had some affinity to the first type, Calvinism to the second, and sectarianism to the third. But a genuine Protestant interpretation of history was missing. It was the historical situation itself, the gap between conservative Lutheranism and socialist utopianism in Germany, which forced upon us the question of a Protestant interpretation of history. The answer given so far centers around three main concepts: "theonomy," "kairos," and the "demonic." The first of these concepts and its relation to the Protestant principle has already been explained. For the concept of "kairos" I can refer to the chapter "Kairos" in this book. The concept of the demonic is fully explained in my book, *The Interpretation of History*. In this introduction there remains the task of showing the relation of the concepts of "kairos" and of the "demonic" to the Protestant principle.

"Kairos," the "fulness of time," according to the New Testament use of the word, describes the moment in which the eternal breaks into the temporal, and the temporal is prepared to receive it. What happened in the one unique kairos, the appearance of Jesus as the Christ, i.e., as the center of history, may happen in a derived form again and again in the process of time, creating centers of lesser importance on which the periodization of history is dependent. The presence of such a dependent kairos was felt by many people after the first World War. It gave us the impulse to start the religious-socialist movement, the impetus of which was strong enough to survive its destruction in Germany and to spread through many countries, as the work and the decisions of the Oxford conference surprisingly proved. It is the basic trend of the European masses today, as all keen observers agree. "Kairos" is a biblical concept which could not be used by Catholicism because of the latter's conservative hierarchical interpretation of history; and it has not been used by the sects because of their striving toward the final end. The Protestant principle demands a method of interpreting history in which the critical transcendence of the divine over against conservatism and utopianism is strongly expressed and in which, at the same time, the creative omnipresence of the divine in the course of history is concretely indicated. In both respects the concept of "kairos" is most adequate. It continues the Protestant criticism of Catholic historical absolutism; it prevents the acceptance of any kind of utopian belief, progressivistic or revolutionary, in a perfect future; it overcomes Lutheran individualistic transcendentalism; it gives a dynamic historical consciousness in the line of early Christianity and the early Reformation; it provides a theonomous foundation for the creation of the new in history. The idea of "the kairos" unites criticism and creation. And just this is the problem of Protestantism (see the chapter entitled "The Formative Power of Protestantism").

The third concept decisive for my interpretation of history is that of "the demonic." It is one of the forgotten concepts of the New Testament, which, in spite of its tremendous importance for Jesus and the apostles, has become obsolete in modern theology. The thing responsible for this neglect was the reaction of the philosophers of the Enlightenment against the superstitious, abominable use of the idea of the demonic in the Middle Ages and in orthodox Protestantism. But abuse should not forbid right use. The idea of the demonic is the mythical expression of a reality that was in the center of Luther's experience as it was in Paul's, namely, the structural, and therefore inescapable, power of evil. The Enlightenment, foreshadowed by Erasmus' fight with Luther and by theological humanism, saw only the individual acts of evil, dependent on the free decisions of the conscious personality. It believed in the possibility of inducing the great majority of individuals to follow the demands of an integrated personal and social life by education, persuasion, and adequate institutions. But this belief was broken down not only by the "Storms of Our Times" [1] but also by the new recognition of the destructive mechanisms determining the unconscious trends of individuals and groups. Theologians could reinterpret the badly named but profoundly true doctrine of "original sin" in the light of recent scientific discoveries. The powerful symbol of the demonic was everywhere accepted in the sense in which we had used it, namely, as a "structure of evil" beyond the moral power of good will, producing social and individual tragedy precisely through the inseparable mixture of good and evil in every human act. None of the concepts used by our interpretation of history has found as much response in religious and secular literature as has the concept of the demonic. This response may be interpreted as a symptom of the general feeling for the structural character of evil in our period. If evil has demonic or structural character limiting individual freedom, its conquest can come only by the opposite, the divine structure, that is, by what we have called a structure or "Gestalt" of grace. Luther's fight with Erasmus is typical for the Protestant interpretation of grace. We are justified by grace *alone,* because in our relation to God we are dependent on God, on God alone, and in no way on ourselves; we are grasped by grace, and this is only another way of saying that we have faith. Grace creates the faith through which it is received. Man does not create faith by will or intellect or emotional self-surrender. Grace comes to him; it is "objective," and he may be enabled to receive it, or he may not. The interest of early Protestantism was, however, so much centered around individual justification that the idea of a "Gestalt of grace" in our historical existence could not develop. This development was also prevented by the fact that the Catholic church considered itself as the body of objective grace, thus discrediting the idea of a "Gestalt of grace" for Protestant consciousness. It is obvious that the Protestant principle cannot admit any identification of grace with a visible reality, not even with the church on its visible side. But the negation of a visible "Gestalt of grace" does not imply the negation of the concept as such. The church in its spiritual quality, as an object of faith, is a "Gestalt of grace" (see the chapter on "The Formative Power of Protestantism"). And the church as "Gestalt of grace" is older and larger than the Christian churches. Without preparation in all history, without what I later have called the "church in its latency" (abbreviated to the "latent church"), the "manifest" church never could have appeared at a special time. Therefore, grace is in all history, and a continuous fight is going on between divine and demonic structures. The feeling of living in the center of such a fight was the basic impulse of religious socialism, expressing itself in a religious and, I think, essentially Protestant interpretation of history.

[1] In the unabridged edition.

[4]

In all these ideas—theonomy, the kairos, the demonic, the Gestalt of grace, and the latent church—the Protestant principle appears in its revealing and critical power. But the Protestant principle is not the Protestant reality; and the question had to be asked as to how they are related to one another, how the life of the Protestant churches is possible under the criterion of the Protestant principle, and how a culture can be influenced and transformed by Protestantism. These questions are asked, in one way or another, in every article of the present book. And, in every answer suggested, the need for a profound transformation of religious and cultural Protestantism is indicated. It is not impossible that at some future time people will call the sum total of these transformations the end of the Protestant era. But the end of the Protestant era is, according to the basic distinction between the Protestant principle and Protestant reality, not the end of Protestantism. On the contrary, it may be the way in which the Protestant principle must affirm itself in the present situation. The end of the Protestant era is not the return to the Catholic era and not even, although much more so, the return to early Christianity; nor is it the step to a new form of secularism. It is something beyond all these forms, a new form of Christianity, to be expected and prepared for, but not yet to be named. Elements of it can be described but not the new structure that must and will grow; for Christianity is final only in so far as it has the power of criticizing and transforming each of its historical manifestations; and just this power is the Protestant principle. If the problem is raised of Protestantism as protest and as creation, a large group of questions immediately appear, all of them insufficiently answered in historical Protestantism and all of them driving toward radical transformations. Many of them are discussed in this book, several of them in other places by myself, some of them hardly at all. A short account of these problems may show their character and their importance. The sharp distinction between the principle and the actuality of Protestantism leads to the following question: By the power of what reality does the Protestant principle exercise its criticism? There must be such a reality, since the Protestant principle is not mere negation. But if such a reality does exist, how can it escape the Protestant protest? In other words: How can a spiritual Gestalt live if its principle is the protest against itself? How can critical and formative power be united in the reality of Protestantism? The answer is: In the power of the New Being that is manifest in Jesus as the Christ. Here the Protestant protest comes to an end. Here is the bedrock on which it stands and which is not subjected to its criticism. Here is the sacramental foundation of Protestantism, of the Protestant principle, and of the Protestant reality.

It is not by chance that a chapter on sacramental thinking appears in this book. The decrease in sacramental thinking and feeling in the churches of the Reformation and in the American denominations is appalling. Nature has lost its religious meaning and is excluded from participation in the power of salvation; the sacraments have lost their spiritual power and are vanishing in the consciousness of most Protestants; the Christ is interpreted as a religious personality and not as the basic sacramental reality, the "New Being." The Protestant protest has rightly destroyed the magical elements in Catholic sacramentalism but has wrongly brought to the verge of disappearance the sacramental foundation of Christianity and with it the religious foundation of the protest itself. It should be a permanent task of Christian theology, of preaching, and of church leadership to draw the line between the spiritual and the magic use of the sacramental element, for this element is the one essential element of every religion, namely, the presence of the divine before our acting and striving, is a "structure of grace" and in the symbols expressing it. C. G. Jung has called the history of Protestantism a history of continuous "iconoclasm" ("the destruction of pictures," that is, of religious symbols) and, consequently, the separation of our consciousness from the universally human "archetypes" that are present in the subconscious of everybody. He is right. Protestants often confuse essential symbols with accidental signs. They often are unaware of the numinous power inherent in genuine symbols, words, acts, persons, things. They have replaced the great wealth of symbols appearing in the Christian tradition by rational concepts, moral laws, and subjective emotions. This also was a consequence of the Protestant protest against the superstitious use of the traditional symbols in Roman Catholicism and in all paganism. But here also the protest has endangered its own basis.

One of the earliest experiences I had with Protestant preaching was its moralistic character or, more exactly, its tendency to overburden the personal center and to make the relation to God dependent on continuous, conscious decisions and experiences. The rediscovery of the unconscious in medical psychology and the insight into the unconscious drives of the mass psyche gave me the key to this basic problem of the Protestant cultus. The loss of sacraments and symbols corresponds to the exclusive emphasis on the center of personality in Protestantism; and both these facts correspond to the rise of the bourgeois ideal of personality, for which the Reformation and the Renaissance are equally responsible. A the same time, personal experience, the intimate observation of many individuals, the knowledge provided by psychotherapy, the trend of the younger generation in Europe toward the vital and prerational side of the individual and social life, the urgent desire for more community and authority and for powerful and dominating symbols—all these seemed to prove that the Protestant-humanist ideal of personality has been undermined and that the Protestant cultus and its personal and social ethics have to undergo a farreaching transformation. This impression was and is supported by the general development of Western civilization toward more collectivistic forms of political and economic life. The demand for a basic security in social, as well as in spiritual, respects has superseded (though not removed) the liberal demand for liberty. And this demand can no longer be suppressed, for it is rooted in the deepest levels of the men of today, of personalities and groups. Reactionary measures may delay the development, but they cannot stop it. Organization of security (against the devastation coming from the atomic bomb or from permanent unemployment) is impossible without collectivistic measures. The question of whether Protestantism as a determining historical factor will survive is, above all, the question of whether it will be able to adapt itself to the new situation; it is the question of whether Protestantism, in the power of its principle, will be able to dissolve its amalgamation with bourgeois ideology and reality and create a synthesis, in criticism and acceptance, with the new forces that have arisen in the present stage of a revolutionary transformation of man and his world.

This is a challenge for both the individual and the social ethics of Protestantism. In the section on "Religion and Ethics" the attempt has been made to meet this challenge, most comprehensively in the chapter on "The Idea and the Ideal of Personality." Here the relation of the personal center, first, to nature, second, to community, and, third, to its own unconscious basis is discussed, and ideas for the transformation of these relations in the coming period of history are suggested. A special point is elaborated in the chapter on "The Transmoral Conscience," which tries to connect Luther's experience of the "justified conscience" with the psychotherapeutic principle of "accepting one's self" and with the emphasis on the creative venture of thinking and acting in the different forms of "the philosophy of life" and pragmatism. With respect to social ethics the chapter on "The Protestant Principle and the Proletarian Situation" is the most representative, though all chapters of the last section, "The Present Crisis," [2] bear on the subject. Protestantism has not developed a social ethics of its own as Roman Catholicism has done (and codified) in terms of Thomism. The Protestant principle cannot admit an absolute form of social ethics. But, on the other hand, it need not surrender its development to the state, as it did on Lutheran soil, or to society, as it did on Calvinistic soil. Protestantism can and must have social ethics determined by the experience of the kairos in the light of the Protestant principle. The chapter on "Ethics in a Changing World" deals with this problem. The main answer given there is: Ethics out of the kairos is ethics of love, for love unites the ultimate criterion with the adaptation to the concrete situation.

It is a shortcoming of Protestantism that it never has sufficiently described the place of love in the whole of Christianity. This is due to the

[2] See the unabridged edition.

genesis and history of Protestantism. The Reformation had to fight against the partly magical, partly moralistic, partly relativistic distortion of the idea of love in later Catholicism. But this fight was only a consequence of Luther's fight against the Catholic doctrine of faith. And so faith and not love occupied the center of Protestant thought. While Zwingli and Calvin, by their humanistic-biblicistic stress on the function of the law, were prevented from developing a doctrine of love, Luther's doctrine of love and wrath (of God and the government) prevented him from connecting love with law and justice. The result was puritanism without love in the Calvinistic countries and romanticism without justice in the Lutheran countries. A fresh interpretation of love is needed in all sections of Protestantism, an interpretation that shows that love is basically not an emotional but an ontological power, that it is the essence of life itself, namely, the dynamic reunion of that which is separated. If love is understood in this way, it is the principle on which all Protestant social ethics is based, uniting an eternal and a dynamic element, uniting power with justice and creativity with form. In the chapter on "Ethics in a Changing World" the attempt is made to lay the foundation of a Protestant doctrine of love.

The formative power of Protestantism in theology and philosophy is indicated in several articles but is not applied constructively. It is my hope that parts of the theological system, on which I have been working for many years, will appear in a not distant future. In the present volume only some results are anticipated, especially in the chapter on "Philosophy and Theology." I have traveled a long way to my present theological position, a way that started in my first larger book, *Das System der Wissenschaften nach Gegenständen und Methoden* ("The System of Knowledge: Its Contents and Its Methods"). In many respects the ideas developed in this book have determined my thinking up to the present moment, especially those on biology, technical sciences, history, and metaphysics. Theology is defined as "theonomous metaphysics," a definition that was a first and rather insufficient step toward what I now call the "method of correlation." This method tries to overcome the conflict between the naturalistic and supernaturalistic methods which imperils not only any real progress in the work of systematic theology but also any possible effect of theology on the secular world. The method of correlation shows, at every point of Christian thought, the interdependence between the ultimate questions to which philosophy (as well as prephilosophical thinking) is driven and the answers given in the Christian message. Philosophy cannot answer ultimate or existential questions *qua* philosophy. If the philosopher tries to answer them (and all creative philosophers have tried to do so), he becomes a theologian. And, conversely, theology cannot answer those questions without accepting their presuppositions and implications. Question and answer determine each other; if they are separated, the traditional answers become unintelligible, and the actual questions remain unanswered. The method of correlation aims to overcome this situation. In the chapter on "Philosophy and Theology" (as well as in all my work in systematic theology) the method is explained and applied. Such a method is truly dialectical and therefore opposed to the supernaturalism of later Barthianism as well as to any other type of orthodoxy and fundamentalism. Philosophy and theology are not separated, and they are not identical, but they are correlated, and their correlation is the methodological problem of a Protestant theology.

In this connection I want to say a few words about my relationship to the two main trends in present-day theology, the one called "dialectical" in Europe, "neo-orthodox" in America, the other called "liberal" in Europe (and America) and sometimes "humanist" in America. My theology can be understood as an attempt to overcome the conflict between these two types of theology. It intends to show that the alternative expressed in those names is not valid; that most of the contrasting statements are expressions of an obsolete stage of theological thought; and that, besides many other developments in life and the interpretation of life, the Protestant principle itself prohibits old and new orthodoxy, old and new liberalism. Since the latter point is especially important in the context of this book I want to enlarge on it in a few propositions which, at the same time, show the main lines of my own theological position.

It was the Protestant principle that gave liberal theology the right and the good conscience to approach the Holy Scripture with the critical methods of historical research and with a complete scientific honesty in showing the mythical and legendary elements in both Testaments. This event, which has no parallel in other religions, is an impressive and glorious vindication of the truth of the Protestant principle. In this respect Protestant theology must always be liberal theology.

It was the Protestant principle that enabled liberal theology to realize that Christianity cannot be considered in isolation from the general religious and cultural, psychological and sociological, development of humanity; that Christianity, as well as every Christian, is involved in the universal structures and changes of human life; and that, on the other hand, there are anticipations of Christianity in all history. This insight, which is deadly for ecclesiastical and theological arrogance, is strengthening for Christianity in the light of the Protestant principle. In this respect also Protestant theology must be liberal theology.

It was the Protestant principle that destroyed the supra-naturalism of the Roman Catholic system, the dualism between nature and grace, which is ultimately rooted in a metaphysical devaluation of the natural as such. And it was the Protestant principle that showed liberal theology a way of uniting the antidualistic emphasis of the Reformation with the ontological universalism and humanism of the Renaissance, thus destroying holy superstitions, sacramental magic, and sacred heteronomy. In this respect above all, Protestant theology must be liberal theology and must remain so even if challenged and suppressed by a period which will prefer security to truth.

But it is also the Protestant principle that has induced orthodox theologians (both old and new) to look at Scripture as Holy Scripture, namely, as the original document of the event which is called "Jesus the Christ" and which is the criterion of all Scripture and the manifestation of the Protestant principle. In this respect Protestant theology must be "ortho-dox" and must always maintain the ground in which the critical power of the Protestant principle is rooted.

It was the Protestant principle that showed orthodox theologians (both old and new) that the history of religion and culture is a history of permanent demonic distortions of revelation and idolatrous confusions of God and man. Therefore, they emphasized and reemphasized the First Commandment, the infinite distance between God and man, and the judgment of the Cross over and against all human possibilities. In this respect also, Protestant theology must be always orthodox, fighting against conscious and unconscious idolatries and ideologies.

Again, it was the Protestant principle that forced the orthodox theologians (both old and new) to acknowledge that man in his very existence is estranged from God, that a distorted humanity is our heritage, and that no human endeavor and no law of progress can conquer this situation but only the paradoxical and reconciling act of the divine self-giving. In this respect above all, Protestant theology must be orthodox at all times.

Is the acceptance of these propositions liberal, is it orthodox theology? I think it is neither the one nor the other. I think it is Protestant and Christian, and, if a technical term is wanted, it is *neo-dialectical.*

This Introduction is written in the confusing period after the end of the second World War. What are the chances of historical Protestantism in this period? What are its possible contributions to this period? Will the new era be in any imaginable sense a Protestant era, as the era between the Reformation and the first World War certainly was? Only a few indications for the immediate future and its spiritual needs are given in the last chapter. Much more could be derived from the whole of this book. A few things are obvious. The wars and the revolutions that mark the first half of the twentieth century are symptoms of the disintegration of life and thought of the liberal *bourgeoisie* and of a radical transformation of Western civilization. In so far as Protestantism is an element in the changing structure of the Western world—and nothing beyond it—it takes part in the processes of disintegration and transformation. It is not untouched by the trend toward a more collectivistic order of life, socially as well as spiritually. It is threatened by the dangers of this trend, and it may share in its promises. We are not yet able to have a picture of this coming era and of the situation of Christianity and Protestantism within it. We see elements of the picture which certainly will appear in it, but we do not see the whole. We do not know the destiny and character of Protestantism in this period. We do not know whether it will even desire or deserve the name "Protestantism." All this is unknown. But we know three things: We know the Protestant principle, its eternal significance, and its lasting power in all periods of history. We know, though only fragmentarily, the next steps that Protestantism must take in the light of its principle and in view of the present situation of itself and of the world. And we know that it will take these steps unwillingly, with many discords, relapses, and frustrations, but forced by a power that is not its own.

May I conclude with a personal remark? It was the "ecstatic" experience of the belief in a kairos which, after the first World War, created, or at least initiated, most of the ideas presented in this book. There is no such ecstatic experience after the second World War, but a general feeling that more darkness than light is lying ahead of us. An element of cynical realism is prevailing today, as an element of utopian hope was prevailing at that earlier time. The Protestant principle judges both of them. It justifies the hope, though destroying its utopian form; it justifies the realism, though destroying its cynical form. In the spirit of such a realism of hope, Protestantism must enter the new era, whether this era will be described by later historians as a post-Protestant or as a Protestant era; for, not the Protestant era, but the Protestant principle is everlasting.

10
RUDOLF BULTMANN

Rudolf Bultmann is at once the most creative and influential New Testament scholar of the twentieth century and a theologian who has had an enormous impact upon theology both in Germany and in America. In 1941 he published a programmatic essay which founded the Demythologizing school of Protestant theology. However, his earlier book on Jesus, published in 1926, already contained many of the major motifs of his later work. No contemporary theologian has generated more controversy than Bultmann; this is largely due to his own language, which moves back and forth between scholarly exposition of the New Testament and modern theological statements. In his most important work, *Theology of the New Testament,* a program of radical Demythologizing is carried on in the context of historical and linguistic analysis. Most theological interpretations of Bultmann largely ignore his exegetical work, but it is here that his writing is both most powerful and most successful in terms of his own purpose.

The following selection is taken from the section on the Gospel of John in the *Theology of the New Testament.* The reader should be aware of Bultmann's conviction that the Gospel of John is the most loyal of the four gospels to the intention of Jesus. Bultmann is also persuaded that demythologizing itself originated with the Gospel of John, inasmuch as this gospel succeeds in transcending the original apocalyptic form of the proclamations of both Jesus and the primitive Church. Particular attention should be paid to the full meaning of Bultmann's statements that the divinity of Jesus is invisible in the Fourth Gospel and that in it Jesus reveals nothing but that he is the revealer.

| Rudolf Bultmann | # Passages from Theology of the New Testament |

THE OFFENSE OF THE INCARNATION OF THE WORD

[1]

How does God's Son come into the world? As a human being. The theme of the whole Gospel of John is the statement: "The word became flesh." [1] This statement is defended by I and II John against the false teachers. These are evidently Christian Gnostics who deny the identity of the Son of God with the human Jesus either by asserting that their union was only temporary or by flatly rejecting the reality of the human Jesus and docetically regarding the human form of the Son of God as only a seeming body. John's answer to them is: every spirit that does not confess that Jesus Christ came in the flesh, that does not confess Jesus (the man as the Son of God) is not "from God"; indeed, such false doctrine is nothing less than the work of Antichrist.[2] Just because John makes use of the Gnostic Redeemer-myth[3] for his picture of the figure and activity of Jesus, a demarcation of his own position from that of Gnosticism is particularly incumbent upon him.

It is clear to begin with that for him *the incarnation of the Son of God is not,* as it is in Gnosticism, *a cosmic event* which sets into motion the

---

[1] 1:14. [Chapter and verse numbers of this type refer to the Gospel of John. When an epistle of John is meant, the reference is given as in footnote 2.—T. J. J. A.]
[2] I Jn. 4:2f.; II Jn. 7.
[3] *Theol.* II, pp. 10-14. [*Theol.* in the footnotes to this selection refers to the complete Grobel translation of Bultmann's *Theology of the New Testament*—T. J. J. A.]

REPRINTED with the permission of Charles Scribner's Sons from *Theology of the New Testament,* Vol. II, pp. 40-42, and 49-69, by Rudolf Bultmann, translated by Kendrick Grobel. Copyright 1955 Charles Scribner's Sons. Also with the permission of SCM Press, Ltd., publisher.

eschatological occurrence (the unfolding of redemption) as a process of nature by which the union of the essentially opposite natures, light and darkness, is dissolved. The Gnostic Redeemer releases the preexistent human selves, who by virtue of their light-nature are related to him, out of the matter (body and "soul") that trammels them, and then leads them to the world of light above. John eliminated both the Gnostic concept of physis ("nature") and the Gnostic notion of the preexistence of human selves and their unnatural imprisonment in the material world. He does not accept the Gnostic trichotomy of man, according to which man's true *self* is imprisoned in a *body* and a *soul*.[4] Neither is the incarnation of the Son of God for John a device for transmitting "Gnosis" to men in the form of teachings about cosmogony and anthropology or for bringing them secret formulas and sacraments, on the strength of which their selves can safely make the journey to heaven.[5]

The Revealer appears not as *man-in-general,* i.e. not simply as a bearer of human *nature,* but as a *definite human being in history:* Jesus of Nazareth. His humanity is genuine humanity: "the word became flesh." Hence, John has no theory about the preexistent one's miraculous manner of entry into the world nor about the manner of his union with the man Jesus. He knows neither the legend of the virgin birth[6] nor that of Jesus' birth in Bethlehem—or if he knows of them, he will have nothing to do with them. Jesus comes from Nazareth, and this fact, offensive to "the Jews," is emphasized[7] rather than deprecated. "The Jews," knowing Jesus' place of origin and his parents[8] are not in error as to the facts, but err in denying the claim of this Jesus of Nazareth to be the Revealer of God. They err not in the matter upon which they judge but in making a judgment at all *kata sarka* (according to the "flesh"—according to external appearances).

Neither does the Revealer appear as a mystagogue communicating teachings, formulas, and rites as if he himself were only a means to an end who could sink into unimportance to any who had received his "Gnosis." Though Jesus says in departing from the earth, "I have manifested thy name to the men whom thou gavest me out of the world" [9] still he has imparted no information about God at all, any more than he has brought instruction about the origin of the world or the fate of the self. He does not *communicate anything,* but *calls men to himself.* Or when he promises a gift, he is, himself, that gift: he himself is the bread of life that he bestows;[10] he himself is the light;[11] he himself is life.[12]

---

[4] *Theol.* I, pp. 165, 168. [5] *Theol.* II, pp. 66-69.
[6] In some Latin witnesses to the text of Jn. 1:13 *"qui . . . natus est"* (who . . . was born) is found instead of "who . . . were born"; this is certainly a "correcting" of the original text.
[7] 1:45; 7:52.   [10] 6:35.
[8] 7:27f; 6:42.   [11] 8:12.
[9] 17:6; cf. v. 26.   [12] 11:25; 14:6.

Jesus, the Son of God who has become man, is a genuine man—which again does not mean that in his personality the divine became visible so as to fill men with enthusiasm and touch their feelings or to fascinate and overwhelm them. If that were the case, the divine would then be conceived of simply as the human exalted and intensified. But according to John, the divine is the very counter-pole to the human, with the result that it is a paradox, an offense, that the Word became flesh. As a matter of fact, the divinity of the figure of Jesus in John is completely lacking in visibility, and the disciples' relation to him as "friends" [13] is by no means conceived of as a personal relation of human friendship. It is the farewell discourses especially that strive to teach this distinction by making clear that the disciples will not achieve the right relation to him until he has departed from them—indeed, that he is not in the full sense the Revealer until he has been lifted up and glorified.[14]

✠ ✠ ✠

[2]

[. . . Jesus'] work as a whole, which forms a unity framed by his coming and his departure . . . *is both revelation and offense.* His departure or "exaltation" (i.e., upon the cross) not only belongs to the whole as its culmination but is that which makes the whole what it is: both revelation and offense. The possibility considered by Jesus in the meditation which is John's substitute for the Gethsemane scene of the synoptic tradition, "What shall I say? 'Father, save me from this hour'?" Jesus immediately rejects: "No, for this purpose I have come to this hour." [15] In his passion the meaning of the sending of Jesus is fulfilled. And by his conceiving and accepting it as the fulfillment of the mission enjoined upon him by the Father,[16] it becomes the hour of exaltation, the hour of glorification. Seen from the vantage-point of this fulfillment the whole work of the man Jesus is a revelation of the divine glory. Whereas in the Gospel of Mark we can recognize the historical process by which the unmessianic life of Jesus was retrospectively made messianic, in John the inner appropriateness of that process is made clear. This is expressed by the evangelist by means of the petition of Jesus which follows the deliberation mentioned above: "Father, glorify thy name" [17] and by the heavenly voice which answers this prayer, "I have glorified it, and I will glorify it again." [18] Hence, the glorification

[13] 15:14f.
[14] See especially 14:28; 16:7; *Theol.* II, pp. 84-88.
[15] 12:27.
[16] 14:31.
[17] 12:28.
[18] *Ibid.*

of God's name which begins with Jesus' exaltation by crucifixion and the glorification of God's name by the ministry of the earthly Jesus[19] are a unity. Neither exists without the other; each exists only through the other. But the glorification of the name of God is also the glorification of Jesus himself, and Jesus' other prayer, "Father, the hour has come; glorify thy Son," [20] corresponds to this one ("Father, glorify thy name"). And the motive for this prayer—"that the Son may glorify thee"—makes the unity of God's glory and Jesus' glory evident. And when the motive is further developed in the words "since thou has given him power over all flesh," [21] the unity of his glory after the exaltation with that before it is once again made clear. Both unities are once more expressed in the words which pronounce the granting of this prayer:

> "Now is the Son of man glorified,
>   and in him God is glorified;
>   if God is glorified in him,
>   God will also glorify him in himself
>   and glorify him at once."

In the "now" of the "hour" when the Son of God departs from the world the past and the future are bound together, as it were. And since not until the future will the past be made into what it really is (*viz.,* the revelation of the "glory"), the disciples can only be glad that Jesus is going away.[22]

Faith in Jesus, then, is faith in the exalted Jesus, but not as if he were a heavenly being who had stripped off the garment of earthly-human existence as the Gnostic Redeemer was conceived to do. Rather, the exalted Jesus is at the same time the earthly man Jesus; the "glorified one" is still always he who "became flesh." In other words, Jesus' life on earth does not become an item of the historical past, but constantly remains present reality. The historical figure of Jesus, i.e., his human history, retains its significance of being the revelation of his "glory" and thereby of God's. It is the eschatological occurrence. Of course, this is not visible to the world, for the exalted Jesus does not reveal himself to it[23]—indeed he cannot, for it cannot receive the Spirit of truth which gives knowledge to those who believe.[24] But those who believe can now look back upon Jesus' earthly life and say, "We have beheld his glory." [25] What, then, is the picture of that life at which faith arrives?

[19] 17:4.
[20] 17:1.
[21] 17:2.
[22] 14:28; 16:7.

[23] 14:22.
[24] 14:17; 16:13f.
[25] 1:14.

[1]

In the hour of Jesus' departure Philip asks him: "Lord, show us the Father, and we shall be satisfied." The answer he gets is: "Have I been with you so long, and yet you do not know me, Philip? He who has seen me has seen the Father . . . . Do you not believe that I am in the Father and the Father in me?" [26] In the person of the man Jesus—and only in him—is God Himself to be met, for: "no one comes to the Father, but by me." [27] In constantly varying expressions *this unity of Jesus the Son with God the Father* is insisted upon: "I and the Father are one." [28] With a formulation from the Gnostic myth it is said: he is not alone, but the Father who sent him is with him.[29] Formulations from mysticism are pressed into service to describe this unity: the mutual knowledge of Father and Son[30] and the mutual immanence of each in the other.[31] Or, in mythological language once more, we read that the Father "loves" the Son[32] and that the Son "abides in his love." [33] The continuation of the answer to Philip nevertheless indicates that in none of these expressions is either mythology or mysticism really present, nor is a metaphysic in the sense of the later two-nature doctrine. This continuation is an exegesis of "I in the Father and the Father in me": "The words that I say to you I do not speak on my own authority; but the Father who dwells in me is doing his works." [34] In the work of Jesus, therefore, God appears, but God is not perceptible, as Philip's request implies, to the gaze of an observer. He is perceptible only to that man who has the openness to let himself be reached by the work of Jesus, the man who can "hear" his word.[35] Yes, God in Jesus encounters even him who shuts himself up against his word—encounters him to judge him. In I Jn. the unity of Father and Son often has the peculiar result that it is impossible to decide whether the author is talking of God or of Jesus.[36]

God Himself encounters men in Jesus, a Jesus moreover who is a man in whom nothing unusual is perceptible except his bold assertion that in him God encounters men. In that fact lies the *paradoxical nature of the concept of Revelation,* a paradox which John was the first to see with any distinctness. It never occurs to Paul to reflect about the revelation which took place in the human figure of Jesus and his work and fate. For him the earthly Jesus is only the "emptied" one,[37] the "impoverished" one,[38]

---

[26] 14:8-10.
[27] 14:6.
[28] 10:30.
[29] 8:16, 29; 16:32.
[30] 10:14, 38.
[31] 10:38; 14:10f., 20; 17:21-23.
[32] 3:35; 5:20; 10:17; 15:9; 17:23f., 26.

[33] 15:10.
[34] 14:10.
[35] 8:43.
[36] E.g., 5:14f.
[37] Phil. 2:7.
[38] II Cor. 8:9.

not one who in his earthly interlude bears heavenly glory and riches. But John emphatically expresses this paradox. He accordingly presents the fact that in Jesus God encounters man in a seemingly contradictory manner: in one direction by statements that declare that Jesus has equal dignity and rights with God, or even that God has abdicated His rights to Jesus, so to speak. In the other direction, John declares that Jesus speaks and acts only in obedience to the will of the Father and does nothing on his own authority. Returning to the former direction, we read that God gave Jesus His (God's) name, gave "all things" into his hand,[39] gave him "power over all flesh," [40] granted him "to have life in himself," as God Himself has life, [41] and correspondingly gave him "authority to execute judgment." [42] Consequently, he wakes the dead as the Father does and makes alive whom he will;[43] he works as the Father does,[44] and is entitled to claim the same veneration as He.[45] But in the other direction, we find Jesus declaring: "I have come down from heaven, not to do my own will, but the will of him who sent me." [46] He acts in obedience to the "charge" which he received from the Father.[47] Only in that charge does he have his existence: "My food is to do the will of him who sent me, and to accomplish his work." [48] In keeping with this saying, the last word uttered by the crucified Jesus is: "It is accomplished." [49] His work is to accomplish the task enjoined upon him by the Father,[50] which he does, not to his own glory but for the sake of the Father's glory.[51] As for Jesus' own glory, the Father sees to that.[52]

The negative formulations of this theme are repeated again and again: Jesus did not come of his own accord or on his own authority.[53] Of himself he can do nothing; he acts only according to the Father's instruction.[54] He speaks and teaches not of his own accord, but only speaks the words which the Father has bidden him speak.[55] Of course, the intent of such statements is not to diminish the authority of Jesus and his words, but just the opposite: to establish it. Just because he does not speak of his own accord it can be said that he speaks the words of God,[56] or that whoever hears him hears the words of God unless his mind is hardened,[57] or that whoever hears his word has life insofar as he believes.[58] These negative formulations are not in the least meant as descriptions of Jesus' humility; the high priest does not speak "of his own accord," either,[59] any more than long ago Balaam did.[60] The notion that it is Jesus' humility that is being

[39] 3:35; 13:3.
[40] 17:2.
[41] 5:26.
[42] 5:22, 27.
[43] 5:21.
[44] 5:17.
[45] 5:23.
[46] 6:38.
[47] 10:18; 12:49f.; 14:31; 15:10.
[48] 4:34.
[49] 19:30 tr.

[50] 5:36; 9:4; 10:32, 37; 17:4.
[51] 7:18; 8:49f.; cf. 11:4.
[52] 8:50, 54; cf. 16:14.
[53] 7:28f.; 8:42; cf. 5:43.
[54] 5:19f., 30; 8:28.
[55] 7:17f.; 12:49; 14:10, 24; 17:8, 14.
[56] 3:34.
[57] 8:47.
[58] 5:24.
[59] 11:51.
[60] Num. 24:13.

described by them is refuted by 5:17f.; for "the Jews" are quite right in being enraged at Jesus' words; regarded from the human standpoint they would be blasphemous presumption. But it is just this standpoint, from which Jesus' character would be measured by ethical standards, which is the wrong one; and what the author is trying to make clear is not Jesus' humility but his authority: the paradoxical authority of a human being speaking the word of God. In other words, it is the idea of the Revelation that the author is setting forth.

[2]

But now let us inquire what *the works* are that Jesus accomplishes in his Father's commission. Or what is his one *work?* For the "works" which Jesus does at his Father's behest[61] are ultimately one single work. At the beginning of his ministry we read: "My food is to do the will of him who sent me, and to accomplish his work," [62] and in retrospect we are told a very similar thing at the end of it: "I glorified thee on earth, having accomplished the work which thou gavest me to do." [63]

In the *kerygma* of the Hellenistic Church Jesus' death and resurrection are the *facts of salvation.*[64] Being a unity, they might have been called "the work" of Jesus, though this terminology does not occur. Neither does Paul speak of "the work" of Christ, even though he, too, might very appropriately have so spoken of Jesus' death and resurrection.[65] Though for Paul the incarnation of Christ is a part of the total salvation-occurrence, for John it is the decisive salvation-event. While for Paul the incarnation is secondary to his death in importance,[66] one might say that the reverse is true in John: the death is subordinate to the incarnation. But on closer inspection it turns out that incarnation and death constitute a unity as the coming (incarnation) and the going (death) of the Son of God.[67] But within that unity the center of gravity is not in the *death,* as it is in Paul. In John, Jesus' death has no preeminent importance for salvation, but is the accomplishment of the "work" which began with the incarnation:[68] the last demonstration of the obedience[69] which governs the whole life of Jesus. The phrase "obedient unto death," [70] quoted by Paul from a Christ-hymn,[71] is developed by John in the whole sweep of his representation of

[61] 5:20, 36; 9:4; 10:25, 32, 37; 14:12; 15:24.
[62] 4:34.
[63] 17:4.
[64] *Theol.* I, pp. 80ff.
[65] "The work of Christ" in Phil. 2:30 is not what the earthly Jesus accomplished but the *work* of Christian missions carried on in the service *of Christ.*
[66] *Theol.* I, pp. 292-94.
[67] *Theol.* II, pp. 33-35.
[68] Theol. II, pp. 47-49.
[69] 14:31.
[70] Phil. 2:8.
[71] See *Theol.* I, pp. 131, 298.

Jesus. Thus Jesus' death takes on a double aspect in John: it is the completion of his obedience, but it is also Jesus' release from his commission, and he can return to the glory he previously had in preexistence.[72] Therefore the crucifixion, which John, of course, narrates, is regarded from the outset as Jesus' *elevation* (*hypsothenai*) a peculiarly ambiguous word,[73] or as his glorification.[74] But the Pauline vocabulary, the *cross* and *the crucified*,[75] is not found in John; and in Jesus' predictive words about his death the terms *be exalted* (or elevated) and *be glorified* have supplanted the terms *be killed* and *be crucified* known to us from the synoptic predictions of the passion. Of course the way to exaltation leads through death,[76] in which the sending of Jesus finds its meaning fulfilled.[77] But his death is not an event whose catastrophic nature could be removed only by his subsequent resurrection. On the contrary, his death itself is already his exaltation. And that means: John has subsumed the death of Jesus under his idea of the Revelation—in his death Jesus himself is acting as the Revealer and is not the passive object of a divine process of salvation. John does not use the term *suffer* (*paschein*) of Jesus, nor speak of his *sufferings* (*pathemata*). The synoptists said that Jesus "must suffer." [78] A similar unfathomable *must*[79] occurs once in John, but its complementary infinitive is not *suffer* but *be exalted*.[80] And 14:31 does not say *so it must be*[81] or the like, but simply "so I do." John's passion-narrative shows us Jesus as not really *suffering* death but *choosing* it—not as the passive victim but as the active conqueror.

The common Christian *interpretation of Jesus' death as an atonement for sins*[82] is not, therefore, what determines John's view of it. At the most, one may wonder whether in using certain expressions John was adapting himself to this common theology of the Church. When John the Baptist points out Jesus with the words: "Behold the Lamb of God who takes away the sin of the world," [83] *take away* is the literal translation of what Jesus does; I Jn. 3:5 is parallel: "he appeared to take away sins." The figure of the Lamb, probably taken from Christian tradition by John, compels us to think of sacrifice. But nothing compels us to conclude that the evangelist sees this sacrifice only in Jesus' death rather than in his whole ministry. The latter view would correspond to John's total view of Jesus. I Jn. 1:7, I admit, is a different matter: "the blood of Jesus . . . cleanses us from all sin"—certainly the common Christian conception of Jesus' death as an atoning sacrifice is present here. But the clause lies under suspicion of being redactional gloss. It competes with v. 9, just below, "If we confess our sins, he [God] is faithful and just, and will forgive our sins

---

[72] 6:62; 17:5.
[73] 3:14; 8:28; 12:32, 34.
[74] 7:39; 12:16, 23; 13:31f.; 17:1, 5.
[75] *Theol.* II, p. 6.
[76] 12:24.
[77] 12:27; *Theol.* II, p. 47.

[78] Mk. 8:31, etc.
[79] See *Theol.* I, pp. 46f.
[80] 3:14.
[81] Cf. Mt. 26:54.
[82] *Theol.* I, pp. 46f., 84f.
[83] *Theol.* I, p. 29.

and cleanse us from all unrighteousness." The two sentences which refer to Jesus as "the expiation for our sins" [84] are probably likewise redactional glosses.

Outside of I Jn. 1:7, Jesus' blood is mentioned a few other times. In the Gospel we find it in 6:53-56—i.e. within the passage[85] inserted by an ecclesiastical editor, which reinterprets the preceding discourse or discussion (in which Jesus had revealed himself as the bread of life) as referring to the sacrament of the Lord's Supper.[86] It occurs again in 19:34b, where the ecclesiastical editor has given the spear-wound a deeper significance by adding: "and at once there came out blood and water." This deeper meaning can only be that both sacraments, Lord's Supper (blood) and baptism (water) are founded upon Jesus' death. The case of I Jn. 5:6 is different: "This is he who came by water and blood, Jesus Christ." For here *water* and *blood* denote not the sacraments but the points of time at which his ministry began and ended: his baptism by John and his death. The purpose of the remark is to assert the reality of the Redeemer's human life against the views of the docetic Gnostics. That is why the sentence continues: "not with the water only but with the water and the blood"— i.e. let no one think that the *Redeemer* united with the human Jesus only at his baptism and then departed from him before his death; no, the Redeemer also suffered death. There is no allusion at this point to the death or blood of Jesus as having significance for salvation.

Whatever may be the origin of these passages, the thought of Jesus' death as an atonement for sin has no place in John, and if it should turn out that he took it over from the tradition of the Church, it would still be a foreign element in his work. It is significant that John does not narrate the founding of the Lord's Supper, in the liturgy of which[87] the atonement idea occurs in the words *for you* (or *for many*). He substituted for it the farewell prayer of Jesus, in which the words, "And for their sake I consecrate myself," [88] are a clear allusion to those words of the Lord's Supper. These words do characterize Jesus' death as a sacrifice, it is true, but here, as everywhere else in John, his death is to be understood in connection with his life as the completion of his work. His life-work as a whole is sacrifice—an idea well expressed in the description of Jesus as he "whom the Father consecrated and sent into the world." [89] Neither does "he gave his only Son" [89] specifically mean God's giving him up to death, but His sending Jesus to men. Neither is it said that his sacrifice is an atoning sacrifice for sins. Neither Jn. 17 nor the other farewell discourses deal with forgiveness of sin. In the whole Gospel, in fact, forgiveness of sin is mentioned only once—20:23—where the authority of the disciples to forgive sins is attributed to a saying of the risen Jesus. This passage alludes to ecclesiastical practice; so does I Jn., which takes ecclesiastical terminology

[84] I Jn. 2:2; 4:10.
[85] 6:51b-58.
[86] *Theol.* II, pp. 58f.
[87] *Theol.* I, p. 146.
[88] 17:19.
[89] 3:16.

into account more than the Gospel does. Twice forgiveness of sin is mentioned in I Jn.: it is conferred by God upon him who confesses his sins[90] and it is a characteristic of members of the Church that their sins are forgiven.[91] In the Gospel, however, it is promised that release from sin will come through Jesus' word, or through the "truth" mediated by his word: "If you continue in my word, you are my disciples, and you will know the truth and the truth will make you free"—free from sin, as the sequel says.[92] A parallel to this is the statement that whoever accepts Jesus' ministration is "clean";[93] for this service of his consists in his having revealed to his own the name of the Father, and given them the words that the Father had given him.[94] And 15:3 says: "You are already made clean by the word which I have spoken to you." So now at last the full meaning of [95] ("for their sake I consecrate myself") becomes evident, for it continues: "that they also may be consecrated in truth." This clause, however, only says how a fulfillment of the prayer, "Consecrate them in truth," is to come about (the explanation in 17:17b explicitly identifies "truth" with "thy word": "thy word is truth"). Jesus' death, therefore, is not a special work, but is conceived as of one piece with the whole life-work of Jesus, being its completion.

[3]

If Jesus' death on the cross is already his exaltation and glorification, *his resurrection* cannot be an event of special significance. No resurrection is needed to destroy the triumph which death might be supposed to have gained in the crucifixion. For the cross itself was already triumph over the world and its ruler. The hour of the passion is *krisis* (of the world) and means the fall of the "ruler of this world" and his condemnation.[96] As a conqueror over whom the "ruler of the world" has no power, Jesus strides on to meet his passion.[97] There is not a word in John of the idea that not until the resurrection and exaltation after his death was Jesus made lord of all cosmic and demonic powers.[98] For the Father did not delay the gift of life-creating power to him until the resurrection but gave it to him from the outset: "he has granted the Son also to have life in himself." [99] It is as he who is the resurrection and the life, or the way, the truth and the life[100] that he encounters men and calls the believer into life now,[101] as the raising of Lazarus demonstrates.[102] That is why we also fail to find in

[90] 1:9.
[91] 2:12.
[92] 8:31-34.
[93] 13:10.
[94] 17:6, 8.
[95] 17:17.
[96] 12:31; 16:11.

[97] 14:30 and see above, *Theol.* II, p. 53.
[98] Cf., for example, Phil. 2:11; Eph. 1:20f.; I Pet. 3:21f.; Pol. Phil. 2:1.
[99] 5:26.
[100] 11:25; 14:6.
[101] 5:24f.; 11:25f.
[102] Ch. 11.

Jesus' words in John the prediction of his "rising" or "being raised" as we know it from the synoptics. The evangelist himself mentions it only in an aside:[103] "When therefore he was raised from the dead, his disciples remembered. . . ." But as a substitute for it we find in 12:16: "but when Jesus had been glorified, then they remembered" . . . (tr.). *To rise* (*anastenai*) occurs only in a redactional gloss at 20:9 and *to be raised* (*egethenai*) only in the redactional epilogue.[104] Both terms are completely lacking in the Epistles of John.

It is not surprising that the evangelist, following the tradition, narrates some *Easter-stories*. The question is, what do they mean to him? The original close of the Gospel[105] just after the Easter-stories says, "Now Jesus also did many other signs." Evidently, then, the resurrection appearances just like the miracles of Jesus[106] are reckoned among his "signs." They symbolize the fulfillment of the prediction of 16:22: "So you have sorrow now, but I will see you again and your hearts will rejoice." [107] So far as they are actual occurrences—and the evangelist need not have doubted their reality—they resemble the miracles in that ultimately they are not indispensable; in fact, there ought to be no need for them, but they were granted as a concession to man's weakness. The Thomas-story is used to make this idea clear: his wish to see the risen Jesus in the body, even to touch him, is granted. But in the same moment he is reprimanded: "Because you have seen me have you come to faith? Blessed are those who though they do not see me yet believe." [108] It is hard to believe that the evangelist closes his representation of Jesus with this as his last word without a deep intention behind it. In it lies a criticism of the small faith which asks for tangible demonstrations of the Revealer. It also contains a warning against taking the Easter-stories for more than they are able to be: signs and pictures of the Easter faith—or, perhaps still better, confessions of faith in it.

The same conclusion can be drawn from the promises made in the farewell discourses. Parallel to the Easter-promise ("but I will see you again," 16:22, already mentioned above, within the whole passage 16:16-24) is another, 14:18; "I will not leave you desolate; I will come to you." This is the promise of his "coming," i.e. his parousia. But when it continues: "Yet a little while, and the world will see me no more, but you will see me; because I live, you will live also," the promise of the parousia is merging into the Easter-promise. What this means is that Jesus' resurrection and parousia are identical to John. Not only that, but parallel to these parallel promises stands a third, the promise of the Spirit,[109] i.e. the promise of Pentecost. Hence, for John, Easter, Pentecost, and the parousia

[103] 2:22.
[104] 21:4.
[105] 20:31.
[106] *Theol.* II, pp. 44f.

[107] Cf. 16:16.
[108] 20:29 tr.
[109] The Paraclete 14:15; 16:33.

are not three separate events, but one and the same. Consequently, the terminology appropriate to Easter again and again mingles with that appropriate to the parousia—reunion with him is mentioned in 14:19; 16:16, 19, 20; the fact that he lives, 14:9; his appearing to the disciples, 14:21f. But out of the traditional parousia-expectation these themes occur: his coming, 14:3, 18, 23, 28; and the phrases characteristic of eschatology, "in that day" 14:20; 16:23, 26, and "the hour is coming," 16:25. And into the midst of these the promise of the Spirit is thrust: 14:15-17, 26; 15:26; 16:7-11, 13-15. But the one event that is meant by all these is not an external occurrence, but an inner one: the victory which Jesus wins when faith arises in man by the overcoming of the offense that Jesus is to him. The victory over the "ruler of the world" which Jesus has won, is the fact that now there exists a faith which recognizes in Jesus the Revelation of God. The declaration, "I have overcome the world," [110] has its parallel in the believer's confession: "this is the victory that overcomes the world: our faith. Who is it that overcomes the world but he who believes that Jesus is the Son of God?" [111] In the short dialogue between Judas and Jesus it is explicitly stated that this is a matter of inward occurrence: "Lord, how is it that you will manifest yourself to us, and not to the world?" Jesus answers, "If a man loves me, he will keep my word, and my Father will love him, and we will come to him and make our home with him." [112] The same is said of the sending of the Spirit—"the Spirit of truth, whom the world cannot receive, because it neither sees him nor knows him; you know him, for he dwells with you, and will be in you." [113]

If, as John maintains, Jesus' original coming is already the κρίσις (judgment), then it is evident that for him the parousia is not an impending cosmic drama.[114] Accordingly, John contains none of the synoptic parousia-predictions of the coming of the Son of Man in the glory of his Father, on the clouds of heaven, or the like.[115]

[4]

As we have seen, the "facts of salvation" in the traditional sense play no important role in John. The entire salvation-drama—incarnation, death, resurrection, Pentecost, the parousia—is concentrated into a single event: the Revelation of God's "reality" (*aletheia*) in the earthly activity of the man Jesus combined with the overcoming of the "offense" in it by man's accepting it in faith. It is only consistent with this concentration that *the sacraments* also play no role in John. It is true that he clearly presupposes that baptism is a practice of the Church when he reports in 3:22 that

[110] 16:33.
[111] I Jn. 5:4f.
[112] 14:22f.

[113] 14:17.
[114] See *Theol.* II, pp. 17-21.
[115] Mk. 8:38; 13:26f., etc.; see *Theol.* I, p. 29.

Jesus is winning and baptizing disciples. (The reader is assured by way of correction in 4:2 that not he himself but his disciples did the baptizing. Is this an ancient gloss?) But in the text that has come down to us in 3:5 ("unless one is born of water and the Spirit, he cannot enter the kingdom of God") the two words *water and* are clearly an interpolation made by an ecclesiastical editor, for what follows deals only with rebirth by the Spirit with no mention of baptism. Besides, it would contradict the untrammeled blowing of the Spirit[116] if the Spirit were bound to the baptismal water. The foot-washing[117] has often been taken to represent baptism, but this is an error. It depicts, rather, the service of Jesus in general which makes his disciples clean; according to 15:3, it is the word Jesus has spoken to them that has made them clean. The ecclesiastical redaction of the account of the spear-wound[118] made a gloss,[119] and saw in the blood and water flowing from the wound symbols of both sacraments.[120] The knowledge-bestowing ointment (*chrisma*) which I Jn. 2:20, 27, says the Church has received (it "abides in you . . . and teaches you about everything, and is true . . ." v. 27) is the "Spirit of truth," of which the same statement is made.[121] Whether the author thinks of this Spirit as mediated by baptism—the term *ointment* would make it a natural assumption—is a question one may properly ask. But since the Spirit of truth in the Gospel[122] is the power of the word at work in the Church,[123] the epistle's *ointment,* too, is probably the word filled with power.

The Lord's Supper is introduced by the ecclesiastical redaction not only at 19:34b but also in 6:51b-58.[124] For in the latter passage the "bread of life" of Jesus' preceding words surely does not mean the sacramental meal, but (like "water of life" and "light") means Jesus himself as the one who brings life in that he is life.[125] Again the notion of a "medicine of immortality" contained in 6:51b-58 does not agree with John's eschatology.[126] Finally, the offense which the "Jews" take at Jesus' offer of his own flesh as food is of a quite different sort from the Johannine *skandala* that arise from the peculiar Johannine dualism which is missing here. In John's account of Jesus' last meal there is no mention of the institution of the Lord's Supper, and for it the farewell prayer of Jesus is substituted.[127] John also substitutes the "new commandment" [128] for the "new covenant," of which the traditional eucharistic sayings speak.[129] But the editorial appendix, ch. 21, reports in v. 13 a mysterious meal which the risen Jesus grants the disciples, and this evidently does mean the Lord's Supper.

It is therefore permissible to say that though in John there is no direct

---

[116] V. 8.
[117] 13:4f.
[118] 19:34a.
[119] 34b, 35.
[120] *Theol.* II, p. 54.
[121] 14:17: "it dwells with you and will be in you" [tr.]; 14:26: "it will teach you all things" [tr.].
[122] 14:17, 26; 16:13.
[123] *Theol.* II, pp. 88-91.
[124] *Theol.* II, p. 54.
[125] 11:25; 14:6.
[126] *Theol.* II, pp. 37-40.
[127] *Theol.* II, p. 54.
[128] 13:34.
[129] I Cor. 11:25.

polemic against the sacraments, his attitude toward them is nevertheless critical or at least reserved.

THE REVELATION AS THE WORD

[1]

We have still to ask what the works are that Jesus accomplishes and that "bear witness" to him.[130] Are they the "signs," the miracles which Mt. 11:2 calls the "works of the Christ" (tr.)? No, at least not in the sense of being an unambiguous legitimation. For, as we have seen,[131] they are ambiguous signs whose meaning can only be found in faith. In that respect they resemble Jesus' words, which are just as ambiguous and open to misunderstanding.[132] In fact the miracles in John are neither more nor less than words, *verba visibilia*. Otherwise, it would be incomprehensible how Jesus' ministry could be called in retrospect a "doing of signs," [133] whereas in the actual account of his ministry the "signs" are secondary in importance to the "words"—and the farewell prayer, looking back, describes Jesus' ministry as the passing on of the *words* God gave him.

That is the fact—the *works of Jesus* (or, seen collectively as a whole: his work) *are his words*. When Jesus says, "The works which the Father has given me to accomplish, these very works which I am doing, bear me witness that the Father has sent me," [134] the words of the preceding discussion[135] indicate what the true works of Jesus are: "judging" and "making alive." They also indicate how these works are accomplished: by Jesus' word. Numerous formulations indicate that to John deed and word are identical.

> 8:28: "then you will know that I am he and that on my own authority I *do* nothing; but as the Father taught me, that I *speak*."
>
> 14:10: "The *words* that I *say* to you I do not speak on my own authority; but the Father who dwells in me *is doing* his *works*" (tr.).
>
> 15:22, 24: "If I had not come and *spoken* to them, they would not have sin . . . . If I had not done among them the *works* . . . they would not have sin."

In addition cf. in 8:38 the interchange between "speak" and "do"; in 17:4, 8, 14, the equivalence of "work," "words" (*rhemata*) and "word" (*logos*). There is a corresponding interchange between "see" and "hear" in 8:38, etc.; on which see below. 10:38 and 14:11 seem to contradict our assertion that the works are not added to the words to substantiate them

---

[130] 5:36; 10:25.
[131] *Theol.* II, pp. 44f.

[132] *Theol.* II, pp. 45-47.
[133] 12:37; 20:30.

[134] 5:36.
[135] 5:19ff.

but are nothing but the words themselves. Both times we read: "even though you do not believe *me,* believe the *works"* (in one case "for the sake of the works"). Does not *me* mean "my works"? But 14:11 is the continuation of 14:10, and together they indicate that the "works" of v. 11 are neither more nor less than the "words" of v. 10. When Jesus thus points away from himself to his working, that can only mean that he is rejecting an authoritarian faith which will meekly accept what is said *about* Jesus. In its place he is demanding a faith that understands Jesus' words as *personal address* aimed at the believer—i.e. as Jesus' "working" upon him. This is the sense in which Jesus refuses the demand of "the Jews" that he openly say whether or not he is the Messiah[136] The answer to that they ought to gather from his works—or workings—which bear witness for him.

The identity of work and word can be further seen in what is said of the effect of the word. "The words that I have spoken to you are spirit and life." [137] This is followed by Peter's confession: "You have the words of eternal life." Whoever believes the word of Jesus and Him who sent him, has eternal life, has stepped over from death into life.[138] Whoever keeps his word will never see death.[139] *His word therefore bestows life.* And neither more nor less than that is meant when it is said that his word leads to knowledge and hence to freedom.[140] His word cleanses and consecrates.[141] Therein, of course, the word is *also the judge* over unbelief:

> "If any one hears my words and does not keep them,
>   I do not judge him . . . .
> He who rejects me and does not receive my words
>   has a judge:
> the word that I have spoken judges him." [142]

[2]

Now what of *the content of Jesus' word* or words? *What Jesus saw or heard with the Father* he speaks. (Or, as a consequence of identifying word and deed, John may also say that he "shows" it or "does" it.) This is in accord with the final sentence of the prologue: "No one has ever seen God; the only Son, who is in the bosom of the Father, he has made him known." [143]

Jesus testifies or speaks what he saw with his Father[144] or what he saw and heard [145] or simply what he heard.[146] He speaks what the Father taught

---

[136] 10:24f.
[137] 6:68.
[138] 5:24.
[139] 8:51.
[140] 8:31f.
[141] 15:3; 17:17.

[142] 12:47f. Blt. [The abbreviation Blt. indicates that the original text was rephrased by Bultmann.—T. J. J. A.]
[143] 1:18; cf. 6:46.

[144] 3:11; 8:38.
[145] 3:32.
[146] 8:26, 40; 15:15; cf. 5:30—the same thing is said of the Spirit in 16:13.

him to speak,[147] or commanded him to speak.[148] He speaks the words that the Father gave him.[149] He does what he sees the Father do, what the Father shows him.[150] Expressed also in a very general way: he reveals the Father's name.[151] It makes no difference whether the present tense is used of what the Son sees and hears,[152] or a past tense of what he saw and heard (all the other passages), any more than there is a difference between "all that the Father *gives* me"[153] and "my Father who *has given* them to me."[154]

But the astonishing thing about it is that Jesus' words never convey anything specific or concrete that he has seen with the Father. Not once does he communicate matters or events to which he had been a witness by either eye or ear. Never is the heavenly world the theme of his words. Nor does he communicate cosmogonic or soteriological mysteries like the Gnostic Redeemer. His theme is always just this one thing: that the Father sent him, that he came as the light, the bread of life, witness for the truth, etc.; that he will go again, and that one must believe in him. So it is clear that the mythological statements have lost their mythological meaning. Jesus is not presented in literal seriousness as a preexistent divine being who came in human form to earth to reveal unprecedented secrets. Rather, the mythological terminology is intended to express the absolute and decisive significance of his word—the mythological notion of preexistence is made to serve the idea of the Revelation. His word does not arise from the sphere of human observation and thought, but comes from beyond. It is a word free of all human motivation, a word determined from outside himself, just as men's speech and deeds can only be determined from outside themselves when they oppose themselves to his word as enemies—determined in the latter case, of course, by the devil.[155] Therefore his word is not subject to men's scrutiny or control. It is an authoritative word which confronts the hearer with a life-and-death decision.

The same thing is meant by the solemn affirmation that Jesus does or says nothing on his own authority.[156] Such statements have the purpose of underlining the authority of Jesus, whose words, although spoken by a man, still are not human words: "No man ever spoke like this man."[157] To a certain extent, the word of the Old Testament prophets is analogous in that they also do not speak by their own authority but are inspired by God. But the analogy also uncovers the difference: Jesus' words are not *from time to time* inspired, but he speaks and acts *constantly* from within his one-ness with God.[158] Unlike the prophets' words, Jesus' words do not thrust the concrete historical situation of the People into the light of God's demand with its promise or threat; they do not open men's eyes to what

---

[147] 8:28, cf. 7:17.
[148] 12:49.
[149] 17:8.
[150] 5:19f.

[151] 17:6, 26.
[152] 5:19f., 30.
[153] 6:37.
[154] 10:26.

[155] 8:38, 41.
[156] See *Theol.* II, pp. 59-61.
[157] 7:46.
[158] *Theol.* II, pp. 59-61.

some present moment demands. Rather, the encounter with Jesus' words and person casts man into decision in his bare, undifferentiated situation of being human. None of the prophets was of absolute importance; one followed upon another. No new revealer follows Jesus; in him the Revelation of God is once for all given to the world, and this Revelation is inexhaustible. For whatever new knowledge may yet be given the Church by the Spirit, it will all be only a reminder of what Jesus said [159]—or, as Jesus says, "he will select from what is mine and declare it to you." [160]

Thus comes to light the deeper meaning of that peculiar fluctuation of expression between "speak" and "do" and between "word" and "work." Jesus' words communicate no definable content at all except that they are words of life, words of God. That is, they are words of life, words of God, not because of their content, but because of *whose* words they are. They are something special and decisive not in and by their timeless content, but in and by the act of being uttered—and that is why they are just as much "works" as "words": Whatever Jesus does is a speaking, whatever he says is a doing. His actions speak, his words act.

For that very reason practically all the words of Jesus in John are *assertions about himself,* and no definite complex of ideas can be stated as their content and claimed to be the "teaching" of Jesus. Hence the radical difference between Jesus' preaching in John and that in the synoptics; John took over only a minimal quantity of the traditional words of Jesus.[161] His words are assertions about himself. But that does not mean christological instruction, or teaching about the metaphysical quality of his person. On the contrary, to understand them in that way would be to misunderstand them; for it would be a failure to understand that his "words" are "deeds." Anyone so understanding him would have to let himself be referred to Jesus' deeds, as were "the Jews" who required of him a clear statement whether he were the Messiah or not.[162]

His words are utterances about himself; *for his word is identical with himself.*[163] What is said of his word is also said of himself: his words are "life," they are "truth";[164] but so is he himself—"I am the way, and the truth, and the life." [165] Whoever hears his word and believes Him who sent him has Life,[166] but that is what he himself is—"I am the resurrection and the life; he who believes in me, though he die, yet shall he live." [167] His words,[168] his "testimony," [169] must be "accepted" (*lambanein*)— so must he.[170] To reject him (*athetein*) is identical with not accepting his words.[171] That his own "abide" in him and he in them means the same

---

[159] 14:26.
[160] 16:14; *Theol.* II, pp. 88-91.
[161] *Theol.* II, pp. 3-5.
[162] 10:24ff.; see *Theol.* II, p. 16.
[163] *Theol.* II, p. 19.
[164] 6:63; 17:17.
[165] 14:6.
[166] 5:24.
[167] 11:25.
[168] 12:48; 17:8.
[169] 3:11, 32f.
[170] 1:12; 5:43; cf. 13:20.
[171] 12:48.

thing as that his words "abide" in them.[172] He is the judge[173]—so is his word.[174] No wonder, then, that the evangelist can confer upon him for his preexistent period the mythological title: *Word* (Logos)!

Certain though it is that *Logos*[175] is meant not as a common noun but as a proper noun, it is also certain that the everyday meaning ("Word") behind the name "Logos" is present in the evangelist's mind. For he is hardly likely to have begun his Gospel with the sentence, "In the beginning was the Logos," without thinking of "In the beginning" at Gen. 1:1 and of the recurrent phrase "God said" in the creation story of Gen. 1. And the same conclusion is to be drawn from I Jn. 1:1, where instead of the personal Word the common noun *word* ("of life") is used as a synonym ("That which was from the beginning, which we have heard . . . concerning the word of life"); here its everyday meaning is clear. The title *Logos* is not derived from the Old Testament, for in it—as also in Judaism—we hear of the "word of God" but never find the unmodified expression, "the Word." But "word of God"—like the rabbinic equivalent *memra d'Adonai*—does not mean a concrete figure (neither a person nor a cosmic power or "hypostasis"), but the manifestation of God's power in a specific instance. Nor is the title *Logos* derived from the Greek philosophical tradition in general or from Stoicism in particular and transmitted to the evangelist by Philo of Alexandria, for the philosophical idea of *logos* as the rational orderliness of the divine cosmos is quite foreign to John. The figure of the "Logos" is derived, rather, from a tradition of cosmological mythology which also exercised an influence upon Judaism, especially upon Philo. In the literature of the Old Testament and of Judaism there is a figure "Wisdom," which is a parallel to John's "Word." Both figures, "Word" and "Wisdom," appear side by side in Philo. In Gnosticism, which also influenced Philo, the figure "Logos" has not merely cosmological but also soteriological functions. It is within this sphere that the origin of the Johannine Logos lies.

His words are utterances about himself. Accordingly, all the Revelation that he brings is concentrated in the great *"I-am" statements*.

> The bread of life—it is I. He who comes to me shall not hunger, and he who believes in me shall never thirst.[176]
>
> The light of the world—it is I. He who follows me shall not walk in darkness but shall have the light of life.[177]
>
> The door is I.[178]
> The good shepherd is I.[179]
> The resurrection and the life are I.[180]

[172] 15:4-7.
[173] 5:22, 27.
[174] 12:48.

[175] 1:1ff.
[176] 6:35 cf. 6:51a Blt.
[177] 8:12 Blt. tr.

[178] 10:9.
[179] 10:11, 14 Blt.
[180] 11:25.

The way, the truth, and the life are I.[181]
The true vine is I.[182]

In fact, Jesus can pronounce this "It is I" absolutely, without any real subject: "unless you believe that it is I, you will die in your sins"[183] and: "when you have lifted up the Son of man, then you will know that it is I."[184] What is to be supplied as the real subject in place of "it"? Obviously nothing definite or specific, but something of this sort: "all that I say is I"—or perhaps better: "he upon whom life and death, being and nonbeing depend"—"he for whom all the world is waiting as the bringer of salvation." For let it be observed that in these "I"-statements the "I" is a predicate nominative and not the subject. The meaning is always: "in *me* the thing mentioned (bread of life, light, etc.) is present; it is I."[185]

All these figures of speech—that of the bread and the light, the door and the way, the shepherd and the vine—mean what John, without using a figure, calls life and truth. That is, they all mean that which man must have and longs to have in order to be able truly to exist. With his "It is I" Jesus therefore presents himself as the one for whom the world is waiting, the one who satisfies all longing. This is symbolically represented in the scene at the well in Samaria. The woman of Samaria says, "I know that Messiah is coming . . . when he comes he will show us all things." To which Jesus replies: "I who speak to you am he."[186] He similarly answers the healed blind man's question who the Son of Man is: "You have both seen him and it is he who is speaking to you."[187] The world's longing takes form in the concept of the *salvation-bringer* in his various forms, with his various titles. So the titles of the salvation-bringer from both the Jewish and the Hellenistic tradition[188] are conferred in John upon Jesus. Jesus is he in whom the old hope is fulfilled; his coming is the eschatological event.[189] But all the traditional titles are insufficient, as is suggested by the title which occurs in Peter's confession: "and we have come to believe and to know that you are the Holy One of God."[190] Only one other time does this title occur in the New Testament: in the demon's confession at Mk. 1:24; it has no tradition (at least no recognizable one), for though Jesus is called "the holy one" at I Jn. 2:20 and Rev. 3:7, in these passages it is not a title but means simply "he who is holy." The title designates Jesus as the absolutely transcendent one whose place is at the side of God and who stands over against the world as the representative of God. At the same time, however, the reader is probably expected to hear in it the etymological overtone: holy—hallow (*hagios*—*hagiazein*) and to remem-

---

[181] 14:6 Blt.
[182] 15:1, 5.
[183] 8:24 Blt.
[184] 8:28 Blt.

[185] *Theol.* II, pp. 26f.
[186] 4:25f.
[187] 9:37.
[188] *Theol.* II, pp. 35-37.

[189] *Theol.* II, pp. 37-40.
[190] 6:69.

ber that Jesus is he "whom the father hallowed and sent into the world" [191] and he who hallows himself for his own.[192]

[3]

Thus it turns out in the end that Jesus as the Revealer of God *reveals nothing but that he is the Revealer*. And that amounts to saying that it is he for whom the world is waiting, he who brings in his own person that for which all the longing of man yearns: life and truth as the reality out of which man can exist, light as the complete transparence of existence in which questions and riddles are at an end. But how is he that and how does he bring it? In no other way than that he says that he is it and says that he brings it—he, a man with his human word, which, without legitimation, demands faith. John, that is, in his Gospel presents only the fact (*das Dass*) of the Revelation without describing its content (*ihr Was*).

In the Gnostic myth, whose language John uses as his means of expression, it suffices that the Revelation consists of nothing more than the bare fact of it (its *Dass*)—i.e. the proposition that the Revealer has come and gone, has descended and been re-exalted. For even though Gnosticism speaks at length in cosmogonic and soteriological speculations about the content of the Revelation, nevertheless the decisive thing for it is the bare fact of Revelation. The reason for this is that for it the Redeemer is a cosmic figure and that redemption is ultimately a cosmic process by which the light-particles imprisoned in the material world are released and guided to the world of light above.[193] Cosmic connection between the Redeemer and the redeemed—that is to say, the identity of their nature (*physis*)— is the presupposition for redemption. By virtue of this identity his fate is theirs, and to know this—i.e. to know one's own nature (*physis*) and its unity with the Redeemer's nature—is the content of the Revelation and is the Gnosis ("knowledge") in which the Revelation is appropriated. But since John eliminates from the myth its cosmological presuppositions, since he does not speak of the "nature" common to the Redeemer and the redeemed or of the fate of human "selves," he appears to retain in his book only the empty fact of the Revelation. He does not give content to the Revelation by filling it with rational or speculative insights, nor by reproducing the message preached by the synoptic Jesus. Consequently, it was natural enough for investigators to declare John a mystic. For the negation of all definable Revelation-content has a counterpart in mysticism: the soul's experience, the content of which goes beyond any possibility of expression. But John is no mystic. The mystic formulas adopted by him he wishes to be understood in the sense of his Revelation-idea.[194] Any

---

[191] 10:36.
[192] 17:19; *Theol.* II, p. 55.

[193] *Theol.* II, pp. 40f.
[194] *Theol.* II, pp. 49-52.

interest in disciplining the soul or cultivating experiences of the soul ("mystical experiences") is lacking. The negative predications of God characteristic of mysticism are missing. And the negation of the world in John does not have the same meaning that it has in mysticism. That is, it does not have the ontological meaning of describing God's mode of being by the *via negationis*. John's negation of the world does mean the condemnation of man, because John sees the "world" as a historical force —*viz.*, as the world constituted of men in rebellion against God.[195] Therefore, his negating of the world means the rejecting and condemning of man's presumptuous independence and of the norms and evaluations emanating therefrom.

But if the Revelation is to be presented neither as the communication of a definite teaching nor as the kindling of a mystical experience of the soul, then all that can be presented is the bare fact of it. This fact, however, does not remain empty. For the Revelation is represented as the shattering and negating of all human self-assertion and all human norms and evaluations. And, precisely by virtue of being such negation, the Revelation is the affirmation and fulfillment of human longing for life, for true reality. That the Revelation is this positive thing can only be seen by such a faith as overcomes the "offense" and subjects itself to that negation, acknowledging its own blindness in order to receive sight.[196] Then it becomes clear that the man called to have faith can ask for no credentials, no legitimation, no "testimony" (*martyria*) to the validity of the word of the Revelation.[197]

Jesus cannot legitimate himself, cannot present "testimony" in the sense in which such is demanded by the world. The "Scriptures" do indeed bear witness to Jesus[198] but their meaning has been perverted by "the Jews." [199] God, too, bears him witness.[200] But this witness is not accepted by the world because it does not know God.[201] And how does God bear him witness? Through Jesus' own "works"! [202] But these works, as we have seen, are identical with his word[203]—identical, that is, with his claim to be the Revealer. The testimony, therefore, is identical with that which is to be substantiated! Hence, contradictory statements can stand in the Gospel, one of which says that Jesus does not bear witness to himself[204] and the other that he does.[205] He bears witness to himself with his "It is I." But only by faith is this testimony understood as testimony: "He who accepts his testimony has affixed his seal that God is true." [206] "He who believes in the Son of God has the testimony in himself. He who does not believe God has made him a liar . . . ." [207] The paradox is that the word of Jesus does not find its substantiation by a backward movement from the attesting word to the thing attested—as it might if the thing itself were confirmable

[195] *Theol.* II, pp. 15-32. [199] *Theol.* II, p. 28.   [202] 5:36f.   [205] 8:14, 18.
[196] 9:39.   [200] 5:31f.   [203] *Theol.* II, pp. 60ff. [206] 3:33.
[197] *Theol.* II, p. 45.   [201] 5:37; 7:28; 8:19, 55; 16:3. [204] 5:31ff.   [207] I Jn. 5:10.
[198] 5:39.

irrespective of the word—but finds it only in a faith-prompted acceptance of the word. This is also what is meant by the following saying: "if any man's will is to do his will (i.e. God's), he shall know whether the (i.e. my) teaching is from God or whether I am speaking on my own authority." [208] For "doing the will of God" here is not meant morally, as if the sentence were urging men to begin with ethics and promising that from it an understanding for dogmatics would of itself arise. No, the will of God demands nothing more nor less than faith.[209] Only in faith is the attested matter seen, only in faith is the witness recognized as legitimate. In other words, the object of faith makes itself accessible to nothing but faith. But whoever, having such faith, "has the testimony in himself," thereby has Life itself: "And this is the confirmation: the fact that God gave us eternal life." [210]

Now it also becomes clear that the Revealer is nothing but a definite historical man, Jesus of Nazareth. Why this specific man? That is a question that must not, may not, be answered—for to do so would destroy the offense which belongs ineradicably to the Revelation. This Jesus had to meet men in a definite form, of course, but John confines himself to letting only that about Jesus become visible which was an "offense." If he presupposes that a traditional picture of Jesus and his proclamation lives on in the congregations for which he is writing, he, at any rate, wishes that picture to be understood in the light of his Revelation-idea. That would mean that he sees the meaning of the synoptic message of Jesus to be that ultimately it is the shattering and negating of the "world's" understanding of itself. In any case, he does not consider the task of the Church's proclamation to be the transmitting of the historical tradition about Jesus. The testimony of the Church is the testimony of the Spirit that was given it. The Spirit, as the "other Counselor," is Jesus' substitute.[211] And when the Spirit "reminds" believers of all that Jesus said,[212] this reminding is not an evocation of the past by historical reproduction. Rather, it is that which makes present the eschatological occurrence which with him burst into the world.[213] When it is said that the Spirit "will guide you into the whole truth," [214] that means that the Spirit teaches the believer by the light of this occurrence to understand each particular present hour.[215]

Beyond the mere statement that the Revelation in Jesus took place, is it only by describing it as the "offense," the judgment over the "world," the negation of human self-assertion that anything can be said about that Revelation? There is one way left to try. Since it is to *faith* that it makes itself available as Revelation, the meaning of the Revelation can be further clarified by showing what happens when *faith* takes place.

[208] 7:17.
[209] 6:29.
[210] I Jn. 5:11.

[211] 14:16.
[212] 14:26.
[213] 16:8-11.

[214] 16:13. Blt.
[215] *Theol.* II, pp. 88-91.

11
HERBERT
BRAUN

The Bultmannian school, if it can be spoken of in the singular, harbors more diversity than any other grouping of Protestant theologians; in it one finds positions ranging all the way from an orthodox Lutheranism to a death of God theology. The latter position is represented by Herbert Braun, who incorporates the radical thrust of Bultmann's work while discarding Bultmann's own apparent bondage to much of the traditional language of faith. Like most Bultmannians, Braun is a New Testament scholar, and he has been affected by the currents of modern German theology. We can see the impress of Barth in Braun's belief that atheism is impossible and illusory, even though this belief takes a strange turn indeed in Braun's attempt to consistently follow through Bultmann's program of transforming theological language into anthropological language. Braun is now a center of controversy in Germany, and a leading Barthian theologian, Helmut Gollwitzer, has recently published a book, *The Existence of God as Confessed by Faith,* largely inspired by a polemic against Braun. The following article was published in 1961 in the German journal *Zeitschrift für Theologie und Kirche,* a periodical which has published a great deal of the significant new work coming from the Bultmannian school.

The Problem of a New Testament Theology

Herbert Braun

The problem of a theology of the New Testament has a double aspect. If one takes "theology" in the broader, customary sense he must define the problem in this way: The authors of the New Testament make statements dealing with man's salvation and with his relation to God which cannot be brought into harmony with one another, and which prove by their disparateness that their subject matter is not what they state, *expressis verbis,* in mutual contradiction. On the other hand, if one conceives of theology in the narrower sense—as doctrine concerning the deity—it is clearly seen that the New Testament reckons naively with the existence of a deity, just as do Old Testament and Jewish literature and a good part of Hellenistic literature as well. The New Testament is thus alienated from us who are no longer able to make such a presupposition. Both types of problems hang closely together in point of view of their essence; here, however, they shall be dealt with separately. Only then, in a third section of this essay, can the effort be made to break through this twofold problem.

[1]

The New Testament makes divergent statements about central theological subjects. We shall ponder one after another christology, soteriology, relation to the Torah, eschatology, and doctrine of the sacraments.

(1) The whole New Testament, of course, agrees that Jesus teaches.

FROM "The Problem of a New Testament Theology," translated by Jack Sanders, *The Bultmann School of Biblical Interpretation: New Directions?* edited by Robert W. Funk (New York: Harper & Row, 1965), pp. 169-83. Copyright © 1965 by J. C. B. Mohr (Paul Siebeck), Tübingen, and Harper & Row, Publishers, Incorporated, New York.

The preaching of the Synoptic Jesus[1] (where, I am still convinced, one is more likely to find fragments from the preaching of the historical Jesus) demands from man radical obedience to God and standing up unconditionally for his neighbor. This preacher of unconditional obedience thereby takes sides precisely with the religiously outcast among his contemporaries. The person of this preacher, on the other hand—apart from his demand and apart from his friendship with tax collectors and sinners—appears to have been of no interest during the period of the public ministry. The same would also be true if one wished to suppose that the historical Jesus considered himself to be the Messiah. He evidently did not himself demand such an acknowledgment from those around him. It is with the Easter faith that the earliest community confesses Jesus to be the Messiah who is shortly to come. Christology thus becomes central. Jewish, Hellenistic, and gnostic honorific titles are now applied to Jesus and are recast, step by step, back into Jesus' life. The Fourth Gospel is an end point of such development. Here Jesus speaks exclusively of the necessity of knowing and acknowledging him as the bearer of salvation. It is in keeping with this that the call which the historical Jesus addresses to men is repressed by the growth of christology. The Pauline Christ effects salvation by dying and rising; his exhortation, however, does not play a central role. The Johannine Jesus, finally, does not make a general call for obedience to God's commands and for love of neighbor in general; he calls for acknowledgment of himself. The New Testament picture of Jesus cannot on the surface be reduced to a common denominator.

(2) The New Testament as a whole looks toward the final salvation that man is to gain before God. Man gains this final salvation, according to the preaching of Jesus, through obeying the instruction of Jesus and through allowing, in this obedience, all his claims before God to be shattered. A specific view about Jesus' dignity is not here demanded of the one who obeys. Beginning with the rise of the earliest community, the Yes to Jesus as the bringer of salvation serves as the condition for the attaining of salvation. This Yes simply goes alongside the demanded ethos, without an organic bond being established between the Yes to the bringer of salvation and the ethos that is demanded. This is the case in parts of the Catholic Epistles, and also in Acts. The Yes to Jesus as the bringer of salvation can, however, also be interpreted in a very sharply defined way: as renunciation of fame; as being sustained by God's miraculous action (*pneuma*), out of which the responsibility for right conduct grows (so Paul); as Yes to the true reality, measured by which what is materially or religiously pregiven becomes unreal, Yes to the reality in which the obedient one first learns the proper understanding of himself (so John). In the Synoptic pattern, the problem of gaining final salvation is indeed sighted, but the final

---

[1] The Synoptic Jesus refers to Jesus as portrayed in the synoptic or first three gospels of the New Testament—T. J. J. A.

salvation is considered to be endangered by the disobedience of man; the obedient one, on the other hand, will be saved. There is no mention yet of a *christological* overcoming of this danger. The naive juxtaposition of christology and conduct signals, to be sure, the basic impossibility of man's gaining salvation, but does not make this impossibility very evident. Paul and John, on the other hand, underscore salvation as a human impossibility. Here Christ becomes the cipher for the organic abrogation of this impossibility by means of the divine miracle. The soteriological question, viewed from the surface, does not receive an unequivocal answer in the New Testament.

(3) The same is true of the relation of the New Testament to the Torah, to the law of the Old Testament and Judaism. Various aspects come into play here, and we must consider them one after the other. There is first the question of the content of the specific instructions. As the Synoptics show, Jesus basically viewed the contents of the Torah as entirely binding. Jesus even sharpened the Torah. Existence for one's neighbor is meant more seriously than the contemporary interpretation of the Torah and even the wording of the Torah itself advise. It is precisely the radicalizing of the Torah which leads, of course, to its concrete breakup. Cultic purity is made altogether unimportant by Jesus. He appears to have broken the Sabbath provocatively by his healings. This concrete freedom over against the Torah does not remove for Jesus, however, the basic Yes to the contents of the Torah. Whoever keeps the Ten Commandments will obtain life. This attitude, which is in itself not unequivocal, is now subsequently modified. A severely Jewish-Christian point of view sees in Jesus the one who requires observance of the Torah to the last letter.[2] Jewish food and marriage laws even become important in certain circles of Hellenistic Christianity.[3] Other circles of Hellenistic Christianity display a certain freedom, but also a conscientious obligation to the food laws,[4] whose content, however, is now mixed with aspects of Hellenistic oriental asceticism. In the post-Pauline period (John, James, the Pastoral Epistles) the ritual content of the Torah has become irrelevant. Only the command of love and its concrete, paraenetic application were held onto through the whole development covering the period of the composition of the New Testament writings.

From the question concerning the content of the Torah is to be separated the question concerning the Torah as the way of salvation. In this regard, Jesus does not dispute the basic statement that right doing results in life. To be sure, he seems to see that precisely the obedience of the Torah can become spiritually dangerous for man. Thus, the son of Luke 15 who behaves legally is the one who is really lost, and the calculating claim of the twelve-hour workers misunderstands God's goodness that gives sovereignly.[5] But neither with Jesus nor with the earliest community does that

[2] Mt. 5:17-19.
[3] Acts 15: 28f.

[4] I Cor. 8:10; Rom. 14, 15.
[5] Mt. 20.

lead to a fundamental renunciation of the Torah as way of salvation. That occurs first with Paul. Here the Torah as way of salvation is forbidden because it necessarily leads man into self-praise. This wrong way is inherent, according to Paul, in every legal way. Thus the non-Jew also has an ethical observance similar to the Torah, and boasting in it too must be excluded by faith. Law may not be used as a way of salvation. From here derive the harsh words that the Torah comes from the demons.[6]

This extreme position, faith or (exclusively) legal works as way of salvation, is soon given up. The Deutero-Pauline and Pastoral Epistles still reproduce the formulas; but the emphasis now lies on faith as the way of salvation, while the warding off of the legal way becomes irrelevant. The law is considered now as an unbearable yoke,[7] no longer as a dangerous inducement to self-praise. One sees only its ethical contents, purified of ritual observances. Thus there comes into use the slogan, considered to be Pauline, "Law and Faith." [8] There are even whole bodies of literature that are no longer interested at all in the question of the Torah as way of salvation (Johannine literature, Catholic Epistles).

Even where the New Testament understands the law as oracular text which looks forward to the messianic period and the Messiah and thus confirms the present Christ event—and hence ignoring the demands of its contents, ignoring its use as a means of attaining salvation—even there no unanimity prevails. The Old Testament and the Torah, to be sure, are cited throughout the New Testament as authority. But the use of this authority is of quite varying intensity. Alongside of Paul, Hebrews, and Matthew, with their repeated scriptural proofs, stands the more cautious use of the Old Testament in John, in the Pastoral Epistles with their quotations (*pistos ho logos*) of *Christian* formulations, and in Acts, where partly formulated *topoi* of the diatribe are used alongside the Old Testament.

The attitude of the New Testament to the Torah is an oscillating color chart.

(4) The movement around Jesus is rooted in Jewish apocalypticism. Like the Qumran community,[9] Jesus expected the end of the world as being very near. Resurrection of the dead and general judgment are essential pieces of this expected final drama. Jesus' exorcisms signalize the immediate nearness of the moment in which God will begin his reign, and Jesus' preaching wishes to prepare the hearer for the proper endurance of the threatening judgment. Since with the Easter faith Jesus is considered to be the Messiah, this belief in the near end is preserved both in the earliest Jewish-Christian community and in the Hellenistic community. Now, however, it is Jesus' coming as Messiah that lies ahead. His earthly life likewise receives in retrospect, at first by degrees, a messianic character. Thus

---

[6] Gal. 3, 4.   [7] Acts 15:10.
[8] Acts 13:38f.; James 2; cf. I Clem. 31:2.
[9] Commonly identified as the Essenes, who produced the Dead Sea Scrolls—T. J. J. A.

Paul[10] and his congregations[11] still expect the parousia in their lifetime, even though they now consider the final salvation as present and, accordingly, the present time as end time.

This expectation is given up in the rest of the New Testament in a double way. First, the date of the parousia is extended. This occurs in a hesitant way in Mark and Matthew (some will experience the end, Mk. 9:1); more decidedly with the third evangelist (for whom the Son of Man sits at the right hand, without saying about his coming within the limits of time; Lk. 22:69 compared with the parallels), for whom the apostolic age has become historical; in II Thessalonians ("the day of the Lord is at hand" is a false slogan); and in II Peter 3 ("a thousand years as one day"). Alongside this way of extending the date stands the resolute absorption of the end into the present in such a way that the temporal future falls out, and judgment, life, and resurrection occur in the present stance of the hearer toward the message of Jesus. That is the way in which the Fourth Gospel interprets eschatology. This consistent eschatologizing of the present which renounces the temporal future did not succeed, however. Some glosses reintroduce the temporal future into the Fourth Gospel, and now make it just barely possible to understand the Johannine text in the sense of the extended eschatology. The eschatological views of the New Testament are, in any case, full of strong tensions.

(5) For the entire development of the history of dogma and of piety during the first Christian centuries, it is no doubt valid to say that the intensifying of what is sacramental corresponds to the subsiding of the eschatological tension. In the New Testament itself, to be sure, imminent eschatology and sacrament still overlap at least partially. Jesus let himself be baptized with the baptism of John as though it were the eschatological sign, and it is possible that he himself baptized. We possess, however, no word from him which indicates to what extent the baptism of John was meaningful for him or for his adherents. Baptism in the name of Jesus is then practiced in the earliest community as placing one under Jesus' protection, as cleansing from previous sins, and, perhaps not immediately from the beginning, as bestowing the spirit—that is, placing one under God's action upon man to effect his final salvation. The Hellenistic community interpreted baptism, furthermore, in analogy to the mysteries as the *neophytes* taking part in the fate of the cult hero. Paul, to be sure, then applies the brake to the aspect of pure naturalism connected with this view in order to emphasize the character of the new life as obligation. He does this without breaking through the frame of nature categories in his own thinking, not to speak of later theology. The sacrament is there.

Something similar holds true for the Lord's Supper. I am still unable, in spite of attempts to link Qumran to the Lord's Supper, to regard Mark 14

---

[10] Rom. 13:11; Phil. 4:5.   [11] I Thess. 4.

and parallels even partially as an authentic report of the Last Supper. I consider rather that the tradition about the *last* Supper, together with the words of institution, is of Hellenistic origin. But even if the saying about the bread, for example, were authentic, precisely Qumran would show that the eschatological meal is no more a sacrament than the regular meal of the daily breaking of bread in Acts is sacrament. Here also that which is really sacramental begins with the Hellenistic community. In this community, participation in the elements means taking part in the blood and body of Christ, and an improper use of this holy matter brings about, so one supposes, illness and death, i.e. the opposite of *the* life which is expected from the sacrament. Paul can use these magical trains of thought; he merely stresses that the sacrament does not produce life if one's conduct is bad. A massive, sacramental doctrine of the Lord's Supper is unorganically inserted into the Fourth Gospel. There thus follows upon the unsacramental attitude of the Jewish Christian beginning a more or less marked sacramentalizing on the soil of Hellenistic Christianity. In keeping with this the cult in which the Jewish Christian community at first also took part—the Temple and sacrificial cult in Jerusalem—becomes unimportant for the further development on the way into the Hellenistic world; it makes room for a Hellenistic Christian cult. Thus, alongside the Jewish calendar of festivals still used in Acts, there comes in the *hemera kyrion,* the first day of the week, which is influenced by Hellenistic oriental religion.

The New Testament does not have a uniform doctrine of sacrament and cult.

[2]

We escape the perplexity and the problems indicated by this disparateness of New Testament theological views too cheaply and too simply if we merely state that these differences must be neutralized in a higher unity. This is certainly the case. But we must be cautious lest we locate the point of coincidence, the higher unity, as too close at hand, shortsightedly and over-hastily. To this end, a deepening of the problems just pointed out is required.

The situation with regard to the disparate standpoints which are advocated in the New Testament is by no means such that we should simply have to choose between the two or more advocated positions and should in this choice have to decide for one of them. Each of the positions, including the point of departure of the whole, i.e. that which can be made out about the views of Jesus of Nazareth, appears in problematical light and brings up a number of questions which we ought not to suppress if we are interested in finding out what the statements of the New Testament may have to say to us today. I shall now discuss such questions in the same order as the five groups of theological statements dealt with above.

(1) All the designations of dignity which the community applied to Jesus in confessions—Messiah, Son of Man, Kyrios, Soter, Logos—fit for the Jew of that time as well as for the religious person in Hellenism into a firmly outlined system of coordinates. That there is such a figure as the Messiah or the Kyrios is beyond discussion for the man of that time; it is rather an obvious presupposition everywhere. This prerequisite which the man of antiquity meets in his religious world view without being expressly conscious of it is not diminished in its character as prerequisite by the fact that the contents of these titles are modified by what the community brings in as peculiar and independent, e.g. the Messiah dies as the atoner, something which is not originally contained in the concept of the Messiah. We today with our world view are not able to meet this prerequisite, namely that there is a Messiah, a Kyrios. Thus, the New Testament question, "Do you hold Jesus to be the Messiah, to be the Kyrios?" becomes a problem for us in the sense that neither our Yes nor our No can have as an answer the meaning which is, on the surface, attached to it in the New Testament.

(2) Final salvation is gained, according to the assertion of the New Testament, through an obedience which makes no claim before God, or through belief in Jesus. Let us put aside for the present the christological side of the problem. Final salvation is conceived either in a Jewish way, as life free from toil upon the renewed earth, or dualistically, as an unearthly, otherworldly condition in the place where God and the heavenly beings are. Both ways of thinking are foreign to us. One should not object that their foreignness is merely a question of a different way of viewing things. Such a prolonged earthly-thisworldly or heavenly-otherworldly form of what we here call life is in its naiveté neither believable for us nor worth striving for. Final salvation as an extension of life or living on upon an otherworldly plane, which is in the final analysis again thought of as thisworldly, is problematical for us.

(3) The colored scale which is reproduced above of New Testament attitudes toward the Torah is governed by a pervading presupposition. That is, that God has decreed binding orders which man is to accept. This acceptance occurs first naively and heteronomously. Old instructions, to be sure, are broken through and replaced by new contents; the Jewish ritual elements as divinely willed content gradually vanish from the New Testament. Such vanishing is again, however, at least as it looks on the surface, legitimized by a heteronomous authority. Authentic sayings of Jesus or sayings of the exalted one in the mouth of the apostles now give the modified order. Casuistry, which lays down God's will precisely, is lacking, to be sure, in the oldest layer with Jesus himself. But the on-going paraenesis of the community in the form of secondary sayings of Jesus, the concrete admonitions of Paul in spite of the ground rule that it is love which fulfills the law—all make clear that the theonomy as heteronomy is not fundamentally overcome. Even Paul's replacing of the law as way of salvation with

faith, even the proclamation that everything that does not proceed from faith is sin,[12] does not change the fact that the orders given by God stand firm with regard to content. The law is holy and the commandment is holy, right, and good. The dulling, following upon Paul, of the exclusive antithesis between legal works and faith is the very return to the heteronomy of the content imposed by God upon man. Precisely this presupposition, however, that God has proclaimed in an authoritarian way instructions of a definite content which are therefore, i.e. heteronomously, binding, is not within our reach and is unattainable in its naive heteronomy. Thus we are also able to grasp the oracular character of the Torah only as a phenomenon of the history of religion; for the concept of God which lies behind it (that there are holy texts full of profound divine meaning) is unattainable for us.

(4) Of the three forms of New Testament eschatology the oldest, the consistent imminent expectation, is obviously an error and is accordingly, for all practical purposes, no longer advocated today at all—irrespective of peripheral instances in Christianity. The form of extending the time limit, on the other hand, which dominates in the later New Testament and which also overlies the original form of the Gospel of John, still has numerous advocates. This is due to the fact that we do not make clear to ourselves what kind of a concept of God is active in each temporal conception of eschatology, be it near expectation or extended eschatology. It is the deity existing in itself, which directs the course of history, which establishes beginning and end. Is God not here, however, naively taken as given? And is it not this naive acquiescence which brings it about that the hearer plunges into the desperate adventure—desperate in terms of our world view—of extending the time limit, after the near expectation has proved to be error? The genuine Johannine renunciation of the temporal future of the final drama is, to be sure, not affected by this reproach. And yet it is difficult to see how it is fitting to call the eschatological terms now actualized in John—judgment, life, resurrection, damnation—eschatology. They are called that in the Fourth Gospel with the historical justification that they originated in the discussion with the temporal eschatology of that day. But precisely this presupposition is not valid for us when we read the Fourth Gospel. The interpretation of temporal eschatology which the Fourth Gospel undertakes is for us merely beating the air.

(5) There is no doubt that Paul resists the materializing of salvation; baptism and Lord's Supper offer no guaranty of salvation. But this resistance occurs nevertheless against the background of a basic Yes, which is able to acknowledge that baptism incorporates one into the *soma* of Christ, that chalice and bread unite with Christ's blood and body. Salvation is

[12] Rom. 14:23.

palpable; the sacrament attaches the receiver to the sphere of the deity. But even the old regular meal, in which the near final salvation is anticipated with rejoicing, as well as baptism understood unmysteriously, which takes away previous sins in view of the near judgment, even these older, not specifically sacramental concepts remain within the sphere of a way of thinking in which the coming of the deity is taken temporally and objectively—that is, in the area of a naive concept of God.

If one takes all these aspects of the deepened problems together, one arrives at the following statement. Each of the groups of concepts which has been mentioned has a considerable sector within which an objectifying thinking takes place which, in its statements concerning the deity, disregards man. The world of God is thought here to be a reality existing in itself, in a definite place, present or to be present at a definite time. Thus God too is, in this view, a quantity existing in and for himself. Here faith means to reckon with the fact that God *exists* and rewards those who seek him.[13] And this prerequisite which man meets reigns to a great extent in the New Testament. For this God who exists in himself makes his will public, which is then to be accepted by man heteronomously. He sets up the variously named bringer of salvation; he prepares the final salvation in his world; he establishes the moments and the end of the course of time; he, with his transcendent world, becomes concretely palpable in the sacrament. To realize all this means at the same time to recognize the impossibility of this view and of this concept of God.

[3]

The New Testament itself, of course, has enough statements on the basis of which even this, its own conception, is broken open. Thus we stand now before the final step, in which an effort will be made to overcome the problems which have been presented up to now. One should be able to break through these problems of New Testament theologizing, previously set out, in such a way that he overcomes the disparateness of New Testament statements with the same step that also leaves behind the objectifying thinking about God and his world permeating the New Testament. We shall now attempt to think through again, from this point of view, the five groups of New Testament statements we have been dealing with.

(1) We recognized that, upon an old nonchristological stage, the life of Jesus, there follows, after the formation of the community, the christological epoch. In this epoch the meaningfuless of Jesus is expressed with

[13] Heb. 11:6.

Jewish, then with Hellenistic titles, in the form of the Easter faith, which itself often varies in individual details. The old stage, the preaching Jesus, puts man under radical obligation ("Why do you call me 'Lord, Lord,' and do not do what I tell you?" Lk. 6:46) and brings him under the sovereignly giving God ("Do you begrudge my generosity?" Mt. 20:15). Precisely this, however, is also the meaning of the explicit Pauline christology. Faith in Jesus means to renounce boasting[14] to obey the God who gives and commands ("You present yourselves as slaves to obedience," Rom. 6:16). With John, however, faith knows that man can truly live only by the miracle of the radical renewing of existence, the new birth;[15] the new birth is attached to man's experiencing the critical love that uncovers him.[16] In the last analysis, the prechristological and the christological epochs are one in the interrelationship of "I may" and "I ought." The "I may" is obviously attached in the beginning of the whole development to an experience that men had in encounter with Jesus of Nazareth. Where this "I may" and "I ought" again become event—in the community by means of the proclamation—there is Jesus; Jesus now, to be sure, in christologized form, now as Christ, as Kyrios. Jesus is therefore not simply there—the Messiah, Kyrios is not simply there—although this naive givenness, this naive objectivity is not excluded in the New Testament. The fact of a prechristological *and* a christological stage in the New Testament, and again the disparateness of the statements even within the christological stage show rather that Jesus always occurs in my "I may" and "I ought"—in the realm of the relation with one's fellow man. And such occurrence breaks down the objectivity of the given.

(2) We recognized that the preaching of Jesus demands obedience and renunciation of any claim before God as a way to final salvation, and that the preaching of the community and of the apostles demands faith in Jesus and right conduct. Faith and conduct can thereby stand unorganically alongside each other; they can also, however, be organically combined. Insofar as faith in Jesus and conduct stand unorganically alongside each other, Jesus becomes—contrary to the proper sense of christology just explicated—an object, and christology becomes naive, more or less massive metaphysics. Where, however, conduct arises from the "I may" as something experienced, or in christological terms from faith in Jesus, there Jesus is understood as "I may" and "I ought," there he is an event analogous to what occurred historically with regard to Jesus of Nazareth. To that extent the New Testament soteriological teaching is, however, *in the last analysis* uniform if one has in view the interpreted version of Christology. Only where Christology stands uninterpreted *alongside* conduct, would one have to speak of two ways of salvation within the New Testament: Of obedience and renunciation of all claims in the teaching of the

---

[14] Rom. 3:27.   [15] 3:5.   [16] 3:16-21.

Synoptic Jesus on one hand, and on the other hand the combination of faith in Jesus and conduct, in the texts which have an uninterpreted christology. In the latter, final salvation would then also have no inner connection with the way of salvation.

For we further recognized that the New Testament understands the final salvation to a considerable extent naively as thisworldly, prolonged life or as continued life upon an otherworldly plane, which is in the last analysis, however, also thought of in thisworldly terms. Now, beside this naiveté which is foreign to us today, we find precisely in the texts that do not show the naive coexistence of faith in Jesus and conduct just discussed —i.e. in some Synoptic, Pauline, and Johannine sayings—a way of viewing things for which final salvation and the way of salvation hang together in an organic and suitable way. This way of viewing things does not oppose the naive, metaphysical expression of final salvation *explicitly*. The breaking up of the naive lengthening of life or continuation of life ensues instead as a natural consequence, from the logic of the subject matter, when e.g. according to Jesus the obedient one is only like a slave who is never entitled to recompense for his fulfilling of his obligation;[17] when the reward that Paul expects consists in his preaching without remuneration;[18] or when life according to John is not something that is coming, but something that the one who believes in Jesus has, i.e. deciphered, the one who allows his worldly and religious standards to be shattered.[19] Thus final salvation is brought down from the heights of a metaphysical so-called world of God onto the profane floor of the true relation with one's fellow man. *Here* then might the salvation of God be found. This is of course, as has been said, a consequence—a justified consequence, to be sure—alongside of which final salvation conceived in a naively objective way continues to exist in the New Testament.

(3) We recognized that the contents of the New Testament instruction fluctuate because the ritual element of the Torah slowly retreats into the background and finally disappears, having become irrelevant, while the command of love holds throughout the entire New Testament. This clear tune at the basis of all variations of paraenesis is particularly underscored in its unity—a unity that holds everything together—in that love toward God is interpreted as love toward one's neighbor. The help and kindness demonstrated or not demonstrated to the oppressed neighbor is in fact demonstrated or not demonstrated to Jesus.[20] *Agape* for Paul is directed toward the neighbor.[21] Love toward God is actualized concretely in the demonstration of love toward one's neighbor.[22] The true relation with one's fellow man is *the* often varied content of New Testament instruction. Thus the paraenetic materials of the diatribe appear alongside the Torah, whose ritual content one soon no longer accepts as source of command. The

[17] Lk. 17:7-10.
[18] I Cor. 9:18.
[19] Jn. 17:3; 9:39.
[20] Mt. 25:31ff.
[21] I Cor. 13.
[22] I Jn. 4:20.

paraenetic materials have in certain circumstances passed through the filter of Hellenistic Judaism, which had already used these contents in its own service. Thus there is present here a far-reaching unity in the New Testament. The problems set in with the question of the basis. I do not mean now the basis of conduct, of the "I ought" in the nonchristological or christologically coded "I may," which we have just considered in the passage on soteriology. Rather we wish to investigate who gives the authorized contents of the instruction—the previous contents, the contents radicalized by Jesus, those deritualized more and more strongly by Jesus and the later development.

We recognized above that God is widely understood as the giver of the Torah; then it is Jesus and the Spirit speaking in the apostle that are the stages which legitimize the radicalizing and the deritualizing. Theonomy is therefore widely taken as heteronomy. Now the New Testament *also,* to be sure, makes considerable beginnings which break through this heteronomy. Man is lord of the cultic day,[23] which is subordinated to man.[24] This is perhaps an authentic saying of the Lord and not a christologizing saying formed by the community. What defiles comes not from without, but from the heart.[25] Such words of Jesus certainly do not mean that their contents are valid because of Jesus' authority; rather they count on the conscientious Yes of the hearer simply on the basis of their content. In fact, therefore, we have theonomy as autonomy, not as heteronomy. Thus Paul too is of the opinion that the pagan knows about the proper norm[26] and is therefore, just as the Jewish student of the Torah, properly informed. Thus Paul renounces casuistry and binds the norm for right doing to the conscience of the believer.[27] The reflection of the believer upon what is right to do in the given case is meaningful.[28] With John, the unquestionable certainty of believing existence is promised to the believer.[29] All that means that it is not God or Jesus as outside authority who legitimizes, heteronomously, the content of an order. Rather it must read the other way; to be able to act in this way or that with a conviction, with confidence, conscientiously, means to act upon God's order, according to God. Theonomy and autonomy coincide. God is thus the expression for the phenomenon of being able to act conscientiously, confidently, and with conviction. Of course, as has been said, these are only beginnings. They are not thought through in the New Testament. The New Testament as a whole is ambivalent at this point, and herein lie its inner problems.

The ground for this ambivalence becomes clear when we remember that the spiritual danger of the Torah as the way to salvation, and thus the Pauline exclusiveness of faith or works, is not at all unanimously accepted

[23] Sabbath-Day—T. J. J. A.
[24] Mk. 2:27-28.
[25] Mk. 7:15.
[26] Rom. 2:14.

[27] Rom. 14:23.
[28] Phil. 4:8-9.
[29] Jn. 16:23.

in the New Testament. There is also in the New Testament a soteriology in which uninterpreted faith in Jesus and conduct stand unorganically alongside one another. Precisely in the non-Pauline and non-Johannine passages with an uninterpreted christology the "I ought" does not grow organically from the "I may." If then even Paul, who relates conduct strictly to salvation and leaves the knowledge of the norm to the conscience of the believer,[30] designates the content of the law as holy and good[31] and consequently still remains bound to the theonomous heteronomy, how could this heteronomy not become completely active at those points in the New Testament where, contemporary with and after Paul, faith in Jesus and conduct stand again unconnectedly alongside one another? The measure in which theonomy becomes autonomy or heteronomy in the New Testament therefore corresponds to the interpreted or uninterpreted christology and to the available or not available interrelatedness of faith and works.

The Torah as prophetic text is widely used in the New Testament, but in subsiding intensity, as we established. Christian and also profane quotations take the place of the Torah. The concept of God connected to this view, however, that God speaks full of profound meaning in holy texts, is foreign to us. But this static concept of God is nevertheless broken through, at least to the extent that it is now assumed that even people outside the Old Testament know something of the proper meaning of faith. Theonomy, in this widening of the quoted texts to include profane writings, is at least faintly perceived as human autonomy.

(4) We recognized that the imminent eschatology is an error of the first generation, which the prolonged eschatology seeks to correct in an inconsistent and implausible way, while both forms presuppose the deity existing in itself and appointing beginning and end. The intention of these eschatological statements however, as it imposes itself upon us, becomes comprehensible when one lets go of the conception of the deity existing in itself and of the conception of the temporal periods fixed by this deity. Precisely the near expectation conceals, in the lap of this objectifying thinking, something which in fact breaks through all these objectivisms. For the man of the near expectation is *now* to repent,[32] *now* to treat properly his fellow human beings entrusted to him,[33] *now* to build the house with right conduct upon the rock instead of sand [34] *now* to watch.[35] Here in the near expectation it is not therefore a matter, properly understood, of the calculating of an objective course of time which an objective deity fixed; here it is a matter of perceiving the proper *kairos*.[36] *Kairos*, to be sure, not understood in the sense of the imminent end taken literally, not in the sense

---

[30] Rom. 14: 23.
[31] Rom. 7:12.
[32] Mk. 1:15.
[33] Mt. 24:43-51 and parallels.

[34] Mt. 7:24-27.
[35] I Thess. 5:1-11.
[36] Rom. 13:11.

of the calculation which all too obviously has been proved to be a miscalculation. Rather imminent eschatology signalizes the filledness, the irretrievable once-and-for-all-ness, and the inevitable urgency of my being addressed, challenged, and sustained in the sense of final validity. Thus extended eschatology would be proved to be precisely a pronounced misinterpretation of imminent eschatology, by the fact that it takes the temporal character of near eschatology, its objectifying scheme, seriously, and disregards what is really intended in imminent eschatology, the urgency of the now. What is really intended does become active in John in an excellent way—but only as interpretation of the *topoi* of the apocalyptic world view that is lost to us. Imminent eschatology, however, properly understood, leads us to the decision here and now—*hic Rhodos, hic salta*. God would then be where the moment is received and lived in its filledness.

(5) We recognized that a sacramental, material thinking with regard to baptism and the Lord's Supper grew up in the New Testament out of older, not specifically sacramental ideas in the course of the development of the first and second generations. Presacramental and sacramental stages, however, take the presence of the deity, either expected or believed at hand, objectively and materially. Now this objective thinking, as had also become clear to us, is not at all the only dominant way of thinking. Jesus let himself be baptized and perhaps himself baptized; but from none of his words can we infer that baptism as such possessed central significance for him and his. What is now stressed in the Christian presentation of the Baptist will have also been Jesus' opinion. Repentance cannot be ritually compensated for by baptism;[37] the Yes to the baptism of John presupposes obedience to the Baptist's preaching.[38] And with Paul the life mediated in baptism and in the Lord's Supper is not primarily a gift (*Gabe*); it is rather at the same moment a task (*Aufgabe*) to be carried out in one's conduct.[39] The Fourth Gospel mentions baptismal water when speaking of the new birth that establishes Christian existence only *en passant,* if the mention belongs to the original text at all. Over against this, the miracle of God and the descent and ascent of Jesus the Son of Man stand in a central position.[40] Briefly, the palpable character of participation in salvation is broken through in the New Testament in many places; God is understood not as a holy given, but in the system of the coordinates "I may" and "I ought." The ambiguity, the ambivalence of the New Testament teaching regarding the sacrament is certainly to be conceded. It is an act of venturous interpretation when we state that the sacramentalizing which is indeed noticeable in the New Testament opposes the personal "I may" and "I ought," opposes the nonobjective concept of God in which the New Testament, according to its own statements, is so decisively interested.

We stand at the end and draw the conclusion. The New Testament con-

[37] Mt. 3:7-10.
[38] Mk. 11:30-31.
[39] Rom. 6:4; I Cor. 10:1-13.
[40] Jn. 3:5-13.

ceals within itself disparate ideas; we have made them clear for ourselves in terms of christology, soteriology, attitude toward the Torah, eschatology, and doctrine of the sacraments. These diversities refer, for their part, to a still deeper problem within the New Testament statements, God as palpable and given and God as not palpable and not given. What is finally God in the New Testament sense? Here the knot of the several problems is tied, and here the breakthrough of the problems, which we attempted in this last part, must prove successful. That God and his world are *also* considered as object, as thing, in the New Testament cannot be disputed. We think we have pointed out, however, in the case of the five areas mentioned, that such objectifying does not correspond to the real trend of the New Testament. As what, however, would God then be understood?

At any rate, God would not be understood as the one existing for himself, as a species which would only be comprehensible under this word. God then means much rather the whence of my being agitated. My being agitated, however, is determined by the "I may" and "I ought"; determined by being taken care of and by obligation. Being taken care of and obligation, however, do not approach me from the universe, but from another, from my fellow man. The word of proclamation and the act of love reach me—if they really do reach me—from my fellow man. God is the whence of my being taken care of and of my being obliged, which comes to me from my fellow man. To abide in God would therefore mean to abide in the concrete act of devoting oneself to the other; whoever abides in *agapan* abides in God.[41] I can speak of God only where I speak of man, and hence anthropologically. I can speak of God only where my "I ought" is counterpointed by "I may," and hence soteriologically. For even according to the New Testament, God in the final analysis, i.e. the inadequate objectifying of the doctrine of God set aside, is where I am placed under obligation, where I am engaged; engaged in unconditional "I may" and "I ought." That would mean then, however, that man as man, man in relation with his fellow man, implies God. That would always have to be discovered anew from the New Testament. God would then be a definite type of relation with one's fellow man. The atheist misses *man*. One may even ask, Is there really such a thing as an atheist? For does not every instance of a relation with one's fellow man already contain something of the intimate connection between the "I may" and "I ought" that is so close to the heart of the New Testament?

[41] I Jn. 4:16.

Part
Three

**THE DEATH
OF GOD
THEOLOGY
IN AMERICA**

12
JACOB
TAUBES

In the ten-year period following the Second World War American Protestant theology was primarily if not entirely devoted to the final phase of assimilating and recreating in an American context the major achievements of German theology between the two world wars. Toward the end of this period, however, rumbles of a new and disturbing nature began to shake the theological world. The new orthodoxy, as established by Barth, had been grounded in a presumed autonomy of faith wherein the reality and truth of faith are in no way whatsoever affected either by interior experience or by the changing currents of consciousness and society. This stance, provoked in part by the collapse of European Christendom which was already manifest in 1914, had never seriously influenced American theology. Indeed, it was not until after the Second World War that American theology became open to the historical or cultural reality of the death of God. Jacob Taubes, a European-Israeli theologian who is now a professor of religion at Columbia University, most forcefully posed the dilemma deriving from the coming together of a world in which God is dead with a theology affirming the gracious sovereignty of God. Taubes's essays of the mid-fifties became almost a sacred text to many younger theologians who were being drawn in a radical direction by the very problem which lies at the center of these essays. The selection which follows is one of these essays; neither Tillich nor any of his defenders replied to Taubes's critique, and it was just this kind of silence which seemed to witness the end of a theological era.

On the Nature of the Theological Method:

*Jacob
Taubes*

Some Reflections on the Methodological Principles of Tillich's Theology

[1]

The term *theology* occurs for the first time in Plato's critique of Homeric religion, and ever since Plato's critique theology signals a crisis in religion. The hour of theology is come when a mythical configuration breaks down and its symbols that are congealed in a canon come into conflict with a new stage of man's consciousness. When the symbols coined to express man's encounter with the divine at a unique moment of history no longer coincide with his experience, theology tries to interpret the original symbols in order to integrate them within the context of the new situation: what was present in the myth is then only "re-presented" in the theological interpretation.

Theological reflection transforms both the original symbols of the canon and man's consciousness by establishing an equilibrium between them. No human situation is given in absolute nakedness. Only through the symbols of language, through the logos, can man orient himself in his surroundings. The symbols demarcate his horizon and govern, as long as they are meaningful, his thought and action. Theology thus recasts man's horizon by interpreting his situation in terms of the canonic symbols, and acts at once as a conserving and as a catalytic force. As apologetics it tries to preserve the original symbols, but, by transferring the symbols of the canon to a changed situation, theology functions catalytically in the birth of a new symbolism. Therefore the task of theology may be described as a dialectic of "perseverance in changing." The equilibrium between symbol and situation is rarely achieved and never more than temporarily. The symbols have their life-cycle in the course of theological interpretation and die when theology can no longer translate them into the temporal situation.

Almost from the very beginning of its history the Christian community sought the services of theology, so that the Christian canonic scriptures not only present a body of original symbols but already represent different stages of theological interpretation. Therefore some could assume that the Christian religion had a specific affinity to theological interpretation and that theology is the legitimate successor of revelation. I do not think that such an interpretation does justice to the beginnings of theology in the Christian religion. Christianity had to make use of theological interpretation already in its earliest stages because its symbols of faith expressing the expectations of the first generation conflicted very early with the actual situation of the community. For the Christian community was thrown into history against her expectations and against her will, and the hiatus between the eschatological symbols of faith and man's continuing existence in history is as old as the history of the Christian church.

The function of theology in the Christian church remained the same throughout its history. Theology continually transformed the eschatological symbols to an ever-changing historical situation and carried through this transformation with the help of the Platonic and, later, of the Aristotelian philosophy, turning the eschatological symbols into ontological symbols. Without this perpetual act of transformation the Christian community would have degenerated into a "narrow and superstitious" sect and the general culture would have bypassed this community without taking notice of it. But no religion can have the luxury of theology without paying a price for it. Secularization is the price the Christian community had to pay for its development from an adventistic sect to a universal church, and the history of theology is the spiritual account of this price. It would be iconoclastic to deny to a community any right of development, to outlaw all transformation, to declare all commentary as fake, and to argue that only the text is valid. It would be idolatrous, however, to overlook the perennial conflict between text and commentary and to fail to emphasize that the canonic text is "broken" through the prism of interpretation. The history of the development of Christian theology is a tragic history because there is no "solution" to the conflict between eschatological symbols and the brute fact of a continuing history. One may admire the achievement of theology but at the same time be aware of the price involved in such an achievement.

But a situation can arise which makes it impossible for theology to fulfill its task of interpretation. Christian theology, like all theology bound to a canonic text, uses the method of allegorical interpretation and does so by necessity. The entire history of theological interpretation is a running commentary to the original text. But what if the very method of allegorical interpretation becomes suspect? Is a theological exegesis of a Holy Writ possible together with a historical analysis of the text? Does not historical interpretation qua method imply a criticism of all theological exegesis? Whereas theological exegesis must "transfer"—this is the original meaning of translation—the original symbols by the method of allegorical interpretation into a given situation, the historical analysis interprets the text, the canonic symbols, in their original historical context.

In the nineteenth century the historical criticism of religion reached its height. The nineteenth century was a period of Old and New Testament criticism, it was the century of *Leben-Jesu-Forschung*,[1] it was the century of the history of dogma. It remained obscure, however, to most historians, why they were driven into this tempest of historical inquiry. Ferdinand Christian Baur[2] wrote his classical history of dogma under the Hegelian assumption that this development had come to an end. Even if Harnack did not subscribe to the speculative assumptions of the Tübingen school,[3] he nevertheless arrived at the same conclusion when he, the historian of Christian theology, pressed the "essence" of Christianity into a "religion of Jesus," discarding all Christological doctrines as dead weight. It was Nietzsche who discovered (what Hegel and his pupils may have known but did not admit) the driving force behind the passion of historical research: the death of the Christian God. Historical research, Nietzsche observed, works only as a post mortem, dissecting the body for the sake of anatomical study and writing an obituary.

After the first World War, however, a new generation of Christian theologians arose that experienced the catastrophe of war in terms of eschatological symbols. The apocalyptic symbols of the New Testament, symbols that had been the stumbling block for theology throughout the entire history of the Christian church, suddenly spoke with an immediacy and self-evidence that needed no further interpretation. No allegorical translation seemed necessary, for only apocalyptic symbols could express the actual situation. With the first World War a "world" broke into pieces. Man experienced himself as estranged in his social and cosmic setting and did not feel at home in a world he had so painstakingly cultivated to make his own. When the façades of culture and civilization crumbled under the impact of the first World War man was confronted with the realities of life: hunger, destitution, and death. I do not minimize the significance of dialectical theology when I suggest that the situation of the twenties

[1] Quest for the historical Jesus—T. J. J. A.
[2] A nineteenth-century German Protestant theologian—T. J. J. A.
[3] A nineteenth-century German Protestant Hegelian school—T. J. J. A.

was catalytic for its development, for a theology is significant only when it responds to a concrete situation.

Karl Barth's commentary on Paul's Epistle to the Romans marks the birth of dialectical theology after the verdict of death had been announced by Nietzsche in the nineteenth century. His commentary is a powerful and penetrating analysis of man's situation and gave voice to man's self-estrangement long before philosophy had taken notice of it. The divine and the human were put in antithesis and any attempt to approach the divine was unmasked as human *hubris* and illusion. Karl Barth's critique of religion did not fall short of the criticism by Feuerbach, Marx, and Nietzsche. In fact his theological criticism of religion aimed to outdo all secular criticism—in order to bring all human thought and action under divine judgment and to open it to the paradox of redemption. God was experienced in his strange otherness to the world and the last trace of the divine was erased from the human realm so that for all practical purposes the earth was left under the rule of the secular. This analysis of man and his cosmos strangely coincided in its diagnosis with the atheistic interpretation of man's actual situation.

As an analysis of man's situation, Barth's commentary is highly significant; but as a commentary on Paul's Epistle to the Romans, it remains a dubious enterprise, combining revolutionary insight into the meaning of the original symbols with an anachronistic exegesis. The program of a pneumatic exegesis only veiled the confusion concerning the historical method. By stressing the antithesis between the divine and the human to the point of paradox, dialectical theology spelled out concretely man's self-estrangement, but under the cloak of paradox it smuggled in some very unparadoxical stereotypes of Protestant orthodoxy. And the later development of dialectical theology into a theological positivism only confirmed the fears of a critic like Harnack that this revival in theology would but contribute a Quixote episode to the history of theology, because neither the presuppositions of a pneumatic exegesis nor the conditions for an orthodox supernaturalism could be revived at will. When the first revolutionary impetus of dialectical theology came to a halt and the conservative restoration of dogmatics began (a shift more significant as a general sign of our time than dialectical theology would like to admit), the attempt to develop theology out of man's actual situation had proven itself abortive.

[2]

It is in such a period of orthodox restoration that Paul Tillich has published the first volume of his *Systematic Theology*. This work presents a challenge to the verdict that the creative development of theology has come to an end. Tillich seriously considers the charge that the history of theology represents a progressive amnesia, suppressing the eschatological meaning of the canonic symbols. He tries to escape the verdict of historical criticism by a solution that is as bold as it is simple: by interpreting ontology in terms of eschatology he charges ontology with eschatological dynamics. Thus he thinks it is possible to interpret eschatological symbols in ontological terms without sacrificing their original meaning. In short, he eschatologizes ontology and ontologizes eschatology in the light of man's present situation.

The starting point of his theology is the experience of despair that marks so much of contemporary art and literature, that comes to voice in existential philosophy and is analyzed in the psychology of the unconscious. Man is seen in an extreme situation that cannot be treated in the traditional stereotypes: neither the ontological speculations of the early Greek church nor the concern of the Reformation with a merciful God and the forgiveness of sin nor the modernistic problem of personal religious life or of the Christian community in the general civilization is at stake. His entire system rotates around the one eschatological problem: man's self-estrangement in his being and his reconciliation in the "new being." When after the first World War the social antagonism between the bourgeois society and the proletarian class seemed to determine man's situation, Tillich tried in a theology of *kairos* to meet the challenge of Marxism in terms of a Christian socialism. Tillich's theological criticism of the bourgeois society wanted to integrate the Marxistic critique of capitalism. The second World War has brought a clear shift in his emphasis from social concerns to psychological problems: not the class struggle determines man's self-estrangement, but man's despair transcends the social division of classes. Tillich tries to meet the challenge of existential philosophy and psychiatry, and his theological analysis of man's despair aims to reveal the unuttered theological a priori of their inquiry. Tillich's theology is apologetic, based on a method of correlation. This method determines the scaffolding of the system which in the first volume is built around the main problem of "I. Reason and Revelation (1. Reason and the Quest for Revelation; 2. The Reality of Revelation)" and "II. Being and God (1. Being and the Question of God; 2. The Reality of God)."

The technique of correlation is not entirely new in the field of apologetic theology and was employed by the Lutheran theologian Karl Heim in a masterly way. In his analysis of the categories of the natural sciences and the concepts of epistemology and ontology Karl Heim unearthed the inner contradictions in their basic axioms and used this crisis in the foundations of science and philosophy to drive man's search for knowledge from intellectual skepticism into an existential despair. Having brought human knowledge to the impasse of despair, Karl Heim turned about to reveal the answer of theology in which all contradictions were resolved and all antagonisms reconciled. Even if the student could not help but admire the author's skill, this technique left him more skeptical toward theology in the end than in the beginning because it gave him the feeling that the method of correlation works like a trick where the theologian, not unlike a magician, pulls the theological answer out of the dark. The analysis of man's situation in no way affected the terms of the theological answer. The crisis of man's knowledge left no scars on theology, and the theological answer did not pass through the mills of the dialectic but appeared superimposed on the analysis.

Tillich's method of correlation is dialectical. His interest in sociology, psychology, and philosophy is not peripheral, but he participates in the cleavages and contradictions, and his analysis of the human situation shapes the theological answer decisively. The theological element of the correlation is forged in his dialectic as much as the anthropological pole. Our interest is not the apologetic technique of correlation but the dialectical principle it involves.

In order to unravel the dialectic of Tillich's method of correlation we would have to discuss his work chapter by chapter. Such a procedure would go beyond the limits of an essay and would, moreover, remain fragmentary since the second volume of his *Systematic Theology* has not yet been published. Therefore I have chosen to treat two methodological points. First, I will consider the necessary presuppositions of a theological system written from an apologetic point of view; this problem centers around the question of theology and authority. Next I will consider the method of correlation; this problem centers around the relation between theology and philosophy.

[3]

The first sentence of Tillich's introduction contains in a nutshell the problem of theology and authority. For theology is defined "as a function of the Christian church" which must serve the needs of the church. Since the dogmatic part constitutes the most significant element in a system of theology, dogmatics is another name for systematic theology and the term "dogmatics" is justified because theology "exercises a function of the church within the church and for the church." [4] The church rests on a foundation whose formulation is given in the creeds, and the function of the creeds "as a protection against destructive heresies" makes their acceptance necessary for the church. With the complete union of church and state after Constantine, the doctrinal decisions of the church became also the civil laws of the state, so that the heretic was considered a criminal who endangered the foundations of the Christian society. The destructive

[4] P. 32. All page references, unless otherwise indicated, refer to Tillich's *Systematic Theology* (Chicago: University of Chicago Press, 1951), Vol. I.

consequences of the union of church and state have discredited the term *dogma* and *dogmatics* and brought the subject of dogmatics into disrepute. But this disrepute is, according to the author, only a historical calamity and does not reduce the significance of formulated *dogmata* for a systematic theology, because the function of systematic theology is a necessary consequence of the nature of the church.

What are the presuppositions of such a claim? The basis of theology as a function of the church rests, according to Tillich, on the doctrine of the logos that became flesh, of the principle of divine self-revelation that has become manifest in Jesus as the Christ, who is the "head" of the "body" of the church. But the idea of a theology as a function of the church is meaningful only if this doctrine is exposed in a direct way. For there must be a nonsymbolic point of reference beyond all dialectics, the rock on which theology as a function of the church may rest. The dialectical method, however, must always turn the logos that became flesh into a symbol. Surely Tillich is right to insist that a symbol is much more than merely a technical sign. But a symbol remains a *"chiffre."* [5] Can, however, a *chiffre* carry the burden of a theology as a function of the church?

The tension between the theology of logos and the doctrine of the church not only marks Tillich's theology but comes to the fore at the most critical juncture of the history of the Church. Since the Alexandrian school of theology[6] has turned the logos of the particular event into a symbol of the "pneumatic logos," the idea of theology as a function of the church has become problematic. A theology of the logos must face three major turning points in the history of the church: the theology of Origen, the prophecy of Joachim of Fiore,[7] and the philosophy of Hegel. The church could not but anathematize Origen after long controversies because his theology of the logos tends, even against his will, to overcome the unique event of the logos in the flesh. It is true that neither Origen nor Joachim of Fiore nor even Hegel state that the creeds of the church are fulfilled and superseded. Nevertheless, this statement is implicit in the dialectical principle. The dialectical method is not a coach that can be stopped at will. The arguments around Origen and his pupils in the old church, around Joachim of Fiore and the Franciscan Spirituals in the medieval church, and around Hegel and his pupils in the modern church give abundant testimony to this contention.

A theology that has a function in the church cannot function without the authority of the church, and this authority is derived from the credo that Christ as the logos has a continuous life in the community, the church

---

[5] Cipher—T. J. J. A.
[6] An early neo-Platonic school of Eastern Christian theology whose foremost spokesman was Origen—T. J. J. A.
[7] A thirteenth-century Italian visionary who proclaimed the advent of the third age of the Spirit following the ages of the Father and the Son—T. J. J. A.

representing the mystical body of Christ. Theology as a function of the church is meaningful only as a continuation of the incarnation, as the logos that became flesh in the *dogmata*.

If the theological task is understood in this rigorous way (and this is one possible interpretation of Tillich's first sentence), then, it seems to me, theology cannot be treated in a systematic way. Not because it is too difficult to prepare a systematic account of the *dogmata* of the church (every catechism does that) but because the incarnation of Christ cannot be treated as a systematic axiom. I do not wish to say that one cannot for pedagogical purposes present the doctrines of the church in a systematic treatise, but one would fail to understand Tillich's basic assumption if one would suppose that he presents theology in the form of a system for pedagogical reasons. The form of his system is connected with the very nature of his theology and he states explicitly that it has always been impossible for him to think theologically in any other than a systematic way. *Systematic Theology* as a title implies that theology is a system. Perhaps theology as a totality of consistent assertions about the *dogmata* can be systematic, but a theology that is the function of the church is not so much a totality of consistent assertion as an exegesis of the logos that became flesh. Such a theology is possible only as an interpretation of the divine word of revelation. To know does not mean to construct a system but to understand the word of the Scriptures in the light of the authorities of the church. Ecclesiastical theology is based on an *argumentum ex verbo* and not on an *argumentum ex re*.[8]

But Tillich's theology is not an *argumentum ex verbo*. It cannot be accidental that with Tillich "the elaboration of the line of thought has consumed all effort and all space," [9] preventing him from making extensive reference to the Scriptures and the classical theologians. In an ecclesiastical theology reference to the Scriptures and classical authorities is not an embellishing ornament to prove the author's knowledge but belongs to the very core of the argument.

Tillich's theology, however, necessarily takes the form of a system, since the method of commentary by pneumatic exegesis, as it appears in Barth's dogmatics, is rendered anachronistic through the impact of historical criticism. But at the same time Tillich would like to preserve the role of theology as a function of the church under conditions that render the very premise of such a role questionable.

If the proposed interpretation of theology seems too rigorous, one would have to consider its possible alternative and to understand theology and the *dogmata* of the church as the product of creative human imagination. For the historical interpretation of Holy Writ and of the development of dogma in no way permits any conclusion about a continuous act of revela-

[8] Argument from the word and not argument from the thing—T. J. J. A.
[9] P. vii.

tion. The historical interpretation of canonic writings ranges from a conservative reconstruction of minute details in the life of Jesus to a radical denial of any historical existence. Both extremes and the interval between them have to be taken into account by a systematic theology that accepts the results of historical criticism. In fact, the historical interpretation tries to unmask all history as human and only human. A comparison of a historical commentary with any pneumatic exegesis reveals the "unbridged gap" [10] between the two methods. A theology that accepts historical criticism not only "suffers" because of this situation but is actually paralyzed as long as it wants to steer a middle course between historical interpretation and pneumatic exegesis.

It is precisely the "philosophical" element[11] in historical criticism that opposes the assumptions of a pneumatic exegesis. In fact, the philological method was developed in opposition to the allegorical interpretation in order to break the "prejudice" of theology. In charging theology with prejudice, historical criticism aims to emancipate itself from the theological presupposition that truth is *given* to man only by the divine word of revelation. A theology of the church that understands itself in the light of a divine word of revelation would have to unmask the assumption of historical criticism to work without the presuppositions of the given word of revelation as an illusion of the autonomous mind. In order to legitimize pneumatic exegesis, theology would have to carry through a "critique of historical reasoning" and to show that the driving principle of historicism, the "historical consciousness," actually epitomizes human *hubris* and illusion. Leo Strauss, in his study of Spinoza's critique of religion, has developed the genesis of this problem and shown the philosophical implications of historical criticism in such a pertinent way that I do not need to repeat his argument in detail.[12] But not even theological positivism dared to go so far and left the problem of historical criticism in a confused limbo. Erwin Reisner, who pointed out that historical criticism was not only a question of philological accuracy but had philosophical implications that shake the foundations of Christian revelation, remained a voice in the desert.[13] The church could tolerate the historical interpretation of the canon and the dogma only at the peril of its existence, since such an interpretation reduces the church to one sociological group among others immersed in the conflicts of the world.

Perhaps the time has come when theology must learn to live without the support of canon and classical authorities and stand in the world without authority. Without authority, however, theology can only teach by an indirect method. Theology is indeed in a strange position because it has to

[10] P. 36.
[11] P. 18.
[12] Leo Strauss, *Die Religionskritik Spinozas* (Berlin, 1930).
[13] Erwin Reisner, *Die Geschichte als Suendenfall und Weg zum Gericht* (Munich, 1929).

prove its purity by immersing itself in all the layers of human existence and cannot claim for itself a special realm. In losing itself in the forms of the world, theology would not betray its destiny. Richard Rothe, the teacher of Ernst Troeltsch, knew something about this destiny of theology. Theology must remain incognito in the realm of the secular and work incognito for the sanctification of the world. Theology should not strive for the vainglory to present a sacred science "separated" from the sciences by special doctrines or dogmas but rather serve in "lowliness of mind" the secular knowledge and life. Would theology miss its point if instead of insisting on a separating circle it would make itself of no special reputation and take upon itself the form of incognito? Theology would in such a fashion become more likely to present the relation between the divine and the human in our time.

[4]

Tillich's systematic theology is not only a theology of the church; it is philosophical theology, and therefore he develops his theology in a continuous correlation with philosophy. His purpose is to define within the limits of a philosophic theology the special *topos*[14] of theology and to establish a criterion for distinguishing it from philosophy. While philosophy inquires into the structure of being, theology deals with the meaning of being for us. The subject matter of theology is what concerns us ultimately. Only those propositions are theological which deal with their object insofar as it can become a matter of ultimate concern for us.

But here we must ask, "Is there any criterion for determining what should be of man's ultimate concern? Could not everybody put his ultimate concern as theology?" Only those statements, answers Tillich, are theological which deal with their object insofar as it can become a matter of being or not-being for us. The question, to be or not to be, implies a specific theological point. But even the second criterion remains formal. Man's ultimate concern is fundamentally rooted in the ontological question. Ontology is not a theoretical doctrine but an act of questioning in which man asks about the ground of his being. Only in the chapter following the exposition of the two formal criteria of theology does Tillich discuss a material criterion of theology by defining theology as a methodical interpretation of the contents of the Christian faith. This statement remains obscure, however, in its relation to the two formal criteria and makes sense only if we remember that theology is by definition a function in the church. It is the ecclesiastical element in the texture of Tillich's theology that leads him to limit the theological circle and to demarcate the line between the-

[14] Sphere or arena—T. J. J. A.

ology and philosophy. But this theological circle has a very wide radius. For the only criterion whereby the circumference of the circle can be drawn is again man's ultimate concern with the Christian message. His ultimate concern can express itself through opposition no less than through submission. Are Feuerbach and Nietzsche, then, within the theological circle?

Tillich's division between philosophy and theology poses a crucial problem for philosophy. If philosophy should deal, as Tillich assumes, only with the structure of being in itself, whereas theology deals within the meaning of being for us, then philosophy *qua* philosophy would have to remain in a detached objectivity and forget about man's concrete condition. But is it at all possible to inquire into the structure of being without first considering its meaning for us? For all ontological inquiry into the structure of being, though it develop the most elaborate system of categories, remains fundamentally empty until it has clarified the meaning of being for us. I do not see any possible split between theology and philosophy in the ontological question. For an inquiry into the structure of being, its categories and concepts, which does not beforehand establish the meaning of being for us is doomed to failure. An ontology that stops short at describing objective structures without recourse to the subjective source of this act remains ungrounded.

The division between the universal logos and the concrete logos cannot be interpreted in terms of Tillich's theological circle. The universal logos must at all times be bound to the concrete, otherwise it becomes a mere phantom of generalities. The union between the universal and the concrete cannot be ontologically "dependent" on an event in the course of history. If ontology is eschatologized and eschatology ontologized, then the drama between "being" and the "new being" must be a perennial act. The act of reconciliation must either be an eternal event or it must put an end to man's being in history. The original eschatological symbols of the antagonism and reconciliation between the *protos adam* and the *eschatos adam*[15] had an inner coherence that is lacking in a theology that has to reckon with the fact of a Christian history and to turn the eschatological symbols into ontological concepts and make the eschaton break into history at an arbitrary moment within history.

It is probable that such or similar considerations have prevented Martin Heidegger from accepting the ontological interpretation of theology which would seem to be the most natural correlatum to his philosophy of being. In sentences that could be taken as a direct comment on Tillich's theology, Heidegger remarked, "If I were to write a theology, which I am sometimes tempted to do, [then] the term *being* would not be allowed to appear in it. Faith does not need the thought of being, and if it needs it it is no longer faith. This Luther understood. Even in his own church one seems to forget

---

[15] The original or primal man and the final or eschatological man—T. J. J. A.

it." [16] Heidegger remains cryptic as to how he would develop the categories of his theology, but this much is clear: that he separates ontology from theology like Kierkegaard and Barth. I cannot but take Tillich's side in this argument, although I doubt whether the ontological interpretation of theology can be confined within the limits of the theological circle.

Is Tillich's *systematic* theology, however, confined ultimately to the theological circle? It is the paradoxical destiny of logos-theology to end in a theology of immanence. This consequence is implicit in the very principle of dialectic. It cannot be denied that Tillich's theology describes the disruptive cleavages of reason and man's alienation in general. But is the reconciliation described theologically, as a "supernatural" breakthrough, as a miraculous healing of the conflict in man? If the supernatural pole is dialectically drawn into the orbit of the world and the divine interpreted in the light of the mystery of incarnation, then the divine becomes immersed in the world, becomes an immanent principle. The divine no longer stands over and against man but is in the depth of his own being. The law of God (theonomy) is no longer a divine decree to man but only "autonomous reason united with its own depth." [17] In such a situation it "is as atheistic to affirm the existence of God as it is to deny it," [18] for God is not a being standing over and against man, calling him, commanding him, arguing with him, but "being itself."

It is important, I think, to inquire into the "topology" of the symbols that are basic to the ontological interpretation of theology. According to Tillich, they are all located in a "depth." The "depth" of reason expresses something that is not reason but that precedes reason and is manifest through it. That which transcends reason is not located "beyond" reason, but the arrow of transcendence points "downward" into the depth. The depth of reason is interpreted as "substance" which appears in the rational structure of reality. Substance also marks the "depth," the "below," and points to that which is "underlying" reality (sub-stantia). The ontological metaphors are even more pointed. The depth is called the "ground" which is creative in every rational act, or the "abyss" which "cannot be exhausted" by any act of creation, or the "infinite potentiality of being and meaningful" which "pours" into the rational structures of mind and reality. The depth is the center of power, and out of the depth all rational structures receive their form.[19] All these symbols are metaphorical variations of the unsymbolic term *being itself*. The religious symbol for what is called the "ground of being" is God.[20]

The point of reference for all these ontological symbols lies in the depth. Since Tillich interprets theology in ontological terms, his basic theological and religious symbols must retain the quality of depth characteristic of

[16] Zurich, November, 1951. Published for private circulation (Zurich, 1952).
[17] P. 85.
[18] P. 237.
[19] P. 79.
[20] P. 156.

Dionysiac theology. Dionysiac theology is an "ecstatic naturalism" that interpets all supernaturalistic symbols in immanent terms. The ecstasy does not lead to a "beyond," in a supernaturalistic sense, but signifies an "intensity" of the immanent. In the last analysis, it is the idea of a Dionysiac theology that secretly impels all philosophical theology, and in the convergence and union of the bacchantic dance and the mystery of the cross, I see the mythical original of the dialectical method. Nietzsche's last utterances point in the same direction. At the end of his *Ecce homo,* Dionysos stands symbolically against the Crucified. In the letters and fragments, however, written in a last clarity of mind before he entered into the night of madness, the veil is lifted from Nietzsche's ultimate concern: Dionysos and the Crucified merge into one symbol. It is the same union of Christ and Dionysos that Hölderlin celebrates in his last hymns. And the theoretical blueprint for the mythical union of Christ and Dionysos is given in the philosophy of Hegel and the late Schelling. The method of dialectic is rooted in Böhme's[21] gnostic theogony of the eternal yea and the eternal nay. Hence, Tillich's ontological interpretation of theology, which is his most original contribution, adds a chapter to the history of Dionysiac theology in the Christian frame of reference.

It is unavoidable that in the context of a Dionysiac theology some of the biblical attributes and metaphors for the divine, which belong to a paternalistic frame of reference, become "confusing" symbols. It needs all the power of Tillich's interpretation to hold the paternalistic symbols in line with the Dionysiac symbols of his philosophical theology. In the last pages of the volume, for example, Tillich is concerned with the criticism of the personalistic symbols for man's relation to God. The two "central" symbols of biblical faith, Lord and Father, have become a stumbling block for many people. Christian theology has been "unwilling to listen to the often shocking insights into the psychological consequences of the traditional use of these symbols."[22] No doubt this remark touches upon a crucial point, but I would question whether the "traditional use" can be eliminated; that is, I would question whether the symbols can be removed from their original context. No interpretation of a symbol can ultimately uproot the symbol from its natural soil. A symbol explains itself through itself and breaks through all the veils of interpretation. It is important for theology to take the criticism of psychology and sociology seriously, but perhaps it is worth while to consider, even if only for a moment, whether the fact that the paternalistic symbols have become a stumbling block is not in fact a verdict on our spiritual situation. These symbols were in no way disturbing to many generations that shaped their traditional use, and the symbols would never have become so central to the Jewish and the Christian language of

[21] An early seventeenth-century German mystic who created a new mode of dialectical vision and thinking—T. J. J. A.
[22] P. 288.

faith if their traditional use had conflicted with their meaning. May not the criticism of paternalistic symbols by psychology be the result of a tacit assumption of a theology of immanence?

Tillich's Dionysiac theo-*logy* challenges the ecstatic Dionysiacs like Ludwig Klages, Keyserling, and other disciples of the pagan cult, who descend into the night and worship earth, race, blood, flesh as sacred powers, abhorring reason as the enemy of the soul. The spirit pulses through the Dionysiac elements in Tillich's theology, which tries to reconcile the powers of the deep that are sacred and the powers of light that are divine. The spirit does not live in enmity with life, but even the abyss of being is illuminated by a logos.

[5]

Hegel also understood the dialectical method as an explication of the mystery of the incarnation and centered his ontology around Christian symbols. No one can understand the dialectical method unless he refers to Hegel's analysis of "life" and "love" in his earlier theological writings. This analysis is deeply interwoven with an interpretation of the prologue of the Gospel of John. But in the *Phenomenology of the* [human or divine?] *Spirit,* Hegel reveals the secret inherent in the dialectical method of logos-theology. Logos-theology contains, according to Hegel, the method, the way in the deepest sense, leading from the contradictions of alienation to man's self-recognition. The logos that became explicit in theology is the spirit that recognizes itself; it is reason united with its own depth. Hegel also describes the logos as distinct but no longer outside of man and draws the supernatural pole into the circle of dialectic. The dynamics of the dialectical method break through the limits of a theological circle because the principle of dialectic cannot fulfill itself without sacrificing theology as an objective doctrine. Only in the situation of estrangement can man speak about his ultimate concern in an estranged way, in the way of theology; and, as a doctrine, theology perpetuates the estrangement of man that it set out to overcome. The structure of Hegel's *Phenomenology* testifies to this dynamism of the dialectical method. The *Phenomenology* does not end with a description of the logos-theology but proceeds to a gnostic theory of knowledge, a doctrine that is neither theology nor philosophy in the strict sense but both at the same time. This doctrine has its source in the Alexandrian theology and in the speculations of Joachim of Fiore. Hegel's doctrine is not a philosophy in the sense of a theory that abstracts from man; and it is not a theology in the supernaturalistic sense, for it does not locate the spirit outside of man. In Hegel's logos-theology the supernatural symbols are finally translated into immanent categories.

It is true that Hegel's synthesis crumbled, since he reconciled the contradictions and oppositions of life only in the realm of the idea and relegated nature, matter, and man's material condition to a secondary position. The social and scientific revolution of the nineteenth century burst through the dikes of Hegel's idealistic synthesis. Schelling, in his lectures on the *Philosophy of Mythology and Revelation,* was the first to stress the primacy of being over the "negative" realm of the pure idea—and Tillich started his work forty years ago with an analysis of Schelling's "positive" philosophy. Schelling, who turned the wheel from idealism to a general revolt against Hegel's synthesis, still interpreted being in objective terms, whereas some of Hegel's pupils (Feuerbach and Kierkegaard) shifted the emphasis from the objective pole of being to the principle of subjectivity.

When Tillich defines the object of theology in terms of man's ultimate concern, he tries, if I understand the structure of his ontological theology, to mediate Schelling's primacy of being with Feuerbach's principle of subjectivity. Feuerbach also argued against Hegel that the pure logos needs to be "incarnated" and "realized" in man's concrete existence, and he also understood the principle of subjectivity in reference to Protestant theology. "In contrast to Catholicism, Protestantism has ceased to be concerned with God per se and is interested only in what he means for man. . . . Protestantism is no longer theology but essentially Christology, i.e. religious anthropology." [23] Like Tillich, Feuerbach quotes Luther's famous saying, "As you believe him, so you have him," as his key word. Feuerbach would, like Tillich, insist that theistic religion "has made God a heavenly, completely perfect person who resides above the world and mankind. The protest of atheism against such a highest person is correct. There is no evidence for his existence, nor is he a matter of ultimate concern. God is not God without universal participation." [24] Feuerbach, again like Tillich, no longer envisages matter as an antispiritual principle but interprets spirit as immanent in matter as the ecstasy of nature and the intensity of man's existence. Feuerbach's reference to Protestant theology, however, lost its meaning when in the course of years his naturalism became a positive, undialectical principle. Religion then turned out to be only an illusion and the spirit an ideological instrument. Perhaps all materialism had to end in atheistic revolution in the nineteenth century and sink into a positive materialism, because Protestant theology (against which the revolt was directed) equated the divine with the spiritual, excluding nature and matter from redemption.

Tillich's dialectic tries to break this deadlock. His dialectic does not drive toward a reconciliation in the realm of the idea. It is a dialectic that does not relegate nature and man's material condition to a secondary position; it takes the individual, the ephemeral, as seriously as the idea. But in its methodological structure Tillich's dialectic is, like Hegel's, a dialectic

[23] Ludwig Feuerbach, *Grundsätze der Philosophie der Zukunft,* p. 2.
[24] P. 245.

of mediation that drives toward a coincidence of opposites. Tillich's theology, like all philosophical theology from Origen to Hegel, considers its interpretation of the canonic symbols as an advance over the "naive" belief. Tillich interprets theological reflection as a progress in understanding. Perhaps this is the destiny and the limitation of all theology. For theology must interpret the transition from the myth to the logos as an advance and reflection as an achievement and therefore fails to see that theological reflection presupposes that the original power of the symbol is gone. Theological reflection starts with the resignation that the symbols do not speak through themselves. The ascent to reflection involves a descent from the original relation into an imaginary reconstruction.

Surely, theological interpretation is an achievement, and perhaps it is only by way of dialectic that we can translate the original symbols for the present situation. But perhaps it is the "temporal situation" that *forces* theology to use the dialectical method. That the theologian has to resort to interpretation is only the reverse side of the fact that the symbols have grown mute. It may very well be that only dialectical terms that border on atheism are appropriate to the present situation. But I would not conclude from this that the dialectical interpretation of the symbols is on a "higher level" than their primitive meaning. For the first generation of Christian believers the coming of the Messiah was a reality and not an ontological problem. Many generations did not stumble over the concreteness of central symbols like Father, Lord, or King of Heaven. And I would not hold it against these generations that they could use these symbols naively and did not need to develop an allegorical or dialectical interpretation. Anyone who, after two thousand years of Christian history, thinks that he can ignore the hiatus of time is the victim of an illusion, and Tillich rightly reproves all fundamentalist and orthodox theology. But why make a virtue out of a necessity? The progress in theological interpretation throughout history runs parallel with a gradual withdrawal of divine presence. Theological "re-presentation" and theological interpretation are driven deeper and deeper into the web of dialectics because the divine presence is more and more veiled.

It may seem contradictory to push the dialectical principle beyond the limits that Tillich has set and at the same time to interpret his method of dialectics in the light of the absence of the divine. But perhaps the dialectical method implies precisely such a union of contraries, for it is at once a method of opposition (*dia*-lectic) and a method of reconciliation (dia-*lectic*). The dialectic of mediation (Hegel, Tillich) considers the development of theology only as a path of gradual elucidation and illumination. The dialectic of opposition (Kierkegaard, Barth) tries to bypass history and to jump over the gap that lies between the original symbols and the present situation. Both uses of the term *dialectic* are legitimate and strangely enough, in the last analysis, their results coincide. "Dialectical theology" opposes the divine to the human to the degree that the divine became the totally "other" to the world. The theology of mediation involves the divine in the human dialectic to the point that the divine pole of the correlation loses all supernatural point of reference. The two methods seem to contradict each other but in fact equally testify to the eclipse of the divine in our present situation.

13
JOHN B. COBB, JR.

John B. Cobb, Jr., stands alone in American theology inasmuch as he is at once a judicious and dispassionate critic and an original thinker of much promise. A student of Charles Hartshorne, Cobb is a philosophical theologian of Whiteheadian persuasion who is now professor of systematic theology at the Southern California School of Theology. Along with Daniel Day Williams and Schubert Ogden, Cobb is a member of a triumvirate which is giving expression to a rapidly developing process theology. Unlike his fellow process theologians, however, Cobb has an acute sense of the theological problem posed by the eclipse of God in our history and experience; in part he is drawn to Whitehead because of his conviction that Whitehead created the first purely secular metaphysics. Cobb acknowledges that ours is a post-Christian culture, a culture for which God is dead. As a consequence, genuine theology, which must engage in a dialogue with culture, becomes "totally vulnerable." This abandonment of all protective ground marks a major motif of radical theology; thus far Cobb is the only radical theologian who has chosen to speak about God, and the following essay embodies his most radical statement thus far.

John B.
Cobb, Jr.

From Crisis Theology
to the
Post-Modern World

After the thunder of a great generation of theologians in the twenties and thirties of our century, the theological horizons of the sixties are painfully silent. Even the voices of the great old men are quieter now, and in any case they cannot answer the questions of a new generation. There exists a vacuum in which even the splash of a small pebble attracts widespread attention. Theologians console themselves that the time for great systems is past and the time of the essay has come. Yet the essays for the most part are trivial.

The silence of our time is especially surprising since there is no lack of highly trained and intelligent men keenly interested in constructive theological work. Why are we so inarticulate? Why must so much of our energy be devoted to studying or interpreting our past? And why are the few efforts toward dealing with our own problems so provisional?

I would suggest that the disappearance of crisis theology has led to a situation so difficult for the theologian that he is likely to exhaust himself in taking his bearings. I will attempt in what follows to focus the problem in terms of the renewed openness of theology to culture and of the problem of historical relativism. I will then indicate in a highly personal way a response to this crisis and a possible way ahead.

[1]

Roughly we may characterize the theology of the nineteenth century as one which sought a synthesis between faith and culture. Culture was posi-

FROM John B. Cobb, Jr., "From Crisis Theology to the Post-Modern World," *The Centennial Review* (Spring, 1964), pp. 174-88. Reprinted by permission of *The Centennial Review* and of the author.

tively appraised, and pride was taken in the success of faith in Christianizing it. Further victories were hoped for and worked for. Dissenting voices vigorously protested that faith lost itself in this synthesis, that Christendom is a fraud, and that only by rejecting culture can faith be true to itself. But these voices were not heard until World War I had proved them prophetic.

Crisis theology undertook to distinguish sharply between faith and culture. Culture is human; faith, of God. Faith seeks no sustenance in culture and makes no special claims to benefit culture. It belongs to another sphere which radically transcends culture and is even, essentially, indifferent to it. In fact, of course, the crisis theologians were far from indifferent to the events of history and took an active and creative part in molding them. It was they and not the remnants of nineteenth-century liberalism who gave effective leadership to resistance against Hitler. Within their own thought, the separation of faith and culture gave way, although the insistence on the duality remained. The legacy of crisis theology is therefore a new openness to culture, an awareness of its importance. It is *this* world in which we are called to faith, and though the faith to which we are called is not simply the culmination of culture, still it must learn to provide an authentic witness within it.

In this formal statement, the new recognition of the inescapability of taking culture seriously seems relatively innocuous. The problem, however, is that the culture we are called to take seriously is one increasingly devoid of Christian form and substance. It is a post-Christian culture, a culture for which God is dead. What does it mean for Christian theology to take this culture seriously?

For some, it means that we are to look in the culture for authentic expressions of man's humanity, and to see in them new forms of unconscious and unintended expression of the Christian faith. However, this will not do. We can, of course, as historians point out that the influence of Christianity is not dead even where it is denied, but if we are to take our world seriously we must acknowledge that the existence in which it seeks a new authenticity is not that of its Christian past.

For others, it means that we are to see in modern culture the direction in which man must inevitably fall when he turns away from faith. But this will not do either. That much in the modern world does indeed express just this is beyond question. But this approach presupposes that there is an island of security in the modern world from which it is possible to view it from without and thus take warning not to follow that course. This is precisely *not* to take seriously the modern world. This is to assume that the modern world is optional, that we choose to live in it or out of it as we choose unbelief or belief.

A third alternative is to understand the modern world as asking questions which it cannot answer, questions which can be answered only by faith. But this approach also fails. The modern world does not in fact seem to be asking those questions to which the Christian gospel provides an answer. To achieve a correlation of question and answer we seem forced to destroy the integrity both of the world and of the gospel.

A fourth alternative is to take from the modern world only a new conceptuality in which faith can express itself. Surely this is acceptable and commendable as far as it goes, but it does not deal frontally with the problem of faith and culture. What is to be expressed in the conceptuality taken from the culture? Is it something which challenges the culture, which roots itself outside the culture and claims autonomy from it? Then again the modern world is not being taken with full seriousness, for the modern world denies every transcendent perspective. Then again one presupposes an island of refuge from which one may decide how and in what way to be a part of the modern world and how and in what way to transcend it.

We seem to be confronted finally by only two choices. We may really take the modern world seriously, acknowledge that it is the only world we know, accept it, affirm it, and live it. To do so is to accept and live the death of God. On the other hand, we may refuse the modern world, distance ourselves from it, fence in our world of traditional faith, and seek to preserve it from the corrosion of the world outside. Both expedients are desperate ones. It is no wonder that theologians find it difficult to speak relevantly in such a time.

The problem for contemporary theology is acutely compounded by historical self-consciousness. Since we are accustomed and compelled to think historically, we are accustomed and compelled to think in terms of the variety of ways in which men seek understanding and fulfillment. We see that Christian faith is one among these ways, that it arose in particular circumstances in conjunction with particular beliefs and expectations, that it spread in some direction and not in others, and that it is fundamentally an historical accident that we happen to be Christians rather than, for example, Moslems.

We may, of course, argue that the historical origins of a belief have nothing to do with the responsible judgment of its truth or falsity. But if so, we must at least assume that we do have some criteria for judging. When our suggestions of such criteria in their turn are found to be products of a peculiar history, we begin to feel the ground sinking beneath our feet. We seem plunged into an infinite regress in which every possibility of normative thinking is destroyed.

If we argue that we must believe something, and then by a leap of faith choose to be Christian, we find ourselves still confronted by the most bewildering diversity. Faith does not seem to mean the same thing for Eastern Orthodoxy, for Roman Catholicism, and for Protestantism. Even within Protestantism the variety is great. Having leapt into Christianity, are we to leap into one or another form of Christianity as well? And what attitude are we to take toward those who leap in another way? Having leapt in our particular way, are we given to know that they have leapt wrongly? Or do we simply confess our own commitment and accept other commitments as equally valid?

It is clear that one of the reasons for the power of crisis theology was that it placed faith radically outside this relativism. For it faith is the gift of God and is validated in its giving. It does not have to claim superiority over unfaith or over competing religions in any other way. Nevertheless, this solution above all sounds like special pleading. Are we really prepared to say that God has given faith overwhelmingly to Westerners and that all the religious attainments of the East are to be seen as so much vain human striving? Is not our belief that this is so clearly a function of our historical conditioning? Can we really claim that this belief is given with the gift of faith so that it too is validated by the act of God? Or if we affirm that God has given faith to all men, what can faith mean any longer? And what happens to the Biblical distinction between believers and unbelievers?

That these difficulties can be multiplied indefinitely goes without saying, and with the passing of crisis theology they have come very much to the fore: The Christian must now recognize that his faith is one among many and that it cannot be set over against all other human phenomena as that one point at which God has acted. Yet the alternative seems to be to return to that relativistic sea from which crisis theology seemed briefly to save us.

[2]

In the above I have called attention to the two features of the contemporary situation which seem to be most critical for the theologian. Our culture, the culture in which we do and must live, is characterized by the death of God. We cannot but understand ourselves and our beliefs historically and hence relativistically.

These two problems are intimately interconnected. The death of God is caused in part by the historicizing of all our thinking. Since we understand an idea by understanding how it arises and develops, we can no longer view the idea as having a one-to-one correlation with reality. We can talk seriously about ideas of God but are not able to speak directly of God. More broadly, we can enter imaginatively into many ways of perceiving reality, but just for that reason we cannot affirm any of them as true. Indeed, the word *true* we are forced to italicize, not knowing any longer what we can mean by it.

It is also the case that the death of God is a *cause* of relativism. As long as God's reality remained a fixed pole for thought, the relativity of human experience and belief could be understood as reflecting varying ways of grasping one ultimate reality. Truth was found in God's knowledge, and even though we might not claim any final criteria for identifying the content of truth, that there existed a final truth about all things was clear. With the death of God, however, truth and reality are alike relativized. They exist nowhere.

This world in which God is dead and truth and reality are without meaning is indeed our world. Yet it is not our total world. If it were, no such statement about it could be understood. If God were wholly and unequivocally dead for us, the statement that it is so would not be made. Indeed, all discourse would be at an end. Every statement assumes that it somehow transcends total relativism, that it points to some kind of reality, that it participates in some kind of truth. We do still live in a world formed by a past that remains alive even in its decay.

I do not mean to seize the point that total relativism is self-contradictory as a basis for setting relativism aside. The *affirmation* of total relativism is self-contradictory, but there is a sense in which relativism can be lived unspoken. The complete relativist would never apply the term relativism to his own thought, for he would not think in such universals. It is the reality of lived relativism, not its philosophical defense, that seems to lie ahead for our world.

I do mean to say, however, that the reality of the death of God and of the concomitant relativism does not exhaust our contemporary world. If we take seriously the historical consciousness which we have already seen to play such havoc with traditional forms of faith and theology, we must also see that the death of God and the concomitant relativism are likewise a function of time and place, one way of being among others, in themselves neither absolute nor final. History shows us that just at that point at which a *Zeitgeist* seems to have swept all before it, it may already be giving way in the minds of the most creative and authentic persons to something quite different, something that certainly will not repeat the past, but something which may yet recover out of the past just what seemed in greatest danger of being destroyed. Perhaps even today at the point at which all rational structure and all human meaning seems to be evaporating, new structures and new meanings may be emerging.

If this is so, and I earnestly hope that it is so, then we may escape the desperate choice indicated above between affirming the modern world and reacting against it defensively. We may refuse the modern world not by defending the past but in the name of the new world which *may* be born. We cannot of course know that it will be born. We cannot even know whether our decision for it may help it to be born. But we can affirm it, and in doing so we can repudiate the modern world in the name of the world we will to be the post-modern world.

The picture I am proposing may be sketched as follows. The *Zeitgeist* of our world is one in which God is dead and all truth and reality have collapsed in relativity. That *Zeitgeist* is working its way into ever more consistent expression in thought, art, and existence. It leads to the death of man in the sense of self-conscious, responsible, historical, individual man. Its chief obstacle to total victory is the vast deposit of centuries of Christian thought, art, and existence which, partly consciously but more largely unconsciously, is expressing itself in a still powerful humanism. This is our contemporary post-Christian situation.

If this were the total situation, I have argued above, then the theologian could only decide between throwing his lot with the new and reacting defensively against it by appealing to the authority of the past. He has learned, as many of his colleagues have not, that there is no resting place in the midway point of rationalistic or romantic humanism. But I am suggesting now that this is not the total situation. In addition to the remnants of Christendom and to the demonic powers released by the death of God, there are other thrusts here and there, thrusts which are as authentically modern as any nihilism, but which refuse nihilism in the name of truth.

These emergent claims upon the future are endlessly varied, and there is no place to stand from which one may judge the likelihood of the success of one or another. Nor is there a place to stand from which one may safely baptize one or another such thrust as Christian. Yet I believe that, ignoring the question of success and risking the danger of apostasy, the Christian thinker today must reach out for a novelty that disdains all appeal to the authority of the past and dares to think creatively and constructively in the present.

Teilhard de Chardin is a recent figure who represents such daring. The world he knew, however strange, was surely authentic, genuinely contemporary. He discounted nothing of the magnificent intellectual achievements of science. He did not appeal to the authority of the past. He took the risk of apostasy. Whether in the end his vision is durable we cannot yet know, but that it struck a responsive chord in the minds of many is clear. That it *could* point to a new world, the beginnings of a new *Zeitgeist,* cannot be denied. For my part I would far rather live in that world than in the world being fashioned by dominant modernity.

The work of Teilhard is instructive in that though it fundamentally eschews the authority of the past it affirms Jesus Christ as the center of reality. Sceptics will understandably regard this as a nostalgic remnant of inherited faith or as a concession aimed at placating the church. But I do not believe this. Whether by historic accident or by supernatural purpose, there is an absoluteness in Jesus Christ which can speak not only through the continuity of Christendom but also across the gulf of centuries and cultures. To refuse the authority of the past need not mean to ignore its truth and reality.

I mention the work of Teilhard de Chardin not to hold it up as the one great hope for the future or for the theologian. On the contrary, I find it often vague, confusing, and unsatisfactory. But it represents a mood which challenges the predominant *Zeitgeist* on its own terms, defending nothing on the ground that "it is written" or that "it is Christian," avidly open to all truth—yet still *believing*. This mood is one with which I can identify myself as theologian, as Christian, as man.

My own effort to share in the work to which this mood gives rise is directed toward thinking into the new world opened up in the philosophy of Alfred North Whitehead. To enter Whitehead's world is to experience a psychic revolution as great as or greater than the Cartesian and Kantian revolutions. To experience that revolution is to enter into possibilities of thought and self-understanding at which Whitehead himself barely hinted. I believe that from within this new Whiteheadian world one can appropriate also the world of Teilhard de Chardin—as of other revolutionary thinkers of our day—with greater clarity than they themselves could achieve.

[3]

Although any serious exposition of Whitehead's thought is beyond the scope of this paper, it is appropriate that some indication be given of the aspects of his thought which seem relevant to this context. Whitehead himself speaks of his speculative philosophy as like a poem, mutely appealing for understanding. One cannot begin with terms and objects as defined within some other vision of reality and then state unambiguously that which Whitehead intends. This procedure is impossible wherever there is genuine novelty of sensibility and vision. Hence, all the more, a few brief paragraphs on his thought can hardly hope to be intelligible. Yet, one must try.

Whitehead alters the locus of concreteness as over against modern common sense. Especially with the decay of idealism, modernity has identified concreteness either with things presented to us in sense experience or with the sense data themselves. Whitehead declares this to be "the fallacy of misplaced concreteness." What is concrete is experience as such, just as it occurs in each particularized moment. Whitehead's "actual occasion of experience" has close affinities with the "shining present" of Brightman[1] and the *"Dasein"* of Heidegger. To this extent, what I have called the psychic revolution demanded by Whitehead is seconded by personalistic idealism and by existentialism.

However, Brightman and Heidegger alike, although in quite different ways, limit this revolution to human (or at least animal) reality. Bright-

---

[1] A twentieth-century American theologian whose philosophy of religion has had a major impact upon much American Protestant theology—T. J. J. A.

man sees the "shining present" in the context of the "illuminating absent." Heidegger sees *"Dasein"* in the midst of other *"Seiende."* [2] For both of them, the physical world, the world of objects, remains something fundamentally other than the experience to which they rightly direct us as the starting point. Whitehead, in contrast, sees the whole physical world as itself also composed of "actual occasions of experience" and of societies of such occasions. There is and can be no object which is not itself a subject or a society of subjects. The physical is one dimension of all experiences including the human, but it is not at all the name of a realm over against that of experience. Whitehead also differs from both Brightman and Heidegger in perceiving experience as a momentary becoming and perishing rather than as a continuum of becoming.

The profoundly distinctive character of Whitehead's vision is apparent in his understanding of relations. All real relations are the reenactment in new experiences of elements of old experiences. All causality is to be understood in this way. Through its causal efficacy the past always profoundly affects the becoming present but never determines exactly how it will become. Causal influence and free self-determination alike characterize every entity in the world.

In terms of these briefly identified principles almost all the traditional problems of thought receive new answers or new versions of old answers. Furthermore, light is shed upon the special problems of modern mathematics and physics that relates these disciplines to human existence in a quite new way. In this context, however, we can note only the relevance of Whitehead's thought for the two acute problems previously discussed—the death of God and universal relativism.

Whitehead's earlier work reflects the death of God at least by its silence. But it gradually became clear as his philosophical speculations broadened that the philosophical reasons for the death of God were repudiated by him. Hence once again the questions of being and becoming emerged in his thought in such a way as to cry out for belief in God. It is fascinating to watch the uncompleted process whereby step by step—reluctantly, it seems at times—Whitehead unfolded a doctrine of God.

Whitehead's doctrine of God has many points of contact with traditional Christian thought—more, I think, than either he or his critics generally recognize. Nevertheless, it is profoundly new. It has been transformed by modern science and mathematics, on the one hand, and by the revolutionary vision of the world as a society of societies of occasions of experiences, on the other. The understanding of God's relation to the world is further transformed by the new understanding of space-time and of relation as reenaction and by Whitehead's special doctrine of God's providing each

---

[2] Heidegger employs the German words *Dasein* and *Seiende* to distinguish between the being which is manifest in human existence and that which is present in all existing beings—T. J. J. A.

momentary occasion with its ideal aim. After generations in which theologians and religious philosophers have struggled to defend some one relation in which God's importance for the world can be argued, we are confronted with a new world of thought in which all manner of modes of relatedness to God are affirmed. Within the Whiteheadian context we can understand both the person-to-person encounter of modern Protestantism and the mysticisms of both East and West. We can agree with those who have seen the relation of man to God in the ethical dimension and with those who have reasoned to God from the order and directionality of nature. We can see both the reality and the all-determinativeness of grace and also the freedom and responsibility of man. But we see all this in a frame of reference that to some degree transforms the meanings of all the traditional terms and problems.

The point of the above is not to explain Whitehead's doctrine of God —that again would be impossible in a few paragraphs—but simply to stress that once one enters the strange new world of Whitehead's vision, God becomes very much alive. The understanding of the world begins and ends with him to a far greater extent than Whitehead himself made explicit in his writings. Insofar as I come existentially to experience myself in terms of the world to which Whitehead introduces us, I experience myself in God; God as in me; God as law, as love, as grace; and the whole world as grounded in him. And I experience this not as in some separation from or tension with what I know of myself physiologically and psychologically, but precisely as illuminative of the fragmentary knowledge afforded by these and all other disciplines. If Whitehead's vision should triumph in the years ahead, the "death of God" would indeed turn out after all to have been only the "eclipse of God."

The problem of the relation of Whitehead's vision to the encompassing relativism of our time is still more complex. Obviously his vision is one among many, conditioned by time, place, and circumstance, subject to interpretation biographically, psychologically, and historically. Unlike most philosophers, Whitehead's philosophy articulates itself as just such a relative undertaking and achievement. One cannot *prove* its truth; one can only display its extraordinary coherence, relevance, and adequacy. And, of course, even the acceptance of such criteria is also conditioned and relative. There is and can be no escape from the circularity of all thinking.

Yet if we take seriously also the conditionedness and relativity of relativism, we will cease to see in the relativity of a position a reason for its rejection. Furthermore, within the position we may find an explanation of how relativism is transcended that seems to account both for relativism and its transcendence more satisfactorily than can be done while one remains, or tries to remain, at the merely relativistic level. Just this is the achievement of Whitehead's thought.

For Whitehead there is no reality that is not relational. For example, one cannot talk first of what occurred at a given time and then separately of what was experienced or perceived. What occurred was just these experiences and perceptions. If we ask "what really happened," we should always be asking "what was really experienced." And all such experience was that of one subject or another. The question of what happened in general is ultimately meaningless. In this sense, the relativity of truth is absolute.

However, this relativity is limited in two ways. First, it is objectively true that such-and-such experiences occurred. Whether they occurred is not relative to our opinion, available evidence, or taste. The experiences of the past are objectively immortal. Also, what occurred was not limited to the human experiences. There were electronic, atomic, and cellular experiences as well, and the reality of their occurrence does not depend on human knowledge of them.

Hence there is a reality to which our opinions and experiences as a whole correspond more or less well. Truth is an important relation in experience, although certainly not the only important one. Reality as known to us is a function of our interests and our instruments, but reality as it experiences itself is relative only to its own interests. We live in a very real and determinate world, a world in which all things are relative, but determinately relative.

From this perspective, we may indeed understand how human experience and belief are functions of the everchanging situation. Certainly the genesis of ideas helps us to understand them, and appropriately so. The complexity of the reality which confronts us is so vast that our ideas can never have a one-to-one relation with it. Yet our ideas do emerge out of reality in a positive relation with it. The most diverse and even apparently contradictory ideas can have some correspondence to that reality, and the ideal of a greater, more inclusive truth-relation is by no means illusory.

Furthermore, when we combine the Whiteheadian doctrine of God with his triumph over nihilistic relativism, we can see that the truth we seek is already real. There is a perspective which shares all perspectives and relates them all truthfully to each other. And that perspective is already effective for us despite the exceedingly distorted and fragmentary character of our own participation in truth.

[4]

One may well object that the effort to explore a new world of thought beyond the dominant modern world is not "theology" but "philosophy." How then can one whose passion drives him in this direction characterize himself as a theologian? The answer to this returns us yet again to the problem of relativism. I know that when I most totally reject the word of the past as authority for my thinking or respond most affirmatively to ideas suggested to me by Whitehead, I am expressing the vision that has become mine as my very selfhood has been formed by my past. When I realize and acknowledge to myself the conditionedness of my being and my stance, there does emerge some degree of transcendence over that conditioning. I can affirm it or I can reject it. Even if I reject it, it still continues to operate in me, but its power over me is nevertheless broken in principle and incipiently in fact as well. If I accept it, what had operated as a blind force becomes now my own will.

I know that the selfhood I experience is formed in the church, in Christian history. What I see in others and in the world, I see through eyes given vision by a Christian past. Knowing this, I am free also to reject it. I might reject it because there are anguish and estrangement given with the Christian vision, a burden of responsibility for a world that denies Christian truth. I might reject it because I see that it is indeed an historical accident that I am grasped by this vision, that I can show no ultimate rational justification for retaining it. Or I might reject it because so much of the reality I perceive through that vision enters into me as destructive of it and as denying its authenticity.

But I do not reject it; I affirm it. It may seem that in this act I contradict all I have said about refusing the authority of the past. This would be true except that the grounds of affirmation can only be that the Christian vision forecloses nothing, conceals nothing, refuses all self-defense. It is particular, but not exclusive. The belief that this is so is itself, of course, a function of the vision. This circularity cannot be avoided. One can only seek in complete openness to expand the circle indefinitely.

Because I know that my quest for a new world is motivated by my Christian selfhood and that the new world I see is seen through Christian eyes, I must acknowledge that all my thinking is Christian thinking, whether or not it is acceptable to other Christians. I cannot claim, as philosophy seems often to want to claim, that any intelligent person should be able to see the truth of my premises and the validity of my arguments.

But why "theology"? If Christian philosophy is the open quest for truth of a self who affirms the Christianness of the vision which is his, then theology is thinking that reflects upon the giver of that selfhood. Christian selfhood experiences itself as a gift in two modes. Historically, it is a gift of a community of faith grounded in Jesus Christ. Existentially, it experiences itself as a gift of God. Theological reflection must seek to understand how these two modes of giving are connected with each other, and in the process it must reflect on such traditional topics as Jesus Christ, the Holy Spirit, the church, the Bible, as well as God. Furthermore, even if such reflection in our day is prompted by our concern for our selfhood, the reflection itself must turn away from that selfhood toward its source in such a way as to bring that selfhood also under most radical judgment.

But this specific theological reflection upon the gift of Christian selfhood is never separable from the Christian philosophical reflection upon reality as a whole and in its parts. The theological must both illustrate and illuminate the categories of philosophical reflection. Each must act as criterion for the other, and each criterion in turn is modified and reshaped by the total reflection. At every point the decision to affirm rather than to reject the starting point in Christian selfhood and vision is open for re-consideration as reflection modifies its self-understanding or casts doubt upon its adequacy.

In this approach, theology is a part of the total reflective process and is *totally vulnerable*. There is no built-in safeguard to insure that in the end there will be any place in one's world for God, or Jesus Christ, or Christian selfhood. Because I believe God *is,* and that in Jesus Christ we find what it means to know God as he is, I also believe that reflection must ultimately lead us toward rather than away from these truths. But I know also that my belief may be shattered in the process, and I cannot appeal to some protected ground of confidence when all else fails.

14
GABRIEL
VAHANIAN

Coming out of a European and Barthian background, Gabriel Vahanian has represented a strange voice on the American theological scene, but one whose impact is increasing. In 1961 he dared to publish a book entitled *The Death of God,* and remarkably enough, in view of its theme, it was highly praised by Rudolf Bultmann. At the time, it had little effect upon most American theologians. Vahanian's project is truly daring since it involves him in an ultimate paradox for a Barthian, speaking about faith in the context and the language of culture, while nevertheless being persuaded that the era of Christian culture has come to an end. It is Vahanian's conviction, as can be seen in the following essay, that a passage through the death of God in our post-Christian world can be the way to a recovery and renewal of the Biblical God.

The Future of Christianity in a Post-Christian Era

Gabriel Vahanian

[1]

God is man's failure. Never does this become so manifest as in periods of transition, like ours, which are essentially periods of spiritual *interregnum*. Throughout the ages, Christian or not, pre-Christian and post-Christian, God has been man's failure. But in the death of his gods, it is man himself who both fails and overcomes his failure.

It is not sacrilegious to speak of the death of God, or of God as the chief failure of man. After all, the concept of God is a cultural—not to say ethnolatrous—concept, and God often is nothing other than some sort of constant accessory of culture. Concepts can be valid only so long as they spearhead the spontaneous expression of a particular human experience; they can live only as long as their cultural framework lasts. But a culture is also materialized by institutions, and these tend to overwhelm and atrophy the human experience, until they have invalidated it. By thus defrauding the concept, institutions objectify and ultimately transform into empirical datum the human reality which they are supposed to incarnate.

In the gospel of John, the incarnation means the constantly unique event through which destiny is improvised once and for all, and not its objectification. Human existence, because it can never be rehearsed, is not an institution but a necessary improvisation of destiny. Admittedly, institutions too are born of the necessity of improvisation, but they freeze it,

FROM Gabriel Vahanian, "The Future of Christianity in a Post-Christian Era," *The Centennial Review* (Spring, 1964), pp. 160-73. A slightly modified version of this essay appeared in Dr. Vahanian's *Wait Without Idols,* New York: George Braziller, 1964. Reprinted by permission of *The Centennial Review* and by special arrangement with Gabriel Vahanian.

they codify it, just as dogmas and religion betray faith by codifying the acts of faith, through which they are improvised, and forgetting at the same time that, as a spontaneous act of faith, existence itself is an impertinent improvisation on the theme of God's reality, of the presentness of God. Unfortunately, organized religion, with its variegated paraphernalia, by trying to show how pertinent faith is, blunts it and mummifies it. No improvisation thus lasts beyond the moment when it is conceived, and the concept that results from it leads finally to the institutionalization of religion, or to the cultural annexation of God, or the deliquescence of faith into religiosity. To cite Karl Barth, man can only formulate concepts which are not identical with God; there is no adequacy between God and our concepts of God. Religion and its gods are, consequently, as many screens, as many obstacles between the living God and man. No wonder that, according to biblical thought, God in whose image man is created is an imageless God. And we may, quite appropriately, paraphrase Faulkner's sentence when he writes in *The Sound and the Fury*: ". . . it was men invented virginity, not women," by saying: it was men invented religion, not God. It was men invented the God that dies.

Indeed, men take pleasure in inventing religions, if not quite to the point of patenting them, at least to that of "incorporating" them. This stricture is not directed against certain American denominations only; every Christian confession is similarly reprehensible whether it is established officially as territorial or unofficially as cultural church, or whether it is incorporated in Vatican State. Christianity itself, as a whole, comes under this judgment insofar as it has *de facto* become the trademark of Western culture.

To speak of the death of God means, then, that finally at the end of the Christian phase of Western culture, the reality of the living God is freed from the cultural concepts and other institutions which attempt to objectify and domesticate it. The death of God marks the end of Christian culture and especially, of its attempt to assimilate *the other God,* the living God of whom our religion as well as our diffuse religiosity is a desperate caricature. This means that, man being a religious animal, we are groping for a new concept of God and a new attitude, a mode of being congruous with it; a new religiosity is dawning. A new era begins when a new religiosity appears, rises from the empty tomb of the dead God.

It was Montesquieu who said, a couple of centuries ago, that Protestantism was bound to disappear, but that, when it has disappeared, Catholicism will have become Protestant. This might well happen. But what will Christianity itself have become by that time? Will it not have fully and plainly become what it already seems to be—nothing more than the bed of a new religiosity, whether this be the threefold religiosity of America's three-religions-and-no-faith, or the cultural, ethnolatrous theology of the West against its rivals for world domination? Montesquieu had simply overlooked the fact that Christianity (ever since it baptized the pagan, syncretistic religiosity of the Mediterranean world) was creating its own religiosity, just as the craving for a drug replaces the illness it was meant to cure. We cannot help but think of thalidomide, meant to ease some pains but resulting in "monsters." Christianity "eased the pains" of the world into which the Word was made flesh, but the religious monstrosity it conceived then has now become our torment or the object of our disdain.

The dissolution of Christianity into religiosity is what Montesquieu had not foreseen. (We must not blame him for that. After all, is it not true that we can only wear the face of our religion, and that religion can only wear the face of the culture it masks?) Between Montesquieu and ourselves, the death of God has marked this transition from a Christianity resting on the Christianized religiosity of the Roman Empire to our post-Christian religiosity which rests on the ruins of the Christian era.

[2]

Thus the death of God also resulted in the unmasking of the latent, diffuse religiosity to which man is, by nature, inclined. It may well be, therefore, as Mircea Eliade remarks, that the present period will go down in history as the first to have rediscovered "diffuse religious experiences," to have recovered the relevance of raw diffuse religiosity, once overcome by the triumph of Christianity.[1] But it may also be, on the other hand, that this post-Christian religiosity will force Christianity out of its Western cage, will enable it to break through the walls of Occidentalism and develop into a new historic reality and into a new possibility as individual existence. Doubtless, there are concrete obstacles hindering such expectations about the survival of Christianity. And what if the Christian tradition were checkmated by these obstacles? Such an eventuality is not impossible: it is becoming more and more evident if not absolutely inescapable. Nonetheless, everything still depends on the ultimate effect of the transition from radical monotheism to radical immanentism and of the leveling down of transcendental values to immanental ones. Either this effect will consist in the recovery of our classic, transcendental categories, according to which God is distinct from, wholly other than his creation. Or else, God has been, so to speak, *renaturalized* into an immanent force, animating the compulsory ideology of the classless society, at one end of the spectrum, and our more democratic pretensions to deity, at the other end. Either way, one thing is clear: man is not an atheist, except by contrast with an established theism, regardless of whether it be monotheism or polytheism. As

[1] "Note pour un humanisme," *Nouvelle Revue Française,* November, 1961.

Jean Guitton has said, man is essentially an idolator or an "iconoclast," but not an atheist.[2] But this aspect of the problem cannot concern us at this point, except insofar as it helps us to deplore again the loss of the iconoclastic element peculiarly inherent in the biblical view of existence, or the iconoclastic nature of man's obligation to God. Indeed, our present crisis stems from the fact that we have changed the biblical iconoclasm of the Christian tradition into the idolatrous post-Christian religiosity of our cultural institutions, be they social, political, economic, or ecclesiastical.

And let us not pretend that Christianity has never been *really* tried. It is dishonest to do so after nearly twenty centuries of Christian apologetics, intellectually or ethically, religiously or institutionally as well as culturally. Besides, that same claim could be made for all the dead religions which are now preserved in the religious wax museum of mankind. To pretend that Christianity has never been really tried can only imply, not that its ideals have been much too difficult and demanding for mortal men to realize, but that we are seeking dubious excuses to conceal the fact (as Teilhard de Chardin rightly observed) that, because Christianity is neither pure nor demanding enough, it can command our allegiance no longer. The death of God is, after all, not a divine failure but the failure of Christian man, just as it is with human failures that we deal when we deal with history.[3] "Splendid result attained by Christendom!" exclaimed Kierkegaard as he remarked that unfaith, the impossibility or "inability to believe" was now "the sign of a deeper nature." [4]

The repudiation of Christianity does not, of course, entail the repudiation of religion. It does imply, however, that mythological Christianity has given way to a technological religiosity; or that, in Berdyaev's terms, religion used to play a *symbolic* role in the shaping of Western culture, but has now become pragmatic and utilitarian. Technological religiosity simply corroborates the increasing irrelevance of Christianity, now become the syndrome of the death of God. In plain words, Christianity was regressing even while it brought about the cultural development that presided over the birth of our technological society. And yet the de-divinization of nature (as necessitated by biblical thought) need not have resulted in the "desacralization" or secularization of the world. *Secularity,* or involvement in the world for the sake of God's glory, need not have slipped into secularism. Fostered by Christianity, secularism has been the best expression of the immanentist religiosity which has succeeded the radical monotheism of classical Christianity, when nature, because it was de-

[2] Quoted by Henri Fesquet, *Le catholicisme, religion de demain?* (Paris: B. Grasset, 1962), p. 105.

[3] Cf. Nicolas Aleksandrovich Berdyaev, *Le sens de l'histoire: essai d'une philosophie de la destinée humaine,* translated from the Russian by S. Jankélévitch (Paris: Aubier, 1948), p. 182.

[4] Søren Kierkegaard, *Fear and Trembling* and *The Sickness unto Death* (New York: Doubleday Anchor Books, 1954), p. 246.

divinized, was still conceived as made for grace. Man's preeminence over the creation was an act of faith. His conquest of the universe is today a technological act of prowess if not simply a technical problem. This deterioration had already set in when in the modern period ". . . reason was cultivated at the expense of spirit." [5] No wonder, then, that today we should consequently cultivate religiosity at the expense of faith in God. That is why one can today reverse Kierkegaard's statement and claim that Western culture is the misfortune of Christianity. And that is also why Christianity has remained a Western if not a strictly European phenomenon. At this point, the question becomes: Can Christianity disentangle itself from the present crisis of Western culture? In other words, is Christianity regressing or developing?

[3]

But we must further clarify the problem. To begin with, it must be borne in mind that any development of Christianity is by necessity a matter of faith. Unlike economic goals, it will not be achieved through any sort of five-year plan. Insofar as one can distinguish Christianity from its religious and cultural institutions, it is not an empirical datum but the expression of an act of faith. In order to develop, Christianity must, accordingly, dissociate itself from those institutions of Western culture which are catalyzing the present spiritual crisis. And by doing this Christianity would be truly iconoclastic, smashing its own golden calf. To paraphrase St. Vincent of Lerins, the task consists in saying all things in a new way without proclaiming insidious novelties. The time has come to proclaim the gospel in a new, bold manner, yet without proclaiming a new gospel. Never easy, this kind of task is still more difficult today, and the future quite precarious, what with all the new-fangled ideologies that compete with Christianity—and not always unsuccessfully both at home and abroad.

The second point that needs stressing without delay has already been intimated. Christianity has until now been almost exclusively a European or Western phenomenon. But the realities of the present world have forced Europe and America to realize that the destiny of the West must include non-Western countries. The era of geographic narcissism has gone —whether that be a good thing or not. The fact is that the ideological gigantism of the modern world and its economic, political, social, religious, and philosophical ramifications burst through the frame of "European" Christendom, and dislocate Christianity—unless, of course, Christianity should choose to become solely the homegrown religion of the West, for internal use only.

[5] Röpke.

In the third place, as an empirical datum Christianity has regressed, and this precisely because it has fulfilled itself in Western culture, more accurately in the Christian or Constantinian phase of Western culture. This judgment is based on the claim—I should prefer to say, on the fact—that *culturally,* if not theologically, there has been a Christian era. Though every age is in need of God's grace and accordingly no age is Christian from a strict theological point of view, the fact remains that our cultural institutions, from the church to our democratic ideals, are unmistakably Christian and not Buddhist or what-have-you: Christianity has become an empirical datum. We may, therefore, and must, in fact, consider our problem in terms of Christianity as an empirical datum. Before inquiring into its three main aspects, i.e., theological, ecclesiastical-institutional, and cultural, let us state our premises. If God is dead, then it follows that as an empirical datum Christianity is regressing. It follows, too, that such a situation makes it *culturally* impossible to become a Christian under the present circumstances. But it does not follow that no act of faith, no new proclamation of the *"kerygma"* (i.e., the core of the gospel) can ever take place and overcome this self-invalidation of Christianity. The future of Christianity depends, in other words, upon a cultural reconversion. Exactly this is what I understand Tillich to mean when he writes: "the destruction of the ontological argument is not dangerous. What is dangerous is the destruction of an approach which elaborates the possibility of the question of God. This approach is the meaning and truth of the ontological argument." [6] With such a statement we are already dealing with the *first* of the three aspects I have mentioned, the theological.

It is a truism to say that the critical moments of Western history have also involved the greatest theological activity. And there is no self-congratulation—no delusion either—in claiming that in this period of crisis, too, we are witnessing a theological work of such magnitude that it can be advantageously compared with the best examples of the past. From Karl Barth to Father Teilhard, including Tillich and D'Arcy, Niebuhr and Maritain as well as, of course, Rudolf Bultmann, there has emerged a constellation of thinkers who are, as the above quotation from Tillich shows, in no sense lagging behind the times. Nor are they, as some did when Christianity was faring in better circumstances, accommodating the Christian faith to the exigencies of the *Zeitgeist,* even while they do, too, cope with them. This is not the place to review their work individually, or to assess the impact of their thought upon contemporary intellectual life. Like the sociologists, we must content ourselves with generalities and concern ourselves with empirically observable facts.

Let us, then, admit that it would be a sign of intellectual impotence if we should chide our theologians for their comprehension of our spiritual

---

[6] *Systematic Theology* (Chicago: University of Chicago Press, 1951), Vol. I, p. 208.

and philosophical problems. Christian theological activity has seldom been quite so alive. But this activity seems to take place mostly in the areas of Christian existence which are less, if at all, governed by the institutionalism of our ecclesiastical organizations. Indeed, nothing resists so much the institutionalism of Christian confessions as does Barth's *Kirchliche Dogmatik* (ecclesiastical dogmatics). And Teilhard's work is published without the *imprimatur*. There is some irony in pointing out that for the first time we have theologians without churches or theological systems without their corresponding ecclesiastical apparatus. Without doubt, it is permissible to consider today's theological renewal as a part and preparation or even a precondition of the *cultural* reconversion advocated earlier and without which there can be no further Christian development, no new Christian historical departure. At the same time, one must also point out, it seems, that our Christian institutions have not yet proved themselves worthy of such a magnificent renewal. To put the matter differently and, perhaps, in theologically more accurate terms, it is as if we had arrived at the point where one can still sense in our institutions the presence of the Christian tradition, but it does not coincide with contemporaneous Christian thought. Conversely, the best Christian thinking is today cut off from the tradition as represented by its institutions. Which means, in the words of Isaiah, that:

> We have become like those thou hast never ruled,
> like those who are not called by thy name.

The theological evidence thus points to the practical possibility of God's absence. And even more strange is the fact that the reality of God is eclipsed by the very institutions of the Christian tradition. This brings us to the *second,* the ecclesiological-institutional aspect.

From this angle, what we must note is that Christianity lives on under the form of secularism and that, for this reason, the demarcation line between regression and development is here almost imperceptible. As a result, most of what is left of Christianity flirts with pluralism, while the rest of it has degenerated into a thoroughgoing syncretism. As Dostoevski said, when the gods lose their indigenous character they die, and so do their people. A few believers, of course, survive, headed against the stream of "churchgoers," those ardent supporters of the perennial institutionalism of the Christian churches. But the thing that draws our attention, without surprising us really, is that institutionalism and secularism always seems to go hand in hand. And yet, it is to the sclerotic institutions of Christianity that some have invited us to turn "with some hope," claiming as does Martin Marty that ". . . we already possess the institutions we need to undertake the religious tasks set before . . ." us. Possibly, a certain degree of hopefulness is permissible, but we should not neglect to use caution, lest these institutions be like the lips with which we honor God while our hearts are far from him. To cite Isaiah again: ". . . because this people draw near with their mouth and honor me with their lips, while their hearts are far from me . . . the wisdom of their wise men shall perish, and the discernment of their discerning men shall be hid."

For this reason, I should rather find myself on Peter Berger's side, when he reminds us that the Church is an article of faith, not an empirical datum. He writes:

> Now, it is certainly true that no human culture is so designed as to facilitate conversion. The Jewish culture of Jesus' own time was not so designed. Neither was the Graeco-Roman into which the Christian message was carried by Paul. In other words, the Christian faith will always be in tension with the world. What is characteristic of our situation is that the religious establishment itself obscures this tension and produces the illusion that what tension there is can be understood as growing pains.[7]

Indeed, to be less iconoclastic than those outside the Church would be the greatest treason of Christianity. Nor can one force happiness down other people's throats, let alone faith; and yet this is exactly what our institutions have generally attempted to do so far. Or they keep over and again fighting old battles not only in theological matters but also in the spheres of politics and economics if a battle is engaged at all. For example, it is doubtful whether the separation of Church and State is a valid *theological* issue of our time. Our ecclesiastical factions waste their energy, it seems, either when they radically argue in favor of it, or when, casuistically, they defend the principle while at the same time they seek, if they do not actually draw, support from the State for various purposes, such as education. But the real problem lies behind what the principle of Church and State separation has come to mean or not to mean today, and this problem comes from the fact that the State no longer needs the Church, being itself a sort of clerical organization that has taken over many responsibilities which used to be ecclesiastical.

Incidentally, let us make it clear if we must that none of this is meant to minimize the importance of the Ecumenical Movement and of the world-wide council which is being held at the Vatican; whether they are any indication that the Christian tradition may yet enjoy a new lease on life depends, of course, on whether they are dominated by the institutionalism of the various Christian confessions they represent. Are they not in fact part of the process toward gigantism so characteristic of our age? They are. To be sure, there is nothing intrinsically evil about gigantism, whether or not it is a necessity of the modern world. But when Christianity sanc-

---

[7] *The Noise of Solemn Assemblies* (New York: Doubleday, 1961), p. 117.

tions this particular trend, the danger is that it may be doing so for merely social and institutional reasons, for the sake of maintaining its status. Should this be the case, not only the Christian ecumenical concern would be misplaced or misguided; it would merely serve to accelerate the petrifying grip of institutionalism and sanction the definitive surrender of the Christian tradition. It is more likely, however, that the leaders of both the World Council of Churches and the Vatican Council have also sensed the danger that has faced the Christian tradition. In this case, they should also realize that the divisions of Christianity rest, in the last analysis, on a conception of faith and existence which is descriptive of, and dependent on, the word-view of the so-called Christian era. That is to say, even granting that they were at one time valid for theological reasons, the divisions have today become purely social and institutional: they have lost their theological justification. Nothing less than a radical about-face, like for example an adjustment of dogmas to the realities of our post-Christian era, would convince us of an unsuspected vitality on the part of the Christian tradition. In a post-Christian era, the sociological divisions of Christianity make no sense. They should not be sanctified, but denounced. True iconoclasm begins with oneself, with the smashing of one's own idols, i.e., of one's superannuated conception of God, of faith and religious allegiance.

[4]

We come now to the third aspect, the cultural one. Actually, all that has been said so far has largely been determined by it. Instead, then, of a repetitious elaboration, we shall rather try to sharpen our focus, and for that we must be ready for paradoxes.

On the one hand, our cultural incapacity for God stems from the radical immanentism which informs human experience today. On the other hand, we are no less religious today than those of the previous era. Religiosity, in other words, has set in, sometimes merely concealing religious anarchy and sometimes hardly concealed by religious pluralism, under the guise of tolerance. But pluralism is a misnomer. Really, should we not, instead, characterize the present phenomenon and plethora of religious experiences as the subtle expression of henotheism? Doubtless, it is not here a question of national henotheism. The gigantism of the modern world would prevent that, to begin with. But we may legitimately speak of cultural henotheism, whether it be in terms of the legacy of the Judaeo-Christian tradition to the West, or in terms of a more diffuse reality which actually rests on roughly economic, social, political, or ideological allegiances. Is not denominationalism but a concealed form of the modern version of henotheism—not to mention the latest fad, the tripartite religiosity of democracy? Clearly, I am not advocating religious bigotry and intolerance. But tolerance need not be syncretistic or lead to that institutional pluralism for which God is a social commodity—as was the case exemplified in the emperor cult of the dying Roman empire. And like the syncretism of the Graeco-Roman world before the rise of the Christian tradition, in the last analysis, pluralism can only be an interlude. It often represents nothing other than the lack of vision on the part of a people which is religiously tired, whose God is dead. Obviously, then, if any hope is left that Christianity might somehow recover certain attributes that will make it again relevant to the future of Western culture, it must first of all substitute new cultural patterns for the old ones with which it is identifying itself without any theological justification. Nothing less than a cultural renovation of Christian institutions—and that means a radically new approach to the question of Christianity's cultural embodiment—is necessarily prescribed if any theological renascence is to have some effect outside the walls of the Church as well as within.

That is why, as we have already underlined, an iconoclastic reconversion, a cultural revolution is sorely needed, and all the more urgently because neither institutions nor cultural patterns in general are so "designed as to facilitate conversion" to Christianity, if they are not, as they seem to be today, so designed as to make it altogether superfluous. By comparison, a much easier task, indeed, confronted the early Christians. To begin with, they were not immobilized nor was their vision obscured by already existing institutions, not to mention the fact that the non-Christian institutions were not only religious but also sacral, at least supernatural in their significance, while our culture has lost its sacral dimension. It follows, therefore, that the survival of the Christian tradition is handicapped rather than helped by the existence of cultural structures that are Christian in name only. It was doubtless easier to make the conversion from pre-Christian to Christian than it is from post-Christian to Christian, and the reasons for this are obviously not merely chronological. The conclusions we have reached may be summarized in the following manner:

First, in its deepest recesses, Western culture is practically immunized against Christianity. Conversely, there has occurred what we should like to call a cultural neutralization of the Christian tradition. This means that the once powerful and culturally pregnant symbols of the God-man, of the real presence of God's transcendent immediacy, of communion, are now become words of a forgotten language. Our customs still exhale a Christian flavor, but our hearts are not Christian.[8]

Second, assuming that it was Christianity which began to kill the pagan gods of nature, by de-divinizing nature, until modern science simply confirmed their death, it is possible that, in the last analysis, the death of God means the death of those pagan deities which had somehow survived

[8] Cf. Alain, *Propos sur la religion,* 8th ed. (Paris: Rieder, 1938), p. 41.

in the Christian cultural conception of God. Accordingly, the absence of God, as the only divine reality that can be experienced today, may thus enable Christianity further to clarify the biblical concept of God as the Wholly Other, because he is the Creator and not a natural force.

Third, the era of Western religious narcissism is gone, and this, certainly, is a significant contribution of our post-Christian era to the Christian tradition. The national egotism of emergent countries will perhaps force Christianity to become more kerygmatic at home as well as abroad, that is to say, to help or to awaken the need of a cultural renovation by becoming iconoclastic again and, thus, relevant to the culture of the West.

Fourth, the debunking of religious obscurantism and the absence of supernatural crutches may equally force us to formulate our "cultural will" (Berdyaev), whether as Christians or not, but certainly not as pseudo-Christian Westerners or as pseudo-Western Christians.

Our final point will be made by way of a question borrowed from Saint Augustine: "How could the City of God," he wrote, ". . . either take a beginning or be developed, or attain its proper destiny, if the life of the saints were not a social life?" [9] How could the Christian tradition survive or develop without a concomitant, congruous, cultural reality manifest in all realms of the spirit from theology to art and literature as well as on all levels of life from morality to economics and politics.

In short, the Christian tradition has been regressing insofar as it has not been relevant to the present crisis of our cultural situation. On the other hand, Christian thought has been developing, but it is no longer relevant to the situation of our post-Christian age and its cultural postulates—nor will it be relevant so long as it is tied down by its institutions and by the dogmas of a forgotten language. And should Christianity perchance survive the dishabilitation of its institutions, the least that still must be said is that Western culture is not "ready" for it, as the pre-Christian world once was ready for the Christian gospel.

[9] *De civitate dei,* Book 19, Chap. 5.

15

WILLIAM HAMILTON

William Hamilton was the first theologian to break through the barriers of Protestant neo-orthodoxy and formulate a theological acceptance of the death of God. Having studied with Reinhold Niebuhr and been profoundly influenced by Karl Barth, Hamilton chose the path of entering into an open dialogue with modern culture. Then, in his article on Dostoevski, "Banished from the Land of Unity" (1959; reprinted in his *Radical Theology and the Death of God,* 1966) Hamilton was led to the decision that Ivan Karamazov tells even the Christian how in fact he, as a Christian, believes. Since that time Hamilton has gradually but decisively become the most articulate spokesman and the most dynamic leader of the death of God movement in America. While his thinking is still in process of development and may well move beyond its present focus upon the death of God, Hamilton's crucial break with the theological tradition may best be studied in his *The New Essence of Christianity,* first published in 1961. The following selections are from that book; they include his deeply honest wrestling with the modern theological problem of suffering, his discussion of the death of God, and his understanding of Jesus as the suffering Lord who destroys and transforms all that divinity apart from Himself.

William
Hamilton

The New Essence
of Christianity

BELIEF IN A TIME OF THE DEATH OF GOD

We cannot objectify God, but we must speak about him. So we get into trouble, our words become distorted, and we raise questions about his location and behavior that we cannot answer. If we objectify him, we make him part of the world, but a part we cannot see. We make him part of the causal sequences of the world, and try to fit him into the order and disorder that we see. But then we find that we must say that he made the world or that he caused the evil and suffering of the world, or we refuse to say this. And so we have on our hands either a capricious tyrant causing evil as well as good, or an ineffectual thing, impotent before evil and causing only the good. We seek for words that express God as something other than personal, and we fall into the danger of making him less than personal. The God seen as a person, making the world, manipulating some people towards good, condemning other people to damnation—the objectified God, in other words—this is the God many have declared to be dead today. This is the God who must disappear, so that we may remake our thinking and our speaking about him. "The courage to be," Dr. Tillich writes in one of his most elusive and profound statements, "is rooted in the God who appears when God has disappeared in the anxiety of doubt." [1]

---

[1] *The Courage to Be* (New Haven: Yale University Press, 1952), p. 190.

FROM William Hamilton, *The New Essence of Christianity*, rev. ed. (New York: Association Press, 1966), pp. 41-45, 55-68, 89-96. Reprinted with the permission of the Association Press.

These two affirmations suggest the contours of the rediscovered Augustinian-Reformed portrait of God in our time. They point to what might be called a recovery of God's divinity, his holiness, his separateness from men. Each of the two basic statements we used to describe this portrait carried a positive and a negative component. The first declared that we cannot know God, but that he has made himself known to us. The second stated that God cannot be properly spoken of or treated as an object, but that we can still praise, adore, speak to him. Put technically, the generally received portrait of God today supports the Reformed insistence that the finite cannot contain the infinite (*finitum non capax infiniti*) and rejects the Lutheran tradition which declares that in the humanity of Jesus the finite has received, and thus can contain, the infinite (*finitum capax infiniti*).[2]

There is a great deal to be said for this rediscovery of the divinity of God, but it may be that we are beginning to pay too dear a price for it. Are we not, perhaps, beginning to lose the delicate balance between negation and affirmation that this position requires? We have come to find it far easier to say "we cannot know" than to say "he can make himself known." His holiness and separateness are beginning to look like an indifference. Now it comes as no great surprise to remind ourselves that the most scrupulously correct theological statements have their own built-in difficulties. One of the reasons why theological moods change is that men come to a time when they want to live with new kinds of difficulties. Theology is always like having six storm windows to cover eight windows. One is quite free to choose which six windows to keep the cold air from entering, and you can live pretty well for a while in the protected rooms. But the uncovered windows will let the cold air in sooner or later, and the whole house will feel it. This contemporary portrait of God is serving well at many points, but some leakage is beginning to be felt.

The Problem of Suffering

I am convinced that the most serious leakage caused by this traditional and correct portrait of God today is at the point of the problem of suffering. There is something in this correct doctrine of God that keeps it from dealing responsibly with the problem, and therefore, because of this silence

[2] Eberhard Bethge has recently noted that the Lutheran *finitum capax infiniti* was very close to the center of Bonhoeffer's thought:
"While other dialectical theologians thought of the sovereignty of revelation as gloriously manifest in its freedom and its intangibility, Bonhoeffer, quite after Lutheran fashion, thought of it as apparent in its self-disclosure. Bonhoeffer differed from the other dialectical theologians of those years in his emphasis on the *finitum capax infiniti*." "The Editing and Publishing of the Bonhoeffer Papers," *The Andover Newton Bulletin*, LII, No. 2 (December, 1959), p. 20. See also Bonhoeffer, *Gesammelte Schriften*, II (Munich: Kaiser Verlag, 1959), p. 278.

and carelessness, one can claim today that the problem of suffering has become a major barrier to faith for many sensitive unbelievers.[3]

It is not that the theology dominated by this doctrine of God does not mention the problem. It does, but when it does it is just not good enough. It may, for example, make much of the mystery of iniquity and ask us to shy away from questions about suffering on the grounds that we have no right to put impious questions to the holy God. It may speak of the ontological impossibility of evil; it may say that we are not asked to understand, but only to fight evil; it may say that God is the source of all, good and evil alike, and this is what it means to affirm the divinity of God, and if we don't like it we don't need to affirm him.

Now this kind of evasion may be correct, may even be true, and is certainly very safe. But we miss something: we miss the curious fact that participation in the reality of suffering sometimes destroys the very possibility of faith. The special power of the problem of suffering is that it can really dry up in a man any capacity or wish to call out for the presence of God. If theology cannot reshape its statements about God to face this fact, many men will continue to prefer some sort of humanism without answers to a correct doctrine of God without answers . . . .

The Death of God

I am not here referring to a belief in the nonexistence of God.[4] I am talking about a growing sense, in both non-Christians and Christians, that God has withdrawn, that he is absent, even that he is somehow dead. Elijah taunted the false prophets and suggested that their god may have gone on a journey, since he could not be made to respond to their prayers.[5] Now,

---

[3] "The insurmountable barrier to Christianity does seem to me to be the problem of evil. But it is also a real obstacle for traditional humanism. There is the death of children, which means a divine reign of terror, but there is also the killing of children, which is an expression of a human reign of terror. We are wedged between two kinds of arbitrary law." Albert Camus, quoted by John Cruickshank, *Albert Camus and the Literature of Revolt* (New York: Galaxy Books, Oxford University Press, 1960), pp. xii-xiii.

[4] "The world has become an entity rounded off in itself, which is neither actually open at certain points where it merges into God, nor undergoes at certain observable points the causal impact of God . . . but it points to God as its presupposition only as a whole, and even so not very obviously. . . . We are experiencing today that we can make no image of God that is not carved from the wood of this world. The educated man of our time has the duty, painful though fruitful, to accept this experience. He is not to suppress it by a facile, anthropomorphic 'belief in God,' but interpret it correctly, realizing that, in fact, it has nothing in common with atheism." Karl Rahner, "Wissenschaft als Confession?" *Wort und Wahrheit*, November, 1954, pp. 812-13. Quoted by Hans Urs von Balthasar, *Science, Religion and Christianity* (London: Burns & Oates, 1958), p. 95. Published in America by The Newman Press, Westminster, Md.

[5] I Kings 18:27.

many seem to be standing with the false prophets, wondering if the true God has not withdrawn himself from his people. This feeling ranges from a sturdy unbelieving confidence in God's demise to the troubled believer's cry that he is no longer in a place where we can call upon him. Arthur Koestler represents the confident mood:

> God is dethroned; and although the incognisant masses are tardy in realising the event, they feel the icy draught caused by that vacancy. Man enters upon a spiritual ice age; the established churches can no longer provide more than Eskimo huts where their shivering flock huddles together.[6]

The patronizing and confident tone of this announcement reminds us of both Feuerbach and Nietzsche. In the famous passage in "The Gay Science" where the idea of the death of God is put forward by Nietzsche, a madman is portrayed as searching for God, calling out for him, and finally concluding that he and all men have killed him. The man's hearers do not understand his words, and he concludes that he has come with his message too early. He goes on to wander about the city's churches, calling out, "What are these churches now if they are not the tombs and sepulchers of God?" Koestler's igloos and Nietzsche's tombs are spiritually, if not architecturally, related. But in spite of Nietzsche's statement that the madman had come too soon, his declaration of God's death was heard and believed. And in the nineteenth century, as De Lubac writes, "man is getting rid of God in order to regain possession of the human greatness which, it seems to him, is being unwarrantably withheld by another. In God he is overthrowing an obstacle in order to gain his freedom." [7] Freud shared something of this Nietzschean conviction that God must be dethroned and killed to make way for the proper evaluation and freedom of man. And of course, as against many forms of religion, even this strident cry bears some truth.

But Koestler's confident assurance of God's dethronement and death is not the only way modern man describes his sense of God's absence or disappearance. When Dr. Tillich refers to the death of God he usually means the abolition of the idea of God as one piece of being alongside others, of God as a big person. Death of God for him is thus the death of the idols,

---

[6] "The Trail of the Dinosaur," *Encounter* (London), May, 1955. One should add that Koestler never seems to stand still, and that at the close of his recent book *The Lotus and the Robot* (London: Hutchinson & Co., Ltd., 1960), he has a very modest word of praise for Christianity, and, if not for dogma, at least for "the tenets of Judeo-Christian ethics."

[7] Henri de Lubac, *The Drama of Atheist Humanism* (New York: Sheed & Ward, 1949), p. 6.

or the false gods. The novels of Albert Camus, on the other hand, portray not only a world from which the false gods, and the holy God of the theological revival, have departed, but a world from which any and all gods have silently withdrawn. The world of these novels is a world in which the word God simply refuses to have any meaning. This is not treated as a good thing or a terrible thing; it is just a fact that is ruefully assumed. It is the God described by the best and most sophisticated theologians of our time, who seems to many today to have withhdrawn from his world. When we feel this, we do not feel free or strong, but weak, unprotected, and frightened.[8]

We seem to be those who are trying to believe in a time of the death of God. Just what do we mean when we say this? We mean that the Augustinian-Reformed portrait of God itself is a picture of a God we find more and more elusive, less and less for us or with us. And so we wonder if God himself is not absent. When we speak of the death of God, we speak not only of the death of the idols or the falsely objectivized Being in the sky; we speak, as well, of the death in us for any power to affirm any of the traditional images of God. We mean that the world is not God and that it does not point to God.[9] Since the supports men have always depended on to help them affirm God seem to be gone, little wonder that many take the next step and wonder whether God himself has gone. Little wonder that Lent is the only season when we are at home, and that that cry of dereliction from the cross is sometimes the only biblical word that can speak to us. If Jesus can wonder about being forsaken by God, are we to be blamed if we wonder?

Beyond the Death of God

Now, a believing Christian can face without distress any announcement about the disappearance of the idols from the religious world of man, but

[8] "Men are frightened at the absence of God from the world, they feel that they can no longer realize the Divine, they are terrified at God's silence, at his withdrawal into his own inaccessibility. . . . This experience which men think they must interpret theoretically as atheism, is yet a genuine experience of the most profound existence . . . with which popular Christian thought and speech will not have finished for a long time." Rahner, *op. cit.*, p. 812, quoted by Von Balthasar, *op. cit.*, p. 96.

[9] The classical Reformation conception of Providence depended for its formulation on the presence of a whole series of orders that were self-evident to sixteenth-century man: the order of the celestial bodies, the order of the political realm, the order and predictability of the natural world, the order and inner coherence of the self. Men as diverse as Calvin and Shakespeare drew on this experience of order in their own work. In the *Institutes*, I. 5., Calvin used this external orderliness as a means of illuminating the sovereign care of God over the world. Tragedy, for Shakespeare, was the unusual and odd breakdown of the natural order of human life. Hamlet's perception that "the time is out of joint" is a perception of a disorder that is the basis of Shakespeare's sense of tragedy. See also Ulysses' speech on order in *Troilus and Cressida*, Act I, Scene 3.

he cannot live as a Christian for long with the suspicion that God himself has withdrawn. How is it possible to turn this difficult corner, and to move from an acknowledgment of God's disappearance to a sense of some kind of reappearance and presence? This sense of the separation of God from the world, Ronald Gregor Smith writes,

> does not lead to mere or sheer undialectical atheism. Any assertion of the absence of God and even further of his nonexistence among the phenomena of the world is dialectically confronted by the equal assertion of his presence. I am sorry if this sounds like a mere verbal trick, but it cannot be helped.[10]

There is something disarming about Gregor Smith's unwillingness to look carefully at the connections between the sense of disappearance of God and the problem of his reappearance. But his way of putting it does indeed sound like a verbal trick, and we must try to discover if there are not ways of moving from the one state to the other.

One of the favorite contemporary attempts to do this might be called the Augustinian doubt maneuver. Augustine noted that he overcame his temptation toward skepticism by observing that even skepticism implied some affirmation of truth, the truth at least of the skeptical position.

> Everyone who knows that he is in doubt about something knows a truth, and in regard to this that he knows he is certain. Therefore he is certain about a truth. Consequently everyone who doubts if there be a truth has in himself a true thing on which he does not doubt.[11]

This may or may not be a convincing way to overcome radical skepticism. But it certainly cannot be used to mean that we can, by a kind of interior maneuver, affirm that we know the very thing we doubt. Augustine did not use it thus; we may doubt one truth, but that implies, he tells us, that we know another thing in our act of doubt, namely, that we are doubters. But some Christians have tried to claim that somehow doubt implies faith. God's existence, we are often told, is most profoundly proven in the very experience of doubting or denying him. Of course, passionate doubt has a resemblance to passionate faith. Both have a deep concern for the problem of truth; both real doubt and real faith deeply care. But it is not good enough to suggest that "There is no God" or "I cannot know that there is a God" really bears the same meaning as "Thou art my God." Let us continue to say that doubt is a necessary way for many of us to faith; that faith never overcomes doubt finally and completely; that lively faith can

[10] "A Theological Perspective of the Secular," *The Christian Scholar*, XLIII, No. 1 (March, 1960), p. 22.
[11] *On True Religion*, XXIX. 73.

bear a good deal of doubt around the edges. But the depth of doubt is not the depth of faith; these are two places, not one, and a choice must finally be made between them. We cannot evade such a problem by a trick of redefinition.

This confusion of doubt and faith obscures the problem of moving from an affirmation about the disappearance of God to an affirmation of his presence. I wonder if the following, and quite beautiful, passage from Dr. Tillich, is not also obscure in its apparent identification of having with not-having.

> To the man who longs for God and cannot find Him; to the man who wants to be acknowledged by God and cannot even believe that He is; to the man who is striving for a new and imperishable meaning of his life and cannot discover it—to this man Paul speaks. We are each such a man. Just in this situation, where the Spirit is far from our conscious-ness, where we are unable to pray or to experience any meaning in life, the Spirit is working quietly in the depth of our souls. In the moment when we feel separated from God, meaningless in our lives, and con-demned to despair, we are not left alone. The Spirit, sighing and longing in us and with us, represents us. It manifests what we really are. In feeling this against feeling, in believing this against belief, in knowing this against knowledge, we like Paul, possess all.[12]

Now this is less specious than the doubt-equals-faith position. And it points to a profound truth. Faith is never the claim to own or possess. God comes to us finally when we confess that we have nothing in our hands to bring. Our not-knowing alone leads to knowing; our not-having is the only way to possession. All this is true, and very close to the Protestant conviction that God's access is to sinners and not to saints. But it will not do. Such a word as Dr. Tillich's can do much. It can persuade the man who struggles for God that there is a sense in which he has been found. It can portray the Christian tradition attractively as one which knows, welcomes, and lives with the experience of struggle and not-knowing. But it will not serve to transform an experience of not-having into an experience of hav-ing. For all of our verbalizing, these remain two different experiences, and we are not finally helped by those who do not face openly the distinc-tions.

The curious thing about this matter of God's disappearance is that even in those moments when we are most keenly aware of God's absence we still, somehow, find it possible to pray for his return. Perhaps we ought to conclude that the special Christian burden of our time is the situation of being without God. There is, for some reason, no possession of God for

---

[12] *The Shaking of the Foundations* (New York: Scribner's, 1958), p. 139.

us, but only a hope, only a waiting.[13] This is perhaps part of the truth: to be a Christian today is to stand, somehow, as a man without God but with hope. We know too little to know him now; we only know enough to be able to say that he will come, in his own time, to the broken and contrite heart, if we continue to offer that to him. Faith is, for many of us, we might say, purely eschatological. It is a kind of trust that one day he will no longer be absent from us. Faith is a cry to the absent God; faith is hope.

An identification of faith with hope is possible, but a little more can be said. The absent one has a kind of presence; the one for whom the Christian man waits still makes an impact on us. W. H. Auden has described this presence very accurately.

> In our anguish we struggle
> To elude Him, to lie to Him, yet His love observes
> His appalling promise; His predilection
> As we wander and weep is with us to the end.
> Minding our meanings, our least matter dear to Him. . . .
> It is where we are wounded that is when He speaks
> Our creaturely cry, concluding His children
> In their mad unbelief to have mercy on them all
> As they wait unawares for His world to come.[14]

In this there is waiting, but also something else. God is also the one whom we struggle to elude; as Augustine says, "Thou never departest from us, and yet only with difficulty do we return to thee." [15] He speaks to us at the point where we are wounded. And even though our wound is our separation from him, the separation is not absolute. The reflections of Psalm

---

[13] Perhaps one of the reasons why Samuel Beckett's *Waiting for Godot* has fascinated us is that Beckett has portrayed so many of the ambiguities in our feeling about God today. Godot, for whom Vladimir and Estragon wait, seems to stand for the traditional God for whom all of us think we are waiting. This Godot has a white beard (p. 59), he punishes those who reject him (p. 60), he saves (pp. 48, 61), he is the one to whom Vladimir and Estragon offer a "kind of prayer," a "vague supplication" (p. 13). In Godot there is a combination of absence and harshness. He is always postponing his visit; yet he is said to beat the young boy's brother (p. 34). Vladimir asks the boy, Godot's messenger, "What does he do, Mr. Godot?" And the boy replies, "He does nothing, Sir" (p. 59). At the close of the play, when Godot still has not arrived, Estragon asks if they should not drop Godot altogether. To this Vladimir replies, "He'd punish us" (p. 60). Finally, is the Christian critic being over-eager when he notes that the waiting takes place by a tree—the only part of the landscape that has not died (pp. 60-61)? (The page references are to the Grove Press edition, New York, 1954.)

[14] From *The Age of Anxiety,* by W. H. Auden. Copyright 1946, 1947 by W. H. Auden. Reprinted by permission of Random House, Inc. Also with the permission of Faber and Faber, Ltd., publishers.

[15] *Confessions,* VIII. 8.

139 and Genesis 32:24-25 in this fragment from Auden remind us of part of our situation.

Thus, neither "death of God," "absence of God," nor "disappearance of God" is wholly adequate to describe the full meaning of our religious situation. Our experience of God is deeply dissatisfying to us, even when we are believers. In one sense God seems to have withdrawn from the world and its sufferings, and this leads us to accuse him of either irrelevance or cruelty. But in another sense, he is experienced as a pressure and a wounding from which we would love to be free. For many of us who call ourselves Christians, therefore, believing in the time of the "death of God" means that he is there when we do not want him, in ways we do not want him, and he is not there when we do want him.

The rediscovery of the divinity of God which we described at the start of this chapter seems defective on two counts. It gives us a portrait of God that does not seem able to receive honestly the threat posed by the problem of suffering, and it does not accurately enough describe the curious mixture of the disappearance and presence of God that is felt by many today. I am not sure just what ought to be our proper response to this curious mixture. There seems to be some ground for terror here, so that we can partly agree with Ingmar Bergmann when he said recently that "if God is not there, life is an outrageous terror." [16] Yet in another sense we face the special texture of our unsatisfactory religious situation with calmness. Most of us are learning to accept these things: the disappearance of God from the world, the coming of age of the world, as it has been called, the disappearance of religion as a lively factor in modern life, the fact that there are men who can live both without God and without despair. We are coming to accept these calmly as events not without their advantages. Perhaps our calmness will disappear when we face the possibility that God will even more decisively withdraw—that he will withdraw from our selves as he has already withdrawn from the world, that not only has the world become sheer world but that self will become sheer self. For if there are men today who can do without God, it still seems to be true that we cannot do so. We are afraid of ourselves without him, even though what we know of him may be only a pressure and a wounding.

Finally, this portrait of the situation between man and God today, in the time (as we have called it) of the death of God, is not satisfactory if this is all we know. We have really described a bondage, not a freedom; a disturbance and very little else. If this were all there were to the Christian faith, it would not be hard to reject it. Is there, then, a deliverance from this absent-present disturber God? There is, and the deliverance will some-how be connected with another image of God—what we have already

[16] *Time,* March 14, 1960, p. 66.

referred to as the impotent God—that emerges when we try to take our next step and saying something about Jesus the Lord.[17] But I have not stated, and I do not want to state, that we can know nothing of God apart from Jesus. We can and do know something, and it is just this unsatisfactory mixture of his presence and absence, his disturbance.[18] As we move towards the center of the Christian faith, Jesus Christ, will we be able to overcome the instability of our belief in a time of the death of God or, even reckoning with Jesus, will something of this experience remain?

JESUS THE LORD

Lordship as Humiliation Answers the Questions

JESUS AND THE KNOWLEDGE OF GOD   If one begins his reflections on this problem with the statement that Jesus is Lord, a first consequence may be some uneasiness with the formula "divinity of Christ," though not with the meaning behind the formula. Uneasiness, not because the phrase points to something false, but rather because it seems difficult to understand how either an affirmation or denial of it could make any sense. Let us assume you are asked, "Do you believe in the divinity of Christ?" It makes no dif-

[17] In a recent debate on the BBC, Professor Gregor Smith tried to bring together the sense of the disappearance of God from the world and a Christian affirmation about Jesus.

"I recognize in that situation that you describe, for yourself and for us all, what you might call the reappearance of God, a veiled reappearance certainly, and I should focus this in the life of Christ, in his life of being for other people, which is how you can sum it up—just being for other people absolutely. I should focus it there, and also in the constellation of events that gather round that particular bit of human history both before and after. I find it almost impossible to say more than this, just because I recognize at once that though I see here action of God, it is, of course, ambiguous. It is still possible to say: 'Well, I just don't see it.' " *The Listener* (London) January 21, 1960.

[18] At this point the Jew—both ancient Israel and the modern Jew—becomes significant for Christian theological reflection. Jewish existence is an important part of the evidence we cite for our conviction that God is the one who leaves us alone and the one who disturbs us. The Jew is the one who knows what it is to be disturbed by both God and men, and in this sense the Christian never ceases being a Jew when he is a Christian. The reality and integrity of Jewish existence are what prevent the Christian from holding too rigid a Christological definition of God. "Apart from Christ I am an atheist" is false; "apart from Christ I am a Jew" would be closer to the truth. This close theological dependence of the Christian on the Jew (which is a mutual dependence for some Jewish thinkers, but not for others) is one reason why we ought to be deeply disturbed by the lack of really effective theological conversation between Christianity and Judaism today. It is arguable that there is more real theological affinity between Protestantism and some forms of Judaism than between Protestantism and Roman Catholicism. The latter is a Christian heresy, whereas Judaism is in some way a theological necessity. The Protestant needs to learn what it means to stand with the Jew, even when the Jew is not willing to stand with him.

ference whether the questioner is impeccably orthodox and suspects you are not, or wildly unitarian and suspects you of dogmatism. The question implies a comparison between two clearly known categories: one, called the divine or divinity; the other, the man Jesus. And the questioner wishes to know whether or not you find these two known categories commensurable. But the point is this: we do not have two known categories at all. We have Jesus the man. Of him we know something; not enough to satisfy, not enough to provide answers to our ethical problems, but enough to be able to say what was characteristic of him and his way with men. And we have further a decision of faith that Jesus is the Lord, the one through whom God meets us. But we do not know any separate category of divinity, a separate divine essence by means of which we can define Jesus.[19] [Previously] we described man's situation before God today, and what we found there was a "divinity" quite perplexing, dissatisfying, even intolerable. That kind of divinity was both an absence and a wounding presence: an absence or disappearance from the world, and a pressure or presence in the heart of the individual. In this sense, Jesus is not divine; as the suffering Lord he is a protest against this kind of divinity, or, in better terms, he is a correction and a transformation of divinity as seen in that way.

If there is divinity apart from Jesus, it is a form of divinity that Jesus as suffering Lord corrects, destroys, transforms. In Jesus the Lord we see for the first time what Christian "divinity" must be taken to be: it is God withdrawing from all claims to power and authority and sovereignty, and consenting to become himself the victim and subject of all that the world can do. The afflicting God of our previous chapter becomes now the afflicted God. Divinity in Jesus is not withdrawal from the world; it is a full consent to abide in the world, and to allow the world to have its way with it.

This is why we can't be content with the traditional way of formulating the question of the divinity of Jesus. "Divinity, divine essence?" we say. "Yes, we know a little of what this means, and what we know of it haunts and disturbs us, both because of its abdication from the world and because of its wounding presence in our hearts. But what we know of it by itself leads us to reject it, not to welcome it at all. In Jesus the Lord, the whole meaning of what it is to be God is so radically transformed that we can no longer move from divinity to Jesus (and thus to assert the divinity of

[19] "Jesus Christ . . . is not God in a self-evident and explainable manner, but only in faith. This divine being does not exist. If Jesus Christ is to be described as God, then one must not speak about his divine essence, his omnipotence or his omniscience, but only about this weak man among sinners, about his cradle and his cross. If we are dealing with the divinity of Jesus we must speak especially of his weakness." From a reconstructed version of Bonhoeffer's 1933 Berlin lectures on Christology, *Gesammelte Schriften*, Vol. 3 (Munich: Kaiser Verlag, 1960), p. 233. Compare the passage from *Letters and Papers from Prison*, pp. 163-64, quoted [in the complete *The New Essence of Christianity*], pp. 54-55.

Christ) but from Jesus to divinity, and to affirm that our picture of God is ultimately determined by seeing him as the one who has come in the lowliness of Jesus the Lord."

If it is true that "Luther limited our knowledge of God to our individual experience of temptation and our identification in prayer with the passion of God's son," [20] then there are some affinities between our position here and Luther's. God himself, Luther would say, is the remote one who comes to us directly only as law and demand. This is the terrible God whom man cannot abide or compass, for he is hidden from man's knowing. But, Luther went on, God has made himself small, and has willed to enter wholly into the lives of men in the humanity of Jesus. Here he is not hidden; he is manifest. Here the infinite one has put himself completely into the finite space of Jesus the man.

Two passages, characteristic of hundreds more, might be cited to remind us of Luther's powerful, and perhaps even dangerous, concentration of the lowly humanity of Jesus. The first is from the early lectures on the Epistle to the Hebrews, 1516-17:

> It is to be noted that he (i.e., the author of the epistle) speaks of the humanity of Christ before he names his deity, and by this approves that rule of knowing God by faith. For his humanity is our holy ladder, by which we ascend to the knowledge of God. . . . Who wishes safely to ascend to the love and knowledge of God, let him leave human and metaphysical rules for knowing the deity, and let him first exercise himself in the humanity of Christ. For it is the most impious of all temerities when God himself has humbled himself in order that he might be knowable, that a man should seek to climb up some other way, through his own ingenious devices.[21]

The second is from the lectures on Galatians, delivered in 1531:

> But true Christian divinity (as I give you often warning) setteth not God forth unto us in his majesty, as Moses and other doctrines do. It commandeth us not to search out the nature of God: but to know his will set out to us in Christ, whom he would have to take our flesh upon him, to be born and to die for our sins. . . . Wherefore . . . there is nothing more dangerous than to wander with curious speculations in heaven, and there to search out God in his incomprehensible power, wisdom and majesty, how he created the world, and how he governeth it. . . . Therefore begin thou there where Christ began, namely, in the womb of the Virgin, in the manger, and at his mother's breasts. . . . For to this end he came down, was born, was conversant among men, suffered, was crucified and died, that by all means he might set forth

[20] Erik H. Erikson, *Young Man Luther* (New York: W. W. Norton & Co., 1958), p. 253.
[21] Weimar edition, 57.99.1.

himself plainly before our eyes, and fasten the eyes of our hearts upon himself, that he thereby might keep us from climbing up into heaven, and from the curious searching of the divine majesty. . . . Then know thou that there is no other God besides this man Christ Jesus. . . . I know by experience what I say.[22]

In our day, Karl Barth, in the first part of his treatment of the doctrine of reconciliation, insists over and over that we must allow Jesus' lowliness and humiliation to determine what we mean by God. Here are some of his comments:

> How the freedom of God is constituted, in what character He is the Creator and Lord of all things, distinct from and superior to them, in short, what is to be understood by "Godhead," is something which— watchful against all imported ideas, ready to correct them and perhaps to let them be reversed and renewed in the most astonishing way—we must always learn from Jesus Christ (p. 129).
> God shows Himself to be the great and true God in the fact that He can and will let His grace bear this cost, that He is capable and willing and ready for this condescension, this act of extravagance, this far journey (p. 159).
> The meaning of His deity—the only true deity in the New Testament sense—cannot be gathered from any notion of supreme, absolute, non-worldly being. It can be learned only from what took place in Christ (p. 177).
> Has He really made Himself worldly for the world's sake or not? (p. 196).
> God chooses condescension. He chooses humiliation, lowliness and obedience (p. 199).
> . . . in giving Himself up to this alien life in His Son God did not evade the cause of man's fall and destruction, but exposed Himself to and withstood the temptation which man suffers and in which he becomes a sinner and the enemy of God (p. 215).[23]

To speak about God and to know him means, therefore, to shape everything that we say and pray into the pattern of Jesus the humiliated Lord. Can we do this in a pure way? Can we do it so perfectly that all the problems of "belief in the time of the death of God" magically disappear? Is there, for the man in Jesus the Lord, no sense of God's withdrawal and

[22] From Philip S. Watson's revision of the 1575 English translation (London: James Clarke & Co., 1953), pp. 43-44.
[23] The page references are to *Church Dogmatics,* Vol. IV, Part 1. It should be pointed out that this note is sounded in the first part of Barth's three-part study of the person and work of Christ. He would doubtless consider the position being suggested here woefully incomplete without the parallel emphasis on the exaltation of man to God alongside the condescension of God to man. The weakness of my position that I indicate just below is not weakness in Barth.

hounding presence, no waiting for God? I cannot believe that a decision for Jesus as Lord will so simply make irrelevant the situation that we described a chapter ago. The God of the time of the death of God and the God coming in Jesus the Lord are somehow both with us, and as yet no conceptual way has offered itself that will permit us to assign each an appropriate place. A decision for Jesus as Lord is the way we face our difficulties, the way we turn the corner, the way we put off the threat of unbelief in, or rebellion against, that other kind of divinity. Perhaps some new formulation of the doctrine of the Trinity would be a way to fit the two themes together. But now they are both present; each striking, correcting, and violating the other.

One thing is true. We have chosen to live with the dangers of the impotence or weakness of God rather than with the dangers of his power, for we believe that this was God's choice in the crucifixion. We have gained something, and we have lost something. We have gained the power to say: "because of Jesus the Lord, God is always emptying himself to meet us where we are. In joy and in despair, he will never let us go." But if we have one kind of confidence along these lines, we have deprived ourselves of another kind, that kind which can say: "God's rule cannot be violated, his purposes for his creation are sure, his power stands sure over all earthly powers." We have chosen to stand with his lowly presence, but we have so defined power as weakness, that our life in that presence has lost much of the protection and serenity other Christians have known.

16
PAUL
VAN BUREN

Thus far Paul van Buren is the only radical American theologian who has had a major impact upon the world of the theological academies. Once a loyal disciple of Barth, he lost Barth's blessing when he published *The Secular Meaning of the Gospel* in 1963. Van Buren may prove to be one of Barth's most creative followers, however, for he surpasses the master in the great modern theological task of transforming theology into Christology. Like so many recent "secular theologians," Van Buren has chosen a modern secular language as the language of theology; but he stands alone in terms of the clarity, precision, and consistency which he has reached in his own language. In adopting the empirical premises and methods of modern analytic philosophy as the basic tools of theology, he was following the lead of other theologians; yet Van Buren has been the only theologian to do so for a purely theological as opposed to an apologetic purpose. Two crucial assumptions underlie his quest for the secular meaning of the Gospel. The first is that genuine meaning in our world is and can only be secular, and the second is that the Gospel is and must be meaningful in our world. Ironically enough, it is his second assumption which has come under the heaviest theological attack. Van Buren himself refuses any identification with the death of God movement, limiting himself to the assertion that the word *God* is dead in our world. As the reader will see, however, this assertion has radical consequences for theology.

Paul **The Meaning**
van Buren **of the Gospel**

THE GOSPEL AS THE EXPRESSION OF A
HISTORICAL PERSPECTIVE

The Gospel, the "good news" of the apostles concerning Jesus of Nazareth and what happened on Easter, was proclaimed as news of an event which it was good for men to hear. The result of its proclamation was that many responded with joy and became "Christians." They shared the way of life of the apostles and the apostles' conviction that the history of Jesus and the event of Easter had universal significance. We shall introduce our analysis of the language of this Gospel by comparing the positions of those who first preached it on the basis of the Easter experience, and of those who became believers later. After a discussion of particularity and universality in the language of the kerygma, we shall analyze the content of the kerygma itself in its basic form, comparing our result with other analyses of the language of faith. Our result will then be compared with some typical, central Christological assertions of the Gospel and with the "call and response" Christology developed in Chapter 2. Although our analysis cannot cover every detail of the language of the Gospel, we intended to give careful attention to the central assertions of the kerygma, so that the logic of its language will be clear.

In the last chapter, we analyzed the language of those who experienced the appearances of Easter described in I Cor. 15:3ff.[1] Faith in the Gospel of the resurrection was not confined, however, to those who had been "eye

[1] Cf. also I Cor. 9:1.

---

witnesses" of the Easter event. The apostles proclaimed the Gospel to others, and some of their hearers responded positively. Those who became Christians in this way understood themselves as sharing with the apostles in a freedom defined by the freedom of Jesus of Nazareth and in a new perspective upon life and the world. This experience has been traditionally called conversion.

A man who has been converted to Christian faith does not ordinarily go about saying, "I have seen the Lord." He may say, "I have seen the light," however, and this suggests how his experience at once resembles and differs from that of the apostles on Easter. Theology has traditionally accounted for his conversion not by referring to an appearance of Jesus, as in the case of the apostles, but by referring to the work of the Holy Spirit. It should not be necessary at this stage of our argument to explain why saying that a man was brought to faith and freedom "by the operation of the Holy Spirit" is not an empirical assertion, in any unsophisticated sense of the word *empirical*. If a man says this, he may indeed intend to call our attention to certain aspects of how things are in the world, and if we see things as he does, we may also attend to these aspects, which would provide some empirical grounding for his statement. The divine reference ("Holy Spirit") does indicate, for instance, that the new freedom and perspective are received as gifts by the believer and that they are of fundamental importance to him. The divine reference is also at least an indirect reference to Jesus.[2] Christian theology, especially in the classical Protestant tradition, has underscored this reference to Jesus by saying that such an "operation of the Holy Spirit" does not take place apart from the "proclamation of the Word."[3] The story of the man who was free for others even to the point of death, and whose freedom has been contagious, is held up to the listener, who is invited to share in this event.[4] In the context of hearing the Gospel proclaimed, the listener may have an experience of discernment. He may "see" Jesus in a new way and acquire a new perspective upon himself and the whole of life. A long tradition of Christian devotional literature has emphasized the act of historical imagination in which the reader is invited to be "present" at the events of which the Gospel speaks, and this imaginative act has also played its part in much of Christian worship. Although the language of conversion differs from the language of those involved in the Easter event, they function in a remarkably similar manner. The difference between the two lies in the fact that the believers' expression of faith depends logically and historically upon that of the apostles.

The language of faith, whether that of the first apostles or of a modern believer, contains an exclusive element: it claims the universal significance of a particular, historical individual, Jesus of Nazareth. In our interpreta-

[2] John 15:26; 16:14.   [4] Gal. 3:1; Heb. 2:8-9.
[3] Typically, John Calvin, *Institutes,* I, ix, pp. 1-3.

tion of the history of Jesus and of Easter, we emphasized the freedom of Jesus. It is evident, however, that there have been other free men in history. We have already suggested some of the dynamics of interpersonal relations which may result from an encounter with a free man. If our reaction is positive, we may feel attracted to him and we may be encouraged to be more free ourselves, or at least challenged to be more free. Our fears may be calmed simply by the presence of one who is unafraid and free from the fears and anxieties which bind us. On the other hand, our reaction may be negative: we may be threatened by a free person; we may feel judged in our insecurity and bondage. This is an odd experience and if we speak of it at all, we will do so with odd words. We might say that there is a certain mystery about it, a mystery of the depths of human personality and relationships.

Jesus of Nazareth may be distinguished, however, from other men who might have a liberating effect upon men. We must grant a "family resemblance" between the language with which we speak of Jesus and the language used to speak of other free men, of course, in order to be able to describe him at all. Nevertheless, we may use a number of the same words in describing two men without denying that the men are actually quite different. When we compare Socrates as portrayed in Plato's *Dialogues,* for example, and Jesus as portrayed in the Gospels, we may say that both men were "free," but we can also see subtle differences. Two different words for "love," *philia* (the attraction of like to like) and *agape* (a love which makes no distinctions and seeks no return on its investment), may serve to indicate something of the difference which we detect between the two descriptions.

The Gospel, however, is not merely about a free man; it is the good news of a free man who has set other men free, first proclaimed by those to whom this had happened. And it has happened again and again during nineteen centuries that, in the context of hearing this apostolic proclamation, men have been liberated. Their response, which the New Testament calls "faith," consists in acknowledging that this has happened by accepting the liberator, Jesus of Nazareth, as the man who defines for them what it means to be a man and as the point of orientation for their lives. They are "in Christ," which is to say that their understanding of themselves and their lives and all things is determined by their understanding of Jesus. They are a "new creation" in that this orientation to the whole world is new for them.

There is no empirical ground, however, for the Christian's saying that something of this sort could not happen to a disciple of Socrates. Reading the history of Socrates might conceivably have a liberating effect on a person, who might say that he shared in the freedom of the philosopher. If this were to happen, the Socratic's freedom, presumably, would be defined by the peculiar character of Socrates' freedom. He would acknowledge Socrates as his norm. He would be "in Socrates," let us say, not "in Christ." Perhaps the Socratic, like the Christian, would claim that his was the only valid norm. The exclusiveness of such a claim . . . would express the firmness of his conviction. Understanding the claim of exclusiveness in this way, we take this to be its meaning.

The language of the Gospel contains not only exclusive claims; it has a universal aspect also. It claims that in the history of Jesus of Nazareth something universal, eternal, absolute, something it calls "God," was manifested. We discussed the difficulties of such language [earlier], but a further consideration is in order. Whether formulated in terms of eternity in time, the divine in human form, or the transcendent in the historical, the Gospel is expressed traditionally in language which has its roots in that of the New Testament and which reflects the patristic doctrine of incarnation. Its earliest and most basic form is the confession "Jesus is Lord." [5] This confession is held to be valid regardless of circumstances,[6] but a believer might say that if he never saw any love among men, he would find it almost impossible to make this confession. In that case, part of the meaning of the confession would be to call our attention to the experience of human love. If we grant that human love or its absence is a part of how things are in the world, we can say that the confession has, in this sense, an "empirical" grounding. Our impression from the New Testament, however, is that this confession implies that the believer is saying, "Even if I never saw any love in others, I have nevertheless seen it in the man Jesus and I recognize the claim of love on me." In this case, the empirical anchorage of the confession is in the history of Jesus and in the actions of the believer. The logic of this confession is at least implied by the traditional assertion that there are practical consequences for the man who confesses the Lordship of Jesus, that Christian faith involves a way of life.

Those who first said, "Jesus is Lord," expressed a particular perspective upon life and history.[7] This confession, ascribing universality to a particular man, indicated that faith constituted a certain understanding of self, man, history, and the whole world, and that this universal perspective had its norm in the history of Jesus of Nazareth and Easter. This perspective upon life and the world was understood not as a point of view selected by the believer, but as a "blik" by which the believer was "grasped" and "held." The perspective of faith was spoken of as a response "drawn from" the believer. The language of the Gospel implies consistently that faith is "given," that the believer cannot and does not want to take any credit for it. By its very nature, faith excludes all boasting.[8]

[5] I Cor. 12:3; Phil. 2:11; O. Cullmann, *Die ersten christlichen Glaubensbekenntnisse* (Zollikon-Zürich: Evang. Verlag, 1943).
[6] Rom. 8:35-39.
[7] Acts 2:36-42; cf. Phil. 2:1-11.
[8] Rom. 3:27; I Cor. 1:27-29; Gal. 6:14.

The issue between those whose perspective on life and history is defined by the history of Jesus and those whose perspective is defined by another reference is notoriously one that cannot be settled by argument. This shows that the function of the Gospel is to indicate not only the norm of the Christian's perspective but also the character of the perspective itself. This perspective cannot be held as one point of view among many. It is not a logical conclusion to a chain of reasoning. Of either of these, a man might say, "This is the position which I chose." The language of faith says, "I did not choose; I was chosen. I did not take this piece of history as the clue to my life and understanding of all history; it took me." The language of faith, by referring to a transcendent element, indicates that something has happened to the believer, rather than that he has done something.

On the other hand, if in response to the proclamation of the free man who has set men free the hearer finds himself to some extent set free, if Jesus of Nazareth has in fact become the historical point of orientation for his own perspective upon history, then this response is certainly his own act also. It is a historical perspective which *he* holds. This paradox finds classic expression in the words of Paul: "I worked harder than any of them, though it was not I, but the grace of God which is with me." [9] This paradox is related linguistically to the peculiarities we have noted in speaking of the effect of a liberated man upon men who are not free. It points to the fact that the new discernment and its accompanying commitment to a way of life is experienced as a response. This perspective arises in connection with hearing the Gospel concerning Jesus of Nazareth and it looks back to him continually as its historical point of orientation. To affirm the Gospel is to express this historical perspective.

The man who says, "Jesus is Lord," is saying that the history of Jesus and of what happened on Easter has exercised a liberating effect upon him, and that he has been so grasped by it that it has become the historical norm of his perspective upon life. His confession is a notification of this perspective and a recommendation to his listener to see Jesus, the world, and himself in this same way and to act accordingly. It is an important perspective and it can be distinguished from other points of view. We may illustrate the difference by comparing the perspective of Christian faith and the point of view of the man whose perspective upon life is founded on the life of his nation. The nationalist understands himself first of all as a patriot and he defines his freedom in the context of loyalty to his country. He can understand the Gospel only as making a relative claim at most. He may allow that there is some freedom to be found in Jesus and in loyalty to him, but it is secondary to his freedom as a citizen. For the Christian, however, the situation will be reversed. His assertion, "Jesus is Lord," expresses the fact that Jesus has become his point of orientation,

[9] I Cor. 15:10.

with the consequence that he is freed from acknowledging final loyalty to his nation, family, church, or any other person and is liberated for service to these other centers of relative loyalty. Because he sees not only his own history but the history of all men in the light of the one history of Jesus of Nazareth and Easter, he will not rest content when his nation, family, or church seek to live only for themselves; he will try to set them in the service of others.

He who says, "Jesus is Lord," says that Jesus' freedom has been contagious and has become the criterion for his life, public and private. As Jesus was led, because of his freedom, into the midst of social and political conflict, so it is with one who shares his freedom. The Gospel asserts that Jesus is Lord of the whole world.[10] This means that the freedom for which the Christian has been set free allows him to see the whole world in its light. When the Christian says that Jesus' Lordship is not limited to the church, he is saying that he understands all free men, regardless of where they may say they have found their freedom, as having "caught" their freedom from the same source as he. He will regard them as the ten cleansed lepers of Luke 17:11ff., who were all set free from their burden, although only one acknowledged Jesus as his liberator. If someone were to object that Jesus is the Lord and Saviour only of believers, he would be saying that he does not see the freedom of unbelievers with the perspective arising from his discernment and commitment as a Christian. The difference is more than a case of theological hairsplitting. It is empirically significant and it has led to serious human consequences in history.

This interpretation of Christian faith is related to Hare's concept of *blik*. The language of faith expressed in the Gospel may be understood if it is seen to express, define, or commend a basic presupposition by which a man lives and acts in the world of men. That is why we call it a historical perspective. As Hare has pointed out, a "blik" is not an explanation of the world or of anything else, but without a "blik" there can be no explanations.[11] He appeals to Hume in support of his conclusion that "the difference between *bliks* about the world cannot be settled by observation of what happens in the world." Although the assertions of the Gospel are meaningless if they are taken empirically, they do have a use. As Hare suggests, "The earth is weak and all the inhabitants thereof: I bear up the pillars of it," has a meaning, if it is taken as the formulation of a "blik." As an explanation it would "obviously be ludicrous. We no longer believe in God as an Atlas—*nous n'avons pas besoin de cette hypothèse.*" [12] The "blik" of the Christian finds its adequate expression in the Gospel, how-

---

[10] Matt. 28:18; Eph. 1:20-22; Phil. 2:9-11.
[11] R. M. Hare, essay in *New Essays in Philosophical Theology*, ed. A. Flew and A. MacIntyre (London: SCM [Student Christian Movement] Press, 1955), p. 101.
[12] *Ibid*. [The phrase quoted is Laplace's famous reply to Napoleon's inquiry about God: "We have no need of that hypothesis"—T. J. J. A.]

ever, and it is related always, if sometimes indirectly, to the history of Jesus of Nazareth. This is why we call this perspective *historical*.

Ramsey has suggested how a "blik" arises. It comes out of what he calls a situation of discernment or disclosure, a situation which is seen suddenly in a new way demanding a commitment of the viewer. The languages of revelation, Easter, the "illumination of the Holy Spirit," and conversion reflect just such a situation. The decisive discernment situation for Christianity is Easter and the Easter proclamation concerning Jesus of Nazareth. Men may come to Christian faith in all sorts of ways, of course. A man may have begun to be a Christian from reading the book of Genesis, or he may have come through a more distant point of entry. When he has "arrived," however, when he has heard and accepted the whole of what the Gospel has to say, the norm of his perspective will always be the history of Jesus and Easter. Because the sources for this history present Jesus as fulfilling the destiny of his people in his own life, his history receives illumination from that of the people from which he came, but in the last analysis, the Christian will read Genesis, Exodus, and all the rest of biblical history in the light of the history of the Gospels.

Our interpretation has underscored an element in Christian faith not immediately evident when it is considered as a "blik" or the consequence of a disclosure situation. We pointed out that on Easter the disciples came to see Jesus in a *new* way. That implies that they *had* seen Jesus in an *old* way. Their new perspective depended upon prior acquaintance with Jesus as a free man. Even Paul had some prior knowledge concerning Jesus. Conversion to the Christian historical perspective depends in part upon some acquaintance with the history of Jesus. To speak of a sheer discernment, whatever that would be, resting on no prior acquaintance with at least some elements of the situation in which it arose, would be like speaking of a sheer experience concerning which we could not say what was experienced. The various illustrations which we have used along the way make the same point. Lincoln's Gettysburg Address presupposed some awareness of the Civil War and the American Revolution. Hamlet's recognition of his father's ghost rested on prior acquaintance with his father. So Easter faith depended on the disciples' memory of Jesus, and Christian faith requires minimal acquaintance with the Gospel narratives.

Miles[13] has spoken of faith as the way of silence qualified by parables. Certainly the Christian possesses no special sources for the scientific description of the universe. Before such questions as whether there is some absolute being, even "Being itself," which is "behind" or "beyond" all we know and are, some final "ground and end of all created things," he will be wise to remain silent. He may qualify his silence, however, by telling something beside a parable. What he has to tell is the history of Jesus

[13] T. R. Miles, a contemporary English theologian—T. J. J. A.

and the strange story of how his freedom became contagious on Easter.

Finally, Braithwaite[14] has taken religious statements to be assertions of an intention to act in a certain way, together with the entertainment of certain stories. As far as it goes, this analysis agrees with our interpretation. We would clarify the "intention" with such words as *discernment* and *commitment,* and we would define the "certain way" as a response to and a reflection of the way of Jesus of Nazareth. It is a way characterized by a freedom "caught" from him. We would go further than this, however. In order to live in the "freedom for which Christ has set us free," we need indeed to "entertain" again and again that piece of history, for it does not just provide an encouragement to walk in the way of freedom; it is the context in which the light dawns anew and in which that freedom proves again to be contagious for us. Braithwaite's presentation of the relationship between "entertaining" the story and the "intention to behave" is not adequate to the language of the Gospel of Easter, helpful as it has been in indicating of what sort that language is, because he has not done justice to the historical aspect of the Gospel and has completely neglected the peculiar "story" of Easter.

THE LANGUAGE OF NEW TESTAMENT CHRISTOLOGY

The foregoing interpretation of the history of Jesus, Easter, and of the Gospel provides a logical account of the language of Christian faith without resort to a misleading use of words. The word *God* has been avoided because it equivocates and misleads. It seems to be a proper name, calling up the image of a divine entity, but it refuses to function as any other proper name does. Circumlocutions such as "transcendence," "being," and "absolute" only evade but do not overcome the difficulty. An interpretation of the language of the Gospel which does not necessitate assertions concerning "the nature and activities of a supposed personal creator," in Flew's[15] phrase, involves discarding some of the traditional language of Christianity, no matter how much other ages have revered this language. When Flew assumes that this language is of the essence of Christianity, he passes judgment on cherished traditions, not on every expression of faith. Nevertheless the question that Flew asks applies: Is this interpretation "Christian at all"? The interpretation must therefore be measured against the assertions of the Christology of the New Testament and of the Christology of "call and response" which summarizes the concerns of the theological "right."

---

[14] R. B. Braithwaite, a contemporary English analytic and empirical philosopher—T. J. J. A.

[15] Anthony Flew, a contemporary English analytic philosopher—T. J. J. A.

To what extent do biblical-Christological statements and our interpretation's statements about Jesus and Easter function in the same way? An important New Testament statement about Jesus is that made by the Gospel of John, claiming that he who has seen Jesus has seen the Father,[16] an assertion which summarizes the New Testament witness to Jesus as the full and adequate revelation of God. This saying occurs in the context of a discussion with his disciples on the night in which he was arrested. One of the disciples has asked Jesus to "show" them the Father, as though something were still lacking in what Jesus has "shown" them until that time. Jesus answers, "Have I been with you so long, and yet you do not know me, Philip? He who has seen me has seen the Father; how can you say, 'Show us the Father'? Do you not believe that I am in the Father and the Father in me?" [17]

Father is the word which Jesus apparently used frequently in cases where his contemporaries might have used the word *God*. It presents all the problems which arise when we try to analyze the word *God*. The further explication of this word, however, is not the only, and not even the best, way to understand this passage, for the passage itself suggests a *via negativa* of an odd sort. The author asks us to stop "looking for the 'Father,' " for we shall not find him and the quest is beside the point in any case. Silence is the first and best answer to questions concerning the "Father." There are "many 'gods' and many 'lords' " [18] but for those for whom the freedom of Jesus is contagious, who have been so touched and claimed by him that he has become the criterion of their understanding of themselves, other men, and the world, there is but one "Lord": Jesus of Nazareth. Since there is no "Father" to be found apart from him, and since his "Father" can be found only in him, the New Testament (and this passage specifically) gives its answer to the question about "God" by pointing to the man Jesus. Whatever men were looking for in looking for "God" is to be found by finding Jesus of Nazareth.

The assertion that Jesus is "in" the Father and the Father "in" Jesus suggests just this transposition of the question concerning "God," which lies deep in the Christology of the New Testament. Whatever can be known concerning "God" has been answered by the knowledge of Jesus made available in the event of Easter. Whatever "God" means—as the goal of human existence, as the truth about man and the world, or as the key to the meaning of life—"he" is to be found in Jesus, the "way, the truth, and the life."

We have no idea what would count for or against the assertion that in seeing Jesus one had seen the Father. Unless we knew already the meaning of the word *Father,* how could we verify or falsify this claim? The New Testament, and the Gospel of John especially, insist, moreover, that apart

[16] John 14:9.　　　　[17] John 14:9-10.　　　　[18] I Cor. 8:5-6.

from Jesus we can have only false conceptions of "God." [19] But if this passage is understood as a recommendation to turn away from asking about the Father and to ask about Jesus of Nazareth instead, its meaning becomes clear. We *can* say what would tend to verify a man's saying that Jesus is the key to his understanding and living of life. One could ask him questions and examine his actions. One could compare his words and actions with the teachings of the New Testament to see what correlation there was. This would be a subtle business, certainly, but it is not in principle beyond the realm of human investigation. In fact it is exactly what the church has been doing, under the name of "pastoral care" or "the cure of souls," throughout its history.

The passage at which we have been looking is followed by a sentence which deserves attention in this context: "The words that I say to you I do not speak on my own authority; but the Father who dwells in me does his works." [20] This has many parallels in the Gospel of John, for in spite of the author's many assertions of the functional equivalence of "Jesus" and "God," there is also a strong emphasis on the submission of Jesus to the "Father." In the later Christology of the church, this became the basis of the problem of the "subordination" of the Son to the Father.

The verification principle precludes taking this assertion of cosmological obedience as a straightforward empirical proposition. Its function is to say something about Jesus which we have already noticed in speaking of his freedom to make no claims for himself. We called attention then to the characteristics of humility, service, and living for other men. Undoubtedly Jesus believed he was obeying some "one," whom he called "Father," but the Gospel of John, as well as the logic of language, forces us to silence before all questions concerning that "one." We can only follow the recommendation of the evangelist to look at Jesus himself; questions about "God" will receive their only useful answer in the form of the history of that man.

A second important aspect of the New Testament witness to Jesus is seen in the assertion that he is not only the revelation of God, but also the act of God: his history is God's decisive act of love for this world. This idea may be summed up typically in Paul's words: "in Christ God was reconciling the world to himself." [21] This is a more difficult passage

---

[19] Matt. 11:27 (Luke 10:22); I Cor. 1:21; John 1:18; 8:19; 17:25. Conversely, "with" Jesus, one has no need to seek a conception of God, a point argued by Luther. Cf. B. A. Gerrish, *Grace and Reason* (London: Oxford University Press, 1962), pp. 76ff.

[20] John 14:10.

[21] II Cor. 5:19. An alternative translation, asserting first that "God was in Christ" and then saying that he was "reconciling the world to himself," breaks the temporal emphasis in the verb form. If this alternative reading were followed, the first assertion would be parallel to the "in me" of John 14:10, which we have already analyzed. Only the second assertion would speak of what was accomplished in the history of Jesus of Nazareth.

to understand than the one from the Gospel of John because it is so largely a "God"-statement. Its verification would depend upon knowing what to do with the word *God,* and that is just the problem. The statement may be taken in another way, however. Does it not suggest that the history of Jesus, including the event of Easter, is the history of a reconciliation of a peculiar sort? Jesus was the cause of division as well as reconciliation among men. As we pointed out, a free man can antagonize as well as attract men, and this was certainly the case with Jesus. He who asserts that the history of Jesus was a normative history of reconciliation means that he is committed to the *sort* of reconciliation revealed in that history. Reconciliation, for the Christian, will always have something to do with the freedom for which Christ has set men free, with being free for one's neighbor. To accept and live such a conception of reconciliation will tend to have serious personal, social, and political consequences, for the Pauline passage has a wide range: the world. The Christian understanding of reconciliation has no limit to its application. It will bear upon all areas of human life, personal and public, local and foreign. It will bear upon the way in which the Christian thinks and acts concerning the relations between nations, peoples, and political groups, as well as upon relationships in his own family. Wherever he sees at work in the world any reconciliation at all like that which characterized the history of Jesus of Nazareth, he will support it, and he will rejoice over signs of such reconciliation accomplished, however partially, as much as he rejoices over the reconciliation with his neighbor which has been made possible by his having been set free for that neighbor.

This verse from chapter 5 of II Corinthians is in the past tense. Then and there, in the history of Jesus, in his life, death, and resurrection, the world was being reconciled to "God." According to the words which immediately follow in Paul's letter, this means that "God . . . did not count men's trespasses against them and entrusted [to the apostles] the word of reconciliation." What can this mean? It cannot be a straightforward empirical assertion, for who can say how the world would be different if men had not been pardoned? We can say, however, how we should treat men if we regarded them as pardoned and accepted in some "final" sense which qualifies all human judging and forgiving. Would it not make a difference in our attitude toward a man who had been found guilty of a crime if we were convinced that his guilt was "born by another," that he was pardoned in some "final" sense? This is another way of expressing the Christian's historical perspective, which leads him to take sides with reconciliation, mercy, and forgiveness and to oppose enmity, retribution, and revenge. Jesus' parable of the unforgiving servant[22] helps us to see the meaning of this perspective and its ethical consequences. The "word of reconciliation" expresses a perspective which leads the Christian to under-

[22] Matt. 18:23-34.

stand and act in the world under the criterion of the freedom of Jesus for his neighbor.

The New Testament frequently speaks of that which "God accomplished" in the history of Jesus by saying that Jesus died for our sins.[23] This has been influential in a theological tradition which says that Jesus became the representative of sinful men by the will of God and suffered the "wages of sin" in their place. Paul said of Jesus that God had made him to be sin who knew no sin,[24] and that in that one died for all, "all have died." [25] The same theme is developed in the Epistle to the Hebrews around the image of Jesus as the perfect and eternal high priest who became also a sacrificial offering.[26] This strain of the tradition has been important in Western theology, especially since Augustine; it received a particularly clear expression in the theology of Calvin and, in our time, in that of Karl Barth.[27] How are we to understand this language?

We have seen that Jesus' freedom was freedom for his neighbor, that he was free from self-concern and therefore open to the concerns of others. We might speak of his solidarity with men: he "put himself in their shoes"; he carried their burdens. In addition, by daring to regard men classed as "sinners" as forgiven and by proclaiming their forgiveness, he convinced them that they were released from the burden of guilt and the consequences of their acts.[28] But what can it mean to say, "He *died* for our sins"? The emphasis is on his death, but we need to remember that theology, as well as the New Testament, speaks of the "cross" or the death of Jesus as the consequence of his life. "The cross" and other references to Jesus' death became summary ways of speaking of his whole history, as indeed his end seemed to his disciples, after the fact, to have been foreshadowed in all of his life. Since his life was one of solidarity with men, compassion for them, mercy toward their weakness and wrong, it is not surprising that his death, which was the consequence of his freedom to be related to men in this way, was spoken of as a death "for us." His death (which could so easily have been avoided if he had taken the way of caution, calculation, and self-interest) was regarded as the measure of the freedom for which he set other men free. The man for whom the history of Jesus and of his liberation of his disciples on Easter is a discernment situation of prime importance will say, "He died for me, for my forgiveness and freedom." When the New Testament says that he died not only for "our" sins, "but also for the sins of the whole world," [29] it reflects the fact that

[23] I Cor. 15:3.
[24] II Cor. 5:21.
[25] II Cor. 5:14.
[26] Heb. 5:1ff.; 8:1ff.; 9:11ff.
[27] Calvin, *op. cit.*, II, xvi, pp. 5ff.; Van Buren, *op. cit.*, Part II, *passim;* Barth, *KD,* IV/1, § 59, 2, *passim.*
[28] E.g., the story of the woman taken in adultery, usually found in John 8:3-11.
[29] I John 2:2.

Jesus was free for every man, those who did not acknowledge him as well as those that did, and it articulates a perspective by which all men, not just believers, are seen.

On the basis of these considerations, we can clarify the dilemma posed by Bultmann: "Does he [Jesus] help me because he is God's Son, or is he the Son of God because he helps me?" [30] The question as it stands only invites confusion. We may say that Jesus helps me because of "what" he is ("Son of God"), and we may also say that such titles as "Son of God" were given to him because of the help he provided. When we say both of these, however, we are using the words "Son of God" in two different ways and are also playing tricks with the slippery word "is." The problem is more clearly expressed if we ask: Does the Gospel speak of a "saving" event which has happened already and which is reported to the listener, who is invited to acknowledge and give thanks for it (a so-called "objective" atonement), or does it announce the possibility of a "saving" event which takes place in the act of acknowledging it (a so-called "subjective" atonement)? Does the Gospel announce a reality accomplished, or a possibility to be actualized by the hearer? This way of phrasing the question makes it clear that we are speaking about *words* (the Gospel) spoken presumably by a believer.

Now of what precisely does the believer speak? He speaks in part of a piece of history, which is certainly in the past. It is the history of a free man and the peculiar character of his freedom. But the Gospel goes on to speak of the moment in which this freedom became contagious in the Easter event, and the speaker, by his very speaking and by the way in which he does it, indicates that this contagious freedom has also touched him. All this constitutes an invitation to the listener to share this discernment and commitment. Perhaps (but also perhaps not) the listener will "see" for the first time, or he will see again, or he will see more clearly than he has in the past. The light will dawn; he will be possessed of a new way of seeing himself, the world, and all things, and he will "catch" something of the contagious freedom of Jesus.

Now, when was he liberated? Or rather, when will he say he was liberated? He will surely say that he became free at the time he acquired his new perspective. But he will be even readier to point to his liberator. It belongs to the language of a discernment situation that we speak of that situation as containing already ("objectively"), prior to its becoming the occasion of a discernment, what was only "seen" at a later time. As the lover might say to his beloved, "I must have passed you a thousand times and spoken to you a hundred, and there you were, the most beautiful girl in the world, and I did not see you. And then, that night, all of a sudden I realized." She did not become the most beautiful girl in the

[30] Rudolf Bultmann, *Glauben und Verstehen* (Tübingen: J. C. B. Mohr, 1952), Vol. II, p. 252; *Essays Philosophical and Theological,* p. 280.

world for him only "that night." He will insist that she always was that, and that he, poor fool, woke up only later to the fact.[31] Such is the language of the "objective" liberation of mankind in the death and resurrection of Jesus. To insist that this is incorrect and that the actual liberation takes place in the moment of believing, which is perfectly true in a psychological sense, is to misunderstand the language appropriate to a situation of discernment which leads one to a commitment embracing all of life.

An analysis of the language of the Christology of "call and response" presented in Chapter 2 [of *The Secular Meaning of the Gospel*] confirms our conclusions about the function of biblical-Christological statements. The statements that Jesus was "called by God" to be the one man who was free to be for all the others, that he "bore the divine election" of Israel to be a light for the Gentiles, that his history "was the enactment of God's eternal plan and purpose," if taken to be cosmological assertions, are meaningless in the terms of the empirical attitudes in which this study is grounded. These statements, however, belong after the words "I believe," and the word *I* is important. The statements, in the form of a confession of faith, reflect or suggest a situation in which the history of Jesus has been or might be seen in a new way. They also express the commitment of the speaker to what he has now "seen." To speak of Jesus' "call" or "election" is to speak of Jesus as one with a history which is different from that of any other man, and of Jesus as one who is "set apart" from all the others and for all the others. As the language of one who, in seeing Jesus as the free man who has set others free, has also been set free himself, the statement is appropriate and logically meaningful. This clarifies also the statements concerning Jesus' "response," for his response was only the other side of the coin. To speak of Jesus' "response" is another way of speaking of his history as a free man. Since according to the New Testament his response of obedience was authenticated as perfect obedience by the event of Easter, we may say that it is the contagious aspect of his freedom which authenticates the language which the believer uses of Jesus. To say that Jesus embodies the plan of God and that he was perfectly faithful to this election is to make the sort of final statement which Ramsey says takes the form "I'm I." In this case, however, the "I" is what "I" have become as a result of the liberation arising from hearing the story of Jesus, his life, his death, and Easter.

Finally, the "eschatological" hope, in this interpretation of the language of the Gospel, is the conviction that the freedom which the believer has

---

[31] The case of "love at first sight" is a compressed variation. The "prior acquaintance," which we have already discussed, would in this case be prior acquaintance with other people and prior knowledge of the fact of "falling in love," together with at least the first impression of the beloved as a person distinct from these other people.

seen in Jesus and which has become contagious for him, and the reconciliation which he sees to be associated with this freedom, will prevail on this earth among all men. That is his conviction, not a prediction. To say that this hope is "eschatological" is to say that one would die rather than abandon it. It indicates the unqualified, undebatable aspect of the Christian's historical perspective.

As Hare points out, there is no arguing about "bliks." Another man may find some other piece of history to be his key to the understanding of life and history: that of the Buddha or Mary Baker Eddy. Or his perspective might be informed by some idea or ideology. It might be a dialectic of history and the Communist Manifesto, an eighteenth-century Declaration of Independence, or the economic theory of Adam Smith. He who has his freedom from Jesus will not agree, however, with those who would say that all sources of freedom are the same. The fact remains that the history of Jesus is not the same as the history of the Buddha, the Communist Revolution, or Henry Ford. It is one thing to say that Christians have always taken the history of Jesus to be indispensable and definitive for their faith, but it is quite another to think that this "uniqueness" can somehow be proved. Christians have never been able, however (and when they were at their best have not tried), to *prove* the "superiority" of their historical perspective over other perspectives. Claims of "finality" are simply the language appropriate to articulating a historical perspective. The logic of these claims can be illuminated by setting them alongside the statement "I'm I."

The meaning of the Gospel is its use on the lips of those who proclaim it. The Christian has seen a man of remarkable and particular freedom, and this freedom has become contagious for him, as it was for the apostles on Easter. The history of this man and of Easter has become a situation of discernment, reorienting his perspective upon the world. If he should have occasion to tell that story, therefore, he can only do so to express, define, or commend this historical perspective, for this is the secular meaning of that Gospel.

That assertion is itself, of course, a recommendation to the reader to see the language of faith in the way expressed, on the assumption that there is a possibility of his holding empirical attitudes similar to those in the light of which this interpretation has been made. This commendation may also be made in the form of two principles which sum up what we have done:

(1) *Statements of faith are to be interpreted, by means of the modified verification principle, as statements which express, describe, or commend a particular way of seeing the world, other men, and oneself, and the way of life appropriate to such a perspective.* A restatement of the Gospel should allow the logical structure of its language to become clear. With this first principle we indicate that we share certain of the empirical attitudes

reflected in the "revolution" in modern philosophy. This principle more than meets the concern of the theological "left" to accept the modern criticism of ancient ways of thinking.

(2) *The norm of the Christian perspective is the series of events to which the New Testament documents testify, centering in the life, death, and resurrection of Jesus of Nazareth.* We have approached the problem of Christology by way of an investigation of the peculiar way in which Christians talked from the first about the man Jesus of Nazareth. Following our first principle, we explored the logic of the language of the New Testament authors concerning Jesus. Our aim has been to discover the *meaning* of their words and to find appropriate and clear words with which to express that meaning today, asking after a functional equivalence between a contemporary Christology and the language of the New Testament. With our second principle, we acknowledge the concern of the theological right wing that Christology be central, and that the norm of Christology be Jesus of Nazareth as the subject of the apostolic witness. These two principles have guided us in the constructive task of interpreting the Gospel in a way which may be understood by a Christian whose empirical attitudes are such as to lead us to call him a secular man.

17

THOMAS J. J. ALTIZER

Since the summer of 1955 I had been torn between an interior certainty of the death of God in modern history and experience and a largely mute but nevertheless unshakable conviction of the truth of the Christian faith. At first I believed that Christianity could be reborn if it were to reverse its own history and return to its original apocalyptic faith by way of absorbing the higher and more universal mystical forms of the Orient (see my *Oriental Mysticism and Biblical Eschatology,* 1961). Then I realized that there is no possibility for us of reversing our history and that our only hope lies in moving through our radically profane consciousness to a new and yet Christian coincidence of the radical sacred and the radical profane (*Mircea Eliade and the Dialectic of the Sacred,* 1963). Throughout these years I had been most deeply influenced by Nietzsche, but at this time I became immersed in the world of Blake's vision, while slowly but decisively becoming overwhelmed by what I came to believe were the Christian ground and form of Hegel's dialectical logic. Now I saw that it was not history, or, at least, not the living and future reality of history, which must be negated and reversed by the Christian faith. Instead, if Christianity is to preserve its unique direction and form, it is now called to a total negation and reversal of the religious movement to a primordial God or primordial Beginning. Hegel's central idea of *kenosis,* or the universal and dialectical process of the self-negation of Being, provided me with a conceptual route to a consistently kenotic or self-emptying understanding of the Incarnation, an understanding which I believe has been given a full visionary expression in the work of William Blake. The initial result of this quest is contained in my book *The Gospel of Christian Atheism*. The last chapter of this book, which probably should have been its first, is included here; I regard this chapter as my freest piece of theological work.

Thomas J. J.
Altizer   **A Wager**

THE LIVING CHRIST

From the point of view of radical Christianity, the original heresy was the identification of the Church as the body of Christ. When the Church is known as the body of Christ, and the Church is further conceived as a distinct and particular institution or organism existing within but nevertheless apart from the world, then the body of Christ must inevitably be distinguished from and even opposed to the body of humanity. Only a religious form of Christianity could establish such a chasm between Christ and the world: for it is the backward movement of religious Christianity which retreats from the world, regressing to a primordial deity which it dares to name as the cosmic Logos and the monarchic Christ. We must not be misled by the emergence of Catholic Christianity into thinking that an increasingly universal form of the Church gives witness to a genuinely forward movement of the Church. A forward movement evolving by means of an extension and enlargement of its given or original form cannot evolve to a truly new and comprehensive universality, nor can it embody the kenotic process of the Incarnation. Thus a forward movement in this sense is finally the expression of the will to power, an all too human regression to an inhuman or prehuman state, which necessarily entails a reversal of the true humanity of Jesus. Once the Church had claimed to be the body of Christ, it had already set upon the imperialistic path of conquering the world, of bringing the life and movement of the world into submission to the inhuman authority and power of an infinitely distant Creator and Judge.

FROM *The Gospel of Christian Atheism,* by Thomas J. J. Altizer (Philadelphia: Westminster Press, 1966), pp. 132-57. Copyright © 1966, W. L. Jenkins, The Westminster Press. Used by permission.

But by identifying the Church's Christ as a reversal of the incarnate Christ, a reversal effected by a backward movement to the now emptied preincarnate epiphanies of God, the radical Christian points the way to the presence of the living Christ in the actuality and fullness of history. It is precisely because the orthodox image of Christ is an image of lordship and power that it is a reversal of a kenotic Christ. The mere fact that the Christ of Christian orthodoxy is an exalted and transcendent Lord is a sufficient sign to the radical Christian that Christianity has reversed the movement of the Incarnation. Simply by clinging to the religious image of transcendent power, the Church has resisted the self-negating movement of Christ and foreclosed the possibility of its own witness to the forward movement of the divine process. Consequently, the radical Christian maintains that it is the Church's regressive religious belief in God which impels it to betray the present and the kenotic reality of Christ. So long as the Church is grounded in the worship of a sovereign and transcendent Lord, and submits in its life and witness to that infinite distance separating the creature and the Creator, it must continue to reverse the movement of the Spirit who progressively becomes actualized as flesh, thereby silencing the life and speech of the Incarnate Word.

Only by recognizing the antithetical relationship that radical faith posits between the primordial and transcendent reality of God and the kenotic and immediate reality of Christ, can we understand the violent attack which the radical Christian launches upon the Christian God. Even the remembrance of the original glory and majesty of God roots the Christian in the past, inducing him to evade the self-emptying negativity of a fully incarnate divine process, and to flee from the Christ who is actual and real in our present. A faith that names Jesus either as the Son of God or as the prophet of God must be a backward movement to a disincarnate and primordial form of Spirit, a movement annulling the events of the Incarnation and the Crucifixion by resurrecting Jesus either in the form of the exalted Lord or as the proclaimer of an already distant and alien majesty of God: hence an orthodox and priestly Christianity is inevitably grounded in the sacred authority and power of the past. How can the Christian know the living Christ who is immediately present to us, a Christ who is the consequence of the continual forward movement and self-negation of the divine process, if he is bound to a long-distant epiphany of Christ which has been emptied and left behind by the progressive movement of the Word's becoming flesh? A Christ appearing to our consciousness in his ancient and traditional form cannot be the true and the living Christ, unless we are to deny the real and forward movement of the Incarnation. Above all, a Christ who even now is manifest in the preincarnate form and epiphany of God, and who can be reached only by a total reversal of our history and experience, must be named as the Antichrist, as the dead and alien body of the God who originally died in Christ. Thus it is the radical Christian proclamation of the death of God which liberates the Christian from every alien and lifeless image of Christ.

Radical Christianity poses the real question which must now be addressed to the Christian: is faith speakable or livable in the actuality of our present? Already we have seen that Christianity is the only form of faith which is not grounded in a backward movement of involution and return. Accordingly, authentic Christianity must move forward through history and experience to an eschatological goal. If Christianity refuses the destiny before it, renouncing the actuality of the time and space which it confronts, then inevitably it must regress to a pre-Christian or non-Christian form. Now we must not confuse a Christian and eschatological passage through the actuality of history and experience with a mere submission to the brute reality of the world; such a submission does not affect the world, nor does it embody a self-negation or self-annihilation of the Incarnate Word. We must, rather, understand the forward movement of Christianity to be a truly negative or self-emptying process, a process simultaneously negating both the Word and world which it embodies, and therefore a process transcending and moving beyond the initial expressions of its own movement. Such a process can be actual and real only by occurring in the actuality of experience; it must move through diverse and ever fuller forms of experience to new and progressively more universal goals. A faith reflecting and witnessing to this process obviously cannot retain a static and unchanging form; instead, it must undergo a continual metamorphosis, a progressive metamorphosis embodying the gradual but continual descent of the Word into flesh. Faith must always be able to speak of the Word which is actually present, and to speak to the actuality of the world and experience which it confronts; otherwise, it will relapse into immobility and silence, thereby betraying the very vocation of faith. Perhaps the religious Christian can believe that Christianity need not know the Christ who is immediately present; but a Christianity divorced from the living presence and action of Christ is a Christianity that has abandoned the specifically Christian movement of faith.

Can we truly speak of the Christ who is present to us, of the living Christ who is actually manifest in our world, and who even now is making all things new? We are forewarned that a contemporary Christ will by no means be identical with the Christ of our Christian past, except insofar as he too is a kenotic Christ who is moving ever more comprehensively into the depths of life and experience. By following the way of the radical Christian, we can rejoice in the death of God, and be assured that the historical realization of the death of God is a full unfolding of the forward movement of the Incarnation. Just as the Crucifixion embodies and makes finally real a divine movement from transcendence to immanence, a movement of an originally transcendent God into the actuality of life and experience, so too the dawning of the death of God throughout the totality of experience progressively annuls every human or actual possibility of returning to transcendence. It is precisely because the movement of the Incarnation has now become manifest in every human hand and face, dissolving even the memory of God's original transcendent life and redemptive power, that there can no longer be either a truly contemporary movement to transcendence or an active and living faith in the transcendent God.

Only by accepting and even willing the death of God in our experience can we be liberated from a transcendent beyond, an alien beyond which has been emptied and darkened by God's self-annihilation in Christ. To the extent that we attempt to cling to a transcendent realm, a realm that has become ever darker and emptier in the actuality of our experience, we must be closed to the actual presence of the living Christ, and alienated from the contemporary movement of the divine process. Every death of a divine image is a realization of the kenotic movement, an actualization in consciousness and experience of God's death in Christ; thus a fully incarnate Christ will have dissolved or reversed all sacred images by the very finality of his movement into flesh. We know the finality of the Incarnation by knowing that God is dead; and once we fully live the death of God, we will be liberated from the temptation to return to an epiphany of deity which is present only in the past. Yet to recognize the Christ who has become manifest and real as the result of a total movement from transcendence to immanence, we must be freed from every attachment to transcendence, and detached from all yearning for a primordial innocence. A truly contemporary Christ cannot become present to us until we ourselves have died to every shadow and fragment of his transcendent image.

We must not deceive ourselves by thinking that the faith and worship of the Church must inevitably give witness to a contemporary epiphany of Christ. No doubt, the Incarnate Word is never without witness, but we have little reason to believe that a Christ who has fully and totally entered the world could be known by a Church that refuses either to abandon its transcendent image of Christ or to negate its religious movement of involution and return. If Christ is truly present and real to us in a wholly incarnate epiphany, then the one principle that can direct our search for his presence is the negative principle that he can no longer be clearly or decisively manifest in any of his previous forms or images. All established Christian authority has now been shattered and broken: the Bible may well embody a revelation of the Word but we have long since lost any certain or even clear means of interpreting its meaning as revelation; the Church in its liturgies, creeds, and confessions may well embody an epiphany of Christ, but that epiphany is distant from us, and it cannot speak to our contemporary experience. Even the language that the Christian once employed in speaking of Christ has become archaic and empty, and we could search in vain for a traditional Christian language and symbolism in contemporary art and thinking.

If we are honestly to embark upon a quest for a truly contemporary epiphany of Christ, we must be prepared to accept an ultimate risk, a genuine risk dissolving all certainty and security whatsoever. Let us note, however, that authentic faith always entails a risk of a high order, and this risk must vary in accordance with the time and situation in which it occurs. Already the modern traditional or orthodox Christian has made a wager incorporating such a risk: he has bet that Jesus Christ is the same yesterday, today, and forever, and thus he has bet that finally there is only a single image or epiphany of Jesus, regardless of the time or history in which it appears. The modern dimension of this wager is that our time is so obviously divorced from the time of Jesus, or, at least, our world and history is clearly estranged from the classical world of Christendom, with the consequence that to choose the traditional form of Christ is either to set oneself against the contemporary world or to decide that the actuality of one's time and situation can have no bearing upon one's faith in Christ. Never before has this consequence become so clearly manifest, because, as we previously observed, ours is the first form of consciousness and experience that has evolved after the full historical realization of the death of God. This means than any contemporary wager upon the Christ of Christian orthodoxy must be willing to forfeit all the life and movement of a world and actuality that has negated or dissolved the Christian God. We cannot pretend that an ultimate faith in the transcendent Christ of the Church can have no effect upon the actuality of the believer's life in the world, nor can we imagine that the Church can change its language about Christ in accordance with the actual world which it confronts without in any way decisively effecting its faith in Christ. No, the fact remains that the Christian today who chooses the orthodox image of Christ is making a wager in which he stands to forfeit all the life and energy of a world that is totally alien to the Church's Christ.

Of course, few Christians are consciously or fully aware that they must make such a choice. But true faith is impossible apart from a risk, and the Christian who now chooses the traditional form of Christ is risking not only the loss of the actuality of the present but also the loss of the Christ who may be fully incarnate in that present. Now we must pose a contrary wager. Dare we bet upon a totally incarnate Christ, whose contemporary presence negates his previous epiphanies, with the full realization that we are therein risking both the total loss of Christ as well as the loss of all that life and energy deriving from the presence of a transcendent and eternally given Christ? We must be fully aware that a wager upon a totally incarnate Christ is every bit as much a wager as a wager upon the orthodox image of Christ. Either risks losing both the true reality of Christ and all that life evolving from the presence of Christ. Both are genuine expressions of faith because each enacts a genuine wager, and they are united in repudiating any form of faith that does not demand an ultimate wager. The radical Christian who chooses a fully contemporary Christ not only must be willing to abandon the Christ of our Christian past but he must accept the fact that no clear path lies present to the Christ whom he has chosen, and no final authority exists to direct him upon his quest. Moreover, the Christian who wagers upon a totally incarnate Christ must negate every form and image of transcendence, regardless of what area of consciousness or experience in which it may appear. Thus he must forswear every transcendent ground of judgment and be banished from every hope in a transcendent life or power. He has chosen a darkness issuing from the death of every image and symbol of transcendence, and he must bet that the darkness of his destiny is the present form and actuality of a totally incarnate body of Christ.

GUILT AND RESENTMENT

Nietzsche, the greatest modern master of understanding man, has taught us an ironical and intimately human mode of listening, and this listening is often most effective when it listens to what is not said. The modern Christian, at least to judge by the theological spokesmen of the churches, has very nearly ceased speaking about damnation and Hell, and seemingly is no longer capable of speaking even about an ultimate and final form of guilt. Irony besets every action of that strange creature man, and we can only wonder that the ecclesiastical Christian should have ceased to speak about damnation in a century in which guilt and damnation have become an overwhelming motif in so many of the most creative expressions of consciousness and experience. Is ours not a time in which Hell appears to be the arena of human existence? Yet our theologians no longer speak of Hell, and great masses of Christians seem to have lost all fear of damnation. While we need not doubt that most ecclesiastical Christians practice Christianity as a heaven-sent way of returning to innocence, why is it that even the wisest and most worldly of our theologians are mute on the subject of damnation? Why can the theologian not speak of Hell, whereas the artist and the thinker often seem to speak of nothing else? Is it the modern religious Christian's inability to speak about a God who is actually present in the world which is the ground of his refusal to share a uniquely modern sense of guilt?

Naïve Christians frequently say that damnation and Hell are Old Testament themes which find no place in the "good news" of the New Testament. But the simple truth is that Hell, Satan, and final damnation are almost uniquely New Testament motifs, and these motifs of ultimate terror play a far greater role in the doctrines and liturgies of Christianity than they do in any other religion. Who else but the Christian fears a final and total damnation? Where else but in Christendom do we find records of an experience of total terror? However, in the modern world we find the strange phenomenon of the Christian who is liberated from the fear of damnation, a Christian who apparently is incapable of experiencing terror. Is this the sign of a mature faith which has finally come of age? Or is it but another sign of the truth of Kierkegaard's judgment that the Christianity of the New Testament no longer exists? Why should the contemporary Christian be innocent of the knowledge of Hell unless the Church has succeeded in establishing itself as a haven from the horror of the modern world? Or is the modern religious Christian so numb with guilt that he can no longer name his condition, and must relapse into a state of immobility and silence about guilt if only as a means of existing in its presence? Is it because the Church can no longer speak about Hell and damnation that we hear so much foolish ecclesiastical chatter about forgiveness? What can an ultimate forgiveness mean if it is impossible to speak about an ultimate guilt? When the Church speaks about guilt, can it be no more than the custodian of the law, ever sanctioning the common fears of society and incorporating in its body whatever is left of the restraints and inhibitions of the society of the past? Is the real function of an all too modern ecclesiastical Christianity to actualize whatever faith and hope is possible for all those masses of men who refuse the darkness and terror of our time?

Nietzsche teaches us that we cannot dissociate the phenomenon of guilt from the phenomenon of pain: it is those who suffer most deeply who are most conscious of guilt, and those who suffer the least who are free of a bad conscience. Of course, suffering in this sense is not to be identified with mere physical pain, but instead is the creation of a full and active consciousness. Nevertheless, a guilty conscience cannot naïvely be judged to be a product of illusion, or of an overly active consciousness, or of simple fear. Guilt is always the consequence of a retreat from life, of a reversal of the life and energy of the body, a reversal having its origin in that repression which is Nietzsche's name for the real ruler of a fallen history. Nietzsche joins Kierkegaard in identifying existence as guilt. For everything that we know as consciousness and experience is grounded in repression, and to broaden or deepen our consciousness is to recognize the power of repression, a power creating all those dualistic oppositions or antinomies which split human existence asunder, dividing and isolating the shrunken energy of life. Accordingly, guilt is a conscious realization of the broken or fallen condition of humanity, and it is actualized in the individual insofar as he becomes consciously aware of his own bondage to repression. But humanity, as the poets tell us, cannot bear much reality;

and we escape the pain of our condition by resentment, a resentment attempting to reverse or even to leap out of the actuality of existence. Resentment arises from an inability or refusal to accept the brute reality of the world; it is a rebellion against life itself, a hatred of the pain, the joy, the fullness of existence. Thus, resentment shrinks existence into the narrowest possible bounds, negating every outlet for the release of energy, and condemning every source of movement and life. The great No-sayers are those who have suffered most profoundly, and they have succeeded in creating patterns of resentment which a weak and broken humanity can accept as the way to the dissolution of consciousness and pain.

Yes, we are guilty; or, our given or actual condition is a condition of guilt; but we harden and freeze our guilty condition by a resentment which forecloses the possibility of the abolition of repression. Resentment is a withdrawal from the possibility of life and movement, a negative reaction to the painfulness of the human condition whereby we submit to guilt and alienation by condemning every possibility of accepting and affirming life. Such a submission to guilt is at bottom a submission to pain, or, rather, an attempt to lower the consciousness of pain by shrinking and confining the energy of life. Ultimately, resentment is directed against the cause of pain; and it arises when we become conscious of our painful condition, and attempt to numb our suffering by negating or evading all occasions for pain. Nietzsche commonly associated resentment with the weak, with those who have been defeated and broken by life, and who then negate every challenge to their own submission and withdrawal. Of course, he also teaches us that resentment can express itself in envy, which is itself the expression of an inability to accept the actuality of a given and particular situation. Always, however, resentment is a flight from life, an evasion of the human condition, an assault upon all life and movement as the way to the dissolution of pain. Resentment progressively lowers the threshold of consciousness, reducing experience to ever narrower spheres, or freezing a given state of consciousness by binding it to a hatred of its immediate ground. Thus, resentment must finally sanction the reality of guilt, passively submitting to the brokenness of the human condition and ruthlessly refusing every promise of forgiveness and life.

A guilty humanity is inevitably conscious of an opposing other, an imperative appearing whenever we become aware of our confinement by recognizing the repressed state of our own energy. The law, Paul teaches, makes us conscious of sin; but we might reverse Paul's dictum and also say that sin and guilt make us conscious of the law. As Augustine so wisely teaches, the deepest attraction of sin is the attraction of the forbidden. The temptation to do the forbidden becomes present only when we become conscious of our own state of repression, and then our attraction to the forbidden deepens our bondage to the law, submitting us ever more fully to its distant and inhuman power. Consequently, repression and guilt are inseparable, or, at least, we become conscious of our guilt only to the extent that we become aware of the power of repression within us. Thence our guilt demands that we be punished, and we indulge in orgies of self-hatred if only as a means of appeasing our bad conscience, a bad conscience which is itself the product of a consciousness of repression. A repressed humanity is a guilty humanity, whether it is conscious of its guilt or not, and to the extent that it becomes conscious of its guilt it must submit to the alien authority of the imperative, an authority sealing the finality of guilt, and binding humanity to perpetual repression. Already in the proclamation of Jesus, however, and in the New Testament messages of Paul and John, we discover the Christian promise of the forgiveness of sin, or the release of the sinner from his bondage to law and judgment, a liberation effected by his participation in the body of Christ or the dawning Kingdom of God. Paul insists that the reign of the law extends throughout the body of a fallen humanity, but it is confined to all that human sphere which does not yet exist in faith, for insofar as we exist in faith we are delivered from the bondage of the law. Indeed, it is only by the gift of freedom in Christ that we become aware of the terrible burden of the law, and only by faith in Christ do we receive the power to name the darkness of sin and guilt. It is by faith alone that we become aware of the true meaning and the overwhelming power of guilt and repression: thus we need have little hesitation in assigning Nietzsche to a tradition of a radical Christian understanding of sin, a tradition going back to Paul by way of Dostoevski, Kierkegaard, Pascal, Luther, and Augustine.

Moreover, it is of vital importance to realize that while existing in a state of alienation and guilt we ourselves must oppose the other, imposing upon all others the obligation under which we live. When Jesus said, "Judge not," he was calling for an end of all moral judgment, a judgment that must inevitably arise from a condition of guilt. Judgment and forgiveness are poles of an opposing continuum; we judge to the extent that we exist in sin, and we become incapable of judgment to the extent that we are forgiven. The Christian is liberated from the alien power of the moral imperative by virtue of his life in Christ, and faith itself calls upon us to acknowledge that we can be aware of a moral demand only insofar as we are estranged from Christ, and thereby closed to the reality of forgiveness. A guilty humanity can exist only by way of judgment and resentment, a judgment sanctioning its own state of alienation, and a resentment opposing every call to forgiveness. In this perspective we can see that resentment is a flight from the presence of Christ, an opposition to his promise of forgiveness. All too naturally a religious Christianity has known the most awesome and terrifying form of the divine Creator and Judge, for a religious reversal of the Incarnation must resurrect the deity in the form of an absolutely majestic and sovereign power, a power that has now lost its ground in the kenotic movement of the divine process. Thus, too, Christendom has known the most terrible guilt in history, and as a religious Christianity has progressively and ever more fully reversed the movement of the Incarnation, the Christian God has increasingly become alien and abstract, until in our own time he has only been present and real in actual experience in a totally alien form, and the whole body of Western humanity has been initiated into a radical and total state of guilt.

Once again we are called upon to make a wager. Dare we bet that the Christian God is dead, that the ultimate ground of guilt and resentment is broken, and that our guilty condition is created by our clinging to the wholly alien power of a now emptied transcendent realm? If we can truly know that God is dead, and can fully actualize the death of God in our own experience, then we can be liberated from the threat of condemnation and freed from every terror of a transcendent beyond. Even though we may be mute and speechless in confronting the terror of our time, we cannot evade its pervasive presence, and to relapse into immobility and silence is to foreclose the possibility of being freed from its life-negating power.

Yet the "good news" of the death of God can liberate us from our dread of an alien beyond, releasing us from all attachment to an opposing other, and freeing us for a total participation in the actuality of the immediate moment. By wagering that God is dead, we bet that the awesome and alien power of an infinitely distant and wholly other is finally created by our own guilt and resentment, by our refusal of the life and energy about and within us. Of course, every man who negates and opposes life becomes bound to an alien power. But the Christian knows that Christ is the source of energy and life: hence the Christian must identify all No-saying as a refusal and resistance of Christ. When the Christian bets that God is dead, he is betting upon the real and actual presence of the fully incarnate Christ. Thus a Christian wager upon the death of God is a wager upon the presence of the living Christ, a bet that Christ is now at least potentially present in a new and total form. No, we are not guilty, says the Christian who bets that God is dead. His very bet denies the alien authority of the imperative, and refuses all that guilt arising from a submission to repression. He bets that he is even now forgiven, that he has been delivered from all bondage to the law, and that guilt is finally a refusal of the gift of life and freedom in Christ.

Needless to say, such a wager entails a risk, and an ultimate risk at that. For the Christian who bets that God is dead risks both moral chaos and his own damnation. While the religious or the ecclesiastical Christian has increasingly become incapable of speaking about damnation, the radical Christian, who has been willing to confront the totally alien form of God which has been manifest in our time, has known the horror of

Satan and Hell, and can all too readily speak the language of guilt and damnation. He knows that either God is dead or that humanity is now enslaved to an infinitely distant, absolutely alien, and wholly other epiphany of God. To refuse a deity who is a sovereign and alien other, or to will the death of the transcendent Lord, is certainly to risk an ultimate wrath and judgment, a judgment which Christianity has long proclaimed to be damnation. Nor can we pretend that it is no longer possible to envision damnation; the modern artist has surpassed even Dante in envisioning the tortures of the damned. So likewise modern man has known a moral chaos, a vacuous nihilism dissolving every ground of moral judgment, which is unequaled in history. The contemporary Christian who bets that God is dead must do so with a full realization that he may very well be embracing a life-destroying nihilism; or, worse yet, he may simply be submitting to the darker currents of our history, passively allowing himself to be the victim of an all too human horror. No honest contemporary seeker can ever lose sight of the very real possibility that the willing of the death of God is the way to madness, dehumanization, and even to the most totalitarian form of society yet realized in history. Who can doubt that a real passage through the death of God must issue in either an abolition of man or in the birth of a new and transfigured humanity?

The Christian, however, cannot escape the fact that he must make a choice. He must either choose the God who is actually manifest and real in the established form of faith, or he must confess the death of God and give himself to a quest for a whole new form of faith. If he follows the latter course, he will sacrifice an established Christian meaning and morality, abandoning all those moral laws which the Christian Church has sanctioned, and perhaps even negating the possibility of an explicitly Christian moral judgment. Certainly he will be forced to renounce every moral imperative with a transcendent ground, and this means that he must forswear the possibility of an absolute moral law, and at best look upon all forms of moral judgment as penultimate ways which must inevitably act as barriers to the full realization of energy and life. Indeed, the Christian who bets that God is dead must recognize that he himself has not yet passed through the death of God at whatever point he clings to moral law and judgment. True, he can look forward to the promise of total forgiveness, but the forgiveness which he chooses can only be realized here and now; it must evaporate and lose all meaning to the extent that it is sought in a distant future or a transcendent beyond. Yet the Christian who wagers upon the death of God can be freed from the alien power of all moral law, just as he can be liberated from the threat of an external moral judgment and released from the burden of a transcendent source of guilt. Knowing that his sin is forgiven, such a Christian can cast aside the crutches of guilt and resentment. Only then can he rise and walk.

YES-SAYING

Not only has the modern Christian apparently been forced to retreat ever more distantly from the fullness of consciousness and experience, but he has been forced to bear the humiliation of discovering in Oriental mysticism a totality of bliss which is not even partially echoed in the shrinking boundaries of an ecclesiastical form of faith. At the very moment when Christian mysticism is either collapsing or receding behind the walls of the monastic cloister, an originally alien form of mysticism is increasingly becoming real to the Western mind and is casting its spell upon a contemporary and seemingly post-Christian sensibility. We must note, however, that it has been Western scholarship which has unraveled the depths and subtleties of the Oriental mystical vision; or, at least, it has been Western thinkers who have succeeded in translating the exotic language of Eastern mysticism into the contemporary language of Western experience. When we think of such masters of Oriental mysticism as Mircea Eliade, René Guénon, and Hubert Benoit, we are thinking of uniquely contemporary visionaries, masters who have discovered a new way to the sacred through the labyrinth of our profane darkness. But have we not long since learned that the great poetic visionaries of the modern West have employed a non-Christian mystical language and symbolism as a way to the center of a uniquely modern immanence? One has only to think of the names of Blake, Goethe, Hölderlin, Baudelaire, Mallarmé, Rimbaud, Yeats, Rilke, Proust, and Joyce, to realize that non-Christian and even anti-Christian mystical symbols and motifs can supply a primary source of a symbolic language which is here directed to a total vision of the radical profane. Yet it is Nietzsche's vision of Eternal Recurrence, a vision also employing but inverting the sacred language of the mystics, which most clearly illuminates the thinking and experience of a history which is becoming totally profane.

Few, if any, thinkers have known the sheer horror of existence which Nietzsche unveiled. Casting aside every fixed source of meaning and value, Nietzsche passed through an interior dissolution of an established form of consciousness and selfhood and resurrected a chaos of meaninglessness lying deeply buried within the psyche of Western man. His quest was not simply a movement toward madness, for he prophetically foresaw the darkness of the contemporary world, a darkness arising in response to the collapse of the foundations of our history. Once the ground of an inherited form of experience has been uprooted, that experience will increasingly become formless, and consciousness will lose both the center and the direction which previously made possible its activity and its self-identity. Nietzsche symbolically employed the name of Zarathustra to distinguish two world epochs of history: believing that the Persian Zarathustra created a moral and religious vision which later became the foundation of Western history, Nietzsche created a new Zarathustra whose prophetic proclamation embodies the end of Western history, an end which that history has reached though its own momentum, and an end which will be followed by the advent of a wholly new historical era. All things whatsoever pass into meaninglessness and chaos when they no longer can be known and experienced from the vantage point of a fixed historical or human ground. But it is only by passing through such a chaos that we can reach the new world lying upon our horizon, a world reversing the forms and structures of our inherited consciousness and experience, and a world promising a new life and freedom to that broken and guilty creature, man.

In its initial form, Nietzsche's vision of Eternal Recurrence records the chaos of a world that has fallen away from its original center. It reflects a totality of perpetual and meaningless flux; no longer is there a beginning or an end, or, for that matter, a purpose or goal of any kind. For to affirm that all things eternally recur, and recur eternally the same, is to grasp an absolutely chaotic movement or flow, a movement in which identity and difference flow into one another, and nothing at all either preserves its own identity or remains different from anything else. Then the world appears as sheer chaos, and existence itself becomes an unimaginable horror. This vision, however, allows us to peer into the abyss and thus to perceive the ultimate ground of all No-saying: for guilt and resentment are rooted in the interior reality of chaos and emptiness. Yet the new Zarathustra comes to teach a way to the fullness of life in the midst of chaos, to proclaim a Yes-saying which is the antithetical opposite of No-saying, a Yes-saying embodying a total affirmation of meaninglessness and horror. Yes-saying is, of course, a primary symbol of the higher ways of mysticism, always reflecting a final *coincidentia oppositorum,* a total union of transiency and eternity, of suffering and joy. But the classical mystical forms of Yes-saying are interior expressions of the metamorphosis of a profane emptiness and nothingness into a sacred totality, a totality of bliss drawing all things into itself, and thereby negating their original and given form. Zarathustra's Yes-saying dialectically inverts its mystical counterpart, for it embraces and affirms a radically profane nothingness, and does so only by negating the religious quest for a sacred totality.

We shall not understand the Yes-saying of a New Zarathustra unless we realize that it is a total negation of the human and historical world of Christendom, and a negation following from the modern prophet's proclamation of the death of God. With the death of the Christian God, every transcendent ground is removed from all consciousness and experience, and humanity is hurled into a new and absolute immanence. Our chaos becomes manifest as a uniquely modern chaos when it is ever more comprehensively present in response to the emptying of the transcendent realm, as its darkness fills every pocket of light, and night falls throughout the whole gamut of experience. Now an ultimate choice is thrust upon every man, as he can either turn back in horror at our chaos by engaging in a final No-saying, or he can turn forward and meet our darkness by means of an ultimate Yes-saying, a total affirmation of our actual and immediate existence. Such an acceptance and affirmation is possible only if man will give all of the energy which he once directed to a transcendent beyond to the immediate moment, thus releasing every source of energy so as to effect a total engagement with the actual present before him. Zarathustra, and every authentic modern visionary, points the way to a total affirmation of the world, an affirmation which becomes possible only when the world appears as chaos, and man is liberated from every transcendent root and ground. Here, the disappearance of transcendence actualizes a new immanence, as a total Yes-saying to an immediate and actual present transforms transcendence into immanence, and absolute immanence dawns as the final kenotic metamorphosis of Spirit into flesh.

On every side, scholarly critics and theologians point to Nietzsche's vision of Eternal Recurrence as the antithetical opposite of the Christian gospel. Without doubt, this radically profane vision is absolutely opposed to the established dogmas and religious practices of Christianity, so much so that it only becomes manifest and real with the collapse of Christendom. Nevertheless, must the contemporary Christian be forced to confess that a totally immanent existence is wholly other than the life of faith? Will he not then also be bound to concede that the Christian can never fully exist in the world and the flesh? The consequence would follow, of course, that the modern Christian must repudiate that total immanence which has so fully dawned in our world and stand aside from every contemporary negation of transcendence. Let there be no question about this: to judge Zarathustra as the Antichrist, and Eternal Recurrence as a demonic inversion of the Kingdom of God, is to set oneself against the radical secularity of the modern world and finally to react with No-saying to the uniquely contemporary history of our time. This is precisely the path of the religious or ecclesiastical Christian today, and we might add that this is also the price which now must be paid for choosing the Christian God. On the other hand, if we can find a way to understand and affirm absolute immanence as a contemporary and kenotic realization of the Kingdom of God, an expression in our experience of an original movement of Christ from transcendence to immanence, then we can give ourselves to the darkest and most chaotic moments of our world as contemporary ways to the Christ who even now is becoming all in all. Nothing less is demanded of the Christian who would truly and fully live in our world, and nothing less is promised by the radically kenotic way of Christ.

The religious seer and prophet, whether in East or West, initially appears as one who can name the darkness about him, discovering in its dark emptiness a reversal of the sacred, a reversal banishing the sacred far beyond a present or given state of consciousness. Obviously Nietzsche was such a prophet and seer, and, like his ancient compeers, his vision is an expression of a prophetic community, beginning from at least the time of Blake and extended into our own day. The modern prophet, however, names our darkness as a darkness issuing from the death of God. Only the seer or prophet who knows the original and all-encompassing power of God can realize the catastrophic consequences of the death of God. Like the reform prophets of the Old Testament or the Taoist prophets of ancient China, the modern prophet can name even our light as darkness because he has been given a vision which abolishes all that humanity has thus far known as light. Both the ancient and the modern prophet must speak against every previous epiphany of light, calling for an absolute reversal of a fallen history as the way to life, with the hope that the destruction or dissolution of an inherited and given history will bring about the victory of a total epiphany of light. Thus we discover in Second Isaiah, the fullest Old Testament prophetic vision of redemption, a call to look forward to the coming transformation of all things:

> Lift up your eyes to the heavens,
>   and look at the earth beneath;
> for the heavens will vanish like smoke,
>   the earth will wear out like a garment,
>   and they who dwell in it will die like gnats;
> but my salvation will be for ever,
>   and my deliverance will never be ended.[1]

The triumphant message of Second Isaiah is inseparable from a vision of the coming dissolution of all of reality as man has known it, and it calls for a faith that is wholly directed to this coming event. A disciple of Second Isaiah recorded an oracle of the Lord's which most clearly witnesses to this radical prophetic call:

> For behold, I create new heavens
>   and a new earth;
> and the former things shall not be remembered
>   or come into mind.[2]

May we take these ancient prophetic words as marking the very essence of radical faith? If so, when we greet our chaos with a total Yes-saying, a total engagement with its dark emptiness, then we too can become open to a new and total epiphany of light. It is precisely by a radical move-

[1] Isa. 51:6.   [2] Isa. 65:17.

ment of turning away from all previous forms of light that we can participate in a new totality of bliss, an absolutely immanent totality embodying in its immediacy all which once appeared and was real in the form of transcendence, and a totality which the Christian must name as the present and living body of Christ. Indeed, can the Christian accept those triumphant words in the third part of *Thus Spoke Zarathustra,* where Zarathustra's animals speak ecstatically of the redemptive meaning of the symbol of Eternal Recurrence, as a portrait of such a new totality of bliss?

> "O Zarathustra," the animals said, "to those who think as we do, all things themselves are dancing: they come and offer their hands and laugh and flee—and come back. Everything goes, everything comes back; eternally rolls the wheel of being. Everything dies, everything blossoms again; eternally runs the year of being. Everything breaks, everything is joined anew; eternally the same house of being is built. Everything parts, everything greets every other thing again; eternally the ring of being remains faithful to itself. In every Now, being begins; round every Here rolls the sphere There. The center is everywhere. Bent is the path of eternity."

All things will dance when we greet them with affirmation, and then we will be released from the No-saying of guilt and resentment by being freed from all attachment to a distant and transcendent ground. When the path of eternity is bent or curved, then the way down is the way up, and the final or eschatological epiphany of Christ will occur kenotically in the immediate moment: "Being begins in every Now."

The highest expressions of mysticism also envision a center which is everywhere. But the sacred "center" is an interior depth or a transcendent beyond which reveals itself to be all in all as a consequence of an absolute negation or reversal of the profane, whereas Zarathustra's "center" lies at the very heart of a profane or immanent existence, and it becomes manifest as being everywhere only as the consequence of an absolute negation or reversal of the sacred. The death of God abolishes transcendence, thereby making possible a new and absolute immanence, an immanence freed of every sign of transcendence. Once a new humanity is fully liberated from even the memory of transcendence, it will lose all sense of bondage to the past, and with the loss of that bondage it will be freed from all that No-saying which turns us away from the immediacy of an actual and present "Now." Before singing his drunken midnight song in the fourth part of *Thus Spoke Zarathustra,* Zarathustra announces that now his world has become perfect; and he asks:

> Have you ever said Yes to a single joy? O my friends, then you said Yes too to *all* woe. All things are entangled, ensnared, enamored; if ever you wanted one thing twice, if ever you said, "You please me, happi-

ness! Abide, moment!" then you wanted *all* back. All anew, all eternally, all entangled, ensnared, enamored—oh, then you *loved* the world. Eternal ones, love it eternally and evermore; and to woe too, you say: go, but return! *For all joy wants—eternity.*

Such a love of the world is a total affirmation of an actual and immediate present: but in totally affirming the present, we must will that it recur, and that it recur eternally the same. A refusal to will the eternity of the present, the eternity of this actual present before us, can only proceed out of an attachment to transcendence, a bondage to a power lying outside the present, a power withholding us from a total affirmation of the world. Thus Zarathustra concludes his drunken song of joy with a repudiation of every backward movement to eternity and an affirmation of the new eternity which is *here* and *now:*

> Woe implores: Go!
> But all joy wants eternity—
> Wants deep, wants deep eternity.

Can we join Zarathustra in his hymn of praise to joy? Can we, too, repudiate every reversal of the present, every flight from pain, every backward movement to eternity? But this is to ask the Christian if he dares to open himself to the Christ who is fully present, the Christ who has completed a movement from transcendence to immanence and who is kenotically present in the fullness and the immediacy of the actual moment before us. If a contemporary epiphany of Christ has abolished all images of transcendence, and emptied the transcendent realm, then we can meet that epiphany only by totally embracing the world. Dare we bet that Christ is fully present in the actuality of the present moment? Then we must bet that God is dead, that a backward movement to eternity is a betrayal of Christ, and that a flight from the pain of existence is a refusal of the passion of Christ. The radical Christian calls us into the center of the world, into the heart of the profane, with the announcement that Christ is present here and he is present nowhere else. Once we confess that Christ is fully present in the moment before us, then we can truly love the world and can embrace even its pain and darkness as an epiphany of the body of Christ. It is precisely by truly loving the world, by fully existing in the immediacy of the present moment, that we will know that Christ is love, and then we shall know that love is a Yes-saying to the totality of existence.

Christian love is an incarnate love, a self-giving to the fullness of the world, an immersion in the actuality of time and the flesh. Therefore our Yes-saying must give us totally to the moment before us, and if we accept its actuality as the "center" which is everywhere, then we can be delivered from every temptation of regressing to a backward movement which is a reversal and diminution of an actual and immediate present. By turning away from the totality of the present, we engage in a regressive movement dissolving the actuality of the immediate moment, thereby disengaging ourselves from the fullness and the finality of existence. In naming Christ as the full embodiment of love, the Christian confesses that Christ is the fullness of time and the world. Christ is the pure actuality of the total moment, a present and immediate moment drawing all energy forward into itself and negating every backward movement to eternity. Every nostalgic yearning for innocence, all dependence upon a sovereign other, and every attachment to a transcendent beyond, stand here revealed as flights from the world, as assaults upon life and energy, and as reversals of the full embodiment of love. The Christian who chooses the ancient image of Christ as the Son of God, or who is bound to an epiphany of Christ in a long-distant past, must refuse the Christ who is actually present in our flesh. He wagers upon a purely religious image of Christ even at the price of forfeiting the actuality of our time and history. But the radical Christian wages upon the Christ who is totally profane. He bets upon the Christ who is the totality of the moment before us, the Christ who draws us into the fullness of life and the world. Finally, radical faith calls us to give ourselves totally to the world, to affirm the fullness and the immediacy of the present moment as the life and the energy of Christ. Thus, ultimately the wager of the radical Christian is simply a wager upon the full and actual presence of the Christ who is a totally incarnate love.

18

WILLIAM MALLARD

William Mallard, a member of the faculty of the Candler School of Theology of Emory University, has come to radical theology through two routes: the study of Church history and historical theology, and experience as an ordained Methodist minister. Although professionally trained as a specialist in medieval and Reformation Church history and thought, Mallard is acutely aware of the theological problems arising from the contemporary situation and is determined to engage in a full confrontation with these problems in the very context of the witness and worship of the Church. He would seem to be the only radical theologian who at present is capable of speaking from within the Church, just as he is the only radical who speaks as a historian. The following essay by Mallard is published here for the first time.

A Perspective for Current Theological Conversation

William Mallard

Because of the brevity of this paper and the intermediate stage of the work it describes, the term *perspective* is more appropriate than the formal designation, *theological position. Perspective* suggests theology in growth and process and a viewpoint contributing to the varied life and discussion within the range of Christian studies. Many of the elements in the following exposition are but in the early stages of formulation, but it is hoped that the general shape, and force, and inner life of the perspective is clear.

Basis

The following theological statement is understood to be an expansion of and commentary upon the faithful confession, "Jesus is Lord."

Method

A method for theology means a chosen frame of reference which is deemed suitable for expounding the meaning both of the New Testament and of contemporary Christian experience. That is, the Biblical material and the content of present-day awareness are *correlated* with one another when each is appropriately illuminated by the given frame of reference. Examples of such methodology include "the feeling of ultimate dependence," "the supreme value of personality," "the propositional truth of all Biblical statements." The method chosen for the present perspective refers both Biblical and contemporary materials to what may be called technically *the dialectical nature of existence.* Put in more ordinary terms, the central judgment here is that "life" goes on always by the encounter and conflict between opposites, that whatever is "worthwhile" is always known and

PRINTED here for the first time with the permission of the author.

seized upon in such clashes—love is sure only in the presence of potential or actual hate, life is strongest in its encounter with the peril of death. Realities are apprehended always as they move to coincide with their opposite. No simple formula or conventional pattern of belief can therefore determine our activity when we are the most genuinely and concretely ourselves, individually or corporately. The perspective here is therefore "existential" in the sense that no abstract principle, or rational concept, or revealed proposition can fix beforehand the given content of who we are as human beings—before, that is, our free and responsible decisions towards one another. (Our "existence" precedes our "essence.") The perspective here is *not* "existential" in the sense (often used) that only at the "borderline" of individual alienation and despair (in actuality or by implication) can man make authentic utterances regarding himself and his destiny. The rich moments of living self-realization also contribute to valid affirmation. In particular, men are not called upon to focus their attention upon the dialectic or to "engineer" contradictoriness; their task is to sort out the most hopeful and life-affirming choices possible.

Authority

The authority for the method described above is the content of the New Testament witness plus contemporary experience within the Christian community (latent or institutional). Thus the method by which it is proposed to correlate Biblical and contemporary material is presumed to arise freely, without artificial constraint, from these two same sources. "Contemporary material" should include as broad a range of cultural and historical matter as possible, just as the Bible should be accompanied by the unceasing accretion of commentary upon it. Therefore, in the "Tradition" (including Church history and historical theology) the two sources overlap.[1]

Content

CHRIST JESUS   Jesus of Nazareth was a Jewish apocalyptical prophet who proclaimed with urgency the imminent end and consummation of history in the Kingdom of God. He proclaimed, that is, the final and most mighty of God's acts. He saw the world about to be transfigured into the everlasting aeon of God's manifest reign. That Jesus' ministry was dominated by apocalyptical eschatology in some form is now (since Albert Schweitzer's

---

[1] The theological method here described is indebted to Paul Tillich. Tillich proposed, however, to correlate Biblical and contemporary material by employing undialectical categories of "being." It is hoped here to be able to transcend such categories in speaking of matters pertaining to faith and salvation. It could be maintained here that Tillich's "God" is finally continuous with the "world," an implied harmonious depth of "things as they are"; that his immanentalism is finally unrelieved, since transcendent reality is given the status of symbol. Even being, and the abyss of being, must not be considered undialectically.

work) evidently established. Whether he felt or acknowledged that the coming Kingdom was actually, presently, at work—by anticipation—in his own activities continues to be a matter of great discussion among Biblical historians. It would be a reasonable judgment that, in any case, Jesus was so imbued with his prophecy as to manifest in his own doings the *quality* of the End that he so urgently expected. Just what that quality was, however, and the manner of its expression, would seem forever closed to the inquiries of the scientific historian.[2] The expected consummation of course did not occur. Confronted with this failure, the primitive Christian community had to rethink the content of its experience, finding that indeed the Kingdom *had* come, in some sense, in the activity of Jesus himself. They first affirmed this regarding his Resurrection, then regarding the Cross and Resurrection together, then his entire life and ministry taken together and climaxed in the Cross and Resurrection. Only by their testimony can the quality and force and importance of Jesus' life be sensed by us, so that he may be called "Lord." Scientific history may assist us in discarding numerous secondary elements in the Gospel narrative, but at the apex, or positive center of confession, the witness of the early community summons us to faith—through its portrayal of Jesus—and scientific history becomes incompetent.[3] Or, to put it another way, no contemporary his-

---

[2] Note the departure at this point from the aims of the "new quest" for the historical Jesus.

[3] In this entire matter, Schweitzer's work is of high importance, but the work of Bultmann and his school is more nearly adequate. Schweitzer is fundamentally right in proposing that any serious historical work on Jesus' life finds him slipping back to become the mysterious apocalyptic figure of the first century that indeed he was ("He passes by our time and returns to His own . . . ," *Quest*, p. 397). But then having established his criterion of historicity as "consistently futuristic eschatology," Schweitzer and his disciple M. Werner attempt to make too many purely historical judgments about Jesus' life (he expected the Kingdom during his ministry, and it failed; he deliberately sacrificed his life to force the Kingdom in, "threw himself upon the wheel of the world . . . ," but only destroyed the eschatological conditions he had created). Any statement of how Jesus thought of himself must be deduced from the Church's early interpretations; obviously these do not distinguish between literal fact and "poetic illumination" of the truth as the Church saw it. We shall probably never be able to discern confidently just how Jesus regarded himself; but the essence of the testimony is clear: Jesus was a man of dynamic eschatological hope and of a love that reversed conventional values. The Kingdom that he prophesied was so real to him that he fully embodied its nature in himself. These judgments are of course expressed in the Church's witness, looking back through the Cross and Resurrection. Whereas Schweitzer's testimony to the "Spirit of Jesus" would seem to by-pass the Cross via his historical criterion, surely Bultmann is right that any witness to Jesus must be an integral part of the full *kerygma*. It is held here that the *kerygma* does indeed point to a historical person, but that the historical content is completely surrounded by, and carried within, a confession of faith. (Bultmann's work may not after all really abolish historical content from the *kerygma*; rather his caveat against history I take to be against contemporary scientific historical methodology, which he rightly sees will *never* give results positively correlating with the content of faith.) Our task is so to interpret (demythologize) the primitive witness as to point to the content commonly significant for both them and us.

toriography can get "behind" (1) Jesus' apocalypticism and (2) the Christological confession of the early Church. We do not, in other words, have two avenues of approach to Christ Jesus (one, "intellectual"; the other, "believing"), whose results must then somehow be harmonized. Rather we are confronted with one major question: What judgment shall we make regarding the special significance claimed for this apocalyptical figure by the early community? Critical reason works in this matter to distinguish historical data and canons of interpretation, to make possible "demythologizing" and "remythologizing"; but the inquiry is incomplete apart from the "leap" or gap in rationality where we risk an evaluative judgment.

Jesus appeared, then, bearing in himself the nature of the mysterious apocalyptic Kingdom whose prophet he was. The literal "furniture" of his expectation, and that of the early Church (as best we know such "furniture") remained unfulfilled. The theologian's task today, therefore, is to distinguish the passing features of his ministry and to affirm its true significance—essentially apprehensible both then and now. That significance lies in the Kingdom of God and the truth and love that manifest the Kingdom.

Jesus announced "that day" soon to come when the demonic order of Satan and his angels would finally be cast down forever by God's cataclysmic intervention. The world would be shorn of its waste and corrupt elements and transfigured into the Kingdom. Some men would belong to God; others would suffer Satan's lot. All superficial appearances, hypocritical religion, and ordinary self-seeking would be laid bare. Jesus showed special uneasiness towards his people's hunger for a Messiah (he probably never acknowledged this role, as such, for himself). His countrymen invariably saw the Messiah as a means to an end: either "bread," or political conquest, or naked supernatural power. Jesus' activities inevitably put him on the brink of commitment to any or all of these; but he struggled throughout his ministry to clarify that there was no such "Christ," no direct "answer" to things on the world's own terms. Everything of importance turned on preparation for the Kingdom—the mysterious apocalypse that would reverse all the world's values, even its hopes and questions. As he succeeded in clarifying his convictions to those around him, he of course found himself increasingly isolated. Still he insisted, in view of the dawning Kingdom, that no natural power or ordinary authority could help, no matter how enhanced. Only a simple urgent confidence in the reversal of all things by the Kingdom could yield hope. To endure without illusion the cruelty of things; to abandon all legalistic, religious security; to accept one's forgiveness through a simple, "blind" trust; to live by anticipation the transfigured Kingdom life of compassion, joy, and love; to honor God by the simplicity and freedom of one's daily life—these were the childlike responses of the "believer." Neither Jesus nor his disciples realized, except perhaps in a vague manner, that the Kingdom was really present in Jesus himself; nor was this presence fully articulate before the Crucifixion.

At the Crucifixion the issues of Jesus' ministry and the Kingdom are made clear. The shape of our existence finds its expression, though its mystery is not "explained." In the Cross, the relation between the Kingdom and the world is stretched to its ultimate opposition, to the breaking point. In face of the world's most harsh absurdity—the betrayal and expulsion of the true and loving man—the Divine Kingdom is its most totally "other." In this heavy circumstance, the role of Jesus contains an astonishing twofoldness. He is, on the one hand, a model of our human existence. He has taken upon him all the goods and ills of his moment of time and fused them into the shocking actuality of his condemnation and death. He is for three hours the articulation of the death-in-life and life-in-death contradiction that plagues the hopeful efforts of us all. Via his one expression of "forsakenness," he is man caught forever on the indifferent, balanced wheel of circumstance. He is prosaic, alienated man, cut off from his own tradition, caught in this extremity with no religion of "return" to comfort him—neither the sacrifice of a mystery ritual, nor the blissful dissolution of the Buddha. He has only the cycle of a pointless "hell." He is the illumination of "things as they are."

Seen from another perspective, however, Jesus *is* the embodiment of the very transcendent, mysterious Kingdom itself! His despised and rejected condition, his commitment to a love past understanding, make him a complete inversion of all the powers and goods that the world can desire. He is "nothing" to the world—accursed and cast out. He is neither a criminal nor a weakling; he has neither made his bid for power and lost, nor is he by nature powerless, using his weakness for illicit domination. Righteous and strong by nature, he is worse than a criminal or a weakling—he is a fool. He has cast himself away for a Reality too burdensome and wondrous for men to bear. "My Kingdom is not of this world." He knows the outrage that is folly's reward, the fury of business-as-usual intruded upon. And by executing him, his assailants make of him the true image of the Kingdom, i.e., as it must appear to the world in general: a weak and ridiculous "nothing," a visionary folly. More deeply grasped, the transcendent, "wholly-other" Kingdom actualizes and focuses itself at the outer limit of the human world, in the anguished and isolated Jesus. The mysterious "no-thingness" of the Kingdom moves to unite with the suffering grace of Jesus' condemned life. The Kingdom does come, in its veiled epiphany at the Cross.

The twofold situation of Jesus crucified is thus (1) an actualization of the human element and (2) a movement of the Divine Kingdom, concretizing itself and its mystery. (Contrast the formula of Chalcedon:[4] "two natures in one person.") Two opposite realities are brought into a new kind of unity

---

[4] The Council of Chalcedon (451 A.D.), which formulated the dogma that Christ is truly man and truly God—T. J. J. A.

with one another. The dialectic of our existence is manifest, not only richly and fully, but with specially peculiar characteristics. The world and its "other" (i.e., the absurd actuality of human history, and the fearful divine Abyss) have met in a dynamic coincidence. The full dialectic is manifest. We see into the "nature of things."

Yet this manifestation has one peculiar characteristic of overriding importance: The Kingdom negates the world and consumes the life of Jesus of Nazareth, but it does so *in order to move creatively into the future* and bring into being a *new present*. The secret kingdom that Jesus had affirmed *does* turn out to be the Kingdom that meets him at the Cross, a Kingdom that crucifies in order progressively to create anew, again and again, through history. The Kingdom *is* eschatological and apocalyptic; it is the Promise in time, the creative tension towards the future in successive deaths and rebirths; the Kingdom comes and is always coming. Its moment of crucifying actualization, at the Cross, is always a moment that looks forward to the new Possibility; it "straightens out" time into agonizing, progressive strides. This kind of Kingdom-actualization always has its immediate human counterpart in a moment of forward-looking faith, a "leap in being," an "absurd" moment that negates the "absurdities" of existence. Faith is the "foolishness" of *nevertheless*. Faith is the acceptance of existence, but in forward-looking affirmation. Faith is the full awareness of "nature's wheel" that yet announces a Promise for man. It is of the highest importance that the Crucifixion account includes *both* the cry of "why . . . forsaken!" and also the "Father, forgive them . . ." and ". . . I commend my life." The entire direction of the Christian faith turns upon his utter desolation *and* his expiring not apart from faith. The concrete and utter desolation of Jesus would coincide dialectically only with the Void. The chaotic "nothing" or absurdity of Jesus' plight would coincide only with the universal Silence of God's "no-thingness." The dialectic of existence would be resolved simply into the motionless Beyond. But Jesus affirmed the meaningful continuance of the struggle. His movement of faith *outward* from the desperate cycle was dialectically the movement of the Kingdom *into* the turbulent stuff of our physical existence. Thus Jesus' Crucifixion, realized precisely *within* the dialectical nature of our existence, nevertheless exactly *reversed* the movement or direction of that dialectic. Rather than the "stuff of life" coinciding with the Void, which negated it, the mystery of the Kingdom entered the agonies of our temporal existence, in order to transfigure them. *That* is the miracle of Christ. Or, put another way: Instead of Jesus' returning into nothing, the Nothing entered into him—a forward-moving event.[5] By that move-

---

[5] The reference to the Incarnate Kingdom as "Nothing" borrows of course upon the *via negativa* of the medieval contemplatives. Whereas with them, however, the negative "approach" to the Divine led, stage by stage, through the levels of

ment, Jesus was carried forward universally into the selfhood of the concrete human beings that succeeded him on earth. Our actual humanity is the renewed flesh of Jesus precisely because the Kingdom is Incarnate in *him* (the corporate body of us all) and therefore in *us,* as the secret of our existence (cf. implications of John 6:33-58). Jesus is thus our present, and yet passes beyond us always as our future, the crucifixion of our easy confidence that we have contained him, the summons of a striving hope that "all things will be made new." The words of Albert Schweitzer are unforgettable:

> He destroyed the world into which He was born; the spiritual life of our own time seems like to perish at His hands, for He leads to battle against our thought a host of dead ideas, a ghostly army upon which death has no power, and Himself destroys again the truth and goodness which His Spirit creates in us, so that it cannot rule the world. That He continues, notwithstanding, to reign as the alone Great and alone True in a world of which He denied the continuance, is the prime example of that antithesis between spiritual and natural truth which underlies all life and all events, and in Him emerges into the field of history.[6]

The *Resurrection* of Jesus was in its outward form an ecstatic experience of the primitive community, brimming as they were with eschatological expectancy. Jesus had taught his followers primarily to expect and prepare for the Kingdom; it is probable that he taught his own death, should it come, as part of the necessary tribulation prior to "that day." Jesus' Resurrection on Easter Sunday was very likely at the outset just one part of what the community conceived to be the whole consummated eschaton breaking in.[7] It is mere conjecture to propose what, in a modern sense, "literally" took place. A religious ecstasy on the order of Paul's Damascus-road "witness" to the Resurrection, or similar to the "descent of the Spirit" at Pentecost, is most probable. Since, with the passage of days and weeks, the untransformed condition of things-in-general was obvious, the com-

---

Platonic "being," and the sense of the blessed "darkness" was nearest in the realm of "essences," in the perspective presented here the approach is via the distinctive qualities of actual historical events, such that to know the dynamic Kingdom is to sort out by free human decision the fresh, living moments of human justice, kindness, compassion, and meaningful self-giving—their clarity, their force, and their direction. It is to live, therefore, the way of the Cross and Resurrection. The Kingdom itself is *not* just, or kind, or compassionate, or self-giving—because it is *more* than these. It is the Logos, or Dynamic Meaning of our existence right in our present, opening the future—but then it is *not* those, either.
[6] Schweitzer, *Quest,* p. 2.
[7] St. Matthew's assertion that on Good Friday tombs were opened and saints appeared (27:51-53) is apparently a bit of this lingering tradition, that the three days from the Crucifixion to the Resurrection were thought to witness the in-breaking of the consummated Kingdom.

munity discerned that the "eschaton" of that terrible Passover had been limited to Jesus' Resurrection only. His living presence was then known as abiding with them, anticipatory of the final climax yet to come.

If the literal details of the Resurrection are thus unclear, its significance is more certain. The community realized that the Kingdom, so soon to be fulfilled, was already dynamically among them (by way of anticipation) *as* the Resurrected Jesus, and indeed had been in some sense present even in Jesus' ministry. They realized, in other words, the new birth of life, looking out of Crucifixion toward the future, and sensed the movement of the mysterious Kingdom into their very communal existence (as described above in relation to the Cross). Of course, their experience and their understanding of the Kingdom were not highly clarified at this point. (We must never idealize the primitive Church, as even a superficial reading of the New Testament indicates.) The price they paid for nearness to the original event was the rich confusion of data and possibilities poured upon them; our disadvantage today of remoteness from Jesus' time is in part compensated by the wealth of commentary and "sorting out" that has meanwhile taken place. Their sense of the true Kingdom was constantly in danger of compromise by emotional impulses, superstition, "spiritualizing," entrenched traditions, and license (cf. Paul's agony over the churches). The Resurrection became attached to an "Ascension," which apparently mythologized the glory of the Kingdom into a highly inappropriate withdrawal from the anguish of history. Nevertheless, the core of the primitive witness actualized the dynamic truth. Despite incredible distortion, the New Reality opened up in Jesus showed an unremitting power of "resurrection," again and again, through the suffering creativity of Christian men and at the frontiers of their decisive faith.

GOD   For a Christian to speak of God is, in the perspective of this essay, simply to enlarge upon what has already been presented above. That is, the reality of God finds description in relation to the vital events moving towards, through, and beyond the ministry of Jesus. In the interest of clarity, the outline will first suggest the changes in men's *idea* or *awareness* of God through Biblical history. Then some attempt will be made to correlate these with the nature of the Divine Reality itself.

The Old Testament presents us with what may very broadly be described as the increasing problem of God's transcendence. Through the long maturation of Israel's experience the grasp of Yahweh[8] moves from restricted localization to a point almost of transcendent inaccessibility. The most casual student of the Old Testament realizes the very early identification of God even with the hostile spirit of a river or roadway (e.g., wrestling Jacob, the bizarre circumcision of Moses). The association of Yahweh

[8] Yahweh is the primary Hebrew and Old Testament word for God—T. J. J. A.

with Sinai is of course of much deeper significance for the people Israel. The eighth-century prophetic vision of Yahweh's universality opens a much wider ethical imperative for faith. But concomitant problems are realized in the post-Exilic Wisdom literature as God's very universality calls into question the justice of his governance over the world. The powerful ethical authority of God resides in his very transcendence over the natural cycle and therefore over any natural grouping of men (family, tribe, nation). Yet this very transcendence (pressed all the way back to God's creation of the entire cosmos) becomes the occasion for questioning God's righteousness, in view of the inequitable conditions of men. If God's justice is universal and all-authoritative, why do the fortunes of men accord so poorly with their just deserts in God's eyes? Why are the innocent cast down? Why do the wicked flourish? The question most immediately recalls the verse-drama of Job. In Job the heritage of just expectations regarding God is at the collapsing point in view of the ruthless mystery surrounding the Creator. In the light of previous biblical history, Job's cry for an accounting on God's part is entirely appropriate. He confronts the awesome terror of the Creator—he who fashioned the hard contradictions and the rich freakishness of nature—but succumbs to the sheer power of God's immense rebuke. Job's "repentance" is disturbing because it suggests the crumpling of his human dignity without promise of renewal and without any glimmer of a redemptive Divine intention.[9] Man is reduced to a wretched smallness, and God becomes correspondingly the "whirlwind" —the dark and terrifying energy behind the disturbing mask of his created order. Transcendence, the aspect of God originally seized upon as the very guarantor of his high ethical nature, has with Job exploded into a cold and unrestrained Majesty, responsible for the nightmarish indifference of "things-as-they-are." God has become the vast "Beyond." Significantly, in the late Old Testament period, the sacredness of his Name is so intensified in purity as not to be pronounceable except once a year, by the High Priest alone, within the Holy of Holies.

The concept of terrifying, full Transcendence in the book of Job is a kind of prelude to later Apocalyptic expectation. Despite the pressure of despair upon his people, God still has one possibility to "redeem himself." He may do it by a coming cataclysm in which the world will be purged of its horrors and all inequities adjusted. Even the dead will be raised to know the restoration of justice. Thus with the spread of the Apocalyptic hope (c.165 B.C.-A.D. 90) the long-mentioned "day of Yahweh" assumes its grandest scope and depth. Elements of Persian dualism intensify the opposition between God's light and the forces of darkness. Utter Tran-

---

[9] The "happy ending" of the folk-tale, in which Job gains a new array of herds and children for his "faithfulness," is of course no solution, as the author of the verse drama well knows. Actual experience is hardly so even-handed.

scendence has relegated the world to demonic forces. But that Transcendence will soon justify itself by a conquering plunge into the arena of history, catching up a transformed world to itself forever. (Thus a complete gnostic dualism was resisted by an appeal to the future.)

The stage is thus set for an evaluation of Jesus' relation to the apocalyptic "Kingdom of God," which of course simply means God himself in his special and final activity as King. Such an evaluation has already been partly attempted in this paper.

The question arises, then, apart from the progression in men's awareness of God, what may rightly be said about God himself through these developments. God, for man, is the Infinite that stands at the limit of his little structures of knowledge and understanding. That Infinite he has always held at bay by his rationality; but man's rationality is unable finally to comprehend his own actual existence. Any attempt so to comprehend is always brought up short in lively contradiction, the disturbing contradiction of man himself. This moment of concretely acknowledged existence (and of reason's downfall) is the moment when man knows himself on the brink of Infinitude (see Kierkegaard). His primal relation to God has always been the threat (or fascination!) of being engulfed, dissolved by Infinity. His most urgent question has been the possibility of mediating between the abysmal God and the ephemeral meanings of his own daily existence.

Such a mediation was the Covenant of the Old Testament. The Yahweh of Sinai[10] was a movement or "shape" of the Divine that, by calling forth the vision and determination of Moses, related itself to the activities of a people (importantly, to their hope for the future) without abandoning its awesome character as the Holy.[11] Such a tentative movement was, however, but a moderate foretokening of the dramatic changes historically to come. That is, the mediation at Sinai presented the Infinite as a kind of Great and Unspeakable King upon the mountain, a "halfway" movement into man's condition and therefore a sign, or "shadow" of the full and rich

---

[10] The God of the Mosaic Covenant—T. J. J. A.

[11] Statements made here about Divine movement, change, and activity are intended as approximate, literal statements, not primarily as "symbolic" (except of course insofar as all language is by nature symbolic). The only levels of reality acknowledged here are finite existence and its immediately suggested dialectical opposite, the infinite. There is therefore no static "realm" of "eternal truth" or "essences"; these are creatures of man's rational fantasy and of his desire to "fix" things that he supposes are of lasting importance to him. They tend to be idolatrous and most likely are a thin disguise of man's desire to give up the difficulties of his existence, to resolve the dialectic into a quiescent and silent Infinity. But in life all is dynamic: as man strives to relate himself to the Infinite, he knows, through his world and his fellows, the Infinite moving to relate itself to him. Such movements are "real," i.e., they are true as constitutive of actual existential relations between man and the ultimate. They of course are not true in any abstract or rationalistic sense.

Incarnation to appear in Jesus. The "anthropomorphic" movement of God in much Old Testament history was therefore a middle-ground, arousing a sense of the Infinite that yet was somehow in human form and self-involved in men's affairs. God was a person-like Being, dwelling "on high," but ranging far and wide in human activity. The next movement of the Divine, announced through the pre-exilic Prophets, was to repudiate this mediate and more localized form because of man's determination to idolatrize the human side of it and thus to render impossible any moment of faith before the Infinite. God's wrathful withdrawal into his Infinity rendered him at once less "bound," less manipulatable, more abstract, more "ethical," more terrifying. But the Infinite was still sufficiently mediated to the human as to be *meaningful*. The coldness of wrath was somehow justified by man's perverse behavior. God was profoundly "injured"; a broken relationship was still a relationship and still understandable. But as the world became wider and history became more generally terrifying, and the affairs of Israel more distraught and complex, the withdrawal of the Divine became a moment of man's most embittered surprise and horror. God dwelt at the brink of unintelligibility (see Job). Creative power threatened to become mere fortuitous energy within the Abyss. God's withdrawal into abstract darkness, or the Void, seemed an unconscionable punishment, a loss of all discernible meaning in man's contradictory strivings. And yet, even the meaninglessness of God—God as sheer Infinitude, as Gulf—was a kind of Wrath, the engendering of an absurd and pointless guilt in men. (For a contemporary portrayal, see A. Camus, *The Fall*.) If existence is devoid of meaning, then *anything* should be "right." Yet confronted with God as Indifferent Void, men know the burden of an incommensurate guilt—with no bar of judgment before which to stand. Such a situation implicit in Job was likewise the somber background against which Apocalyptic was conceived. An example is the anguish of the Apocalyptic Ezra in his cry to the angel Uriel:

> It would be better for us not to be here than to come here and live in ungodliness, and to suffer and not understand why. . . . I beseech you, . . . why have I been endowed with the power of understanding? For I did not wish to inquire about the ways above, but about those things which we daily experience: why Israel has been given over to the Gentiles as a reproach; why the people whom you loved has been given over to godless tribes, and the law of our fathers has been made of no effect and the written covenants no longer exist; and why we pass from the world like locusts, and our life is like a mist, and we are not worthy to obtain mercy. But what will he do for his name, by which we are called? [12]

[12] II Esdras 4:12, 22-25, Revised Standard Version.

Apocalypticism moves, therefore, to the brink of equating guilt and existence. (To exist is to be wretched and pointless and therefore guilty.) The Infinite had removed to an absolutely intolerable posture opposite men. Transcendence had broadened to the point of Nothingness and yet of extreme Wrath. Further transcendence, logically suggesting freedom and autonomy for man, actually promised the opposite—increased self-hatred and absurdity. God could not set men free by being more and more God "in himself." He not only did not comfort men regarding their death; he threatened to become the Death Principle itself in life, cutting the motivation for all courage and responsibility. This issue of utter Transcendence was at once realized and at the same time turned away from in the Apocalyptical affirmation. The threat of despair simply intensified the claims of hope. The future would justify the present; the Kingdom would solve the agonies of desperation and reunite the blessed. Jesus evidently could know the profound terror of his time and yet address God as "Father" because of his absolute commitment to the coming Kingdom.

The Kingdom *did* come. But the outward form that it assumed was unanticipated, even by Jesus himself. The turn of history was a new movement of the Divine, truly world revolutionizing in its scope and implications. Infinite Death had to die; Transcendence had to be transfigured; Wrathful Majesty had to become a simple, suffering dignity. The movement of the Infinite was a dialectical concretizing into the anguished, faithful selfhood of the crucified Jesus, and through that death, into the re-created body of all humanity. The Infinite in its abstract form became the concrete Infinite of man's meaningful future, known in Jesus. This is to say, in one sense of the word, that Transcendence became Immanence. But to say so undialectically is only to leave things as they were before, to render God into the heavy and brutal absurdity of the factual world-in-general. It is perhaps better to say that Transcendence profoundly revolutionized its nature for us, in Jesus. The union of Transcendent and immanent was not simply for the purpose of return to Transcendence (the "Nothing"); but rather the ordinary direction of the existential dialectic was reversed by Transcendence becoming the nature and meaning of man's secular future. The Infinite assumes, therefore, a *kind* of transcendence with the following forms and implications: the Open Possibility standing before every free human decision, requiring a trusting faith that risks and suffers in order to achieve; the Mystery of the worth of each human being, dialectically coincident with even his barbarous, or his "vegetative" nature; the Way of self-giving, inviting the venture of compassion, or *self*-transcendence; the unlimited Usefulness of material goods for the well-being of humankind; the factor of the New in human affairs, darkly summoning to faith and threatening the judgment of sterile decay if unheeded; the Meaning of human destiny, the *nevertheless* of the Cross that in some unseen way man will prevail—the Promise, indeed, that in the beginning called out Abraham and is alone the full gift of Grace. In each case, the item named is identified with its concrete articulation: bread *is* its usefulness; man *is* his mysterious worth; the "going out" *is* promise and grace. In sum: God has become the radically Incarnate Word, or Logos, in man's history. That Word is intimately signified by human hope, or the faith that affirms the future (Transcendence-for-us). Thus Transcendence takes on something of the character envisioned by Dietrich Bonhoeffer in the fragments of his unwritten book:

> Encounter with Jesus Christ, implying a complete orientation of human being in the experience of Jesus as one whose only concern is for others. This concern of Jesus for others the experience of transcendence. This freedom from self, maintained to the point of death, the sole ground of his omnipotence, omniscience and ubiquity. Faith is participation in this Being of Jesus (incarnation, cross and resurrection). Our relation to God not a religious relationship to a supreme Being, absolute in power and goodness, which is a spurious conception of transcendence, but a new life for others, through participation in the Being of God. The transcendence is to be found not in tasks beyond our scope and power, but in the nearest person to hand. God in human form, not, as in other religions, in animal form—the monstrous, chaotic, remote and terrifying—nor yet in abstract form—the absolute, metaphysical, infinite, etc.—nor yet in the Greek divine-human of autonomous man, but man existing for others, and hence the Crucified. A life based on the transcendent.[13]

The Incarnate Meaning of things *is* Jesus, as he is actualized in each of our fellow human beings—before whom we must decide, with whom we must go forward. The terrible form of the Infinite as the incommensurable meeting of the Void and the Wrathful has moved to become the death and Resurrection of Jesus, the renewal of humankind. This is the sacrifice, indeed the "death" of God. The Infinite has negated its abstract, meaningless form to become the wonder of Christ-for-us, in each moment of our free and decisive striving. To speak therefore of God's "death" is to seize upon the only mythology adequate to these two realities: (1) the vanishing of the Infinite as the abstract, wrathful Abyss of Deity and (2) the realization of this change, and its passageway towards human rebirth, in the literal and anguished death of Jesus. With this Divine "death," existence became either expressly or implicitly "secular," knowing the "sacred" as now specifically the tension of human freedom towards its secular future. All actual abstraction has thus been in a twinkling secularized. No longer

---

[13] Dietrich Bonhoeffer, "Outline for a Book," Ch. 2, *Letters and Papers from Prison,* translated by Ronald Gregor Smith (New York: Macmillan, 1962).

the wrathful Abyss, it has taken on an indifferent quality except in relation to its human usefulness, as in mathematics, science, or ordinary communication. The universe, scientifically considered, is "benignly indifferent" (see A. Camus, *The Stranger,* concluding pages), a neutral ground for man's exploration and discovery, and no longer a terrifying model of the Divine Emptiness. Only when the universe is concretely considered as the full arena of man's meaningful destiny is it seen itself to have an evolving direction, to constitute, with respect to its end, an act of Creation. The Divine itself has now fully entered flesh as the austere summons of human destiny. The relation of the Infinite to man has taken a new and decisive turn. God is now no longer the Abyss, nor an intermediate personal, "anthropomorphic" Spirit, but the Logos of man's hopeful existence. To ask precisely the nature of that Logos, or Meaning, of man's history is not to inquire after a "personal, spiritual Being," but to contemplate the essential Mystery of Jesus' ministry and suffering and Resurrection. And to inquire into that Mystery is necessarily to become not less than a folllower of Jesus, as a way of decisively dealing with our fellow human beings.

A note on terminology Intellectual concepts as provided by developing culture have always been awkward instruments for clarifying the Christian faith. It has been suggested above that the mythology of "the death of God" appropriately expresses the Divine Incarnation, which has also been dealt with in more rigorous, technical terms. Language involving "the death of God" must, however, be used with care in the interest of as complete accuracy as possible. To say, for example, that "God is dead" can leave far too much room for variant interpretations. The statement can mean that, for Christians, a certain specified form of the Deity has negated itself in the Christian revelation. But numerous other responses to the three-word statement are obviously possible. The term, *the death of God,* is probably preferable as an introduction to discussion, since it is more general, does not make an indicative statement, and obviously calls for exposition.

Again, the theological perspective outlined here can be fitted into the different "-isms" of traditional philosophical theology only with obvious difficulty. Notice that the Bible itself has been used as a primary source for numerous different philosophical descriptions of God. Most of early Western theological history, as Charles Hartshorne asserts, apparently saw the Old and New Testaments as supporting "classical theism," a view of God as both purely absolute and yet knowing and loving the world.[14] Hartshorne himself classifies the Judeo-Christian Scriptures as presenting an

---

[14] Charles Hartshorne and William L. Reese, *Philosophers Speak of God* (Chicago: University of Chicago Press, 1953), p. 34.

ancient, or "quasi" form, not of theism, but rather panentheism. In addition, straightforward pantheism has been noted in Scripture, either as acosmism (at the outset of the creation story), or as pancosmism (in the eschatological outlook of the New Testament: "that God may be all in all"[15]). With the discussion of "the death of God," the question of the term *atheism* has also arisen, which historically has both a strict and a more relaxed usage.[16] In its more strict sense, "atheism" has meant denial of any Divine Reality whatsoever; obviously such usage is not applicable to the perspective presented here. In its less strict form, "atheism" has included, for example, deism and pantheism while turning its negative force against theism in particular (thereby becoming an "antitheism"). The proper use of "atheism" may therefore depend upon what disposition is made of the term *theism*.

Notably, the word "theism" is of seventeenth-century English origin, a distinctively modern usage, though freely applied to centuries of theological history that never employed it.[17] Kant was the first clearly to note its English origin and to define it as indicating a transcendent, intelligent, and freely active God, present ruler over the world. Kant saw no means of personal intercourse between man and the theistic God, though only a small theoretical modification had to be made for others to find such a relationship possible. Hartshorne[18] applies "theism" variously to such figures as Philo, Augustine, Aquinas, and Descartes and discerns throughout a fatal flaw in these thinkers: that an absolutely transcendent Deity is irreconcilable with an active, loving Lord. Indeed, Hartshorne finds that theism classically conceived impinges upon atheism for just this reason.[19] It would seem, then, that "theism" points to a rationalistic concept of God as not assuredly either related to the world or unrelated. The theistic theory is thus out of harmony with the substance of this essay primarily at two points: (1) It does not permit the full Incarnation of the Divine, in which the "personality" of God is real only as the actual selfhood of Jesus; (2) it offers a rationalistic description of the divine essence, disallowing the full mystery of the Infinite as approached through the *via negativa*. Or, to summarize, "theism" presents an unsatisfactory middle ground that bears within itself a serious contradiction yet affords no opportunity for serious dialectical conceptualizing. The term "atheism" might therefore be used to designate the perspective here presented, in the careful sense of "antitheism," or as a kind of popular polemic against the very crudely theistic notions found to such a disturbing extent through our

[15] I Cor. 15:20; cf. *Hastings Encyclopedia*, 1922, "Pantheism."
[16] Cf. *Schaff-Herzog Encyclopedia*, 1911.
[17] *Ibid.*, "Theism."
[18] *Op. cit., passim.*
[19] *Ibid.*, p. 434.

society. Since, however, "atheism" properly carries the heavy connotation of rejecting all Deity of whatever sort, it is probably best that it not be used.

If it were insisted that the Christian, in full awareness of the Christian revelation, should identify his view of God by the use of such technical philosophical language, the task of translation would be difficult. From the viewpoint of this essay, the result would be something on this order: a dialectical and humanistic panentheism (God includes, but is more than, all "things"). This would imply the radical Incarnation of the Infinite, yet its openness towards man's future. But the term is stilted and uncommunicative except in the most specialized sense—an entirely inappropriate symbol of faith. It is part of the irony of our situation that we must strive with such instruments to suggest that which, in itself, is essentially simple.

IMPLICATIONS FOR THE REST OF THEOLOGY   Because of the limited aims of the present essay, no attempt will be made to treat with any adequacy the remainder of the topics in the traditional theological spectrum. Rather, certain suggestions will be offered as to the direction of further exposition.

Some of the matters already outlined have obviously indicated materials for an appropriate *view of man*. Man must be seen in the light of Hebraic psychology as a "whole" being, totally an existing creature, an "animated body," not an "encased soul." His existence must be affirmed—the mystery of his birth, the contradictoriness of his life, the reality of his death—if he is to know his Promise as creature. He is properly both social and individual. Each individual is called upon, in faith and courage, to accept responsibility for his life and for his death (no one can live his life or die his death for him). Such is his acceptance of himself and his existence. A strong individual of this sort is the best participant in the life of his society, for he is not fearful of the issues that arise from social interaction. He strives for a just foundation in the law that will provide a secure base for the free development of strong individuality in others. Man thus finds meaning in his existence through the rich interplay of individual and social tendencies.

That is properly called *sin* which in any way alienates a man from decisively dealing with the issues of his existence in faith—and which, therefore, alienates him from himself, his world of human relations, and fundamentally from Christ. The root of sin in man is a double root that may take the form of either "dreaming innocence" or despair. Either leads to concrete acts that divert man from working out the significance of the role that is given him. "Dreaming innocence" indicates man's notion of some uncomplicated bliss in which he either considers himself already a participant or to which he would like to "return"—as if to an idealized childhood. (Many popular concepts of heaven do not present at all the goals of a significant future but are a thinly disguised desire to return to an Eden or Paradise of a preexistent sort.) Despair, on the other hand, seeks to negate life's reality by denouncing or destroying all possible structures of meaning in order to precipitate one's own death, and possibly the death of others. Both elements are in fact expressions of the instinct for death: "dreaming innocence" promotes a kind of "living death" within structures presumed to be beneficent; despair actively and futuristically seeks the breakdown of life through loss of hope for a given situation. The two therefore impinge upon one another in much human behavior. For example, irresponsible sex-behavior may include both a fantasy of pleasurable escape *and* a destructive loss of confidence in the future. Sin understood as idolatry would likewise involve two sorts of "idols," those of legalistic demand and those of easy dissipation (idols with "hard hands" and idols with "soft hands"). Their relation to innocence and despair may vary. Within the Christian household, the central sin, governing all others, is the rejection of Christ Jesus and the cataclysmic change in the divine-human relation that he actualizes. No greater idolatry exists than either the "innocence" or the "despair" of worshipping God in a form appropriate and "true" for another season and another clime. The escapism of honoring a dead God is always accompanied by the consequent misguided destruction of meaningful human relations.

Man's *redemption* effects precisely a reversal of his alienation through a full reorientation of all his relationships. The human form of his redemption is his acceptance of the Cross and Resurrection. Such acceptance is expressed by an articulate, intellectual act of "belief," but is not an intellectual act in its essence. Rather it is man's living acceptance of what we have called here the "dialectical nature of his existence" in the trustful confidence of its meaningful future—or, in other words, acceptance that may be called "discipleship": the finding by man of his own Cross and Resurrection as Christ Jesus is "formed" in the relations between himself and others. Discipleship is, in turn, entirely a work of *grace,* and grace *is* in itself the very Logos that has incarnated itself within meaningful human time. Man knows grace, therefore, as the Mystery of forward-looking, creative power in his life, never apart from human relations. Nor does he ever know the reality of grace apart from his own deliberate, voluntary decisions for the "good" of himself and others; only in such movements (never in "scientific inquiry") can he sense the Ground of hope that is the source of his activity. Furthermore, grace is manifest only in direct proportion to the fullness of the dialectic. That is, man knows it as the infinite "nevertheless" of faith and hope, fully incarnate in the moment of contradiction that apparently crucifies all faith and hope. And by implication, man's unexpressed acceptance, in advance, of his own death is the form of his quiet courage and joy in effective, routine day-to-day living. The dialectic is therefore an all-encompassing "justification by faith," applied not only (as with Luther) to the structures of individual guilt, but also ultimately to the corporate social and cultural structures of history (see Tillich). The Christian, in consequence, never abandons the striving quest for the highest expression of justice and love in all group or corporate relations. He also realizes that the two Great Commandments (love of God and love of neighbor) have in effect become one.

The *Church* occurs, then, wherever men, in full awareness of their real or potential danger to one another, nevertheless relate themselves in the wisdom of faith. Or in other words, the Church realizes herself wherever men genuinely accept one another as they are (knowing the peril involved), yet in the confidence that their destiny of love and justice can be both affirmed and realized. To say these things is to say that the Church must center upon Christ Jesus, even though his name should be only potentially realized or articulate in a given group. Such a "latent Church" is possible because Christian community is not determined by an external form, imposed from without, but by a kind of life, springing from within. The human life of the Church is not "artificial" (cf. religiosity), but "normal." A true sense exists, therefore, in which the latent Church is discovered wherever human responsibility is actualized in constructive, "secular" behavior (secular because accepting of the world—constructive because life-affirming). When the Church becomes "confessing," therefore, and expressive of Christ's name, she still remains a "humanizing" community in the best sense of the word. She lives, not only to realize the simplest and truest, the most unadorned, human existence, but also to stand as a community of revolutionizing protest against the world's generally *in*human procedures. Her vocation is to be simply and courageously human over against the weird distortions perpetrated by culture, most especially "religion." She is to be Christ Jesus "formed" among men and is therefore necessarily both crucified and risen, both existential and apocalyptic. She "bears the Cross" of accepting the conditions of life as they are, of seeking the despised Christ wherever the world has denatured its humanity. She knows, however, the open possibility for men that *is* the new Life, the free response to real choice in a rebirth towards the future.

Her *worship,* therefore, should always concretely dramatize her secular existence, in which the issues of faith are realized. Insofar as possible, the forms of her celebration should present the historic symbols of her life in a contemporary medium and style, to signify that for Christians meaningful history is not past, but has moved into our present and our immediate future. Liturgy is thereby "traditional" more in the sense of expressing the present Gospel (which, after all, *is* the Tradition) than in the sense of being dependent upon past formulations of faith. Litanies, prayers, and confessions from the past always therefore express a communion with previous moments of the Church's life in a way transcendent to the actual words employed. Liturgical language can never therefore be "literal" language, lest the Church should regress. Use of historical modes is helpful and important in providing a sense of the progressive actualization through history of the Incarnate Word. But more important is the community's constant rethinking and restatement of her self-dramatization and confession, so that a living faith may be affirmed.

Worship naturally centers upon the two sacramental movements of the Church's life, *baptism* and the *Lord's Supper*. The significance of these is already, of course, implicit in the theological perspective of this paper. Baptism signifies our acceptance, indeed our devoted affirmation, of the conditions of life and death that are given us, in the faith that they find a significance in the coming Kingdom of Christ. Death is accepted, not as a final principle, but as a means to renewal, through the Grace of the Incarnate Word. Infant baptism is an act of devoting the child to his life and to his death, in their nature as actualized for him in Jesus. Baptism of the infant thus expresses, in a sense, the "normal" grace of his creation and entry upon existence—a creation to be truly realized, however, only in the "new" creation of his own later acceptance of his future in Christ. Through baptism, death is realized as a gift of grace, sealed in the mystery of Christ's promises. The Lord's Supper also enacts for the community the significant movements of death and life. The central symbols are the cup and the loaf, elements of man's ordinary secular manufacture for his own sustenance, and at the same time significantly the substance of Christ's own death. The worship here realizes the profound movement in the Divine life itself, God's moving from his abstract and wrathful form to become in Jesus the sacred significance of our literal, secular bread. By such real and simple bread shared, we know the loving community. And in a deeper sense, in our varied human relations we become a kind of "bread for one another," as he became "bread" for us—not mutually destructive, but nourishing and creative, in the always new realization of Christ Jesus in our midst.

19
MAYNARD
KAUFMAN

Maynard Kaufman, a member of the
department of philosophy and religion at
Western Michigan University, did his
graduate work in the field of literature and
theology at the Divinity School of the University of Chicago. Believing that the time
has come for theology to enter the age of
the Spirit, Kaufman repudiates all theologies
which find their ground in either the God
of the Bible or the Christ of historical
Christianity. He has been deeply affected by
the major intellectual and literary movements of the twentieth century even while
attempting to recover a cosmic and apocalyptic form of faith. The following essay
is published here for the first time; in an
earlier form it was given as a lecture at a
Danforth conference in the summer of
1965.

Maynard Kaufman

Post-Christian Aspects
of the Radical Theology

In 1962 Bishop Robinson concluded the preface of *Honest to God* by saying that although the book may sound too radical, "in retrospect, it will be seen to have erred in not being nearly radical enough." [1] Since then American theologians seem to have been trying to correct that error. Radical theologians today no longer worry about whether God is up there or out there or down there, but assert that God is dead or that God-language, at least, is dead. In this context Christology has also collapsed. Christ is no longer regarded as a "window into God at work";[2] Christology is opaque, and we are left with the historical fact of Jesus of Nazareth who lived an exemplary life. The concept of Christ as a divine saviour is regarded as both unnecessary and incredible to modern secular man. Conclusions such as this seem to follow from the concern over the secular dimension in contemporary life. According to the radical theologians we should not even speak of the secular as a dimension in contemporary life; it is viewed as a comprehensive and totally pervasive phenomenon.

The radical theology with which this essay is concerned is represented by the recent writings of Thomas J. J. Altizer, John B. Cobb, Harvey Cox, William Hamilton, Gabriel Vahanian, and Paul M. van Buren. These are all academic Protestant theologians, and although they differ in starting point and method, and even in their evaluation of the secular, or secularity, they are united by their focus on secularity. As the editors of *New Theology No. 3* point out, there is a growing tendency to affirm

[1] John A. T. Robinson, *Honest to God* (Philadelphia: Westminster Press, 1963), p. 10.
[2] *Ibid.*, p. 71.

PRINTED here for the first time with the permission of the author.

secularity, a tendency exemplified by Harvey Cox's *The Secular City*. And, as the possibility of Christian secularity becomes more acceptable there is a turn from what the editors call the "mere anarchy" of what had been a more centrifugal theological situation:

> This year we have noticed a kind of centripetal direction, a hunger for order, a courage to make affirmations in the context of Christian tradition, a hesitant but visible first step toward new construction. One gets the impression that other theologians, who share so much of the cultural analysis of the God-is-dead theologians, are for the most part saying of these theologians' conclusions, "But that is not what *we* meant!" [3]

There is widespread sympathy among theologians for the concerns which motivate these radicals, even among those who do not think it is possible to do theology this way and therefore retreat back to the faith of their fathers. But if one appreciates the intention of the radical theologians to articulate the positive dimension in secularization it is not possible to do theology as it has been done either. Traditional Christian theology can provide one with criteria for understanding the contemporary situation only in a distorted form which leads either to the articulation of our sense of loss and alienation or to the facile optimism of urban secularity.

Reservations about the radical death of God theology are certainly well-founded, and one wonders at the fact that such antitheology is possible. But even though one perceives the contemporary secular situation as the radical theologians do, it is possible to speak of it positively *and* theologically, and an alternative to their antitheological interpretation of it can be proposed. Let us first note that the antitheistic attitude of today's radical theology followed the nonobjective theism of such classical modern theologians as Tillich and Bultmann. The Christian doctrine of God has died the death of a thousand qualifications, and most of them were caused by the attempt to speak of God as revealed in Christ. The doctrine of Christ was the objective and historical basis for the doctrine of God. In other words, I am proposing that the failure of Christology implicitly preceded the so-called death of God, but that it became explicit only afterwards, and that the contemporary theological situation should therefore be positively affirmed as post-Christian. It is possible to be a post-Christian theist rather than a Christian atheist. Gabriel Vahanian quite correctly understands the contemporary situation as culturally *and* religiously post-Christian, and it is characterized by the death of the Christian God.[4] But because Vahanian judges the immanence of modern religiosity in orthodox Christian terms on the basis of biblical transcendence he is un-

---

[3] Martin E. Marty and Dean G. Peerman, "The Turn from Mere Anarchy," *New Theology No. 3* (New York: Macmillan, 1966), p. 15.
[4] Gabriel Vahanian, *The Death of God* (New York: George Braziller, 1961), Chap. 7.

able either to affirm it or to present a constructive alternative. If we are to speak of the contemporary situation constructively we must speak in terms of a post-Christian theology. In the first part of this essay, therefore, radical theology is interpreted and divided into two types: Christian secular theology and implicitly post-Christian radical theology. Once the post-Christian aspects of a truly radical theology are explicitly acknowledged it is possible to develop a constructive position of post-Christian theism, and this is the burden of the second part of this essay.

The position of post-Christian theism can be emphasized in another way. It used to be possible to talk about God most adequately by talking about Christ. But now these two doctrines seem to be incompatible. Theologians who talk about God find it difficult to talk about Christ or the Jesus of History, while theologians who talk about Jesus or Christ claim it is unnecessary to worry about God. Among the latter are the secular theologians of today who do a kind of glorified cultural anthropology instead of theology. On the other hand, it is interesting to observe that the only really constructive and contemporary work being done on the doctrine of God is done in terms of philosophical or natural theology, such as John Cobb does with Whitehead's process philosophy, and such thinking seems to be done quite independently of Christology. Even though theological process thinkers have always claimed that they were doing Christian theology they were not recognized as Christian theologians by those who spoke out of the tradition because most of them obviously failed to relate their work to the Christian tradition.

This split between theologians and Christians has, of course, been generally recognized, and it is now fashionable to assign the problem to that aspect of secularization which renders metaphysics meaningless and unnecessary. The secular is thus identified with the empiricism of analytic philosophy, as in Van Buren's work,[5] or with the pragmatic and profane outlook of the ordinary man, as in Cox's book. Cox asserts that secularization "has relativized religious world views and thus rendered them innocuous." [6] In this sense the author of *Adventures of Ideas* was surely a secular thinker, but he developed a metaphysics of relativism on the basis of which some theologians still find it quite possible to speak of God. John Cobb suggests that Whiteheadian thought takes the nihilistic sting out of relativism.[7] A commitment to the secular, in other words, does not automatically rule out the relevance of every metaphysical philosophy to theological thought.

Analytic philosophers and positivists have their own methodological

---

[5] Paul M. van Buren, *The Secular Meaning of the Gospel* (New York: Macmillan, 1963).

[6] Harvey Cox, *The Secular City* (New York: Macmillan, 1965), p. 2.

[7] John B. Cobb, Jr., *A Christian Natural Theology* (Philadelphia: Westminster Press, 1965), p. 274.

reasons for investigating the meaning or even questioning the validity of metaphysical and theological language. Theologians who follow their example usually do so with a more vociferous antimetaphysical bias, and one suspects that the reason for this can be found in the prejudice against natural theology which we have inherited from European neo-orthodoxy. Theologians are likely to reject metaphysics for religious and theological rather than philosophical reasons. Cox, for example, can speak of the doctrine of creation in the Bible as the "disenchantment of nature." [8] Secular theologians convey the impression that metaphysics is un-Christian because it inhibits an appreciation of this present age or because it is a form of natural theology which thus fails to do justice to the Christian revelation of man's historicity. One of the greatest contributions of process philosophy is that in it this needless bifurcation between nature and history is no longer necessary because nature is conceived of as a process which includes man and history. Some Whiteheadian theologians, such as John Cobb, affirm the post-Christian character of secular man and find meaning in the phrase "death of God" and thus qualify as radical theologians.[9] Cobb's doctrine of God in *A Christian Natural Theology* is not qualified by Christology or soteriology.[10] In this respect I would call it a post-Christian theology. Christ is no longer the primary and indispensable mediator between God and man in the world. Process philosophy enables a reappropriation of divine immanence in nature. I shall try, presently, to explain why I understand such theology as a theology of the Third Person of the Trinity.

At this point we can provisionally discern two types of radical theology. The one type affirms Christian secularity as the outcome of Christianity as an historical religion. This movement can be traced to the protest against religion, understood as natural religion, in European neo-orthodoxy, and finds expression in the so-called secular theology of today where, as in Harvey Cox, it promotes a process of desacralization. In contrast to those who affirm the secular there are the radical theologians who are in quest of the sacred, either in the Christian atheism of Thomas J. J. Altizer or in some form of philosophical or post-Christian theism. This schematic contrast requires a great deal of refinement, to be sure, since both types of radical theology work toward an erasure of the distinction between the sacred and the profane, or secular reality. For Altizer this distinction is real but dialectical, so that opposites can be expected to coincide, and one can hope to discover the sacred in the midst of the profane reality.[11] William Hamilton, although he can affirm the death of God with Altizer,

[8] Cox, *op. cit.,* pp. 21-24.
[9] John B. Cobb, Jr., "From Crisis Theology to the Post-Modern World," *The Centennial Review,* VIII (Spring, 1964), pp. 175-80.
[10] Cobb, *A Christian Natural Theology,* p. 12.
[11] Thomas J. J. Altizer, *Mircea Eliade and the Dialectic of the Sacred* (Philadelphia: Westminster Press, 1963), pp. 17-19.

can none the less be distinguished from him as a secular theologian when he says that "I am not as anxious [as Altizer] to recover the sacred, since I am starting with a definition of Protestantism as a movement away from the sacred place." [12] Here the death of God functions to free man from religion so that he can be open to the secular world.

The problems of theological and metaphysical language, then, need not and should not be confused with the religious or existential assertion that God is dead. The death of God is asserted for the sake of initiating a radical change in the traditional pattern of Christianity or because it is felt that Christianity has failed. The doctrine of God is not really at stake. The death of God rhetoric is often a way of talking about the contemporary religious situation. If we speak of it pejoratively we call it religiosity; if we affirm it we call it, following Bonhoeffer, religionlessness. It was Bonhoeffer who argued that it has been a mistake to regard Christianity as a religion of salvation, and surely this insight is basic for the radical theologians. It is here that William Hamilton acknowledges his debt to Bonhoeffer and explains that "I take religion to mean not man's arrogant grasping for God (Barth) and not assorted Sabbath activities usually performed by ordained males (the moderate radicals), but any system of thought or action in which God or the gods serve as fulfiller of needs or solver of problems." [13] We must note that the kind of religion rejected here does not consist of celebration or worship, but rather the form of religion peculiar to Western man, a religion of redemption which has served as a crutch to man in bearing the burden of making history and tragedy. Hamilton's provocative essay on the new optimism attempts to describe this shift of sensibility in America from Prufrock (modern pessimism) to Ringo (post-modern play and optimistic celebration) which renders tragedy and the need for redemption obsolete.[14] This may be over-optimistic since we still experience tragedy, but much less of it is caused by taking history and its moral dilemmas so "sinceriously."

A secular, religionless Christianity, we are told, is to be nonsoteriological. Christianity should no longer be understood as a religion of redemption. This is what Nicolas Berdyaev had emphasized for a long time.

> In man there is a divine element, and grace itself, if it is not understood in a legal way and not associated with the idea of authority, is the disclosure of the divine element in man, it is the awakening of the divine in him. . . . True and deep anthropology is the revelation of the

[12] William Hamilton, "The Death of God Theologies Today," reprinted from *The Christian Scholar* (Spring, 1965) in *Radical Theology and the Death of God,* by Thomas J. J. Altizer and William Hamilton (Indianapolis: Bobbs-Merrill, 1966), p. 36.

[13] *Ibid.,* p. 40.

[14] William Hamilton, "The New Optimism from Prufrock to Ringo," reprinted from *Theology Today* (January, 1966) in *ibid.,* pp. 157-69.

Christology of man. . . . What God expects from man is not servile submission, not obedience, not the fear of condemnation, but free creative acts. But this was hidden until the appointed time. The revelation which is concerned with this cannot be divine only; it must be a divine-human revelation in which man takes an active and creative part.[15]

Berdyaev argues that a religion of creativity should replace a religion of redemption. Among other things creativity means that man himself contributes to the revelatory process, or that the possibility of inspiration is genuinely affirmed. Berdyaev is here anticipating the Third Epoch, the age of the Holy Spirit in terms of the Joachimite trinitarian theory of history, a tradition of radical theology which is appealed to by Altizer.

This tradition maintains that we are now living in the third and final age of the Spirit, that a new revelation is breaking into this age, and that this revelation will differ as much from the New Testament as the New Testament itself does from its Old Testament counterpart. Of course, the great Christian revolutionaries of the nineteenth century went far beyond their spiritual predecessors. But we can learn from earlier radical Christians the root radical principle that the movement of the Spirit has passed beyond the revelation of the canonical Bible and is now revealing itself in such a way as to demand a whole new form of faith.[16]

Surely this is the context in which the radical theology of today ought to be understood. The sacred is being revealed in a new form, but something more than a new form of faith is needed. Faith is the posture of man in the Christian epoch, in a religion of redemption, but in this world which has come of age man no longer needs to trust in a *deus ex machina*. Here lies a basic inconsistency in the thought of most radical theologians. Modern man is saved by knowledge and not faith; by creative acts and not by the grace of God in Christ, as those who proclaim the death of God affirm. But those who would articulate the dimensions of this way of life are inconsistent when they slip back into a soteriological terminology and continue to make Jesus the center of their thought. Even the nineteenth-century seers appealed to by Altizer are unreliable on this point if, as he explains, "the name of Jesus is no mere symbol of a higher man to these prophets: rather, they unveil the historical reality and power of his name as concealing a hidden but universal process of redemption and transformation, a process that has only been known in a reversed or religious form to his ecclesiastical followers." [17] It is not enough to set one-

[15] Nicolas Berdyaev, *Truth and Revelation* (New York: Collier Books, 1962), p. 122.
[16] Thomas J. J. Altizer, *The Gospel of Christian Atheism* (Philadelphia: Westminster Press, 1966), p. 27.
[17] *Ibid.*, p. 56.

self against ecclesiastical forms of Christianity, we must find our way beyond them in terms of a post-Christian theology.

The secular radical theologians, in spite of their espousal of a non-soteriological form of Christianity, have also failed to extricate their thought from a soteriological terminology. Although they may have given up all theories of the atonement except the moral-influence theory, their Christianity remains soteriological. Jesus is still the revelation of how to live. Jesus was incarnate in this world, and as he affirmed it and loved it so do his disciples. This is emphasized especially in Hamilton's article on "The Death of God Theologies Today," [18] and what shines through it all so clearly is that simple religious need for models or archetypes to live by. Jesus may not be regarded as a divine archetype, but he functions as a Christ figure whose image redeems the time in which we wait. This is still a redemptive function, but with the difference that the Christ figure now serves to give sanction to secular or popular culture.

The inconsistent affirmation of secularity is the most characteristic and perhaps the most pernicious aspect of secular theology. When this affirmation is stated in abstract theological terms it has a Barthian tone to it, as in William O. Fennell's "Theology of True Secularity." Fennell maintains that God created a secular world and peopled it with autonomous men free to use it, and that "in Jesus Christ, God has rescued the world from man's 'religiousness,' restored it to its original 'secularity,' and in him has given back to man the freedom which he lost when he sought to make his culture a religious and therefore idolatrous thing." [19] Here we must ask what kind of "true" secularity this is if it requires religious justification. This is equally true of Harvey Cox in his secular city when he tries to justify its secularization on a biblical basis. As Daniel Callahan remarked in his review of *The Secular City,* "If secular man and his way of life are self-sufficient, any talk about taking a 'biblical perspective' is beside the point." [20] It is apparent that the idea of a religionless Christianity is a difficult one to maintain.

The perniciousness of the secular theology lies in the fact that it promulgates religiosity with its superfluous justification of the *status quo.* This is surely the most radical acculturation of Christianity in its history, but it is what we have learned to expect since we learned that Christianity is an historical faith. The secular theologian, still informed by that truncated theology which says that God (or Something Ultimate) is active in history, views with indiscriminate seriousness whatever comes to pass. He is in bondage to the givenness and facticity of history. Thus he is com-

---

[18] Pp. 46-50.
[19] William O. Fennell, "The Theology of True Secularity," *New Theology No. 2,* ed. Martin E. Marty and Dean G. Peerman (New York: Macmillan, 1965), p. 29.
[20] Daniel Callahan, "*The Secular City:* Toward a Theology of Secularity," *New Theology No. 3,* p. 38.

mitted to what Christianity has become in its historical development and seeks only to rationalize the result rather than change it or acknowledge its bankruptcy. This is Christian faith today! Langdon Gilkey rightly criticizes Van Buren for pretending that his "secular meaning of the Gospel" was really the intention of the New Testament and Councils instead of acknowledging that it was the result of contemporary empirical standards.[21] The attempts to sanction the pragmatic and technological outlook of contemporary secularism by appealing to the worldly life of Jesus and his disciples could also be criticized as a projection of our secular concerns into the life and message of Jesus. As Bultmann recently reminded us, the message of Jesus was eschatological.[22] He preached the coming of the Kingdom of God as an eschatological consummation, and his human life was lived toward that end. There is a world of difference between a doctrine of the incarnation which sanctions secularity and the incarnate life of Jesus with its eschatological orientation. In view of this it is hard to imagine that the secular theologians would affirm secularity and worldliness, or, as Cox does, that "technopolis" is the long-awaited Kingdom of God.[23]

We can only conclude that Christianity is undergoing the second stage of a dereligionizing process. The first stage was a transformation of Christianity into a noneschatological but metaphysical religion, and it resulted in Christendom. The second stage is the current transformation of Christianity into a nonmetaphysical and nonreligious secularity. It retains only a thisworldly ethic which is still sanctioned by the incarnational principle. The doctrine of the incarnation now functions only to cancel out any distinction between sacred and profane. The distinction between sacred history (*Heilsgeschichte*) and secular history which theologians have tried to maintain thus also collapses. In effect this absolutizes the profane historical process as the only locus of human possibility and self-realization.

By virtue of their radical position the secular theologians of today help us to see the major issues in theology very clearly. The hidden impetus in Christianity is unmasked and its worldliness is revealed. The incipient dichotomy between religion and Christianity is becoming more and more apparent. This juxtaposition is reflected in the title of a recent article by Kenneth Hamilton: "*Homo Religiosus* and Historical Faith." The question he asks is the major question with which Christians are confronted: "Can the spiritual outlook of *homo religiosus* be revived in our modern, historically minded, antimetaphysical age?" [24] Informed by Bonhoeffer, Hamilton

[21] Langdon Gilkey, "A New Linguistic Madness," *New Theology No. 2,* p. 46.
[22] Rudolf Bultmann, *Jesus Christ and Mythology* (New York: Scribner's, 1958), pp. 11-14.
[23] Cox, *op. cit.,* pp. 110-13.
[24] Kenneth Hamilton, "*Homo Religiosus* and Historical Faith," *New Theology No. 3,* p. 66.

doubts that it can be revived, and attempts to refute what he understands to be Mircea Eliade's defense of *homo religiosus*. This is the typical Christian way out of the dilemma which the Christian faces in a post-Christian world. But if we must choose between religion as the quest for the sacred and a Christianity which identifies itself with the oppressive reality of a secularized Christendom, it is Christianity that must be rejected. This is not much of a rejection, of course, given the mutilations and deprivations which characterize secular Christianity. But it does involve the rejection of a Christianity which has progressively identified itself with the historical process to the point where the very idea of the sacred or a nonhistorical mode of being is denied as a possibility for contemporary man. Thus a consciously post-Christian position also implies a post-historical attitude.

There are other and more viable religious possibilities inherent in our contemporary situation, and in the remainder of this essay other ways of talking about these possibilities are explored. In particular, it will be suggested that a positive understanding of the post-Christian situation in terms of a theology of the Third Person of the Trinity can provide the basis for a more constructive radical theology.

In exploring the possibility of a theology of the Holy Spirit we must first see how it is related to the now defunct theology of the Second Person of the Trinity and can thus be conceived of as a replacement for it. We can be aided here by the kind of di-polar theism which emerges in process philosophy because it is here that various modes of relationship between God and the world are affirmed in terms which are relevant to the scientific thought of our own time. Thus Cobb is bold enough to predict that "if Whitehead's vision should triumph in the years ahead, the 'death of God' would indeed turn out after all to have been only the 'eclipse of God.'" [25] The reappropriation of divine immanence by means of process philosophy means that talk about the Holy Spirit need no longer be vague and spooky. The Holy Spirit is not an abstract or disembodied spirit; it is the spirit of life and vitality, and it is manifest as freedom and creativity. It is here, with reference to a post-Christian pneumatology, that Altizer's radical understanding of the Incarnation is helpful.

> The Incarnation must be conceived as an active and forward-moving process, a process that even now is making all things new. . . . What is distinctive to Christianity is a witness to an incarnation in which Spirit becomes flesh in such a manner as to continue to exist and act as flesh. . . . Christian theology has never thought through the full meaning of the Incarnation if only because it has remained bound to an eternal and primordial form of Spirit.[26]

[25] Cobb, "From Crisis Theology to the Post-Modern World," p. 185.
[26] Altizer, *The Gospel of Christian Atheism,* p. 41.

The spirit is active only in and through the body. A disembodied spirit is merely a ghost.

Such a radically incarnational theology, which I regard as post-Christian, can be clarified by means of Charles Hartshorne's analogy of organism. This can be oversimplified for our purposes with the summary phrase "the world is God's body." [27] God is not a disembodied spirit, and if the world we live in is alive God is not dead. The image of the world as God's body, understood in a panentheistic rather than in a pantheistic way,[28] should be appealing to Christians because it is the corollary of the Christian image of the Church as the Body of Christ. The relationship between Christ and his Church would thus be expressive of the relationship between God and the world. Christ and the Church are thus seen as symbolic, not as ends in themselves. Now Altizer suggests that the identification of the Church as the Body of Christ was the original heresy.[29] If this is true it is because Christian theology has absolutized Christ and the Church and thus produced Christendom. That exclusive focus on Christ and the Church was a contradiction of the notion that Christ was the special revelation, within the circumscribed locus of human history, of the nature of God. Now, insofar as the activity of God is perceived only in history, either in profane history or in "sacred history" (Christ and the Church) it is certainly correct to conclude that God is dead. This is implied by secular theologians when they deny the revelatory or religious aspect of Christ and the Church and think theologically in terms of politics. Thus Cox says that "in Jesus of Nazareth the religious quest is ended for good." [30] But we have seen that this focus on the historical life of Jesus as normative leads to the exclusion of other ways through which man can express his humanness. Thus the symbolic dimension or religious significance of this secular and objective social reality, i.e., Christendom, is no longer perceived.

This view of historical institutions as symbolic is most adequately set forth by Berdyaev.

> The most important thing is to grasp that in the process of objectification to which the historical and social life of man is liable, Spirit is symbolized and not realized. The source of the symbolization is to be found in the fact that only prefigurations of the coming realization, signs of the other world, are given. But symbolization loads men with chains when it is regarded as being already realization. In a deep sense

---

[27] Charles Hartshorne, *Man's Vision of God* (Chicago: Willet, Clark, and Company, 1941), p. 185.
[28] God *in* all rather than God understood as being all—T. J. J. A.
[29] Altizer, *The Gospel of Christian Atheism*, p. 132.
[30] Cox, *op. cit.*, p. 265.

of the word both worship and culture are symbolical, but in them a way towards realization is provided if that symbolism is not regarded as static, as though it were a final consummation.[31]

The symbolic dimension in Christianity is now perceived only from a post-Christian perspective. When historical facts or empirical realities are regarded as normative for religion, as in Van Buren's thought, one's style of life is tied to that which has been objectified, and life is patterned after death. For an objectification is only the corpse or material remains of a previous spiritual activity. It is the institutional church as the Body of Christ or as an extension of the Incarnation which has no life in it. Theologians who intend to be relevant to the contemporary situation will thus be frustrated as they cling to historical incarnational models. Berdyaev asserted that "the new spirituality should appear disincarnate; it should rebel against incarnation as a form of objectification or of historical relativism, but actually it will be a reincarnation, a catastrophic rather than an evolutionary reincarnation." [32] We can find evidence for such spirituality in modern nonrepresentational painting and symbolist poetry, which, from Kandinsky the painter and Mallarmé the poet, has found its inspiration in Theosophy and related forms of occultism. It is in this polemic against objectification that the post-historical dimension of a post-Christian culture is expressed. Berdyaev argued that "revelation must be freed and purified from the power of the historical, or, to speak more truly, from the power of historicism, from the process of making what is relative absolute." [33] All of his work urges this transition from historical to eschatological Christianity. History is a great failure; it must be regarded as a transitional phase to a new epoch.

It is not easy to give substance to the charge that history is a failure, if only because the word *history* is itself so equivocal. We speak of history when we refer to the burden of outmoded values and institutions, and we have been trying to "take history seriously" when we have tried to figure out what relevance this history has in the present. Then there is history as an academic discipline and historicism as a more general way of viewing reality, and these have long been under fire by those writers who try to articulate the sensibility of modern man. The critique of history in this sense is brilliantly reviewed and documented by Hayden V. White, and he suggests that "one of the distinctive characteristics of contemporary literature is its underlying conviction that the historical consciousness must be obliterated if the writer is to examine with proper seriousness those strata of human experience which it is *modern* art's peculiar

[31] Berdyaev, *op. cit.*, p. 149.
[32] Berdyaev, *Spirit and Reality* (London: Geoffrey Bles, 1946), p. 170.
[33] Berdyaev, *Truth and Revelation,* p. 91.

purpose to disclose." [34] The historian perpetuates a way of looking at the world which gives the outmoded forms of the past a specious authority. But modern artists, says White, are much more impressed with the discontinuities in modern life.

> This is why so much of modern fiction turns upon the attempt to liberate Western man from the tyranny of the historical consciousness. It tells us that it is only by disenthralling human intelligence from the sense of history that men will be able to confront creatively the problems of the present. The implications of all this for any historian who values the artistic vision as anything more than mere play are obvious: he must ask himself how he can participate in this liberating activity and whether his participation entails the destruction of history itself.[35]

The historian, White concludes, should no longer try to construct a specious continuity between past and present, but should seek ways to educate us to a sense of discontinuity, for "discontinuity, disruption, and chaos is our lot." [36] Such discontinuities are certainly evident in radical theological thought today, but too many Christian theologians are either historians themselves or try too much to take history seriously. They are thus unable to take the present seriously, an attitude exemplified by Martin E. Marty and Dean G. Peerman as they introduce *New Theology No. 3.*

> Of course, Christian theology has been around for almost twenty centuries, and change must always be viewed in the light of a tradition which anticipates much of what appears to be new. Future historians of theology may understandably yawn now and then as they page through journals obsessed with talk about the death of God, the presence of the profane, the problems of the spiritual life. "We've been through all that before" is a proper rejoinder.[37]

Certainly this is the kind of historical consciousness which debilitates thought and discourages creativity.

Much of the radical theology today is stridently antihistorical, but only in a qualified way. It will be obvious to those who have read *The Gospel of Christian Atheism* that Altizer shares in the tendency to reject past history, but he focuses on "historicity"—"the realm of concrete and actual events, of humanly meaningful events" [38]—instead. "We shall not understand the Yes-saying of a New Zarathustra," he says, "unless we realize

[34] Hayden V. White, "The Burden of History," *History and Theory,* Vol. v, No. 2, p. 115.
[35] *Ibid.,* p. 123.
[36] *Ibid.,* p. 134.
[37] "The Turn from Mere Anarchy," p. 11.
[38] Thomas J. J. Altizer, "Word and History," reprinted from *Theology Today* (October, 1965) in *Radical Theology and the Death of God,* p. 133.

that it is a total negation of the human and historical world of Christendom, and a negation following from the modern prophet's proclamation of the death of God." [39] More than any other radical theologian Altizer perceives the discontinuities which actually do alienate us from the Christian tradition, and surely he articulates the only valid Christian response to this situation. But it is, as he rightly claims, a *Christian* response, and it is uniquely Christian in its commitment to the historical process as it is manifest in the present. "The God who reveals himself in history is the God who empties himself of the plenitude of his primordial Being; thereby he actually and truly becomes manifest in history, and finally history becomes not simply the arena of revelation but the very incarnate Body of God." [40] Although Altizer perceives the bankruptcy of the Christian ecclesiastical tradition as an historical religion, it is still in history (understood as historicity) that he seeks the incarnate Body of God.

> Indeed, the Christian confesses that God is most truly or actually himself while in a state of ultimate self-alienation and self-estrangement. For the Christian believes that God most fully reveals himself in Jesus Christ: and the kenotic acts of the Incarnation and the Crucifixion are by no means to be understood as fragmentary epiphanies of the power and glory of an eternal and unchanging Godhead, but rather as historical acts or events whereby the Godhead finally ceases to exist and to be real in its past and primordial manifestations. [41]

This Hegelian dialectic of negation may be appropriate to a philosophy of history in which one event follows another, *nacheinander*. But in another dimension of reality things persist in being *nebeneinander,* and the *nacheinander* and *nebeneinander* are *nebeneinander.* [42]

In terms of Whitehead's or Hartshorne's di-polar concept of God it is not necessary to negate the primordial or transcendent nature of God in order to perceive and affirm the consequent or immanent nature of God. But this can be done only if this doctrine of God is understood cosmologically rather than historically. The agonizing either-or quality of the wager which Altizer proposes is therefore slightly misplaced and its pathos is unnecessary. We do not simply face a choice between "the primordial and transcendent reality of God and the kenotic and immediate reality of Christ" [43] unless we first choose to remain Christians bound to the repressive order of history. And as long as this is what we choose we live a fallen existence, subject to sin and death and requiring atonement and

---

[39] Altizer, *The Gospel of Christian Atheism,* p. 150.
[40] *Ibid.,* p. 86.
[41] *Ibid.,* p. 88.
[42] *Nacheinander:* one after another; *nebeneinander:* by one another, or simultaneously together—T. J. J. A.
[43] *Ibid.,* p. 133.

forgiveness of sin. Even Altizer's radical Christian atheism is a religion of redemption, and these themes are fully integrated within the structure of his antitheology.

But it is no longer necessary to assume that authentic human existence can be found only in historical existence. There are other theological ways of perceiving the discontinuities in the historical process, and this is the value for us of the Joachimite trinitarian theory of history. The polemic against history in many of our greatest writers, from the French Symbolists to Yeats and Joyce and D. H. Lawrence, finds its basis and deepest religious center in a Joachimite theory of history. Berdyaev, speaking with the vision of those nineteenth-century seers whose influence is still felt today, challenges historicistic modes of thought with such a periodic theory of history. Mircea Eliade contrasts the historicistic preoccupation peculiar to Western Christian man with the nonhistorical orientation of archaic man. Altizer points out that both Berdyaev and Eliade judge history from the horizon of the sacred, from a metahistorical viewpoint which is no longer easily intelligible to the secular consciousness engulfed by its historicity.[44] Thus Eliade, like Berdyaev, tries to rescue modern man from the constrictions of his historicity. Berdyaev does this by appealing to neglected elements within the Christian tradition, especially to the doctrines of eschatology and pneumatology, and, of course, such appeals are unheeded because Christianity is itself historicized. Eliade works within the context of the history of religions, and is thus able, as he puts it,

> to confront "historical man" (modern man), who consciously and voluntarily creates history, with the man of the traditional civilizations, who, as we have seen, had a negative attitude toward history. Whether he abolishes it periodically, whether he devaluates it by perpetually finding transhistorical models and archetypes for it, whether, finally, he gives it a metahistorical meaning (cyclical theory, eschatological significations, and so on), the man of traditional civilizations accorded the historical event no value in itself; in other words, he did not regard it as a specific category of his own mode of existence.[45]

Eliade strongly implies that such a nonhistorical experience of time is a possibility for modern man also insofar as remnants of the archaic or ahistorical attitude continue to permeate Christianity, not to mention the eschatological outlook which originally gave rise to Christianity. Although he acknowledges the inevitable increase of historicistic modes of thought and recognizes the legitimacy of such thought as an offspring of the Judeo-Christian emphasis on history as a theophany, Eliade appears to take comfort in the fact that the position of those "who define man as a 'historical

---

[44] Altizer, *Mircea Eliade and the Dialectic of the Sacred,* p. 34.
[45] Mircea Eliade, *Cosmos and History* (New York: Harper & Row, 1959), p. 141.

being' has not yet made a definitive conquest of contemporary thought," and notes the recent resurgence of ahistorical orientations which "disregard not only historicism but even history as such." [46] To be sure, modern man cannot simply regress to the paradise of archetypes, repetition, and cosmic regeneration as a nonhistorical way of life, but Eliade's distinction between cosmos *and* history need not be either cosmos *or* history for a post-Christian and post-historical existence. In a recent article Eliade discovers intimations of archaic cosmic religions emerging in the work of nonreligious modern artists, and he sees this in the context of the radical death of God theology.[47] This is a post-historical rather than a nonhistorical phenomenon.

However, although Eliade laments the neglect of Joachim of Floris' "prophetico-eschatological speculations," [48] he does not overtly seem to regard his own work as a propaedeutic to the Third Epoch as Berdyaev does. What we do find in Eliade is the possibility of human creativity—not in Christianity, the religion of fallen man identified with history and progress—but in and through a renewed involvement with nature. Berdyaev also asserts a cosmic dimension in spiritual religion: "The era of the Spirit can be nothing but a revelation of a sense of community which is not merely social but also cosmic, not only a brotherhood of man, but a brotherhood of men with all cosmic life, with the whole creation." [49] One thinks here of Wordsworth's sense of communion with nature, especially as expressed in *The Prelude,* which contains only one reference to Jesus while the Presence in Nature, which exercised so creative an influence on the growth of the poet's mind, is clearly identified with the Holy Spirit. Or, we are reminded of the post-modern stranger portrayed by Camus who "laid his heart open to the benign indifference of the universe" and was happy as he felt it was "so brotherly." [50] It is needless to multiply instances. The point is that a sense of cosmic sacrality is not absent even in the midst of the secularization of Christianity. And perhaps it is emerging *because* of this secularization. The secular modern man who wills to be historical faces the terror of history because he is unfree with reference to the history he has made.

The strongest case for the possibility—and necessity—of a post-Christian and post-historical epoch is made by Norman Brown in his investigation into the psychoanalytical meaning of history.

> Man, the discontented animal, unconsciously seeking the life proper to his species, is man in history: repression and the repetition-compulsion

[46] *Ibid.,* p. 153.
[47] Mircea Eliade, "The Sacred and the Modern Artist," *Criterion* (Spring, 1965), pp. 22-24.
[48] Eliade, *Cosmos and History,* p. 145, note.
[49] Berdyaev, *Truth and Revelation,* p. 152.
[50] Albert Camus, *The Stranger* (New York: Vintage Books, 1946), p. 154.

generate historical time. Repression transforms the timeless instinctual compulsion to repeat into the forward-moving dialectic of neurosis which is history; history is a forward-moving *recherche du temps perdu*,[51] with the repetition-compulsion guaranteeing the historical law of the slow return of the repressed. And conversely, life not repressed —organic life below man and human life if repression were overcome —is not in historical time.[52]

It is here in Brown's *Life Against Death* and also in Herbert Marcuse's *Eros and Civilization* that the outlines of a post-Christian doctrine of the Holy Spirit can be perceived most clearly and concretely. Perhaps this is most obvious in Brown's stimulating chapter on "The Resurrection of the Body," but the possibility of a resurrected or spiritual body depends upon a post-historical mode of existence.

The elucidation of Freud's metapsychological speculations by Brown and Marcuse has proved to be a powerful lever by means of which the lid can be lifted from civilization so that its inner dynamics can be examined. This new vision provides another challenge to the necessitarian or deterministic aspect of the historical process. We see that the historical process, civilization itself, is the product of repression and the alienation of man from his proper or elementary life. Man is not naturally or essentially an historical being; history is made by man unconsciously desiring to be something other than what he is. He gives up the possibility of happiness and changes himself and his world in order to make something of himself, thereby creating what Freud called the reality principle. Marcuse explains that "a repressive organization of the instincts underlies *all* historical forms of the reality principle in civilization," but he challenges the assumption that this historical development should assume "the dignity and necessity of a universal biological development." [53] It is on the basis of Freud's distinction between the reality principle and the pleasure principle that Brown and Marcuse try to point the way to the possibility of a nonrepressive civilization. Although the pleasure principle is defeated and repressed by the reality principle both in civilization as a whole and in each individual, it lives on in the unconscious and finds an ineffectual expression in art, heretical spiritual religion, and revolutionary sociopolitical movements. This indicates that the triumph of the reality principle is never final and complete; the claims of the pleasure principle constantly reassert themselves and must be constantly repressed. This is work, but it makes work possible, and work makes history and builds civilization —and its discontents. The compulsion to work is attributed to guilt, and it is with reference to guilt that Brown tries to explain Eliade's distinc-

[51] Quest for lost time—T. J. J. A.
[52] Norman O. Brown, *Life Against Death* (New York: Vintage Books, 1959), p. 93.
[53] Herbert Marcuse, *Eros and Civilization* (New York: Vintage Books, 1962), pp. 31-32.

tion between archaic and modern historical time. "In modern man guilt has increased to the point where it is no longer possible to expiate it in annual ceremonies of regeneration. Guilt is therefore cumulative, and therefore time is cumulative." [54] Life for historical man is therefore a futile exercise in overcoming guilt.

Marcuse would like to hope that the real possibility for a nonrepressive civilization at the present time is enhanced as the very achievements of a repressive technological civilization seem to create the preconditions for the gradual abolition of repression. At this point his hope seems to converge with the optimism of the secular theologian with regard to technopolis. But in retrospect Marcuse is not optimistic about the possibility of an evolutionary development toward a nonrepressive civilization.

> The immense capabilities of the advanced industrial society are increasingly mobilized against the utilization of its own resources for the pacification of human existence. All talk about the abolition of repression, about life against death, etc., has to place itself into the actual framework of enslavement and destruction.[55]

It can be claimed that the incarnational principle in Christianity, which sanctioned the development of historicism and severed ethics from its eschatological basis, so that redemption saves man in history rather than from it, is largely responsible for the domination of the reality principle. Brown points out that "current psychoanalysis has no utopia; current neo-orthodox Protestantism has no eschatology" and that "this defect cripples both of them as allies of the life instinct in that war against the death instinct which is human history." [56] Secular Christianity no longer functions to deliver man from guilt, but enables him to go on with his work in spite of his guilt. Cox's chapter on "Work and Play in the Secular City" has a lot to say about work, but a doctrine of play is conspicuous by its absence. In Western civilization Christianity, or Christendom, has become the historical form of the reality principle, and in that unholy alliance it gained its strength and tenacity.

Because Christianity is identified with the reality principle on the ideological grounds provided by the doctrine of the Incarnation, the possibility of a more positive theology depends upon the development of a *post*-Christian theology. Berdyaev is able to speak of the possibility of spiritual religion in relation to Christianity because Eastern Christianity understands the Spirit as proceeding directly from the Father. But the *filioque*[57] clause in Western Christianity, which subordinates the Spirit to

---

[54] Brown, *op. cit.*, p. 278.
[55] Marcuse, *op. cit.*, p. xi.
[56] Brown, *op. cit.*, p. 233.
[57] *filioque:* The orthodox Western (as opposed to Eastern) Christian dogma that the Holy Spirit proceeds from the Father and the Son while yet being co-essential with the Father and Son—T. J. J. A.

the Son, inhibits the possibility of the Third Epoch. As a result of the *filioque* clause a genuine theology of the Holy Spirit can never emerge from within Western Christianity; it must be a *post*-Christian theology. Even Paul Tillich, who tried to emphasize the doctrine of the Holy Spirit, still did so in a Christian way which denied the autonomy and creativity of the Spirit.

> In the divine economy, the Spirit follows the Son, but in essence, the Son *is* the Spirit. The Spirit does not himself originate what he reveals. Every new manifestation of the Spiritual Presence stands under the criterion of his manifestation in Jesus as the Christ.[58]

The Spiritual Presence is thus limited to a phenomenon which is sublimated and repressed under the rule of the reality principle.

A constructive radical theology has no firm basis unless the *filioque* clause is denied, and this denial would result in a post-Christian doctrine of the autonomy of the Holy Spirit. Barth opposes such denial precisely for this reason. It would not only liberate the Spirit, but it would also sanction the possibility of speaking of the immediate relationship between God and the world in a naturalistic manner which is independent of the Mediator.[59] Now, it is interesting to observe that this is exactly what is done by Whiteheadian theologians, and it is not surprising that creativity is a basic category in Whitehead's thought. It is therefore reasonable to suggest that they are doing theology in terms of the Third Person of the Trinity rather than the Second. Most theologies of religious experience and theologies of culture might also be better understood in this way. There is surely some truth to Barth's interpretation of Schleiermacher and nineteenth-century liberal theology as the precocious beginnings of a theology of the Holy Spirit.[60] The cultural context today is even more congenial to this enterprise. The Church, which is supposed to be permeated by the spirit of Christ, is no longer the living context in which theology is done. Most theologians are academic scholars, responsible to the discipline of the university.

Finally, I speak of the Third Epoch as a way of emphasizing some sense of a radical or discontinuous transition. The possibility of a non-repressive civilization gradually evolving under the rule of the reality principle is explored by Marcuse and rejected. As historicism progresses it becomes increasingly exclusivistic and intolerant of other modes of human self-realization. The order of domination becomes more repres-

---

[58] Paul Tillich, *Systematic Theology* (Chicago: University of Chicago Press, 1963), Vol. III, p. 148.
[59] See George S. Hendry, *The Holy Spirit in Christian Theology* (London: Student Christian Movement Press, 1957), pp. 42-46.
[60] Karl Barth, *The Humanity of God* (Richmond, Virginia: John Knox, 1960), pp. 24-25.

sive, even if this happens in the benevolent manner suggested by Aldous Huxley's *Brave New World*. Life in a technological civilization imposes increasingly complex and totalitarian forms of organization until a saturation point is reached. It has now become possible to envisage history itself as a self-conscious transitional phase in the evolution of man. Teilhard de Chardin does this in an imaginative and religious manner with his doctrine of the "noosphere." [61] Mircea Eliade suggests that "it is not inadmissible to think of an epoch, and an epoch not too far distant, when humanity, to ensure its survival, will find itself reduced to desisting from any further 'making' of history in the sense in which it began to make it from the creation of the first empires, will confine itself to repeating prescribed archetypal gestures, and will strive to forget, as meaningless and dangerous, any spontaneous gesture which might entail 'historical' consequences." [62] Roderick Seidenberg, in his book, *Post-Historic Man,* also works with the thesis that history is a transitional phase to a post-historic period. History, or human consciousness, is seen as arising out of the imbalance or tension between instinct and intelligence, or between organic and organizational structures of society. Seidenberg suggests that "in the ultimate state of crystallization to which the principle of organization leads, consciousness will have accomplished its task, leaving mankind sealed, as it were, within patterns of frigid and unalterable perfection." [63]

Seidenberg's vision is deterministic and by no means optimistic. It does not transcend the limits of the reality principle. His view of the post-historic period is simply the infinite extension of the repressive technological aspects in this historical epoch. His view is mechanistic rather than organic. He sees history in purely secular terms as the technological use of intelligence for the sake of the conquest and use of nature. He differs from the secular theologians in that he sees further and spells out the implications of historical determinism. In this respect he is very instructive.

But Marcuse and Brown have helped us to see that a post-historic epoch can be thought of in dialectical terms as an eschatological reality. This would be a catastrophic reincarnation, as Berdyaev said, because it would shatter the repressive order of technological civilization. "Eschatological" does not refer to an imaginary reality beyond time and space but to a time and space transformed by the perspective of a post-historical mode of existence. In mythical terms it would be a regenerated cosmos. Just as the resurrection of Christ was a cosmic event, in mythical terms, and not an historical event, so his second coming can be understood as the resurrection of man in a spiritual (i.e., creative) body reintegrated with a transformed cosmos, a new heaven and a new earth. Here we must resort to

---

[61] Teilhard de Chardin, *The Phenomenon of Man* (New York: Harper & Row, 1961), Book III, Chap. 3.
[62] Eliade, *Cosmos and History,* pp. 153-54.
[63] Roderick Seidenberg, *Post-Historic Man* (Boston: Beacon, 1957), p. 180.

eschatological imagery, and our difficulty with such imprecise and quasi-mythical language is symptomatic of our deprivation. The physical reintegration of man with the cosmos is not a possibility within an historicistic perspective, and our thought and language is truncated by this perspective. But depth psychology and the study of myth in archaic religions has helped us to recover meanings once lost.

Our most pressing need is to escape from the tyranny of historicism and from a deterministic view of history. We must learn to express our sense of being in time without being dehumanized by history. This requires the reappropriation of a cosmic sacrality as described by Eliade, for example, but it should not be understood as a regression to pre-Christian or archaic modes of life, even though aspects of the archaic orientation remain viable even today. A post-Christian cosmic sacrality can best be understood religiously in terms of the doctrine of the Holy Spirit and philosophically in terms of organismic process philosophy. On a cultural level it is implied by the possibility of a nonrepressive civilization in which man would be freed from the neurosis of history. Charles H. Long has suggested that "the 'death of God' as a historical-religious form is an expression of the desire and necessity of human creativity." [64] Surely some radical theologians would agree with this. We do stand at the threshold of a new epoch. If we can accept it as post-historical and post-Christian there is a basis for optimism about the future because it can then be the Third Epoch in which a new sense of physical creativity could be realized. Christianity has now been reduced to an impotent unitarianism of the Second Person which serves only to sanction an uncritical identification with the historical process or with the religiosity of Christendom. But this, like talk about the death of God, already exemplifies a fairly radical discontinuity with traditional Christianity even though it may have been implied by it. In this situation I have proposed a renewed focus on the doctrine of the Holy Spirit, not merely for the sake of any simple answers, and not merely to revive an obscure part of our theological heritage, but rather as a way of perceiving the dimensions and implications of our post-Christian situation.

[64] Charles H. Long, "Critical Review of *Oriental Mysticism and Biblical Eschatology* by Thomas J. J. Altizer," *Journal of Religion*, XLIV (July, 1964), p. 272.

Selected
Bibliography

[1] Roman Catholic Responses
to Modern Atheism

While Catholic theology is now moving into a positive response to atheism, it passed through a full negative response, identifying atheism as the dissolution of man.

Balthasar, Hans Urs von. *Science, Religion and Christianity*. London: Burns & Oates, 1958.

Borne, Etienne. *Atheism*. New York: Hawthorn, 1961.

Chenu, M. D., and Heer, Friedrich. "Is the Modern World Atheist?" *Cross Currents* (Winter, 1961).

Dewart, Leslie. *The Future of Belief*. New York: Herder and Herder, 1966.

Gorres, Ida. "The Believer's Unbelief," *Cross Currents* (Winter, 1961).

Lacroix, Jean Paul. *The Meaning of Modern Atheism*. New York: Macmillan, 1965.

Lepp, Ignace. *Atheism in Our Time*. New York: Macmillan, 1963.

Lubac, Henri de. *The Drama of Atheist Humanism*. New York: Meridian, 1963.

Metz, Johannes (ed.). *Fundamental Theology: Is God Dead?* Vol. XVI, *Concilium*. Glen Rock, N.J.: Paulist Press, 1966.

Murray, John Courtney. *The Problem of God: Yesterday and Today*. New Haven, Conn.: Yale University Press, 1964.

Novak, Michael. *Belief and Unbelief*. New York: Macmillan, 1965.

Zaehner, R. C. *Matter and Spirit: Their Convergence in Eastern Religions, Marx, and Teilhard de Chardin*. New York: Harper & Row, 1963.

———. *Mysticism: Sacred and Profane*. Oxford: Clarendon Press, 1957.

[2] Recent Explorations of the Human Meaning of Atheism

To list even the more penetrating contemporary discussions of atheism would be to write a book. Such discussions commonly occur in response to Marxism, Freudianism, existentialism, naturalism, and the whole world of modern literature. The following is an arbitrary list of a few of those writings that seem to have particular relevance to a death of God theology.

Brown, Norman O. *Life Against Death*. New York: Random House, 1957.
————. *Love's Body*. New York: Random House, 1966.
Earle, William. "Man Is the Impossibility of God," *Christianity and Existentialism,* John Wild (ed.). Evanston, Ill.: Northwestern University Press, 1963.
————. "The Paradox and the Death of God," *Christianity and Existentialism,* John Wild (ed.). Evanston, Ill.: Northwestern University Press, 1963.
Edie, James M. "The Absence of God," *Christianity and Existentialism,* John Wild (ed.). Evanston, Ill.: Northwestern University Press, 1963.
Eliade, Mircea. *Cosmos and History*. New York: Harper & Bros., 1959.
————. *The Sacred and the Profane*. New York: Harper & Bros., 1961.
Findlay, John. "Epilogue on Religion," *Values and Intention*. New York: Macmillan, 1961.
Glicksberg, Charles L. *Modern Literature and the Death of God*. The Hague: Martinus Nijhoff, 1966.
Heller, Erich. *The Artist's Journey into the Interior*. New York: Random House, 1965.
————. *The Disinherited Mind*. Chester Springs, Pa.: DuFour Editions, 1953.
Knight, G. Wilson. *Christ and Nietzsche*. London: Staples Press, 1948.
Kolakowski, Leszek. "The Priest and the Jester," *The Modern Polish Mind*. Boston: Little, Brown, 1962.
Malraux, André. *The Metamorphosis of the Gods*. New York: Doubleday, 1960.
Marcuse, Herbert. *Eros and Civilization*. New York: Random House, 1962.
Poulet, Georges. *Studies in Human Time*. Baltimore, Md.: Johns Hopkins Press, 1956.

[3] Judaism and the Death of God

Martin Buber dominates modern Jewish thinking, and his influence pervades the theological, as opposed to the rabbinic, expressions of Judaism. But the American Jewish thinker has entered new fields (much like his Protestant counterpart), and American Judaism may yet produce a fully secular form of faith, as it promises to do in the work of Richard Rubenstein.

Buber, Martin. *Eclipse of God.* New York: Harper & Bros., 1957.

——. *Israel and the World.* New York: Schocken, 1948.

Cohen, Arthur A. *The Natural and the Supernatural Jew.* New York: Pantheon, 1962.

Fackenheim, Emil. "On the Eclipse of God," *Commentary* (June, 1964).

Fromm, Erich. *You Shall Be as Gods: A Radical Interpretation of the Old Testament and Its Tradition.* New York: Holt, Rinehart and Winston, 1966.

Himmelfarb, Milton (ed.). "The State of Jewish Belief: A Symposium," *Commentary* (Aug., 1966). Thirty-eight responses from leading rabbis to five theological questions, the last of which is: "Does the so-called God is dead question which has been agitating Christian theologians have any relevance to Judaism?"

Rubenstein, Richard L. *After Auschwitz: Essays in Contemporary Jewish Theology.* Indianapolis, Ind.: Bobbs-Merrill, 1967.

Taubes, Jacob. "Dialectic and Analogy," *Journal of Religion* (Apr., 1954).

——. "Theodicy and Theology," *Journal of Religion* (Oct., 1954).

[4] Protestant Responses to Atheism and Secularization

While Protestant theology has met the challenge of atheism with only hesitation and reluctance, it has wrestled with the problem of secularization from almost its beginning, and this is now perhaps the dominant theme of Protestant writing.

Bonhoeffer, Dietrich. *Letters and Papers from Prison.* New York: Macmillan, 1962.

Bultmann, Rudolf. *Essays: Philosophical and Theological.* London: SCM Press, 1955.

——. "The Idea of God and Modern Man," *Translating Theology into the Modern Age,* Robert W. Funk (ed.). New York: Harper & Row, 1965.

——. "What Sense Is There to Speak of God?" *Christian Scholar* (Fall, 1960).

Buri, Fritz. *Christian Faith in Our Time.* New York: Macmillan, 1966.

——. *Theology of Existence.* Greenwood, S.C.: Attic Press, 1965.

Callahan, Daniel (ed.). *The Secular City Debate.* New York: Macmillan, 1966.

Cobb, John B., Jr. *A Christian Natural Theology.* Philadelphia: Westminster Press, 1965.

Cobb, John B., Jr. "Christian Natural Theology and Christian Existence," *Christian Century* (Mar. 3, 1965).

———. "Christianity and Myth," *Journal of Bible and Religion* (Oct., 1965).

———. "Whitehead's Philosophy and a Christian Doctrine of Man," *Journal of Bible and Religion* (July, 1964).

Cochrane, Arthur C. *The Existentialists and God.* Philadelphia: Westminster Press, 1956.

Cox, Harvey. *The Secular City* (revised edition). New York: Macmillan, 1966.

Ebeling, Gerhard. *The Nature of Faith.* Philadelphia: Fortress Press, 1961.

———. *Word and Faith.* Philadelphia: Fortress Press, 1963.

Edwards, David L. *The Honest to God Debate.* Philadelphia: Westminster Press, 1963.

Ferré, Frederick. "A Crisis Déja Vue?" *Centennial Review of Arts and Science* (Spring, 1964).

———. *Language, Logic, and God.* New York: Harper & Bros., 1961.

Funk, Robert W. *Language, Hermeneutic, and Word of God.* New York: Harper & Row, 1966.

Gilkey, Langdon B. "The Concept of Providence in Contemporary Theology," *Journal of Religion* (July, 1963).

———. "Cosmology, Ontology, and the Travail of Biblical Language," *Journal of Religion* (July, 1961).

———. "Dissolution and Reconstruction in Theology," *Christian Century* (Feb. 3, 1965).

———. "Secularism's Impact on Contemporary Theology," *Christianity and Crisis* (Apr. 5, 1965).

Gogarten, Friedrich. *Demythologizing and History.* New York: Scribner's, 1955.

———. *The Reality of Faith.* Philadelphia: Westminster Press, 1959.

Hart, Ray L. "Imagination and the Scale of Mental Acts," *Continuum* (Spring, 1965).

Heim, Karl. *Christian Faith and Natural Science.* New York: Harper & Bros., 1953.

Herzog, Frederick. *Understanding God.* New York: Scribner's, 1966.

Hopper, Stanley Romaine. *The Crisis of Faith.* London: Hodder & Stoughton, 1947.

———. "On the Naming of the Gods in Hölderlin and Rilke," *Christianity and the Existentialists,* Carl Michaelson (ed.). New York: Scribner's, 1956.

Hordern, William (ed.). *New Directions in Theology Today,* Vol. I. Philadelphia: Westminster Press, 1966.

Kaufman, Gordon. "On the Meaning of 'God': Transcendence Without Mythology," *Harvard Theological Review* (Apr., 1966).

Leeuwen, A. van. *Christianity in World History.* New York: Harper & Row, 1965.

Meland, Bernard Eugene. *The Secularization of Modern Cultures.* New York: Oxford University Press, 1966.

Michalson, Carl. "The Task of Systematic Theology Today," *Centennial Review of Arts and Science* (Spring, 1964).

Nicholls, William (ed.). *Conflicting Images of Man.* New York: Seabury Press, 1966.

Ogden, Schubert. *Christ Without Myth.* New York: Harper & Bros., 1961.

————. *The Reality of God.* New York: Harper & Row, 1966.

Pike, James A. *A Time for Christian Candor.* New York: Harper & Row, 1964.

————. *What Is This Treasure?* New York: Harper & Row, 1966.

Robinson, James M., and Cobb, John B., Jr. (eds.). *The Later Heidegger and Theology.* New York: Harper & Row, 1963.

————. *The New Hermeneutic.* New York: Harper & Row, 1964.

Robinson, John A. *Honest to God.* Philadelphia: Westminster Press, 1963.

————. *The New Reformation.* Philadelphia: Westminster Press, 1965.

Scott, Nathan A. *The Broken Center: Studies in the Theological Horizon of Modern Literature.* New Haven, Conn.: Yale University Press, 1966.

Shiner, Larry. *The Secularization of History.* Nashville, Tenn.: Abingdon Press, 1966.

————. "A Theological Perspective of the Secular," *Journal of Religion* (Oct., 1965).

Smith, Ronald Gregor. *The New Man.* London: SCM Press, 1956.

————. *Secular Christianity.* New York: Harper & Row, 1966.

Tillich, Paul. *The Courage to Be.* New Haven, Conn.: Yale University Press, 1952.

————. *The Protestant Era.* Chicago: University of Chicago Press, 1948.

————. *Systematic Theology,* Vols. I, II, and III. Chicago: University of Chicago Press, 1951-63.

West, Charles C. *Communism and the Theologians.* Philadelphia: Westminster Press, 1958.

Wilder, Amos N. *Modern Poetry and the Christian Tradition.* New York: Scribner's, 1952.

[5]   The Death of God Theology in America

Hopefully the following writings represent only the initial product of the death of God theological movement, but it is to be emphasized that even these pieces reflect a wide spectrum of theological opinion. The first conference of radical theologians was held in October of 1966 at the University of Michigan. Bobbs-Merrill will publish the papers from this conference in 1967 in a volume that will include articles by Thomas J. J. Altizer, Langdon Gilkey, William Hamilton, Henry Malcolm, John A. Phillips, Richard L. Rubenstein, and Steve Weissman.

Altizer, Thomas J. J. "Creative Negation in Theology," *Christian Century* (July 7, 1965).
——. *The Gospel of Christian Atheism.* Philadelphia: Westminster Press, 1966.
——. *Mircea Eliade and the Dialectic of the Sacred.* Philadelphia: Westminster Press, 1963.
——. *The New Apocalypse: The Radical Christian Vision of William Blake.* East Lansing, Mich.: Michigan State University Press, 1967.
——. "Theology and the Contemporary Sensibility," *America and the Future of Theology,* William A. Beardslee (ed.). Philadelphia: Westminster Press, 1967.
Cole, Dan P. "Death of God Can Be Christian Affirmation," *Christian Advocate* (Sept. 8, 1966).
Comstock, W. Richard. "Theology After the Death of God," *Cross Currents* (Summer, 1966).
Cooper, John C. *The Roots of Radical Theology.* Philadelphia: Westminster Press, 1967.
Hamilton, William. *The New Essence of Christianity.* New York: Association Press, 1961.
Hamilton, William, and Altizer, Thomas J. J. "The Death of God," *Playboy* (Aug., 1966).
——. *Radical Theology and the Death of God.* Indianapolis, Ind.: Bobbs-Merrill, 1966.
——. "The Shape of a Radical Theology," *Christian Century* (Oct. 6, 1965).
Hudson, Fred M. "Four Meanings of 'The Death of God,'" *Motive* (Apr., 1966).
Lacy, Allen. "Thomas J. J. Altizer: An Attempt to Understand Him," *Church Review* (Apr.-May, 1966).
Mallard, William. "Critical Review of Thomas J. J. Altizer, *The Gospel of Christian Atheism,*" *Christian Advocate* (June 2, 1966).
Miller, David. "*Homo Religiosus* and the Death of God," *Journal of Bible and Religion* (Oct., 1966).
Miller, William Robert (ed.). *The New Christianity.* New York: Dell, 1967.
Noel, Daniel C. "Still Reading His Will? Problems and Resources for the Death of God Theology," *Journal of Religion* (Oct., 1966).
Smith, F. J. "Christianity and Christ," *American Church Quarterly* (Winter, 1964).
——. "God Is Dead: A Philosophical Critique," *Centennial Review* (Fall, 1967).
——. "Where Is God?—A Phenomenology of Belief," *Religion in Life* (Summer, 1967).
Underwood, Richard. "Hermes and Hermeneutics: A Viewing from the Perspectives of the Death of God and Depth Psychology," *Hartford Quarterly* (Fall, 1965).

Vahanian, Gabriel. *The Death of God*. New York: Braziller, 1961.

————.(ed.). *The Death of God Debate*. New York: McGraw-Hill, 1967.

————. *No Other God*. New York: Braziller, 1966.

————. "Swallowed up by Godlessness," *Christian Century* (Dec. 8, 1965).

————. *Wait Without Idols*. New York: Braziller, 1964.

Van Buren, Paul M. "The Dissolution of the Absolute," *Religion in Life* (Summer, 1965).

————. "Linguistic Analysis and Christian Education," *Religious Education* (Jan.-Feb., 1965).

————. *The Secular Meaning of the Gospel*. New York: Macmillan, 1963.

————. "Theology in the Context of Culture," *Christian Century* (Apr. 7, 1965).

[6] Critical Responses to the Death of God Theology

Theological responses to the death of God theology are now appearing in most journals of theology, and for the last three years many journals in both England and America have been occupied with an analysis of the work of Paul van Buren. Many books and articles on the death of God theology are scheduled to appear in the near future, but it is not possible to list all of them here.

Adolfs, Robert. "Is God Dead?" *Jubilee* (July, 1966).

Alexander, W. M. "Death of God or God of Death?" *Christian Century* (Mar. 23, 1966).

Bado, Walter J. "Is God Dead?" *Homiletic and Pastoral Review* (July, 1966).

Beardslee, William A. "A Comment on the Theology of Dr. Altizer," *Criterion* (Spring, 1967).

Bennett, John C. "In Defense of God," *Look* (Apr. 19, 1966).

Berger, Elmer. "On the 'Death of God Theologies,' " *Education in Judaism* (Jan., 1966).

Brown, Robert McAfee. "Critical Review of Thomas J. J. Altizer, *The Gospel of Christian Atheism*," *Theology Today* (July, 1966).

Casserly, J. Langmead. *The Death of Man: A Reinterpretation of Christian Atheism*. New York: Morehouse-Barlow, 1967.

Clark, Bowman. "No, God Isn't Dead," *Georgia Impression* (Fall, 1966).

Cobb, John B., Jr. "Speaking About God," *Religion in Life* (Spring, 1967).

Cox, Harvey. "The Death of God and the Future of Theology," *New Christianity*, William Robert Miller (ed.). New York: Dell, 1967.

Czeglédy, Alexander. "Creative Negation in Theology," *Christian Century* (Nov. 3, 1965).

Dell, Edward T., Jr. "The God Questioners: Old Heresy and New Theology," *Episcopalian* (Aug., 1966).

Evans, J. Claude. "Tilting at Altizer," *Christian Century* (Mar. 30, 1966).

Fackre, Gabriel J. "The Death and Life of God," *Theology and Life* (Fall, 1965).

Foshee, Charles N., and Peden, W. Creighton (eds.). "The Death of God Theology," a symposium published in *Radford Review,* Radford College, Radford, Va. (Fall, 1966).

Gilkey, Langdon B. "Critical Review of Paul M. van Buren, *The Secular Meaning of the Gospel," Journal of Religion* (July, 1964).

————. "God Is not Dead," *Bulletin of Crozer Theological Seminary* (Jan., 1965).

————. "Is God Dead?" *Bulletin of Crozer Theological Seminary* (Jan., 1965).

————. *The Relevance of God Language.* Indianapolis, Ind.: Bobbs-Merrill, 1967.

Gleckler, Dan. "An Open Letter to the God Is Dead Crowd," *Christian Advocate* (July 14, 1966).

Graham, Billy, *et al. Is God Dead?* Grand Rapids, Mich.: Zondervan, 1966.

Hall, Robert. "Theology and Analysis," *Christian Scholar* (Winter, 1965).

Hamilton, Kenneth. *God Is Dead: The Anatomy of a Slogan.* Grand Rapids, Mich.: Eerdmans, 1967.

————. *Revolt Against Heaven.* Grand Rapids, Mich.: Eerdmans, 1966.

Hazelton, Roger. "The Future of God," *McCormick Quarterly* (May, 1966).

Henry, Carl. "A Reply to the God Is Dead Mavericks," *Christianity Today* (May 27, 1966).

Herberg, Will. "The Death of God Theology," *National Review* (Aug.-Sept., 1966).

Hiltner, Seward. "Not Dead Enough," *Christian Century* (Sept. 28, 1966).

Hodgson, Peter C. "The Death of God and the Crisis in Christology," *Journal of Religion* (Oct., 1966).

Holcomb, Harmon R. "Christology Without God: A Critical Review of *The Secular Meaning of the Gospel," Foundations* (Jan., 1965).

Hopper, Jeff. "What 'Gods' Have Died?" *Journal of the Methodist Theological School in Ohio* (Fall, 1966).

Hunnex, Milton D. "Has the Spirit of Confusion Bewitched the Secular Theologians?" *Christianity Today* (Dec. 23, 1966).

Ice, Jackson (ed.). *The Death of God Debate.* Philadelphia: Westminster Press, 1966.

Josey, Charles C. "On the Death of God," *Journal of Religion and Health* (Oct., 1966).

Kirkpatrick, Dow. "A Sermon on God's Death," *Christian Advocate* (Feb. 24, 1966).

Lacey, Paul A. "The Death of 'the Man Upstairs,'" Comments by Chris Downing, J. H. McCandless, and Clinton L. Reynolds, *Quaker Religious Thought* (Spring, 1966).

Long, Charles H. "The Ambiguities of Innocence," *America and the Future of Theology,* William A. Beardslee (ed.). Philadelphia: Westminster Press, 1967.

McBrien, Richard P. "Radical Theology: From Honest-to-God to God-Is-Dead," *Commonweal* (Sept. 23, 1966).

McCracken, Robert J. "Atheism in Our Time," *Theology Today* (Oct., 1966).

McKinnon, Alastair. "The Life of Man and the Death of God," *Christian Outlook* (Apr., 1966).

Mascall, E. L. *The Secularization of Christianity.* New York: Holt, Rinehart and Winston, 1965.

Mehta, Ved. *The New Theologian.* New York: Harper & Row, 1966.

Montgomery, John W. "'Death of God' Becomes More Deadly," *Christianity Today* (Dec. 9, 1966).

————. *The "Is God Dead?" Controversy.* Grand Rapids, Mich.: Zondervan, 1966.

Moulton, Warren L., *et al.* "Death of God: Four Views," *Christian Century* (Nov. 17, 1965).

Neibuhr, Reinhold. "Faith as the Sense of Meaning in Human Existence," *Christianity and Crisis* (June 13, 1966).

Ogletree, Thomas W. *The Death of God Controversy.* Nashville, Tenn.: Abingdon Press, 1966.

Rubenstein, Richard. "Thomas Altizer's Apocalypse," *America and the Future of Theology,* William A. Beardslee (ed.). Philadelphia: Westminster Press, 1967.

Runyon, Theodore H., Jr. "Death of God—One Year Later," *Christian Advocate* (Nov. 17, 1966).

————. "Divine Transcendence Versus Human Responsibility?" *The Death of God Debate,* Gabriel Vahanian (ed.). New York: McGraw-Hill, 1967.

Sanders, James Alvin. "The Vitality of the Old Testament: Three Theses," *Union Seminary Quarterly Review* (Jan., 1966).

Shideler, Emerson W. "Taking the Death of God Seriously," *Theology Today* (July, 1966).

Stob, Henry J. "The Death of God Theology," *Reformed Journal* (Mar. and Sept., 1966).

Stokes, Mack B. "Reflection: Death of God," *Christian Advocate* (Jan. 27, 1966).

Tillich, Paul. "The Significance of the History of Religions for the Systematic Theologian," *The Future of Religions.* New York: Harper & Row, 1966.

Trotter, F. Thomas. "Variations on the Death of God Theme in Recent Theology," *Journal of Bible and Religion* (Jan., 1965).

Wall, James M. "What Do They Mean, 'God is Dead'?" *Together* (June, 1966).

Weissman, Steve. "New Left Man Meets the Dead God," *Motive* (Jan., 1967).

Williams, Alex W. "The Death of God," *Presbyterian Survey* (June, 1966).

Wilson, Kenneth L. "Can We Manage Without God?" *Christian Herald* (Jan., 1967).

Winter, Charles L., Jr. "Radical Theology: Its Message to Orthodoxy," *St. Luke's Journal of Theology* (Oct., 1966).

Wolff, Richard. *Is God Dead?* Wheaton, Ill.: Tyndale House, 1967.

A 7
B 8
C 9
D 0
E 1
F 2
G 3
H 4
I 5
J 6